Female Infanticide and Child Marriage

Female Infanticide and Child Marriage

SAMBODH GOSWAMI

RAWAT PUBLICATIONS
Jaipur • New Delhi • Bangalore • Mumbai • Hyderabad • Guwahati

ISBN 81-316-0112-9

Published by
Prem Rawat for **Rawat Publications**
Satyam Apts, Sector 3, Jawahar Nagar, Jaipur 302 004 (India)
Phone: 0141 265 1748 / 7006 Fax: 0141 265 1748
E-mail: info@rawatbooks.com
Website: www.rawatbooks.com

New Delhi Office
4858/24, Ansari Road, Daryaganj, New Delhi 110 002
Phone: 011 2326 3290

Also at Bangalore, Mumbai, Hyderabad and Guwahati

Typeset by Rawat Computers, Jaipur
Printed at Chaman Enterprises, New Delhi

To

Dr. Pratibha Jain

my guru, guide and philosopher,
with reverence and gratitude.

Contents

Preface

One measure to gauge the refinement of society in a given age and clime is the status enjoyed by women therein. The better the status, the more cultured the society. Judged by this yardstick, society in the Rajputana (now Rajasthan) could not boast of a complementary degree of refinement. Many obnoxious customs and practices surfaced during the ancient and medieval period, which aimed at defining the spheres of women folk, viz., child and unequal marriage, polygamy, female infanticide, sati, etc. These social practices limited the social space of women and even advocated the 'systematic clearing' of the female child. Even after attaining independence, we are still grappling with these problems, despite the claim of the British officers and that of the Government of India that these problems have been eradicated, and that they are the things of the past.

A little girl below five years of age, dressed in colourful bridal costume and a boy, in equally colourful clothes, hanging the sword, as if it were a piece of toy on his waist, being given away in marriage, surrounded by a horde of merrymaking relatives, is a common sight in some parts of the country and more so in Rajasthan. It is an open secret that boys and girls are tied into wedlock at that tender age when they do not understand the significance and implications of marriage.

Another equally heinous practice is female infanticide, which prevailed in many sections of the Rajputana, (and is still prevalent in new forms and ways), aimed at systematic clearing of female species. It is not justifiable to believe that superstitious, religious and orthodox attitude of the inhabitants was singularly responsible for the prevalence of the above mentioned twin baneful practices. There were certain other factors such as uncertain political atmosphere, complex social and religious organization and hierarchy, deteriorating economic condition and lack of educational facilities, which induced the people to perpetuate and adhere to such damaging customs.

The object of this research work is to evaluate the causes and circumstances, which contributed towards the emergence and growth of these nefarious practices of female infanticide and child marriage. And also to know the extent to which these two evil customs were practiced and prevalent in the society and the particular areas, castes, tribes, religions and creeds, in which they were followed. At the same time, an effort will be made to discover the status enjoyed by women, in social, political, economic, education and religious spheres.

For this, the work has been divided into eight chapters. In the first chapter, the historical importance and the role of women in ancient Indian society has been traced. During Vedic times, women had access to education and enjoyed freedom in social and personal matters. The gradual deterioration of their status and position in the later times and the causes responsible for this deterioration has also been dealt in this chapter.

The evil practice of female infanticide was unfortunately prevalent in many societies of the world. It was also widely prevalent in the erstwhile States of the Rajputana. An attempt has been made in chapter 2, to understand the causes and the role of various socio-economic-psychological and political forces, which forced the people to commit this heinous crime.

Some social scientists believe that the State of Rajasthan has been needlessly denigrated for child marriages. An attempt has, therefore, been made in chapter 3, to understand the origin of the custom of child marriage and the various factors which are responsible for this practice in India (as well as in the State of Rajasthan), and its prevalence amongst various castes, communities, erstwhile States and the areas, and also the interrelation of child marriage with other social malpractices. It also brings out the difference between the actual age of consummation (i.e., *gauna* or *muklawa*) and the age of marriage.

In Rajputana, various social organizations did a commendable work in the upliftment of the status of women and in the eradication of prevalent social abuses. These organizations condemned polygamy, child and unequal marriages, *chandni,* dance of the *bhagtans* (i.e., prostitutes) at the auspicious occasions (e.g., at the time of marriage or at the birth of a son) and created awareness among the general public. They also advocated the role of education for the betterment of the status of women. In chapter 4, the significance and role played by social organizations like Desh Hitaishini Sabha, Walterkrit Rajputra Hitkarini Sabha (WKRHS), Arya Samaj, in the social reform process in the Rajputana, has been discussed. The role of Har Bilas Sarda, one of the members of Arya Samaj, will always be remembered for his untiring efforts against child marriages and for passing of an Act against child marriages in 1929. Chapter 4, also underlines his efforts as well as those of some of the women activists of Arya Samaj, who devoted their life for the cause of women education and prevention of child marriages, and improvement of the position of widows.

It is generally assumed that the caste organizations play a negative role in the developmental process and create obstacles in the path of social changes. Significantly, caste organizations played an important role in the social history of the Rajputana as it were they, who framed rules regarding the minimum marriageable age for boys and girls, and imposed limits on the expenditure on auspicious and inauspicious occasions including marriage and *mausar.* These caste organizations started schools and libraries, published newspapers and magazines and even tried to pressurize their native rulers through hunger strikes, *dharnas* (rally or demonstration) and wrote open letters to them and distributed pamphlets in connection with the abolition of the prevalent social malpractices. Chapter 5 highlights the contribution of such caste organizations, which made a remarkable contribution towards prevention of child and unequal marriages and for the amelioration of women situation.

In chapter 6, the significant contribution of the native rulers in the abolition of female infanticide and in prevention of child and ill-matched marriages has been discussed. In fact, some of them initiated social legislation, much before the arrival of the East India

Company in the Rajputana and as such, an attempt has been made here to study their role in the reform process.

Despite the efforts of various social and caste organizations as well as that of enlightened individuals and rulers, the problem of child marriage is still prevalent in our society even in the 21st century and several cases of child marriage come to light on the occasions of Akha-Teej and Basant Panchami. Similarly the heinous custom of female infanticide has reappeared in the garb of female foeticide and more lives have been destroyed by it than by infanticide. Chapter 7 therefore, deals with the new ways and forms which female infanticide has taken in recent times. Chapter 8 highlights the regional variations in the cases of child marriage and in the great imbalance of male/female ratio in various erstwhile states of Rajasthan.

In carrying out this research work, historical methodology has been adopted and archival records, interviews and Census reports of different years have been used, coupled with other literary sources.

Acknowledgement

It becomes my pious duty to express my hearty gratitude towards all those individuals and agencies whom I have constantly troubled during the course of my research work. First and foremost, I owe deep gratitude to Dr. Pratibha Jain, former Head, Department of History and Indian Culture, University of Rajasthan, Jaipur for her kind permission to me to work on this subject. Without her keen interest, cooperation and guidance, I would not have perhaps been able to complete the work. I can never forget her motherly affection and the manner in which she devoted herself to the study of the present thesis, despite her extremely busy schedule. The lengthy discussions with her and the innumerable suggestions offered by her, proved to be of immense help to me. Whatever little I have been able to do, is only because of her motivation.

I express my heartfelt gratitude to Shri Nath Ji Maharaj (head-priest of the Charan community), Rani Laxmi Kumari Chundawat (eminent writer of Rajasthan), Shri Kalanath Shastri (renowned scholar of Sanskrit language and former Director of Rajasthan Sanskrit Academy), Shri Shiv Charan Das (great grandson of Mahakavi Shyamal Das – the legendary historian of Rajasthan), Late Dr. N.K. Singhi (former Head of the Department of Sociology, University of Rajasthan), Prof. Tej Kumar Mathur (former Head, Department of History, M.D.S. University, Ajmer), Dr. Vinod Shastri (Associate Professor, Department of Sanskrit, University of Rajasthan), Dr. Sanjeev Bhanawat (Director, Centre for Mass Communication, University of Rajasthan), Shri Raghunath Prasad

Tiwari Umang (Director of Tiwari Madan Lal Pareek Shodh Sansthan, Jaipur), 'Chitransha' Bindeshwari Prasad Shrivastav (author of *All India Kayastha Conference*) and Shri Arvind Kumarsambhav (national president of Rashtriya Kayastha Mahaparishad and state-head of Rajasthan Kayastha Mahasabha) for bestowing their blessings and offering valid suggestions, from time to time. The interviews with them gave me new facts and thoughts and helped me in understanding the two problems of female infanticide and child marriage in totality. All through the seven years of my research work, they took personal interest and I am deeply indebted to them for their constant inspiration.

Thanks are also due to the authorities and staff of National Archives of India, New Delhi, Jawahar Lal Nehru Library, Teen Murti Bhawan, New Delhi, Rajasthan State Archives, Bikaner, Rajasthan State Archives (Secretariat Library), Jaipur, City Palace Library, Jaipur, Arya Samaj, Jaipur, Central Library, University of Rajasthan, Jaipur, Radha-Krishnan Library, Jaipur, Maharaja Public Library, Jaipur and Tiwari Madan Lal Pareek Shodh Sansthan, Jaipur. I gratefully acknowledge the facilities provided by them in consulting the original as well as secondary records.

I express my sincere gratitude to the management and the Principal, Dr. Man Bhandari as well as the staff members (teaching as well as non-teaching members) of Sant Jayacharya P.G. Mahila Mahavidyalaya, Jaipur, who were always a source of great help and encouragement to me.

The blessings and inspirations of my parents and parents-in-law have enabled me to complete my work. The discussions, which I had with my father, Prof. Vasudhakar Goswami, Sociologist and former Vice Principal, Government P.G. College, Dausa, went a long way in shaping my thoughts and in understanding the significance of research work.

I am also thankful to my wife Swati, my son Pranshu, and my two and half year old daughter Pratichie, who gave me full cooperation in completing my research work and in bringing out this book. Without their help, it would have been difficult or me to pursue my work. The time which I should have spent with them, was consumed in my research activities and I value the patience with which they bore this period of neglect. I would also like to thank Mr. Mohit Goswami (Director, And Things Like That Inc., Jaipur), for designing the cover page of this book.

Finally, I thank Shri Pranit Rawat of M/s. Rawat Publications, Jaipur, for excellent publication of this book.

Abbreviations/Glossary

ABBREVIATIONS

A.G.G.	Agent to the Governor General for Rajputana
A.V.	Atharva Veda
B.D.S.	Baudhayan Dharmasutra
Cons. no.	Consultation number of the Foreign and Political Department
Cf.	Cited from
Encl.	Enclosure
F.&P.	Political Consultations/Foreign and Political Department to Government of India
G.D.S.	Gautam Dharmasutra
M.K.J.R.	Mehkama Khas Jodhpur Records
M.S.	Manu Smriti
N.A.I.	National Archives of India, Delhi
Offg.	Officiating
R.S.A.B.	Rajasthan State Archives, Bikaner
R.S.A.J.	Rajasthan State Archives, Jaipur
R.R.	Rajputana Residency
R.A.R.	Rajputana Agency Record
R.V.	Rig Veda
Th.	Thakur

V.S.	Vikram Samvat
V.D.S.	Vasistha Dharmasutra
W.Y.V.	White Yajur-Veda
Y.V.	Yajur Veda

GLOSSARY

Bhumia	Holder of a small piece of land
Durbar	The Ruler/Court of Princely State
Dharna	Demonstration
Gotra	Family or clan
Gauna/Muklawa	Actual age of consummation
Jagir	Landed Estate
Jagirdar	Landlord
Khaamps	Sects of the clan
Khureeta	Official Letter
Naata or Karewa	Widow re-marriage
Neg	Customary gifts given to the Charans, Bhats etc. on the occasion of joy and happiness
Nukta/Mausar/ Mrityubhoj	Feast given after death
Panchas	Village elder man
Purdah	Veil
Panchayat	Meeting of the members of a caste or a group
Rekh	Land revenue
Shastras	Holy scriptures of the Hindus
Tyag	Presents, money etc. given to Charans and Bhats on auspicious occasions
Tilak/Tika	Presents/money given to the bridegroom or the intended groom by the bride's family at the time of betrothal

1

Status of Women in India

A Historical Background

The status and the position of women in India, has been a controversial subject, as it reflects the contradictory and the paradoxical nature of the Indian society. While on the one hand, woman has been called *devi* or goddess, the abode of gods, the perfect guide or guru of her children; on the other hand, she has been criticized for the weaknesses of her character, for her unpredictable and impulsive nature and has even been denied the basic right of existence as a human being. The staunch supporters of Indian culture, who believe that women enjoyed an honourable, significant and unique position in the annals of Indian history, unlike other civilizations, quote the verses from ancient Hindu literature to support their point of view. Similarly, those who believe that women had a subservient or a secondary place, as far as their social, political, economical and religious rights are concerned, vis-à-vis their male counterparts, also quote the verses from the sacred Hindu literature, to show that women never enjoyed a free and independent status and that their rights in the society were considerably restricted. Moreover, the opinions of different religious scriptures differ from each other, thereby giving birth to many contradictions. This difference of opinion raises many questions, as to the nature, and scope of free will enjoyed by women in different periods of Indian history.

Thus, this situation, or dilemma, demands a thorough and objective probe, to understand the status, position and significance of the role of women as mothers, wives and daughters, and the scope of freedom, free will and personal space as enjoyed by them in their respective roles, along with various social restrictions imposed upon them, from time to time. In order to have a better understanding of the present social structure and position of women therein, it is imperative to know the operation of various historical, political, cultural and economic factors which moulded the society. And such a historical perspective is all the more necessary in the case of a society, with a continuous history of more than three thousand years. It is also crucial to have a brief look at the past society, because some of the norms and values affecting women today have their roots in the past.

For this, one has to look into the various social institutions like marriage, family, caste, society, etc., to have a better and clear picture of the position of women. This will also throw greater light on various social practices like child marriage, female infanticide, polygamy, *sati, jauhar,* etc. It is also necessary to understand the problems of female infanticide, foeticide and child marriage as they are closely related to other social evils (or malpractices) and have played a vital role in shaping the destiny of the Indian women. Though the necessity of reviewing women's status across historical phases is non-controversial, the task is fraught with innumerable difficulties. Sukla Das,[1] observes "First, the subject as it is too wide in scope, defies generalization. Second, various changes occurred in the different periods of our long history to alter the position and status of women. Third, the contradictions in abundant source-materials with no precise dates and their varied interpretations render it rather difficult to assess the quantum of theory and reality. Fourth, vastness of the country where a large number of cultures confluenced and where stages of development were not uniform poses difficulty in drawing any fixed or definite conclusion. Fifth, conglomeration of facts and fantasies about our past have often blurred a rational judgement. Considering these major constraints it would be unwise to brush aside the matter by a general estimate under any positive notion of 'good' or 'bad'." Similarly, eminent sociologist M.N. Srinivas[2] has observed that "it (i.e., the changing position of Indian women) has many facets and generalization is well nigh impossible because of the existence of considerable variation among regions, between rural and urban areas, among classes, and finally among different religious, ethnic and caste-groups. While in certain contexts the Indian subcontinent is a single cultural region, in many others it is heuristically more rewarding to look upon it as a congeries of micro-regions, differences between which are crucial". Similarly, Romila Thapar[3] believes that "within the Indian sub-continent there have been infinite variations on the status of women diverging according to cultural milieu, family structure, class, caste, property rights and morals." Despite these difficulties, an attempt has been made here, to give an account of the position and status of women in India, in different periods of Indian history.

In the Vedic period (i.e., the period from 2500 B.C. to 1000 B.C. when the four Vedas – Rig Veda, Sam Veda, Yajur Veda and Atharva Veda were compiled), women were active participants in different spheres of societal activities.[4] In this period, women enjoyed all the rights in social, economic, political and religious domain, as were enjoyed by their male counterparts. Though the Vedas are essentially works of rituals, ceremonies and of philosophy and references to mundane affairs are very few; yet they show a glimpse of the Aryan society in all its colours and present the condition and the contribution of the women in that age.[5]

In the early stages of the arrival and the expansion of the Indo-Aryans in northern India, they went through a period of long and continuous struggle with the non-Aryan tribes. The constant wars and the resultant calamities demanded a large number of soldiers, who could fight with the enemy in unknown land and who could defeat their rivals, scattered around in large numbers. This very fact forced them to rely upon the masculine power and explains the emergence of a new god Indra, who was more masculine, more aggressive than prior gods and who soon captured the title of Devendra i.e., god of the gods. As the Aryans were driven by a desire to boost up their numerical strength, to make up for the comparative dearth of men, women as progenitors of the race, occupied a central place in the Vedic society.

Their arduous life of expansion had a two-fold impact on the status of women in society. Due to their all-engrossing life on earth, the Aryans showed little concern in the questions related to life after death. Neither had they the time nor the wish to ponder over such sensitive questions at that time. Secondly, this do or die situation forced them to take, as well as respect, the work of every member of their community, and consequently the importance of women in political, social, economic and religious fields was soon felt in the Aryan society. Men at that time, were mostly engrossed in military and semi-military pursuits, hence they had to rely on the help and cooperation of women in other spheres of life. And as such women were not considered as parasites but were useful members of society for securing material prosperity in peace and victory in war. Women, too, used to take active part in production, agriculture and in manufacture. Thus, for such people, writes P. Thomas, "women were not ornaments but co-partners in life, in its pleasure and hazards, in its joys and sorrows and an exuberance of vitality and vigour guided them in forming their institutions of marriage and family life." Similarly, Sukla Das[6] observes that, "the cheap or forced labour of the enslaved population was not available to the early Aryans, hence they could not treat women with disregard or total contempt. Consequently, women had general freedom and a relatively better status in the early Vedic period".

During this period, sons were indispensable as fighters for the family and the clan, but it does not mean that a girl child was neglected or ignored or received a differential treatment by her parents and society, as compared to male children. In Vedic literature there are many hymns which are addressed to gods and goddesses like Agni, Soma, Ashwins, Maruts, Vishwe-deva, Indra, Ribhus, Brahmanspati, Aditya, Appanpata, Raka, Vishwajit, Saraswati, Usha, Anumati, Siniwali, Savitri, etc., which are expressive of the yearning for sons, but at the same time, there are hymns which present the craving for a girl child. Some of the hymns, expressive of the yearning for sons, have been mentioned here:[7]

"*Agni* hath bestowed on me riches and sons and this spouse. Be ye not parted, Dwell ye here, Reach the full time of human life, with sons and grandsons sport and play, rejoicing in your own abode."

"O, Dawn enriched with ample wealth bestow on us the wondrous gift.

Wherewith we may support children and children's sons."

"O, Bounteous Indra, make this bride blest in her sons and fortunate.

Vouchsafe to her ten sons; and make her husband the eleventh one."

"Vouchsafe blessing upon the wombs that bring male children forth."

"Prepare accordingly the mother for the infants' birth. On the right way bring forth the boy. Make him come hither, I am here. The amulet which Aditi wore when desirous of a son, Tvashtar hath bound upon this dame and said, "Be mother of a boy."

"I wish my thought have commenced with divine far-sighted *Dakshina*. Steal not my life. I will not thine, May I, O, Goddess in thy sight find for myself a hero son."

"May he come forth alive, unharmed, yea, living from the living dame."

These hymns can lead one to conclude that the Aryan society was a male-dominated society or it was a gender-biased society. But a close look at the Vedic texts will reveal that an ardent desire for the birth of a daughter is not missing in that society either. There are innumerable references to daughters being fondly and affectionately brought up by parents. A simile which has been drawn to express the Heaven and Earth, reflects upon the relations of the girl child with her parents. "Faring together young, with meeting limits, twin sisters lying on their parent's bosom."[8]

Similarly, in one of the hymns of Rig Veda, the desire of the couple to reach their full extent of life with sons and daughters, has been mentioned.[9] In another passage, a father is commended for having many excellent daughters as his quiver for containing unfailing darts, both being effective in assailing the hearts of men.[10] One passage expresses a desire for brave sons and sagacious daughters.[11] A prayer addressed to Lord Pushan likewise evinces a keen desire for daughters. A prayer in the Yajur Veda while urging for victorious, sagacious and brave youth for the nation also wishes for like-minded women. Besides this, there are several verses in the Vedas, which express keenness for children, which includes both, sons and daughters.[12] It is interesting to note, that for the attainment of wise, educated and erudite daughters, special religious ceremonies were organized in the period of Upanishads.[13] These examples prove beyond doubt, that girls were neither considered as unwanted nor inferior at that time and that they were accorded a status of absolute equality with that of a son at all levels – religious, social and political.

In the Vedic age, women used to be well-educated, well-cultivated and were refined in their manners and etiquettes. Some of the hymns of the Rig Veda have been attributed to female rishis. According to the orthodox tradition recorded in

Sarva-anukramnika, there are as many as twenty women among the authors of Rig Veda.[14] S.R. Shastri has classified these hymns as follows: hymns that are entirely attributed to female rishis; hymns that are partly attributed to female rishis; hymns that are attributed to female rishis, but are of dubious authorship.[15]

The first category includes hymns composed independently by Apala and Vishwa-wara, who belonged to the Atri family. Apala addressed hymn 91 of the tenth book and invokes Agni in Book V of the Rig Veda, while Vishwa-wara has composed hymn 91 of the seventh book.[16] The second category includes hymns which have been traditionally attributed to female rishis, Lopamudra and Sachiyasi, addressed jointly with their spouse or some other seer. Lopamudra has composed a hymn jointly with her husband Agastya.[17] The last category represents hymns of Ghosha, Indrani, Urvashi, Surya Savitri, Shraddha, Kamayani, Shachi, Paulomi, Sarparagini. With the exception of Ghosha the rest are mythological or divine figures, who obviously cannot be accepted as the real authors. The real composers may have been someone else, possibly women, opines S.R. Shastri.[18]

These illustrations demonstrate a healthy tradition of imparting training to daughters, equivalent to that of sons. To impart education to all children and to help them in settling in life were the twin duties of the Vedic parents and in this there was initially no discrimination between a boy and a girl. Upanayana or ceremonial initiation into the Vedic studies at par was the rule. The initiation ceremony of girls used to take place as regularly as that of boys.[19] The Vedas unambiguously underline the indispensability and significance of education for maidens[20] and held such educated maidens in high esteem. In the following hymn of Rig Veda, the qualities of a leading lady are described by comparing her to dawn. Just as the dawn is luminous because she gets all the light from her veritable father, the sun, so the daughter of illuminated parents, it is stated, alone could be the enlightened one:

"O Ideal Lady of the earth, shining as luminous light of dawn. Endowed with inspiring speech and mirth. You are the leader luminous love born. Your glory is sung by the noble ones, your achievements praised by one and all. Creator of refined daughters and sons, to you flock millions, big or small."

Similarly, at other places it is mentioned that:

"An unmarried young learned daughter should be married to a bridegroom who, like her, is learned. Never think of giving in marriage a daughter of very young age."

"A young daughter who has observed *brahmacharya* i.e., finished her studies should be married to a bridegroom who, like her, is learned."

The Atharva Veda also advocates female education categorically.

"A king by observing *brahmacharya* can protect his kingdom easily. An *acharya* can impart education to his students, if he has himself observed his *brahmacharya*. A young daughter, after the observance of *brahmacharya,* should be married to a young man."[21]

Women were imparted training in spiritual and temporal subjects in Vedic period. The spiritual aspect of education comprised training in religious lore, historical tradition and mythology. The scholars were divided into two classes – brahma-vadinis and *sadyo-vadhoos*.[22] The former were life-long students of theology and philosophy and considered the attainment of knowledge and the spread of knowledge as the aim of their lives and for that, they remained unmarried throughout their lives. Brahma-vadinis were women of high scholarship. Many of them composed hymns which enriched the Vedic literature. Ghosha was a celebrated *rishika,*[23] so were Lopamudra,[24] Apala[25] and Vishvavara[26]. Vishvavara not only composed hymns but performed the function of a *ritvij* or priest at a sacrifice,[27] a privilege that was denied to women in subsequent period. Many of the women scholars took to teaching profession and were known as *acharyas*.[27(a)] Vak, the daughter of Abhrma, to whom the authorship of hymn 125 of Book X of Rig Veda is attributed, marks the beginning of the line of the brahma-vadinis "who flooded the later Vedic literature with their number and philosophical discourses, discussions and speculations... The hymn embodies in it the language of tremendous force and vigour, the concept of the unity of the universe. This hymn is one of the earliest precursors of the non-dual doctrine of the later Vedanta philosophy.[28] This proves that not only mythology and tradition were taught to women, but also the intricate principles and concepts of metaphysics. The *sadyo-vadhoos* prosecuted their studies till their marriages at the age of 15 or 16.

The Vedic literature also testifies to women's proficiency in fine arts.[29] From the Taittriya Samhita (VI.6.5), the Maitrayana Samhita

(III.7.3), and the Shatpath Brahman, we know that women were taught to dance and sing, which appear to be recognized feminine accomplishments.

They appeared even in tournaments[30] like horse and chariot races[31] and publicly attended feasts and gatherings[32]. There are certain references in the Rig Veda, which point out that women, too, received military training. It was a necessity for a society, which was engaged in long and continuous struggle with the non-Aryan tribes, to train their women in self-defense. At times, women even accompanied their husbands in the battle field. In the Rig Veda we come across women of military profession like Mudgalini[33], Vispala[34] and Shashiyasi[35] who took active part in battles and who astonished their rivals with their bravery. Mudgalini, Mudgal's wife, was a brave warrior, who in the hour of crisis, drove the chariot for her husband and acted as a *rathi* or *saarthi*. She is said to have overpowered her husband's enemy, who thus defeated, took to his heels chased by her. Similarly, Vispala, the wife of king Khela, accompanied her husband to the battle field, where she lost her leg, which was later replaced with an iron one by the Ashwins[36].

These references to women warriors in the Rig Veda prove beyond doubt that women received some kind of military training in those days.[37] Similarly, in the Atharva Veda, there are several allusions to the bravery of women.[38]

In the Vedic period, women used to take part in the decision-making bodies of the society. In a hymn, in Rig Veda, a desire is expressed in the marriage ceremony that the bride would figure not only as a mere housewife but also as an eloquent speaker in the Vidath (विदथ).[39] This was true about the women of the aristocratic families as well as common ones. In the Rig Veda, the scene of Vidath and the maiden's curiosity/inclination to attend to the discussion and to participate in it is described in more than one hymn.[40] Further, grown up males are described as deputing strong and social maidens to the Vidath. In the deliberative functions women enjoyed an equal voice with men. In the Rig Veda and the Atharva Veda, both men and women were expected to speak to Vidath in their advanced age.[41] Bloomfield's view that the Vedic women had nothing to do with the public life[42] has been refuted by several writers including R.S. Sharma[43] as it pertains to a period when the patriarchal society was established on a firm footing and women had lost their hold over social and political structures. These examples clearly show that the activities of women were not confined to the hearths and homes alone, but they also played an important role at the political front.

The Institution of Marriage in the Vedic Period

The custom of marriage, with its features, qualities and its role as a social institution determines, to a great extent, the position and the status of a woman. A good marriage is harbinger of peace, prosperity, and happiness for the woman, while a bad one is like a nightmare and is worse than a painful chain. Marriage and post marriage problems from the past to the present form an important part in the development of woman. Even in the 21st century, the custom of marriage is considered as a sacrosanct religious sacrament, and it is therefore necessary to understand its significance, in the light of historical facts.

The institution of marriage was a sacred institution in the Vedic times. The need for an organized and settled life and the continuous requirement of the soldiers, for the society, soon led them to understand the significance of marriage as an institution. Moreover the prevalent notions that "gods accepted no oblations offered by the unmarried", and "an unmarried man is unholy and therefore unworthy of doing *yajnas*" enhanced the esteem and acceptability of marriage in the Aryan society.[44] The aims of the marriage in Vedic times were *dharma, praja* (progeny), and *rati* (pleasure) and the ideal marriage of the Vedic period was a religious sacrament which made the couple joint owners of the household.

Considerable freedom seemed to be given to the girl and boy for selecting a match. There is no clear evidence whether the consent of the parents or brother(s) was essential or not. The latter appeared on the scene after the parties concerned had come to an understanding, and their participation as well as that of the wooer *(vara)* in the formal 'wooing' was a mere formality. However it was an essential preliminary to the marriage ceremony. Although the Vedic literature makes no direct comment on the forms of marriage prevalent at that time, yet five kinds of marriages can be inferred from whatever information we have from the scattered sources. They were the *brahma*, the *prajapatya*, the *swayamvara*, the *rakshasa* and the *gandharva* forms of marriage. In the brahma marriage, the bride was offered to a bridegroom who was specially invited for the purpose, by her parents. In the prajapatya form of marriage, the bride was offered according to due rights, but with an injunction to the couple that they should be always inseparable companions in the discharge of their religious duties. In these marriages, the parents, after a close scrutiny of the groom's conduct, his character, his family background, his education, settled the marriage with the help and aid of family members and friends and it was expected from the bride that she would respect her parent's decisions, as far as the choice of groom is concerned. The bride after a formal ceremony, left the house of her father and came to stay over with the bridegroom and his family. This form of marriage was considered as the most ideal and sacred and was popularly accepted, in the Vedic period.[45]

In the swayamvara form of marriage, the bride used to choose her husband, from the different contenders, who presented themselves, before her or her family, for that specific purpose. The details and other relevant information, regarding the different contenders, were passed on to the bride, before the ceremony of swayamvara, so that she could make up her mind about her future husband. At times, in order to check the physical and mental capabilities, of the different contenders, some sort of competition was also held, where due time was given to everyone to prove his worth. In a hymn in the Rig Veda, regarding the marriage rituals of Surya, the germination of the swayamvara form of marriage can be traced out. Similarly, Ashwins were selected as bridegrooms after they defeated Soma in a chariot race.[46]

The gandharva form of marriage can be compared to that of the present day love marriages. Impressed and enamored by the physical and mental attributes of each other, some of the male and female members of the Aryan society, used to marry each other clandestinely and at times openly.

In the rakshasa form of marriage, the girl was abducted forcefully and was forced to marry her abductor. Since in this form of marriage the will and consent of the girl was not taken into consideration and the marriage ceremony was performed in the state of her helplessness, therefore it was considered as heinous and hence the name rakshasa marriage gained currency, as it was believed to be the work of rakshasas (devils) alone and not that of any decent and well-cultivated man. The story of the stealing of Shundhayuv (daughter of Purumitra) by Vimada against the will of her father, but probably with her consent, can be gathered from I.112.19; I.116.1;

I.117.20 and X.39.7 in the Rig Veda, bears a testimony to the prevalence of this form of marriage in the Vedic times.[47] The story of the marriage of Urvashi with Pururava in Chapter X.95 of the Rig Veda, suggests that some sort of contractual marriage was also known to the Rig Vedic Aryans.[48] In the story it is mentioned that Pururava married the beautiful damsel Urvashi, who originally belonged to the Gandharvas, on the condition that he would not appear undressed before her, as it disturbed her aesthetic sense. The Gandharvas, who wished to reclaim Urvashi, managed to wake him up one night and Urvashi saw him in a flash of lightening. This rendered Urvashi free from Pururava instantaneously and she once again went back to the Gandharvas.

In the Vedic period, we also find the prevalence of monogamous as well as polygamous marriages. But the monogamous marriages were more popular and recognized than the polygamous marriages. We come across a number of examples, where the former is commended as well as praised, in the Rig Veda. In its very first chapter, it is mentioned that:

"As the rays of the sun touch roaring clouds, and lightening goads on the burst of clouds, and the clouds thunder and quench the earth, with cooling, cozy showers of mirth; So does the husband shower all pleasures, to his mate of graceful treasures, when enchanted by her hilarious touches, her smiling, bewitching, enfolding approaches; A sun like husband, luminous shining, and his wife alluring smiling, with their mutual attraction and love, like cloud and lightening shower heavenly love."[49]

In the same chapter it is further mentioned that:

"When a man accepts as wife, a lady lustrous as twilight, emerging out of night of darkness, as a guiding light of life; Well-versed in medical science, who keeps her household disease-free, and by her myriad virtues refined, keeps her household full of spree; And so does a lady garland a man, calm like moon, yet vigorous as sun, whoever attracts the charming lady, to his virtues divinely spun. The chariot of such a happy life, moves on to paths of plenty and pleasure, and heavenly virtues all descend, to make such abode a bed of treasure."[50]

Similarly at other places in the Rig Veda, it is stated that[51]:

"I clasp thy hand and enter into the holy state of matrimony so that we may be blessed with prosperity and noble progeny. Mayst thou live with me happily throughout life! Through the grace of the almighty Lord, who is the Creator and Sustainer of the universe and in the presence of this August assemblage, thou art being given away in marriage so that we may together rightly perform our duties as householders."

"With all my strength and resources, I have clasped thy hand; and thus united, we shall together follow the path of virtue. Thou art my lawfully wedded wife and I am thy lawfully wedded husband."

"God, the protector and sustainer of all, has given thee to me. From today, it devolves upon me to protect and maintain thee. Blessed with children, mayst thou live happily with me as thy husband for the full span of human life (a hundred years)."

"Following the divine law and the words of wisdom uttered by the sages, may we make a good couple and may God vouchsafe unto us a shining life of virtue and happiness."

"As God nourishes and sustains all creatures through His great forces like the sun, the moon, the earth, the air etc., so may He bless my wife with healthy and virtuous progeny and may you all assembled here bless her!"

"I accept thee as my partner for life. I will not keep away even mentally anything from thee. I will share with thee all I enjoy. We will persevere in the path of virtue, surmounting all obstacles. Let us be devoted to each other. Let us share each other's joys and sorrows, wish each other well and look upon each other with love and live happily for at least a hundred years. May we live, listening to sweet words for at least a hundred years. Distant though we were, one from the other, we now stand united. May we be of one mind and spirit!"

"Through the grace of God, may the eyes radiate benevolence. Be thou my shield. May thou have a cheerful heart and a smiling face. May thou be a true devotee of God and mother of heroes. May thou have at heart the welfare of all living beings!"

"I pray that henceforth I may follow thy path. May my body be free from disease and defect and may I ever enjoy the bliss of your companionship!"

"First gave the liberal gained a fragrant dwelling, and got themselves a bride in fair apparel (sic)."

"*Agni* hath given him the bride again with splendour and with ample life. Long lived be he who is her lord. A hundred autumns let him live."

The following hymns of the Atharva Veda,[52] also reflect the same mood:

"Same be your drink and common your food, to the same yoke together I bind you; Worship *Agni* together in harmony like spokes round the nave of a wheel."

"Like in heart, of like intent, non – hostile do I make you; One another you should love, as the cow loves her new born calf."

These are some of the examples, which prove the preponderance of monogamous marriages over that of polygamous marriages.

Similarly, the very word *dampatti*, denotes the inseparable duality of husband and wife, and excludes the third person from the conjugal life.[53] The Vedic Index says.... "the evidence points to the first wife wedded alone(sic) being a wife in the fullest sense."[54] The ritual, too, did not provide for the association of more than one wife in the normal sacrifice.

But in the Rig Veda itself, there are evidences of polygamous marriage. "The Rig Veda", observes R.C. Majumdar[55], "certainly permits polygamy (1.62.11; 71.1; 104.3; 105.8; 112.19; 186.7; VI.53.4; VII.18.2; 26.3; X.43.1; 101.11, etc.), though monogamy may have been the rule (I.124.7; IV.3.2; X.71.4). Whether monogamy developed from polygamy in the *Rigveda* age as Zimmer thinks, or whether polygamy is secondary as Weber believes cannot be decided. Probably polygamy, though allowed, was practically confined to the *rajanya* class. Polyandry is not referred to anywhere in the Rig Veda. The few passages in the wedding hymn (X.85.37, 38) in which "husbands" (plural) are spoken of in connection with a single wife can be explained on a mythological basis." Perhaps it was the result of the problem of surplus women, since the Aryans were going through a period of long and continuous struggle with the non-Aryans and this created a shortage of grown-up male members in the society. The large number of casualties faced by both the sides, forced them to find some way to solve the riddle of surplus women and hence polygamy was adopted by the Aryan society.

Some of the examples, which prove the existence of polygamy, are given below:[56]

"Between both poles, the car horse goes pressed closely as in his dwelling moves, the doubly wedded."

"Like rival wives on every side, enclosing ribs oppress me sore."

"........ as yearning wives cleave to their yearning husband."[57]

"The favourite wife neglected.... The favourite wife most dearly loved."[58]

Similarly, the expressions such as "like a king among his spouses, 'and as wives embrace their lord, found in the Rig Veda prove, beyond doubt, the existence of polygamy in the Vedic times.

According to B.S. Upadhyaya[59], "the close association of Aryans with Indo-Aryans may have led the former to conform to some of the customs of the natives. Further, the temptation of the victorious warriors, to appropriate to themselves the 'belles' of the enemy, must have led to the extenuation of the practice."

The paramountcy of sons for reasons secular and religious and the ardent desire for the continuance and preservation of the family line, further motivated the people to opt for polygamy. But in general, the practice far from being esteemed, was an object of social disapprobation and condemnation.[60]

In the Vedic period, the practice of child marriage was not prevalent in India. A perusal of the marriage hymn, which reflects a great deal on the status and age of the bride, shows her to be fully grown and mature at the time of her marriage. Similarly, at another place in the Rig Veda there is mention of "beautiful damsels who selected their own life partners."[61] The tradition of imparting education to the girls and the freedom enjoyed by them in the selection of their husbands, coupled with the respect and love they enjoyed, created an atmosphere of enlightenment in the society and as such the custom of child marriage was not prevalent. There are many hymns in the Rig Veda which clearly show that marriages were held, when both the parties were quite grown up. R.C. Majumdar,[62] observes that "the frequent mention of unmarried girls like Ghosha, who grew up in the houses of their parents (1.117.7; X.39.3; 40.5), the references to the ornaments worn by the maidens at festival occasions in order to win lovers (1.123.11; V11.2.5), reference to a youth's courtship of the maiden he loves (1.115.2), to the lover's gifts' (1.117.18), their mutual love (1.167.3; 1X.32.5, etc.) and to the spell (V11.55.5.8) by which a lover hopes to lull the whole household to sleep while he visits his beloved – are evidences which speak in favour of the custom of girls normally marrying long after they had reached puberty." Thus, 'Surya' is given in marriage by her father only when she is youthful and yearns for a husband.[63] The very use of different words for marriage like *udvaah* (i.e., carrying away,) *parinay, upayam, pani-grahan* etc. in Sanskrit language suggests of post-puberty marriage. In the Rig Veda, a hope is expressed that the bride would immediately take over the command, not only of the entire household, but also of the relatives.[64] This naturally implies that the bride must be mature enough to handle all the affairs of the family, otherwise such thing would not have been said there. In a similar manner, there are several *mantras* in the Atharva Veda through the use of which women's hearts could be captured;[65(a)] also there are mantras, the recitation of which ensured a sooner marriage[65(b)] and there are mantras, to increase the reproductive power of both males and females[65(c)], as well as to keep away the 'other' man or woman from mutual love or married life.[65(d)] These references again contradict the possibility of child marriage in the Vedic society.

The Role and the Importance of Wife

Position of the wife was honourable in the family. She was the centre of the domestic world and an empress or *samrajini.*[66] Without her, a man was incomplete and imperfect.[67] Wife's affection and children made a man *purush* or complete.[68] A wife was considered as *sharir-ardha* or *ardhangini,* i.e., the better half.[69] The husband and the wife were the two wheels of a chariot, each depending on the other, for its better functioning.[70] Woman as wife is denoted by the words *Jaaya, Janani* and *Patni* in the Rig Veda. As Jaaya she was the sharer of her husband's affections; as Janani she was the mother of children and as Patni, she was the partner in the performance of sacrifices.[71] A wife was considered as *sumangali* or *mangalmayi,*[72] *kalyani* or bestower of happiness[73] and most auspicious or *sivtama.*[74] The following seven vows, which were taken by the Aryans at the time of their marriage *(sapta-padi)* bring out clearly the importance and the position of wife:

"May the first step lead to food that is both nourishing and pure. May the second step lead to strength (at the physical, emotional, intellectual and spiritual levels). May the third step lead to prosperity. May the fourth step lead to all round happiness. May the fifth step lead to progeny (noble and virtuous children). May the sixth step lead to long life. May the seventh step lead to friendship (through harmony, understanding)."

After these seven vows were taken by the new couple, the bridegroom expressed his feelings in the following manner: "Having completed the seven steps, be thou my life-long companion. Mayst thou be my associate and helper in successful performance of the duties that now devolve upon me as a householder. May we be blessed with many children who may live the full duration of human life."

On marriage, the bride was accorded the most venerable position in the household. She entered the new home with all the rights of a wife and had the full authority to run the affairs of the family. Perfect harmony and happiness are prayed for in conjugal life, which (it is hoped) will be long enough to bless the couple with sons and grandsons.[75] The following hymns[76] describe the newly married wife as taking up a most respected position as the mistress of her new household, wielding authority over the husband's father, brother and unmarried sisters.

"Be not hostile to thy lord; Be tender to animals; Be amiable; Be very glorious; Be the mother of males; Be devoted to the Gods; Be the bestower of happiness; Be the bringer of prosperity to our bipeds and quadrupeds."

"Be a queen to thy father-in-law. Be a queen to thy mother-in-law.

Be a queen to thy husband's sisters. Be a queen to thy husband's brothers".

"This verse envisages the case," observes R.C. Majumdar[77], "very probably of the marriage of the eldest son in the family, when the old father has retired from active life. The authority exercised must have been more or less the rule of love." In the Vedic age the wife was on a level of equality at the hearth, which was the altar of sacrifice.[78] The Aryan wife, along with her husband, took active part in the spiritual life of the community and as such performed sacrifices, which was considered as the most sacred feature of the religious life of the Aryan people[79]. Singing of the Vedic hymns during the sacrificial session was long considered as the most appropriate function of the wife. Apart from that, her principal function in the Aryan household was to keep the domestic fire kindled at all hours, since Agni was the priest of all Gods.[80] In II.39.2 of the Rig Veda, the very word *Dampativa Kratuvida* shows that household fire was tended by husband and wife. The following hymns of the Rig Veda, clearly reveals this aspect of the Aryan wife.

"O God, with constant draught of milk, husband and wife with one accord. Press out and wash the soma juice...

Serving the Immortal one with gifts of sacrificial meal and wealth.

They satisfy the claims of love and pay due honour to the Gods."

"The married couples anxious to satisfy thee and presenting oblations together celebrate (they worship), for the sake of obtaining herds of cattle."[81]

"He, whom the two, a pair of equal age, dwelling in the same place and engaged in the same ceremony, worship night and day."

"Praiseworthy blessing hast thou laid, Indra laid upon the pair who with uplifted hands, serve thee man and wife."[82]

"*Agni,* great vital power is their, pairs waxing old in their devotion seek thee."[83]

"I cook the offering, I present oblations. Only my wife attends the service."

These passages clearly show that women actively participated in the religious ceremonies and without them the religious ceremonies were considered as incomplete and unfruitful. In the Vedas (the Rig Veda as well as in the Atharva Veda), the occurrence of the word dampatti at several places, itself suggests that the husband and the wife were regarded as one unit of society and as such the wife enjoyed all the privileges as were enjoyed by men of the Aryan society. It is interesting to note that in one of the hymns of the Atharva Veda, the husband declares that, "he is *Saam,* while his wife is *Rka*; he is sky, while his wife is earth; he is *Vishnu,* while his wife is *Laxmi;*" and thus indicates and accepts boldly, the inseparability of the two[84(a)]. Similarly, in the same chapter a blessing is given to the husband and wife that they should love each other like the *chakor* birds (i.e., love birds) and should enjoy all the worldly pleasures together[84(b)]. Regarding the inseparability of husband and wife, Prof. Indra has aptly remarked that, "the wife and husband being equal halves of one substance, were regarded equal in every respect, and both took equal part in all works, religious and social".[85]

Status of Women as Mothers

The Aryan race, for a long time, faced long and continuous wars and was in a state of 'do or die' against the non-Aryan tribes. These wars demanded soldiers, who could take the place of wounded and the deceased soldiers and as such women as progenitors of race soon became objects of veneration for them. "The chief object of the Vedic marriage," observes Sukla Das[86], "being the propagation of race by procreating male children, the woman was always looked upon as potential mother. Multiplication of stock to dominate over the non-Aryans was so vital that impotency, absence or death of a husband was no bar to her giving birth to a child. Hence the society sanctioned the system of *niyoga* and widow re-marriage". There are many hymns in the Rig Veda, which clearly reveal the status of motherhood in the Aryan society.[87] Some of them are quoted below:[88]

"Spare both him and her who have given us birth. O' Rudra abstain from striking the persons who are dear to us."

"Her servants are like sons, brought up in the same house and whom a virtuous wife, as well as, her husband cherishes equally."

"May Aditi receive me, as mother receives her son, and may my prayers go straight to her heart to abide there."

"As mothers care for their nurslings, so do heaven and Earth follow thee with solicited, O' Vigorous and Redoubtable Indra."

"The generous and magnificent soma unites himself as tenderly to the waters, as a nursling attaches itself to its mother."

" O divine dawn-like lady! motherhood indeed, is your coveted goal, cherishing for an inner melody, a child indeed, elevates your soul. Moved by hilarious, caresses, touches of your husband, lovable, adored you bear in your womb, your child adored. Mustered with painful pleasing clutches, offering this present of moonlike baby, you become grand, worshipful lady. Tolerant as earth, and high as sky, deep as ocean, luminous lullaby, with your friendly attitude to all, as a fairy you flutter in all. Salutations to thee ! ideal fair body to tension rid world; a sweet melody(sic)."

The Aryans recognized the importance of motherhood and soon they imposed human attributes on their deities. Aditi, who is believed to be the mother of gods, symbolizes motherhood. She is described as the mother of Mitra and Varuna[89] Aryaman, the Rudras, the Adityas and Indra. In later literature too, Aditi's character as a mother is preserved. In the Atharva Veda and the White Yajur Veda, goddess Aditi is invoked as a generous and mighty mother.[90] The following hymns bring out her motherly traits:[91]

"May Aditi welcome, even as a mother, her dear heart-gladdening son, my song that lauds her."

"Save us in depth and shallow from the foe, thou mother of strong sons. Let no one of our seed be harmed."

"We call to succor in the mother of those whose sway is just the queen of order. Strong rulers, for expanding never decaying, Aditi, gracious guide and good protectress."

"Let us bring hither, in pursuit of riches, Aditi our word, the mighty mother. Her in whose lap the spacious air is lying. May she afford us triply guarding shelter."

Prithvi is also spoken of as "kindly mother earth." Similarly in the *Atharva Veda,* Goddess Prithvi is eulogized as" a benevolent mother".

Saraswati is another goddess, reflecting the inborn kindness of motherhood.

"Best mother, best of rivers, best of Goddesses. We are as it were, of no repute. Dear mother give thou us renown ! In thee, Saraswati, divine, all generations have their stay."

The imposition of motherly traits on the female deities created a divine halo around the very idea of a mother.[92] This glorification and deification of the mother and motherhood in the Vedic mythology, had a far-reaching impact on the position of women. Even in the ages to follow when she was at the lowest ebb, her position as a mother continued to be one of deep veneration, respect and even worship.

From the above account, one can infer that the Vedic age was not a gender discriminatory age, that it was the golden age of Indian womanhood as she had a say in the socio-political affairs and had full and equal opportunities for the development of the self. She enjoyed all the privileges, which were enjoyed by the men of her society and was considered a partner in all affairs, whether domestic or religious. But in spite of that, there developed a school of thought in the Vedic times, which believed that women were inferior, untrustworthy, hypocrite, unfaithful and disobedient. "The tendency to regard women as fragile," observes Sukla Das,[93] "and of a weak moral standard, a means of enjoyment and a commodity crystallized later but their genesis can be detected as early as in the Vedic period." In the Rig Veda itself, in Chapter-VIII and Chapter-X, we find certain passages which held women in positive disrepute[94]:

"...Woman's mind is ungovernable and her intellect has little weight."

"There cannot be any friendship with a woman. Her heart is more cruel (*vrka*) than that of a hyena".

"... Women are evil personified ".

"...even a woman endowed with all virtues and qualities is far inferior to the worst or the lowest man."

" Lord Indra himself has said that women have very little intelligence. She cannot be taught".

Similarly, the Yajur Veda (VI.5.8.2) conveys the same prejudices, when it says – "Women's code says that the women are without energy. They should not get a share in property. Even to the wicked, they speak in feeble manner."

In the later Vedic texts, it is mentioned that:

"The meaning of a dream, the effects of clouds in autumn, the heart of woman, and the character of kings are beyond the comprehension of anybody," and, "it is more easy to discover flowers on the sacred fig tree, or a white crow, or the imprint of fish's feet, than to know what a woman has in her heart."

In the Atharva Veda, in Chapter XIV[95], a husband proclaims that his wife has been given to him by God Brihaspati to serve him and to secure progeny. The husband, even goes to the extent of calling her as his *poshya,* i.e., dependent. Similarly, in the Shatpath Brahman, women are dubbed as liars[96], physically inferior and unworthy of receiving *soma* in religious yajnas[97]. The Shatpath Brahman (XIV.1.1.31), clubs women, shudras (untouchables), dogs and crows together, and declares that falsehood, sin and gloom remain integrated in them.

In the husband-wife relationship, the husband was given an important position and the role of the husband was so much emphasized, that everything belonging to the wife (even her body) was considered as husband's property[98]. In the *Aitreya Brahman,*[99] the daughter has been described as "giver of pain to her relatives at her very birth, taker of family wealth at her marriage and creator of hardships for her parents because of her impulsive nature and exuberances of her youth".

These examples suggest that voices of dissent against the accepted norm of equality of men and women were beginning to raise their ugly head in the Rig Vedic time itself and gradually, these ideas were beginning to penetrate into the hearts of common men. "These uncomplimentary comments", remarks Sukla Das[100], "cannot be brushed aside as light-hearted cynicism. They offer index to social attitudes towards women that was taking root. Subsequent reduction of women to mere expendable commodity derives its origin from the Vedic ethos". It appears, "he further writes, "that just as buffaloes, camels and cattle were presented to the priests by their benefactors so also women were given as gifts as would appear from several hymns which glorified gifts of the generous donors".[101] In the Mahabharata there are several instances, where young girls and maid servants, were offered as *daan*. Raja Bhagiratha, on the completion of a religious yajna, gave away ten lacs young girls as *dakshina* to the priest class[102]. It is striking to note that wives were also offered as *dakshina* in that age. Raja Mitrasaha, offered his wife Madyanti to Maharishi Vasistha and then started his journey to *swargaloka* (heaven)[103]. In the same way, Kalmashapada and Yuvanashva gave away their wives as gifts or *daan*[104]. The period from 1000 B.C. to 500 B.C. witnessed further deterioration in the position and status of woman and womanhood in ancient India. Her educational rights now became a thing of the past as the Vedic studies became long and complicated, covering a period of 12 years. From this period onwards, *Upanayana* became a mere formality for women. Further, the introduction of inter-race marriages (i.e., marriages between Aryan males and non-Aryan females), the evolution of the theory of transmigration and the increasing significance of sons, for religious purposes, went a step further in lowering the status of women.

Towards the end of the Vedic age, especially in the Atharva Veda, we do observe the beginning of the theory of transmigration of soul, which had a direct bearing on the change of attitude towards women, with a firm belief in the endurance of sustenance of manes by means of oblation offered by the living. According to Hindu mythology it is believed that the soul of a parent achieves moksha or nirvana (freedom from material life) only if a son is born. At the funeral of an adult, only a male relative (a son or nephew) should light the pyre.

Over the issue of eligibility of sex to offer oblations, a son alone was thought to be competent. The very word *putra,* i.e., son means one who saves the father from going to a particular hell called *put*. Besides, the evolution of caste system and the availability of forced or cheap labour, made the Aryans ponder over the notions of ceremonial purity. Women were beginning to be considered impure and especially so, during pregnancy, child-birth and menstruation. Since the phase of the Atharva Veda the concept of a good woman had begun to surface round certain qualities. A woman was considered good if she pleased her husband, gave birth to male children and never contradicted her husband.[105] In the Brahman literature the definition of a good woman became more rigid. They were now being dubbed as "mere followers of their husbands, always walking behind."[106]

The patriarchal nature of society also influenced the status of women in the Vedic times. The Vedic marriage rituals emphasized the duty of obedience for the wife. The supreme authority was clearly vested in the husband as it was the bride who was bestowed.[107] Women had to leave their own family after marriage and stay with that of husbands', which influenced their property rights, to some extent. It is significant to note that in the vast range of the Vedic literature there is no instance of a woman sovereign either reigning independently or as a regent.

The prevalence of inter-caste marriages and the appearance of non-Aryan wives in the Aryan household, who had no prior knowledge of the Vedic literature or the religious ceremonies and rituals of their husband's race forced the scholars to impose new restrictions on the participation of women in the religious ceremonies, as they mispronounced words and recited the holy Vedic mantras incorrectly.

Even up to the period of the Ramayana and the Mahabharata, which had been compiled in 6th and 5th century B.C., women used to be fairly well-educated and they participated in the religious ceremonies of the society. They used to perform different *yajnas* themselves, without the aid of any priest. When Lord Rama was selected as the heir-apparent to the throne, his mother Kausalya, performed yajna for his safety, prosperity and happiness.[108] We come across a number of female-scholars, who were revered for their knowledge, and who were known far and wide. Kausalya, Tara, Pratitheyi and Badwa in the Ramayana were celebrated scholars of mantras (*mantra-vids*) and so were Sita and Atreyi[109]. Similarly in the Mahabharata, Sulabha was adept in the studies of Vedanta, while Draupadi was known as "*pandita*" and Kunti (mother of Pandavas) was a scholar of the Atharva Veda[110]. But by this time, a considerable change had occurred in the mentality of the society towards the girl child. The Ramayana tells us that when Sita came of age and her marriage had to be arranged her father's anxiety became as intense as that of a poor man, who suddenly loses all his money. The epic goes on to observe that a daughter's father, even if occupying a position as exalted as that of the king of gods, has to put up with insults not only from his equals but also from his inferiors. In one passage, it is said that it is very shameful for a man, to be the father of a girl child, as it is difficult for him to keep his head high.[111] Further in the epics, a girl child is supposed to be a constant bringer of sorrows and miseries to her family. In the Mahabharata, she is called "an enemy" and an "ill omen", as she takes away the family wealth in the form of *stree-dhan*, and as she could brings disgrace to her family because of her impulsive nature.[112]

"The Mahabharata", according to Sukumari Bhattacharji[113] a Sanskrit scholar, "presents two different pictures of women, one of which emerges from its prescriptive section and the other from the core section and there is a clear dichotomy between the two. Women in the core epic, behave with much greater freedom while those in other sections are presented as mere chattels." Similarly, Uma Chakravarti,[114] a feminist historian, while examining various sources of the Ramayana, remarks: "An analysis of the development of the Sita legend in a historical context, however reveals, that the emphasis on chastity and assumption that ideal marriage is based on female deviation are aspects which are grafted on to an originally simple story. Over the centuries important details added to the story have had a crucial influence on the shaping of the feminine identity".

In the age of the Sutras[115] (i.e., the period from 500 B.C. to 100 A.D., when Shrauta Sutra, Griha Sutra and Dharma Sutras were written) the inequities against women became fairly well-defined. In the Baudhayan Dharma Sutra, we find an exhaustive list of do's and don'ts for men, as far as their relation with women is concerned. Many new restrictions were imposed on them and an attempt was made to curtail their freedom in different social affairs. The Baudhayan Dharma Sutra severely criticizes a man, who dines together with his wife and enjoins that the wife should not eat before her husband; rather she should eat only after all the male members of her family have finished their food.[116] Independent existence was denied to her and it was believed by the Sutrakars, i.e., writers of the Sutras that her mind, her body and everything else which she possessed, belonged to her husband. Thus, she should do all her work with the sole aim of pleasing her husband and should not do anything that displeases or offends her husband. It was further laid down that she should submit herself to every demand or desire of her husband without asking a single question or without showing any hitch. Those who follow every order of their husband, have been glorified as *aprati-vadini* by the Baudhayan Dharma Sutra.[117] Sukumari Bhattacharji rightly observes that society demanded faithful obedience and allegiance from wives and their movements were largely controlled by the dominating males of the family.[118]

The writers of the Dharma Sutras went a step further and insisted upon pre-puberty marriages and held widow-remarriages in disrepute. The introduction and the adoption of pre-puberty marriages in the Hindu society was a revolutionary step and it soon became an accepted norm in the society. Perhaps the invasion of foreign tribes and the resultant chaos that followed thereby, forced the scholars of the day to recommend pre-puberty marriages. Moreover, the emergence of Buddhism and Jainism in 6th century B.C. and the longing of men and women, who were greatly inspired and motivated by the teachings of Lord Buddha and Mahavir, to join their orders, without caring to marry, forced the writers of the Sutras, to lower the age of marriage. The joining by the maidens, disturbed the institution of family upon which the Aryan society rested, and consequently it was thought that boys and girls should be married before they attained an age when they could exercise an intelligent choice in that matter. Further, many people who joined the monastic orders, without a genuine spiritual urge, found themselves unable to live up to the high standard and ideals of their teacher and soon indulged in moral lapses. Their lapses were furiously commented upon by the public and forced the social thinkers to feel that it would be better to prevent such abuses by making marriage obligatory for all girls.[119] Secondly, the marriage of girls came to be compared to the upanayana of boys at about this time. If upanayana was obligatory for boys, marriage which was its counterpart, ought to be absolutely binding on girls. Thus, motivated by these considerations, marriageable age of girls was reduced to 13 or 14 by this time. The Baudhayan Dharma Sutra even went to the extent of declaring that the corpse of a maiden can be burnt only after a formal marriage even after her death.[120]

The writers of the Dharma-Sutras, who flourished from 400 B.C. to 100 A.D. began to advise that marriages of girls should not be delayed long after their puberty. Two of them, viz., Vasishtha[121] and Baudhayan[122] were prepared to recommend that girls may be kept unmarried for a period of three years after their puberty, if there were difficulties in properly settling their marriages. But Gautam[123] and Vishnu insisted that marriages must be celebrated within three months of the time of puberty. It is clear that they were in favour of pre-puberty marriages in normal circumstances. Opinion was obviously divided at this time. Some thinkers pointed out that life was transitory, and if marriage was intended to ensure the continuance of the family, the bride should not be too young when it is performed. Others contended that absolute chastity was to be most desired, and so we should select a bride, who should not have even dreamt of sexual love.[124]

Soon after 100 A.D. this conflict ended and society definitely decided in favour of pre-puberty marriages. An undue premium came to be placed upon absolute chastity; in order to prevent the theoretical possibility of unchastity in any bride, it decreed that marriages should always be performed before puberty. Society was anxious that there should be no room whatsoever even for the possibility of any reports arising or reflecting upon the character of its maidens.[125] Further, an early marriage meant a son, soon after puberty, to ensure the continuity of the family and offer oblations to the manes. That this may mean an undue physical strain on the girl-mother was unfortunately not realized by the writers of the Sutras. The Indian society, like a number of 'classical' societies, was patriarchal in nature at that time. Patriarchal values regulating sexuality, reproduction and social production (meaning total conditions of production) prevailed at that time and were expressed through specific cultural metaphors. Overt rules prohibitting women from specific activities and denying certain rights soon came into existence. But a subtler expression of patriarchy was through symbolism giving messages of inferiority of women through legends, which highlights the self-sacrificing, self-effacing, and pure image of women. It was also through the ritual practices which day in and day out emphasized the dominant role of a woman as a faithful wife and devout mother. Fredrick Engles, in his seminal work, *Origin of the Family, Private Property and the State*, writes that "the overthrow of Mother Right was the world's historic defeat of the female sex". It was replaced by Father Right through the establishment of patriarchal families which made man the lord of the house and an absolute owner of the all movable and immovable property. It also made man as husband: the owner and proprietor of his wife. In this process the woman was reduced from an independent human person to a mere reproductive being whose sole purpose in life was to produce legitimate heirs (obviously sons) for him. This created a structure of unilateral and stringent standards of monogamous marriages for women accompanied by the concepts of virginity of the girl and of chastity and fidelity of the wife.

The period from 200 A.D. to 1000 A.D. was again a period of deterioration for the position and status of women, as the Smriti writers, who flourished at this period, imposed many new restrictions upon the body, soul and the very existence of the women of the day. Manu, for example, believed and insisted that women should never be allowed a free and independent status. In her childhood, she should remain under the control of her father, in her youth, she should remain under the control of her husband and in her old age, she should remain under the control of her sons.[126] "A woman who leads an independent life without any control, can bring ill fame to the family" was the belief of Manu.[127] He believed that the marriage ceremony or the *kanyadan* signifies the handing over of the bride, from the father to the groom and henceforward, the husband becomes the master or the lord of the wife, and as such she should obey, respect and follow every desire of her husband. Manu was not in favour of advocating women's participation in religious yajnas; on the other hand, he believed that by serving her husband faithfully and devotedly, a wife can attain the heaven or swarga. She should not, after her marriage, do anything that displeases or offends her husband. Then only she can expect to get a better husband, in the next birth. He was also not in favour of the remarriage of widows, and advised that after the death of her husband, she should lead an austere and simple life and should not even dream of any other man, even if she had no children from her dead husband. He severely criticizes and condemns a widow who wishes to remarry or who craves for physical pleasure. According to him, the partition of wealth, the marriage of the girls and the utterance of the words can take place only once in the entire life and they cannot be and should not be repeated.[128] Further, if the wife remains barren up to a period of eight years, then according to Manu the husband should remarry. If the wife delivers dead babies, then the husband can remarry in the tenth year and if she delivers only female – children then the husband can re-marry in the eleventh year. If the wife is ill-mouthed (*katuvadi*) then the husband can remarry in the very next year, was the advise of Manu. He also forbid the wife to participate in dance and music programmes of the community, if the husband does not wishes so.

Manu believed that women have been given birth by the almighty to procreate and as such if suitable groom is available, then they should be married, even if they have not attained the age of marriage. But in the absence of any suitable groom, Manu advised that, they should remain unmarried all through their lives but in no circumstance should they be forced to marry an unsuitable or unworthy groom. He also severely criticized the inter-caste marriages and enjoined that the girl of the other caste has no right to perform or participate in the religious ceremonies; and anyone who allows his inter-caste wife to perform such religious ceremonies, will himself lose his caste and should be ostracized by the community. Commenting upon these negations, Veena Das[129] has aptly remarked that, "women were literally seen as points of entrance, as 'gateways' to the caste system. If men of ritually low status were to get sexual access to woman of higher status, then the purity of not only the women, but also of the entire group would be endangered. Since the main threat to the purity of the group came from female sexuality, it becomes vital to guard it. Most groups solved this problem by the custom of pre-puberty marriage." Thus, marriage at an early date, marriage within the caste and even in the sub-caste, prohibition of *pratilom* marriage (where a woman of higher caste, marries a man of lower caste), marriage as a sacrament (whereby a woman is bound in wedlock till she dies), were all practices which suggest the control of female sexuality, according to Veena Das.

It will be interesting to note that even after such negative injunctions, Manu respected and held women in high esteem. According to him "God dwells in, where women are loved and respected" and where they are harassed, tortured, insulted or maltreated; there peace, prosperity, happiness and wealth can't remain.[130] The happiness of a man and of the family, depends upon the happiness of women in that family; if the women are happy, then everything will be well and fine but if they are unhappy then their curse will ruin the entire family. Manu even advocated and accepted the notion of woman's share in the parental property.[131] Manu has defined *stree-dhan* as "that which was given to her before the nuptial fire, in bridal procession, as token of love and which she has received from brother, mother, father or husband."

Yajnavalkya, another Smriti writer, insisted that girls should be married before the age of puberty; otherwise every month their guardians will be guilty of the destruction of an embryo.[132] Yama, who came about four hundred years later, stated that even if a suitable match is impossible, the girl should be married before she comes of age, even to an unsuitable husband.[133] The view of Yama was much more orthodox than Manu, as the latter was willing to allow a girl to remain unmarried even to the end of her life, if a proper husband could not be secured whereas the former did not mind a girl being chained to an unsuitable and undeserving husband for her whole life, if there was the least danger of the fatal line of the age of puberty being crossed before marriage.

The period from 500 A.D. to 1000 A.D. was a period of further decline for the position and status of women in India. The Smriti writers of this period, not content with prohibiting post-puberty marriages, began to encourage marriages much before the time of puberty. They held that a girl should be regarded as having attained puberty at the age of 10 and therefore her marriage should not be postponed beyond that age. At this time the ritual of marriage in the case of girls was regarded as corresponding to that of upanayana in the case of boys, the belief of the Smriti writers was that if the eighth year was the proper time for the latter, it ought to be the ideal time for the former also.

The custom of pre-puberty marriages became common among the Brahmans alone in the beginning and in spite of the universal and terrible condemnation of the post puberty marriages by Smriti writers from 200 A.D., child marriages did not come into vogue among the Kshatriyas for a long time.[134] Heroines of most of the Sanskrit dramas written during the period 300-1200 A.D. are grown up brides at the time of their marriages. Rajya-Shri, Kadambari and Mahashveta were fully grown-up before they were married. In the Kshatriya royal families, the prevalence of swayamvara form of marriage (if the testimony of the *Dvasraya-Mahakavya* of Hem Chandra and the *Prithviraj-Vijay* of Jayanak be regarded as valid for the survey of this period) would show that the girls were mature enough to choose their partners in life: The former mentions a swayamvara in which Mahendra of Nadol (A.D. 1000) held the ceremony for his sisters Durlabha Devi and Lakshmi. The *Prithviraj-Vijay* refers to the swayamvara of Kalavati, for whose hand twelve kings contested, and who was married to the ruler of Kanyakubja or Kannauj (probably Bhoja).

But the people in general, followed the dictates of the Smritis so girls, in the orthodox families of the Brahmans and those who followed their example, were married at a very early age. The twelfth year was the latest limit laid down for a girl to remain as a maiden.[135] A Brahman, found guilty of marrying a girl, after she had attained puberty in her father's house, was not considered fit for conversation and dining in the company of the other members of his caste. Alberuni, who witnessed these things personally, remarked that, "the Hindus marry at a very young age" and that "a Hindu is not allowed to marry a woman above twelve years of age. A number of foreign travellers and merchants tell us that boys and girls were married in India several years earlier than the time of puberty. Fitch,[136] a 16th century English trader, has noted that boys and girls were married at Murshidabad in Bengal at the age of 10 and 6 respectively. Manucci tells that during the 17th century girls were often married before they were able to speak but never after the age of 10. Similarly, according to Tavernier, the usual marriage-age was 7 or 8. In the British period, 8 or 9 was the usual marriageable age of girls.

A.S. Altekar points out certain factors which led to the popularity of early marriages. According to him, the upper section of society began to follow the example of the members of lower classes who married their daughters at a very early age because of the greed of bride-price, a custom which was fairly common among them. Secondly, he thinks that the girl's parents were always keen to avail themselves of the earliest opportunity to get a suitable bride-groom in a caste ridden society, where the field of selection had become confined to a few sub-castes. Thirdly, by marrying their daughters at a young age, the parents got relieved from the worry about their daughter's future. In case, the father died and the mother became a *sati*, the girl had her husband and his family to look after her, if she were married before their death. Lastly, Altekar opines, that as a result of the satisfactory economic condition in the society and the prevalence of the joint family system, people did not feel the necessity of postponing the marriage till the boy became an earning member.[137]

The period from 1000 A.D. to 1900 A.D. was one of rapid decline in women's status and completed the process of women's subordination. Many new practices emerged in the Indian society, which further degraded the status of women.

Practices like polygamy, *sati*, *jauhar*, child and unequal marriages, prohibition on widow remarriages (even those of child-widows), the ill-treatment of the widows and the negations imposed upon them, female infanticide, etc., completed the circle of their exploitation and made them fully subservient and dependent on their male counterparts. Their origin, their interrelationship with each other and the role played by them in Rajasthan, as well as the efforts to put an end to these practices, will be discussed in subsequent chapters.

Genesis of the Two Problems

In the Vedic age as we have seen, boys and girls were married at a fairly advanced age, when they were mature enough to understand the significance of their changing roles.[138] The marriage ceremony was performed only after the completion of the Brahmacharya-ashram. The existence of the Swayamvara form of marriage, is a clear indication of the fact that the women were fairly grown up and they had the right to choose their life-partners themselves. The case of the marriage of Sita in the Ramayana, and of Draupadi in the Mahabharata bears testimony to the above mentioned fact. But in the age of the Sutras, emphasis was laid on lowering the age of the bride. According to the Hiranyakeshi and Gobhil Griha-Sutra,[139] a *nagnika* girl was fit for marriage. Some scholars have interpreted the word nagnika, in a different sense. To them, nagnika girl means one who plays in the dust without properly covering her body, and without having any sense of shame or decency. While other scholars have expressed different version of this word and for them nagnika girl means one who is fit to meet her husband in privacy. In that age, a girl of eight years was called *gauri*, one who was 9 years old was called *rohini*, one who was between 10 to 12 years of age was known as *shyama*, and the one who was more than 12 years of age was called *kumari* and *rajaswala*. In the Dharmashastras, it is laid down that the marriage of a girl should take place before she has had her first menses.[140] Similarly, in the Smritis, the same position has been accepted. According to Manu, a man who is 30 years old should marry a girl of 12 years and one who is of 24 years should marry a girl of 8 years.[141] Kautilya in his famous treatise Artha Shastra has laid down 12 as the appropriate age of marriage for the girls.[142] The same views were held in the Gautam Dharmasutra and the Parashar-Smriti.[143]

Thus, because of the various *shastrik* injunctions, the age of marriage for both the girls and the boys was lowered and it was considered a great sin to have ones unmarried daughter at home, before she even reached the age of puberty.

The second important reason was the chaos created by the invasions of foreigners. The Greeks, the Sakas, the Bactrians, Kushanas, Hunas, Arabs, Mongols, Turks, etc., disturbed the social fabric and beside the wealth and territorial gains, they laid their hands upon the women of their invaded territory. They forced the Indian women to marry their invaders, looted them, and took thousands of them by the might of their brute force and all this forced the scholars of the day to lower the age of marriage. To maintain the purity of blood, to discourage inter-caste marriages, and to keep away their girls from the ill-sight of the foreigners, many restrictions were imposed and thus, child-marriage was a result of such restrictions.

Moreover, because of the influence of Buddhism and Jainism, some women left their homes and became *bhikshunis*. Thus, to discourage this tendency, the concept of child-marriage was introduced, so that their activities could be controlled and they could not use their free will to decide the course of their lives.

Another problem, which was the result of this deterioration of the status of women, was female infanticide. Female infanticide was prevalent in many societies of the world, whether civilized or uncivilized, and is still prevalent in the 21st century in new ways and forms. The origin of this practice and the period in which it started cannot be traced correctly. It was prevalent in various Rajput clans, the Jats, the Meenas, the Charans, the Ahirs, the Kapoors, the Bedis, the Sodhis, the Kallars, and the Khasis, for many reasons. Poverty, pride, superstition, prejudice, polygamy, illicit relationships, the problem of dowry were some of the important causes of female infanticide, in India and Rajasthan.

Because of the foreign invasions and their consequent victories, the territories of the kings shrunk in size and wealth and the constant wars took thousands and thousands of human lives. Such a position created great difficulties before the parents of the daughters as they were not sure about their own lives, about the future of their children and especially daughters and, about the future of their own kingdoms.

Moreover, the feeling of pride and prejudice about the greatness of their lineage and that of their blue blood was prevalent in certain ruling classes which forced them to consider themselves as superior to other clans or castes. Hence with such a false notion, they could not marry their daughters in families with lower rank. While a Rajput boy could marry a girl, of low family-status; such was not the case with the Rajput girl. It was mandatory for her parents to seek an alliance, in an equal, if not a higher family.

At the same time, a Rajput could not marry his children in his clan as the different *khaamps* or sects of the clan were considered as blood relatives. This clan exogamy, forced them to look outside their dynasties. Paucity of appropriate grooms created a new problem which was that of dowry, as it was the ardent desire of every parent to seek a higher alliance for her daughter. With already shrinking resources, it became difficult for them day by day, to cope with increasing demands of the bridegroom's parents, and these circumstances forced them to opt for the practice of female infanticide. A detailed description of the causes, incidences and the role of different social factors in the origin of child marriage and female infanticide are given in subsequent chapters.

Notes

1. Das, Sukla, "Status of Women in the Vedic Period: Genesis of Gender Polarity" in *Dimensions of Indian Womanhood* (Vol. III), C.M. Agrawal (ed.) Shri Almora Book Depot, Almora, 1993, pp. 64-65.
2. Srinivas, M.N. Cf. Bakshi, S.R. and Bala Kiran (eds.), *Social Status and Role of Women*, Deep & Deep Publications Pvt. Ltd., N. Delhi, 2000, p. 177.
3. Cf. Ibid., p. 178.
4. Pinkham, M.W., *Women in the Sacred Scriptures of Hinduism*, Columbia University Press, New York, 1941, p. 1.
5. Shastri, S.R., *Women in the Vedic Age*, Bhartiya Vidya Bhawan, Bombay (Mumbai), 1952, p. 65.
6. Das, Sukla, op. cit., pp. 64-65.
7. For further details on this topic please see Pinkham, op. cit., pp. 9-30.
8. *R.V.*, I.185-5, Cf. Upadhyaya, B.S., *Women in Rig Veda*, S. Chand & Co., N. Delhi, 1974, p. 43.
9. "पुत्रिणां ता कुमारिणा विश्वमायुर्व्यश्नुतः । उभा हिरण्यपेशसा" *R.V.*, VIII. 31.8.
10. *R.V.*, VI. 75.5 Cf. Upadhyaya, B.S., *Women in Rig Veda*, S. Chand & Co., New Delhi, 1974, p. 43.
11. *R.V.*, IX. 159.3 and also, *R.V.*, IX. 67.10 and *Y.V.*, 22.22 Cf. Vedalankar, Ramnath, op. cit., p. 25.

12. *R.V.*, I.23.24; I.136.6; II.33.1; X.18.2; X.85.27; X.85.43; X.128.5; *Y.V.*, XIX.48; XIV.1.53; XIV.1.54; XIV.2.31; XIV.2.64; The word *Praja* in these hymns stands for *santaan* i.e., children. Cf. Vedalankar, Ramnath, op. cit., p. 25.
13. *Brihadarayanak Upanishad*, 6.4.17.
14. Altekar, A.S., *Position of Women in Hindu Civilization*, Motilal Banarsidas, Delhi, 1973, p. 10. And also, Mishra, Jai Shankar, *Pracheen Bharat ka Samajik Itihaas*, Bihar Hindi Grantha Academy, New Delhi, 1992, p. 417.
15. Shastri, S.R., op. cit., pp. 25-27.
16. Upadhyaya, B.S., op. cit., p. 181; and also, Shastri S.R., op. cit., pp. 25-29.
17. Upadhyaya, B.S., op. cit., p. 181.
18. Shastri, S.R., op. cit., pp. 25-29.
19. Altekar, A.S., op. cit., pp 9-10.
20. *R.V.*, III.55.16, and also *Y.V.* VIII.1, and *A.V.*, XII.3.17, 18; XI.5.8 Cf. Upadhyaya, B.S., op. cit., pp. 179-180. And also, Kapoor, Devendra, Kumar, *Success Motivating Vedic Lores*, Deva Vedic Prakashan, Bombay (Mumbai), 1978. pp. 45-46.
21. "ब्रह्मचर्येण कन्या युवानं विन्दते पतिम् ।" *A.V.*, II.5.18.
22. Altekar, A.S., op. cit., p. 10.
23. *R.V.*, I.117; X.179. Samhita and Pada Text with Sayana's commentary, Critically ed. By Vedic Samshodhana Mandala, 4 vols. Poona, 1933.
24. Ibid., I.179.
25. Ibid., VIII.91.
26. Ibid., V.28.
27. Ibid., V.28.1.

27 (a) Altekar, A.S., op. cit., p. 14.

28. Upadhyaya, B.S., op. cit., p. 183.
29. *R.V.*, IX.56.3, 1.116.15; 112.10; 118.8; X.39.8; X.102-103 IX.66.8, Cf. Upadhyaya, B.S, op. cit., pp. 185-187.
30. *R.V.*, I.48.6, 124.8, IV.58.8, VII.2.5; IX.4; X.86.10.
31. Ibid., X.168.2.
32. Ibid., X.86.10.
33. *R.V.*, X. 102.2. And also, X. 102.5, X.102.11.
34. Ibid., I.116.15; 112.10; X.39.8.
35. Sharma, Tripat, *Women in Ancient India, 320 A. D. – 1200 A.D.*, Delhi, 1987, p. 10.

36. *R.V.*, I.17.116.15. And also, *R.V.* I.17.119.8.
37. *R.V.*, V.61; 80.6; VII.78.5; VIII.33; 19.91, Cf. Upadhyaya, B.S., op. cit., p. 187.
38. *A.V.*, XIV.1.47; *Y.V.*, V.10; V.12; X.26; XIII.16; XIII.18; *R.V.*, X.86.9; X.159.2-5; X.159.3; X.159.4; X.159.5, Cf. Vedalankar, R., op. cit., pp. 22-24.
39. "गृहान्गच्छ गृहपत्नी यथासो वशिनी त्वं विदथमा वदासि ।।" *R.V.*, X.85.26.
40. *R.V.*, I.67.3, Cf. Tripat Sharma, *Women in Ancient India*, Ess Ess Publications, New Delhi, 1988, p. 11.
41. "एना पत्या तन्वं स सृजस्वाधा जिव्री विदथमा वदाथः ।" *R.V.*, X.85.27; and also, *A.V.*, XIV.1.21; VIII.1.6.
42. *Journal of the American Oriental Society*, 19, p. 14.
43. Sharma, R.S., *Aspects of Political Ideas and Institutions in Ancient India*, Delhi, 1959, p. 64.
44. Altekar A.S., op. cit., p. 343. And also "अयज्ञियो वा एष योऽपत्नीकः", *Taittriya Brahman*, II, 2.2, 6.
45. Upadhyaya, B.S., op. cit., pp. 75-76.
46. " आ वां रथं दुहिता सूर्यस्य कार्ष्मेवातिष्टदर्वता जयन्ती ।
विश्वे देवा अन्धमन्यन्त ह्रद्भिः समु श्रिया नासत्या सचेथे ।।" *R.V.*, I.116.17; X.85.9, 14.
47. Shastri, S.R., op. cit., p. 43. And also, Majumdar, R.C.; Pusalkar A.D.; Majumdar A.K., *The Vedic Age (The History and Culture of the Indian people)*, Bhartiya Vidya Bhawan, Bombay, 1971, pp. 392-394.
48. Thomas, P., *Indian Women through the Ages*, Asia Publishing House, Bombay, 1964, p. 8.
49. *R.V.*, I., 79.2. Cf. Kapoor, Devendra, Kumar, op. cit., pp. 51-52.
50. *R.V.*, I.123.1, Cf. Ibid., pp. 56-58.
51. " आगधिता परिगधिता वा कशीकेव जंघहे ।
ददाति मह्यं यादुरो याशूनां भोज्या शता ।" *R.V.*, I.126.6; And also, I.127.7; I.131.3; III.53.4; IV.3.2; X.85.23; X.85.39; X.107.9.
52. *A.V.*, III. Cf. Majumdar, R.C., Pusalkar, A.D.; Majumdar A.K., op. cit., pp. 456-458.
53. Altekar, A.S., op. cit., p. 104.
54. MacDonnell & Keith, *Vedic Index I.* p. 476.
55. Majumdar, R.C.; Pusalkar A.D.; Majumdar A.K., op. cit., pp. 392-394.
56. *R.V.*, X.101.11, 1.105.8; Cf. Upadhyaya, B.S., op. cit., pp. 111-112.
57. *R.V.*, I.62.11, VII.18.2; VII.26.3; X.43.1 Cf. Pinkham, op. cit., p. 17.
58. *A.V.*, XX.128.10-11. Cf. Pinkham, op. cit., p. 17.
59. Upadhyaya, B.S., op. cit., p. 111.

60. Prof. Indra, *The Status of Women in Ancient India*, 1940 (Place not mentioned) p. 67.
61. "भद्रा वधूर्भवति यत् सुपेशाः स्वयं सा मित्रं वनुते जने चित।" *R.V.*, X.,27.12.
62. Majumdar, R.C.; Pusalkar A.D.; Majumdar A.K., op. cit.
63. *R.V.*, X.85.9, Cf. Altekar, A.S., op. cit., p. 49.
64. *R.V.*, X.85.46, Cf. Shastri, op. cit., p. 17.
65. (a) *A.V.*, VI.9.99; VI.10.102.
65. (b) *A.V.*, II.6.36.
65. (c). *A.V.*, VI.10.101.
65. (d) *A.V.*, VII.3.36-37-38.
66. " सम्राज्ञी श्वशुरे भव सम्राज्ञीं श्वश्रूवां भव।
ननान्दरि सम्राज्ञी भव सम्राज्ञी अधि देवृषु।।" *R.V.*, X.85.46 and also, *A.V.*, XIV. 2.16-17-26-40-63-64.
67. *Shatpath Brahman*, 5.2. 1.10.
68. *Mahabharata*, Adi Parva, 74.40.; Brihaspati, 25.11; Aparark, 7.40.
69. *Brihat Samhita*, 74.5, 5, 11, 15. And also, *M. S.*, 9.26.
70. *Taittriya Brahman*, 3.75.
71. Shastri, S.R., op. cit., pp. 18-19.
72. "सुमङ्गलीरियं वधूरिमां समेत पश्यत्।
सौभाग्यमस्यै दत्वायाथास्तं वि परेतन।।" *R.V.*X.85.33.
73. Ibid., III.53.6.
74. Ibid., X.85.37.
75. *R.V.*, VIII.31.4-5-6-7-8-9; X.85.25-26-27; X. 85. 33-36-42-43-44-45-46.
76. Ibid.
77. Majumdar, R.C.; Pusalkar A.D.; Majumdar A.K., op. cit., pp. 392-394.
78. Macdonald, *Vedic Religion*, p. 158, Cf. Pinkham, op. cit., p. 18.
79. "संहोत्र स्म पुरा नारी समनं वाव गच्छति।
वेधा ऋतस्य वीरिणीन्द्रपत्नी महीयते विश्वस्मादिन्द्र उत्तरः।।" A.V. XX. 9.126.10. And also, "योषितो यज्ञिया इमाः।" *A.V.*, 2, 36.1; 11.1.17.27.
80. Upadhyaya, B.S., op. cit., p. 140.
81. *R.V.*, I.131.3, and also 1.144.4; Cf. Shastri, S.R., op. cit., pp. 19-20.
82. *R.V.*, I.83.3, Cf. Prof. Indra, op. cit., pp. 85-86.
83. *R.V.*, V.43.15, and also *A.V.*, XII.3.43; Cf. Pinkham, op. cit., p. 19.
84. (a) "O virtuous one! I have accepted thee thoughtfully and so hast thou accepted me. Out of the fullness of love have I accepted thee and so hast thou accepted me. I am the *Saam* and thou art the *Rik*. I am the *Dyau* (heaven) and thou art the earth. We marry each other joyously. May we be blessed with bright, heroic and long-lived children!"

"अमोऽहमस्मि सा त्वं सामाहमस्म्यृक त्वं द्यौरहं पृथिवी त्वम्।
ताविह सं भवाव प्रजामा जनयावहै।" *A.V.* XV. 2.2.71.

84. (b) "इहेमाविन्द्र सं नुद चक्रवाकेव दम्पती।
प्रजयनौ स्वस्तकौ विश्वमायुर्व्यश्नुताम्।" *A.V.* XV.2.2.64.

85. Prof. Indra, op. cit., p. 26.

86. Das, Sukla, op. cit., p. 65.

87. Wilson, *Rig Veda* (ed. 1888), Vol. I, p. 307 V7 Cf. CD Bader; Clarisse, *Women in Ancient India*, Anmol Publications, Delhi, 1988, p. 52.

88. Wilson, op. cit., Vol. I, p. 195, V3, and also p. 303, Vol. V, p. 202, V6, Vol. V.362 Cf. Bader, op. cit., p. 52. And also, Kapoor, Devendra Kumar, op. cit., pp. 53-55.

89. *R.V.*, VIII.25.3.; 47.9; 90.15 and also, II.27.7; X.36.3; 132.6.

90. *A.V.*, VII.6.2; VII.6.1; 2.4; XII.1.8 W.Y.V., 21.5. Cf. Pinkham, op. cit., pp. 9-12.

91. *R.V.*, V.42.2, VIII.56.10-12; X.18.10; II.41-16 Cf. Pinkham, op. cit., pp. 9-12.

92. "माता पुत्रत्वस्य भूयांसि कर्मण्यारभते।
तस्यां शुश्रुषा नित्या पतितायामपि।" *Apastamba Dharma Sutra*, 1.10.28.9.
And also,
"नास्ति मातृसमा छाया नास्ति मातृसमा गतिः।
नास्ति मातृसमं त्र्रणं नास्ति मातृसमा प्रिया।।" *Mahabharata*, 12-266.31.

93. Das, Sukla, op. cit., p. 64.

94. "इन्द्रश्चिद् घा तद्ब्रवीत्स्त्रिया अशास्यं मनः उवो अह क्रतुं रघुम्।" *R.V.* VIII.33.17. And also,
"न वै स्त्रैणानि सख्यानि सन्ति सालावृकाणां हृदयान्येता।।", *R.V.*X.85.15.

95. "ममेयमस्तु पोष्या मह्यं त्वादाद् बृहस्पतिः।
मया पत्या प्रजावति सं जीव शरदः शतम्।।" *A.V.*XIV.1.1.52.

96. *Shatpath Brahman*, 14.1.1.31.

97. *Taittriya Samhita*, 6.5.8.2.

98. *Shatpath Brahman*, 4.4.2.13.

99. "संभवे स्वजन दुखकारिका, संप्रदान समयेऽर्थहारिका।
यौवनेपि बहुदोषकारिका, दारिका हृदयदारिका पितुः।।"
Commentary of Sayana on *Aitreya Brahman*, 33.1, Cf. Mishra, Jai Shankar, op. cit., p. 380.

100. Das, Sukla, op. cit., p. 61.

101. *R.V.* X.34.2-4.

102. Cf. Mishra, Jai Shankar, op. cit., p. 363.

103. *Mahabharata*, 2-298.16, 2.51.8, 2.52.11, 2.33.52, 12.29.65. and also,
"राजा मित्रसहश्चैव वसिष्ठाय महात्मने।
मदयन्तीं प्रियां भार्यां दत्वा च त्रिदिवि गतः।।" *M.B.*, 12.234.30.

104. Ibid., 1.184.20.
105. *A.V.*, XI.5.18.
106. *Brihadarayanak Upanishad*, I. 9.2.14.
107. Upadhyaya, B.S., op. cit., p. 68.
108. *Ramayana*, 2.20.15.
109. Ibid., 2.20.15, 4. 16.12, 5. 15.48.
110. *Mahabharata*, 3, 305-20.
111. "कन्या पितृत्वं दुखं हि नराणां मानकांक्षिणात्।
कन्या हि द्वे कुले नित्यं संषये स्थाप्य तिष्ठति।।"
Valmiki Ramayana, and also, Altekar, A.S., op. cit., p. 5.
112. *Mahabharata*, 1.15.9.11; 6.3.7.
113. Cf. Bakshi, S.R. and Bala Kiran, op. cit., pp. 178-179.
114. Ibid.
115. The prominent *Grihasutras* and *Brahmsutras* were: *Apastamba Grihasutra, Baudhayan Grihasutra, Hiranyakeshi Grihasutra, Parashar Grihasutra, Sankhayana Grihasutra, Asvalayana Grihasutra, Apastamba Dharmasutra, Baudhayan Dharmasutra, Gautam Dharmasutra, Vasistha Dharmasutra*, Cf. Altekar, A.S., op. cit., pp. vii & viii.
116. *B.D.S.*, 1.1.19.
117. Ibid.
118. *Journal of the Asiatic Society*, Vol. 32, No. 1-2, 1990, p. 63.
119. Altekar, A.S., op. cit., pp. 32-33.
120. "तथैव कन्यां च मृतां प्राप्त यौवनां तुल्येन पुंसा प्राप्तगृहवत्तां दहेत्।" *Baudhayan Sumarta Sutra*, V, 9.
121. "ऊर्ध्वं त्रिभ्यो वर्षेभ्यः पतिं बिन्दत्तुल्यम्।
त्रीणि वर्षाणयुदीक्षेत कुमारी ऋतुमती सती।।" *V.D.S.*, XVII.59.
122. "त्रीणी वर्षाणयुदीक्षेत कुमारी ऋतुमती सती।
कुमारी ऋतुमती त्रीणी वर्षाणयुदीक्षेत।।" *B.D.S*, IV.1, 14.
123. "त्रीन्कुमारी ऋतूनतीत्य स्वयं युज्येतानिन्दितेन उत्सृज्य पित्रयानलंकारान।" *G.D.S.*,XVIII.20.
124. *Mahabharata*, XIII, 79, 14.15.
125. "त्स्माद्विशल्ययितुमिच्छसि मां यदि त्वं
वत्से तदुन्मिषति नूतनयौवने ऽस्मिन्।
न स्वेच्छमर्हसि चिरं खलु कन्यकात्व–
मासेवितुं सुलभदुर्लभदुष्प्रवादम्।।" *Kama-Sutra*, 34, 229.
126. *Manu Smriti*, V.150, Manoj Pocket Books, Delhi, First edition (Year not mentioned), p. 167.
127. Ibid., V.152, 155, 158, 168 pp. 167-170.
128. Ibid., IX.46, 80, 83, 87, 88 pp. 282-288.

129. Cf. Bakshi, S.R. and Bala, Kiran, op. cit., p. 186.
130. *Manu Smriti*, III.56, 57, 58, 59, 60, 61, 62; p. 78.
131. Ibid., IX.117, 129, 130, 191, 192, 193; pp. 292-303.
132. Cf. Altekar, A.S., op. cit., p. 56.
133. Ibid; p. 57.
134. Sharma, B.N., *Social Life in Northern India, (AD 600 to 1000)*, Munshiram Manoharlal, Delhi, 1966, p. 14.
135. Ibid., p. 15.
136. Cf. Altekar, A.S., op. cit., p. 61.
137. Altekar, A.S. op. cit., pp. 59-61.
138. "सोमो वधूयुरभवदश्विनास्तासुभा वरा।
सूर्या यत्पत्ये शंसन्तीं मनसा सविता ददात्।।" *Rig Veda*, X.85.9.
139. "नग्निकांतु वहेत्कन्यां यावन्नर्तुमती भवेत।" *Gobhil Griha Sutra*, 3.4.6.
140. "माता चैव पिता चैव ज्येष्ठो भ्राता तथैव च।
त्रयस्ते नरकं यान्ति दृष्टवा कन्यां रजस्वलाम्।।" *Samvarta Smriti*, 1.67.
141. "त्रिषंद्वर्षेदिहेत्कन्यां ह्रयां द्वादशवार्षिकीम्।
त्रयष्टवर्षेऽष्टवर्षं वा धर्मे सीदति सत्वरः।।" *Manu Smriti*, 9.94.
142. "द्वादशवर्षा स्त्री प्राप्त व्यवहार भवति।" *Artha Shastra*, 3.2.
143. "अप्रयच्छन्दोषी" *G.D.S.*, 18.22. and also,
"प्राप्ते तु द्वादशे वर्षे यः कन्यां न प्रयच्छति।
मासि मासि रजस्तस्य पिबन्ति पितरोऽनिशम।।" *Parashar Smriti*, 7.7-8.

2

Origin of Female Infanticide

Infanticide, or the killing of the newborn, has often been interpreted as a primitive method of birth control and a means of ridding a group of its weak and deformed children. Children are put to death (or they allowed them to die) only under exceptional circumstances. Infanticide, in different forms, for different reasons was practiced by various societies of the world. It was prevalent among the Sabines, the Phoenicians, the Carthagians, the Greeks, the Romans, the Persians and the Canaanites, as they sacrificed children of tender age, either to avert an evil or a calamity or for attainment of some desire.[1] The Spartans also practiced it and they killed weak, deformed or diseased infants for the purpose of getting healthy and strong warriors.[2] The practice was prevalent among the Arabs, who buried their female offspring under their altars to save them from falling into hostile hands and thereby getting dishonoured and defiled.[3] It was even practiced by the Greeks,[4] the Italians,[5] the Polynesians, the Chinese and the Japanese (where it was called 'mabiki') to maintain an effective population, or to give up their duties of rearing their children.[6]

The custom of female infanticide was also practiced by the Eskimos, as the conditions of life were so severe that female children were killed shortly after birth, lest they do not find husbands to support them. And the horrible custom of infanticide was also prevalent among the 'civilized' nations of Europe, as late as the 19th century, and it included the practice of 'over-laying' (smothering) an infant, sharing a bed with his/her parents and the abandonment of unwanted infants.[7]

In many societies practicing infanticide, infants were not deemed to be fully human, until they underwent a rite of initiation that took place for some days to several years after birth, and therefore killing before such initiation was socially acceptable. The purposes of infanticide were many: to maintain the purity of blood, child spacing or fertility control in the absence of effective contraception, elimination of illegitimate, deformed, orphaned or twin children or sex preferences, to name a few.

The practice of infanticide was also prevalent in India amongst several communities like the Khatris, the Gakkhars, the Khokhars, the Malhotras, the Seths, the Kakkars, the Bedis, the Kapurs, the Sodhis, the Aroras, the Suyals, the Moyal Brahmans, the Rajputs, the pure Pathans and the Mohammedans of Punjab; the Jarejas (Jadejas), the Jaitwas, the Lewa Khombees of Gujarat; the Jats, the Gujars, the Ahirs, the Tagas and the Koris of North-Western Provinces. Similarly, it existed in the then Western Province (now Uttar Pradesh), among the Bais Rajputs of Kooba Tappa in Deogaon; the Raj Kumar Rajputs of Jaunpur; the Gautam Rajputs of Doulatabad tappa in Nizamabad pargana; the Raghu Vanshi Rajputs of Dhobee tappa in Kerakat pargana in Jaunpur; the Kachwaha, the Bhadauri and the Parihar Rajputs of Bara Pargana; the Chauhans and the Ahirs of Mainpuri; the Hara, the Surajbhans, the Kalhans of Gorakhpur.[8] In Bengal, the infants were thrown in the Ganges, as an offering to the deities.[9] Amongst the Kallars of Tamil Nadu, girl-children were put to death for social and economic reasons.[10]

The practice of female infanticide was also prevalent in certain tribal groups like the Nagas[11] of the North-eastern region; the Khonds[12] of Orissa and the Todas[13] of Nilgiri hills and the main cause for its prevalence among them was inefficient family planning. The Nagas practiced it "in order to save themselves from the annoyance of being harried by wife hunting parties from a stronger clan". The Khonds believed that, "it was better to destroy girls in their infancy, than to allow them to grow up and become causes of strife afterwards".

One of the several reasons, extended for the existence of this practice among the several castes and tribes, mentioned above, was the prevalence of hypergamous marriages, a custom which forbids the marriage of a woman with a person of lower social standing. This invariably led to the giving of large dowry to secure a bridegroom of high social status. The financial burden of marrying off a daughter, and the social stigma of having an unmarried daughter at home, forced people to kill infant girls at birth. There were also certain superstitious beliefs which lent credence to the prevalence of female infanticide. A common belief was that if you kill a female child, the next one is sure to be a male. Another belief was that female children bring ill luck to the family, and could bring possible disgrace to the family honour because of their youthful exuberances. Similarly, the Khonds believed that the souls of girl children, killed as a result of infanticide, would not be born again and hence the number of female children would decrease in their society.

The practice of female infanticide was prevalent in Rajasthan, in certain clans of Rajputs like the Rathores of Marwar,[14] the Bidawats of Bikaner,[15] the Bhumia-Tanwars of Torawati,[16] and the Kachwahas of Jaipur,[17] the Bhatis of Jaisalmer,[18] the Solankis and the Hara Rajputs of Bundi,[19] "the low and the high Rajput classes" of Sirohi[20] the Rajputs of Jhalawar[21] and it was also prevalent "to a considerable extent" in the Shekhawati region.[22]

The Charans and the Bhats,[23] the Meenas,[24] the Ahirs and Jats (of Bharatpur)[25] and the Mers or Mhairs (of Ajmer-Merwara)[26] also practiced female infanticide. The Rathores of Marwar practiced it, since they were afraid of the extortionate demands of Charans and Bhats, at the time of marriage and also considered it as disgraceful to have an unmarried daughter at home.[27] The Charans and Bhats practiced it, on account of the prevalence of dowry expenses (like Rajputs) in their community.[28] The Rajputs of Kutch or Kathiawar and the sandy deserts of Rajasthan practiced it for economic and social reasons.[29] The tribes of Meenas and Mhairs of Ajmer and Udaipur, were equally proud of their lineage as the Rajputs themselves and adopted it from them, as an imitation.[30] The Jats of Bharatpur and nearby regions practiced it, for they took it as disgraceful to give their daughters in marriage to anyone.[31] Among the lesser noteworthy families, it prevailed in the house of Asoph, Kuchamun and Neemuch.[32] It is important to note that no evidence of the prevalence of this evil custom has been found among the Brahmans and the Mahajans of Rajasthan. Neither the local historians nor the English officers have said anything, in this regard, for them. Rao Raja Rial Mal or Rid Mal,[33] the Jodhpur Vakeel, has recorded in this connection that, "it is a practice confined to Rajputs alone and is not carried out by the Brahmans and Mahajans".

The practice of female infanticide in the Rajputana, did not arise from any religious motive. It developed under certain specific conditions and was conditioned by the peculiar political, social and economical circumstances of the age. "Pride, poverty, and avarice were in league to perpetuate this crime."[34] It was a practice which arose out of the social customs, institutions and the prevalent notions of the inferiority or superiority of a particular caste, clan or tribe. The roots of the evil lay deep in the institution of caste and marriage.

It is difficult to say how this practice originated in India as well as in the Rajputana. In fact, female infanticide was an obvious outcome of the gradual degradation in women's position, due to socio-economic and political factors. It is difficult to trace the origin of this evil practice, but it became firmly rooted by the medieval period.

There are no references to this evil custom in the Vedic, epic or classical literature.[35] Some European scholars, e.g., Weber, Zimmer and Dalbruck, have misunderstood and misinterpreted some of the hymns of the Vedic texts and wrongly concluded that the practice was prevalent in the early period of ancient Indian history.[36] Relying upon Taittriya Samhita, they came to the conclusion that female infanticide was prevalent in the Vedic society, but the passage upon which they have based their findings, simply points that the birth of a daughter was not greeted with as much joy as that of a son. The passage in question, merely refers to the traditional habit of Hindu midwives of keeping the child aside on the ground if it were a daughter, and of lifting it up in joy if it were a son. There are many passages in the ancient literature of India which express the fondness for the male child and undesirability of the daughters.[37] Also, there are texts relating to charms and rituals for ensuring the birth of sons.[38] Prayers and ceremonies came into existence as early as the Atharva Veda, as it mentions the *punsuvan* ceremony[39] (VI.11.3) which was one of the 16 *sanskars* to be followed by the Aryans. When a woman conceived, it was desired that she should deliver a male child. Therefore, at a particular time (for example, when the moon entered in *pushya nakshatra*) the expectant lady was given milk of *shami vriksha*, i.e., banyan tree to smell and a water pot full of water, called *purna kumbha* was given to her. Some drops of the juice of the bark of banyan tree, were also dropped in the right nostril of the expectant lady at night to avoid any possibility of miscarriage. During the ceremony it was prayed that: "Almighty God, you have created this womb. Women may be born somewhere else but sons should be born from this womb" and "O Husband, protect the son to be born. Do not make him a woman" (Atharva Veda, II. III.23).

These ceremonies indicated the valour of manhood and were to be performed on a pregnant woman to ensure the inception as well as the safety of a male child in the mother's womb. But from these passages, it cannot be concluded that female infanticide was practiced in ancient India. If the evil had been common, it would surely have been condemned by the Sutra and Smriti writers, who regarded the destruction of an embryo as one of the seven most abominable and heinous crimes.[40] The crime could not have prevailed in the Vedic period, since a girl was not considered as a burden or a source of anxiety to her parents and her marriage was not a problem for them. As we have seen in Chapter 1, women of the Vedic period enjoyed a considerable amount of freedom and personal space and were not in a subservient or secondary position vis-à-vis their male counter parts. Further, there is no evidence to show that inter-caste marriages or inter-dining amongst the four *varnas* was prohibited in the Vedic period.[41] "There is no authority", wrote Max Muller, "whatever in the hymns of the *Veda* for the complicated system of the castes; no authority for the offensive privileges claimed by the *Brahmans;* no authority for the degraded position of the *Shudra;* no law to prohibit the marriage of people belonging to different castes; no law to brand the offspring of such marriage with an indelible stigma".[42]

The complicated system of castes with its elaborate rules, restrictions, taboos and the accompanying privileges of the Brahmans was not present in that society, which later on became a supporting factor for female infanticide. Many works of the later period, mention the rise of mixed castes from the marriages of men and woman of different Varnas, which further complicated the whole social scenario.[43] As a natural fallout of this process, in the later period, we find the growth and development of a complex system of social differences, with innumerable divisions and subdivisions of castes and clans. This paved the way for various new exogamous and endogamous groups, which resulted in a more complicated system of caste distinctions and social precedence. Each caste, now had its own set of rules, which determined the individual's social status, his privileges, his occupation, his mannerism and his social behaviour. Each caste kept itself aloof from the other, as a result of which artificial and rigid barriers were created between one caste and the other. In the Rajputana, endogamy,[44] i.e., "marrying in" or marriage within one's own group was practiced at caste and sub-caste levels by the members of all the castes irrespective of their traditional high or low position in the social structure. It was imperative for a Rajput girl, to marry a husband belonging to either her equal or preferably, to a superior class and it was the ardent desire of every Rajput to establish matrimonial relations in a more powerful, more affluent and more reputed family than his own.[45] Beside endogamous rules, the exogamous restrictions[46] related to *gotra, sapravar* and *sapinda* rules were also followed in the Rajputana for controlling the choice of mates. According to rules laid down in Hindu Dharma Shastras, persons who are *sagotra, sapinda* or *sapravar* are not eligible for marriage. Gotra which probably meant herd, and which later on had come to denote the family or clan, was the exogamous group and hence, marriage within one's own gotra was considered to be incestuous among the Hindus and particularly Rajputs in the Rajputana. Moreover, the ranks of different castes in social hierarchy varied from place to place and region to region and all this created confusion in the then social structure. A marriage outside one's own caste was inconceivable and selection of boys and girls of marriageable ages was limited to a particular caste and region. Restrictions in the field of matrimonial selection were further imposed by banning marriage with certain degrees of kinship, both on the maternal and the paternal sides, particularly among the traditional higher castes. Although the number of generations to be avoided differed from caste to caste as a rule, however, marriage was banned among *chachera* or the family of the paternal uncle, *mamera* or the family of the maternal uncle, *phuphera* or the family of the paternal aunt and *mausera* or the family of maternal aunt. Because of the growing multiplicity of exogamous groups, members were regarded as closely related and they were not allowed to intermarry. Further this exogamy was based on isogamy and hypergamy. Hypergamy[47] or the custom of "marrying up" forbade a woman of a particular group to marry a man of a group lower than her own in social standing and compelled her to marry in a group equal or superior in rank. "The result of these restrictions", wrote Bingley,[48] "is a surplus of women in the higher sects leading to a competition for husbands, and an enormous increase in the cost of getting a daughter married. It is this question of expenses that is the cause of female infanticide which is so prevalent among the Rajputs."

As discussed above, the growth in the rigidity of the caste system and its rules led to the rise of certain constraints and complexities in a girl's marriage. Owing to various restrictions placed upon marriage, it became difficult for a Rajput of poor means to procure a suitable match for his daughter. Firstly, the exaggerated sense of pride restrained a Rajput from marrying his daughter into a clan inferior to his own. An honourable marriage alliance was the one, arranged among equals or in a clan superior to one's own. Sleeman[49] believed that, "the lower clans who can unite their daughters, to those of higher grade commit less murders of this kind than others, but all Rajput clans are more or less addicted to female infanticide. It is the dread of sinking in substance from loss of property, and in grade from loss of caste, that alone leads to the destruction of female infants". Besides, there was also a restriction upon marriage within the same clan which was held incestuous, as the boys and girls belonging to the same clan were considered to be brothers and sisters. The Kachwahas of Jaipur, for example, were divided into sixty-five clans, or *khaamps*,[50] some of whom were feudal-lords ruling over different parts of the Rajputana (Shekhawats in Shekhawati, for example); yet they were considered as brothers and sisters and marriage between them was inconceivable. In the same manner, the Haras or Hadas of Harauti, were divided into nineteen clans; the Rathores of Bikaner were divided into sixteen clans; those of Marwar were divided into twenty-one clans; the Sisodiyas of Mewar were divided into seven clans; the Yadus (or Jadus or Jadon) of Karauli were divided into seven clans; the Bhatis of Bikaner were divided into two major clans which together had thirteen branches and the Bhatis of Jaisalmer, were divided into five clans. Similarly, the Chauhans of Banswara, were divided into eleven clans, three of which were (i) the Madawat clan (ii) the Hathyot clan and (iii) the Keringot clan; and the Sisodiyas of Banswara (who have sprung from the Sisodiyas of Dungarpur) were divided into eight branches.[51] "Although religion nowhere authorizes this barbarity (i.e., female infanticide)", wrote Colonel Tod,[52] "the laws which regulate the marriage amongst the Rajputs powerfully promote infanticide. Not only is intermarriage prohibited between families of the same clan (*khaamp*), but between those of the same tribe (*gotra*); and though centuries may have intervened since their separation, and branches thus transplanted may have lost their original patronymic, they can never be regrafted on the original stem". "For instance", observed Colonel Tod, "though eight centuries have separated the two grand subdivisions of the Gehlots, and the younger, the Seesodiya, has superseded the elder, the Aharya, each ruling distinct States, a marriage between any of the branches would be deemed incestuous. The Seesodiya is yet brother to the Aharya, and regards every female of the race, as his sister. Every tribe has, therefore to look abroad to a race distinct from its own, for suitors for the females(sic)."

The difficulty of marrying their daughters was also felt by those castes, clans and tribes who were cut-off from the rest of their brethrens and were considered as impure or outcasts and who wished to be united again with their original stem. For example, Jahrejas (Jadejas) of Gujarat considered themselves to be Rajputs of a very high order, and had their original settlement in Sindh. At the time of Muslim invasions, many inhabitants of Sindh were converted into the new faith. The Jahrejas found themselves surrounded by tribes who had embraced the new faith. Now, they could not marry their daughters to those castes amongst whom they used to have matrimonial relations earlier. Nor could they afford to incur the expense and risk of travelling far and wide and send their daughters to distant Rajput families of repute, nor could they intermarry amongst themselves.[53] The same was the case with the Bhati Rajputs of Bhatner, the Sodas of Bikaner,[54] the Johiyas (Yaudheyas) of Bhatner,[55] and the Sondia or Sondi Rajputs of Jhalawar.[56] Similarly, the Bauris,[57] the Khanzadas,[58] the Meos,[59] the Sirvis,[60] the Kayamkhanis, some clans of the Meenas (for example the Rawat, Cheeta, Kathaat, Gorat and Barad Meenas), the Lodhas, the Dhakars, the Khaarols, the Sikligars, the Kansaras, the Lakharas, the Mehra-Kahars, the Pinjaras, the Maru Kumhars, the Darzis, the Chitaras, the Gaanchas, the Tambolis, the Kalals, the Lohars, the Malkanas, the Telis, the Nais, the Motisars, the Ghaanchis, the Beesotara Sunars, the Jangra Khatis, the Daroga Rajputs, the Bharbhunjas, the Baridars, the Beldars, the Baldiyas, the Banjaras, the Pitlyaas, the Jagris etc. were either considered as impure, or inferior or outcasts by the higher sections of the society, despite their Rajput origin.[61]

The Bhati Rajputs originally hailed from Prayag or Allahabad, from which place they dispersed in various directions. "The Bhatis of Bhatner", writes Sherring, "were most probably Hindus, who were converted to the Mohammedan faith, later on." Similarly, the Soda Rajputs of Bikaner, because of their long association with the Muslims, embraced their ways and manners, which lowered their status in the social hierarchy. The Sodas displayed a singular blending of Hinduism and Islamism in their social customs and religious institutions, and two of the branches of Sodas – the Umras and the Sumras, embraced Islam.

A tradition goes that in Śamvat 1249 after the death of King Prithvi Raj Chauhan, Shahbuddin Ghori had come to power. Many Rajputs of the Chauhan army were captured by Ghori. Majority of them were converted to Islam. Some of them, however, were let off on the recommendation of a *mali* (i.e., gardener), who declared that they were not Rajputs but members of his own class. The Rajputs who thus escaped gave up their arms and took to agriculture and growing of vegetables and were henceforth called Malis or gardeners. In the same manner, the Johiyas, formerly known as Yaudheyas, were converted to the Mohammedan faith in the medieval period, and thus found it difficult to marry their sons and daughters in other Rajput families. Likewise, the Sondia or Sondi Rajputs, who inhabited Jhalawar, "were a mixed race," according to M.A. Sherring, "who were considered as descendants of outcasts." In the same manner the Bauris claimed to have descended from the Rajputs. A Rajput princess of Gujarat, according to a prevalent anecdote, was being escorted by a party of Rajputs to Delhi, where she was to espouse the emperor. On the way, the party halted one day in Marwar territory, by a large *pukka* well. A Rajput girl of the place, who saw the princess, reproached her with the disgrace she was about to incur in marrying a Mohammedan. Stung by the girl's words, the princess threw herself into the well and was drowned. Her escort got stuck in a dilemma and could not decide whether to proceed to Delhi or to go back and tell her relatives what had happened, and remained at the well. After they had exhausted their means they took to plunder and were referred to by the people of the neighborhood as the *bauri-wallahs* – from *bauri* a well. In course of time they married women of other castes and were in consequence outcasted by the Rajputs. Since then they have formed a separate caste under the name of bauri and some of them adopted theft and robbery as their profession.

Similarly, the Khanzadas were formerly the rulers of Mewat and claimed descent from the Jadon Rajput chief Tahan Pal. When Mohammed Ghori captured Tahangarh in the Karauli State in 1196 A.D., many of the Jadon families dispersed. A descendant of Tahan Pal named Insaraj acquired Sarhata near Tijara in the Alwar state. Insaraj had five sons of whom the eldest Lakhan Pal was the founder of the Khanzadas, while the other four sons were said to have been the progenitors of the Jadon clans of the Meos. Lakhan Pal had two sons Sambhar Pal and Sopar Pal, both of whom became Mohammedans during the reign of the emperor Firoz Shah Tughlak. From these two brothers, the different families of the Khanzadas claimed descent. The brothers embraced Islam, partly to save their lives and partly to regain their estates of Sarhata and Jhirka, which had been annexed by Firoz Shah.

Likewise, the Meos, who inhabited Alwar, Bharatpur and some parts of Haryana, claimed Rajput descent and the names of their chief clans are derived from their reputed Rajput ancestors but there appear to be grounds for believing that some of them have sprung from the same stock as the Minas. And regarding the origin of Sirvis, Sir John Malcolm writes, "they are stated to be the descendants of 24 Rajputs who alone survived their prince, Anand Rao, when the fortress of that name was taken by stratagem, about 600 years ago. These Rajputs were so ashamed at having survived their prince, that they threw aside their swords and shields and dropped the name of Rajput forever taking in its stead, that of Sirvi a derivative of the Rangri word *sir,* i.e., cultivation thereby intimating that they would thenceforward devote themselves to the cultivation of the soil."

During the medieval period, the invasions of the foreign (as well as Indian) caste and tribes, created an altogether new situation and the social fabric was disturbed once again. Hordes after hordes from Central Asia crossed the Indian borders to invade, plunder and take away the booty of the country. The invasions of Arabs, under Mohammed-bin-Qasim in 711-712 A.D., those of Turks from 1000 A.D. onwards, those of Mongols, Afghans, Mughals (and later on by the Marathas) and their successive victories against the-then regional forces, shattered the age old social fabric, social hierarchy and social institutions apart from influencing their political, economical and religious conditions. The emergence of these foreign castes and tribes on the horizon of India, including the Rajputana, and their consequent settlement in India, disturbed the age old social fabric. These invaders, brought new faith, new culture, new traditions, and new philosophy along with them and with the speed of lightening they were able to spread them in all the four corners of the country. "On the destruction of Kannauj, the capital of the ancient kingdom of the same name by Shahbuddin Ghori in 1194 A.D.", remarks Sherring, "the Rathores abandoned their country, which they had governed with wonderful energy so long, and entering the barren wastes of Marwar, founded a new Kingdom there, under Rao Chanda, in 1382 A.D."

Similarly, the Yadu Rajputs of Karauli (it is said that their ancestors founded Jaisalmer in 1157 A.D.), had a belief that in the year 1120, their ancestors erected the fort of Dholpur. "It is probable", writes Sherring, "that they held lands in that territory in those days, but they must have been soon dispossessed, especially as we know that in 1194, Shahbuddin's possession of the kingdom of Kannauj, of which there is reason to believe that it formed a part (sic)." This was equally true of other Rajputs and Jats, who had migrated to far-off places in the North-Western Provinces and Central India. It was found that the obstacles in getting a daughter married, were far greater with those having some impurity of blood or taint or remoteness. Thus, according to Colonel Tod,[62] "this was true of the Raj Kumars of Jaunpur, the Parihar Rajputs in Jijni, Bundelkhand and also of the Jahrejas, who by intermarriage with the Mohammedans, had lost their caste" and thereby lowered in the social hierarchy. "Political causes have disunited them from the Mohammedans and they desire again to be considered as pure Rajputs, but having been contaminated, no Rajput will intermarry with them.... The owner of a hide of land a Seesodiya, Rathore or Chauhan would spurn the hand of a Jahreja princess" (sic).

Since every society and State was facing this crisis and had to indulge itself in long and continuous wars every now and then, the society clamoured more for the boys, who would replace the existing soldiers in near future, and would live and die, for the sake of their honour, religion and State. During this troubled time, the birth of a daughter was looked down upon and it became a liability for the family in which she took birth.[63] In that age, the responsibility of saving their States from foreign and regional aggressions, mainly rested upon the shoulders of Rajputs, as they were one of the important military classes, at that time and were always exposed to danger. Rearing, safety and thoughts about the marriage of daughters always haunted their minds. The economy of the sandy dunes of the Rajputana, which frequently witnessed natural and man-made calamities, made it difficult for them to procure food for themselves and their families, which further worsened the situation. Moreover, the Rajputs could never imagine their womenfolk should suffer being a prey in the hands of the enemies and thus be disgraced and dishonoured. "The Rajput race" remarked Talboys Wheeler,[64] "is the noblest and the proudest in India. With the exception of the Jews, there is perhaps no people of higher antiquity or purer descent. They are brave and chivalrous, keenly sensitive to an affront and especially jealous of the honour of their women." It is, perhaps the reason, why practices like sati and jauhar came into existence and why they were wholeheartedly supported by the warrior classes.

Further, the prevalence of the notions of class consciousness and caste hierarchy among the martial races and especially among the Rajputs, forced them to maintain the purity of their blue blood and this led them to maintain strict adherence to family genealogy which resulted in sharp distinctions between the superior and the inferior Rajput families. The family genealogy became a whim with the Rajputs and the touchstone of affinities and guardian of the laws of inter marriage among them. The selection of a bride or bride-groom for their children or for the ruler of the State was, as a rule, made by their parents or guardians. Even though a boy may have attained maturity, the selection of a bride for him, according to the usage of the country, generally rested with the parents. In the case of grown-up boys, however, the tradition was to consult them before selecting a bride for them. But marriage within the princely circles was rarely a matter of individual choice, it being accepted that the duty of a son or of a daughter was to obey the wishes of parents or grandparents. "The poorest Rajput of this day," observes Tod,[65] "retains all the pride of ancestry, often his sole inheritance. He scorns to hold the plough, or to use his lance but on horseback. In these aristocratic ideas he is supported by his reception among his superiors, and the respect paid to him by his inferiors.... Each of the superior rank is entitled to a banner, kettledrums preceded by heralds and silver maces, with peculiar gifts and personal honors, in commemoration of some exploit of their ancestors." "Reduced in power", wrote Col. Tod,[66] "circumscribed in territory, compelled to yield much of their splendor and many of the dignities of birth, they have not abandoned an iota of the pride and high bearing arising from a knowledge of their illustrious and regal descent." Their towering pride and their superior consciousness proved obstacles in contracting marriages in families of inferior origin and status.[67] In Jaisalmer,[68] for example, if a Rajput entered into matrimonial relations with a lower Rajput gotra, then he was forced to pay a fine and was considered as partial outcaste, for a limited period, by the caste-panchayat. This 'blot' could only be effaced by strictly following and obeying the orders, directions, penalties imposed by the caste-panchayat. But if a Rajput, of Jaisalmer, married a non-Rajput or gave his daughter in marriage to a non-Rajput, then he was permanently ostracized by the society and none held any kind of social relations with the 'offender'. In this context Sherring[69] has rightly observed that, "infanticide as practiced by the Rajputs, arises in the first instance, from the custom of the race to prohibit intermarriages among members of the same tribe. This produces another custom equally pernicious, namely, that of endeavouring to marry a girl into a tribe of a higher rank than that to which she belongs. The lower tribes of Rajputs have consequently a motive of great strength, to induce them to spare the lives of their girls, in as much as their ambition is gratified, by the superior alliances which are formed. But this motive becomes less powerful the higher the rank of the girl, until in tribes of the highest rank, it has no force at all; the marriage of a girl in such case is attended with prodigious expense, with no counter balancing circumstances gratifying the pride or ambition of her family. The result has been female infanticide(sic)."

The inevitable result of this rank consciousness was that all the Rajput families claimed themselves to be of pure race and stock.[70] And to secure their grounds and positions, they claimed to have relations with the mythical heroes and Gods. Out of the thirty-six (36) royal clans of Rajputs, ten (10) belonged to the solar dynasty (i.e., *surya-vansha)*; fifteen (15) belonged to the lunar dynasty (i.e., *chandra-vansha*) and rest of the clans, owed their existence to other dynasties.[71] The Chauhans, the Chalukyas, the Pratihars and the Parmars claimed that they were given birth by the God Almighty from the fires of the *yajna-kunda,* i.e., sacred fire-pit,[72] while the others claimed themselves to be related to the solar or lunar dynasty (surya-vansha and chandra-vansha) or with that of the dynasty of Lord Krishna (i.e., *yadu-vansha*). Under such a social system, no females of superior rank, whether superior in their own estimation or that of the community at large, could ever think of being contaminated by having marital relations with inferior ranks.[73] Thus, their marriage became a real big problem for their family members.

Moreover, the prevalence of the false belief that "the bestowal of a female in marriage betokens inferiority"[74] further worsened the matter. The marriage customs like the hitting of the *torana* (which was an indication of the superiority of the groom's side over that of the bride's side), the touching of knee or taking hold of the knee of the bridegroom, among other divine honours to him, by the bride's father, further worsened the whole scenario and hence persons of high caste, unwilling to humble themselves for the sake of a daughter, destroyed the female infants.[75] The marriage of a daughter not only wounded the pride of a caste or of a family, but brought upon degradation and humiliation of the father at the hands of his son's-in-law's family.[76] Moreover, the daughter had to be married before a certain age, and to remain unmarried after that age meant social disgrace, a blot on the family's honour and name which could not be effaced under any circumstance. This disgrace attending a family, where a daughter, after having attained maturity, remained unmarried was one of the important causes of female infanticide in Marwar.[77] The tenacity with which each clan held on to caste distinctions and rules varied from clan to clan and place to place and in no case, could it be reduced to a general pattern. Nevertheless, the feeling of pride was firmly rooted in the people, that they became restless at the mere thought of accepting and acknowledging inferiority to anyone. The higher the rank, the more difficult it was to secure a match for the daughter. The very act of selection affected their pride since it involved the admission of equality, if not the superiority of a rival clan. This was all the more difficult, since every Rajput family vied with others in claiming superiority of birth and rank.[78]

In this context, Col. Bingley[79] has aptly remarked that "an extreme sensitiveness on all points relating to the honour of their women, is a marked feature in the Rajput character(sic).... As the honour of every family demands that its daughters should be married into the highest possible clans, girls are regarded as a burden, and female infanticide is regrettably common. For this reason also, the higher the grade of Rajput, the commoner is the crime, owing to the greater difficulty of obtaining suitable husbands."

An important consequence of this rank consciousness resulted in the practice of giving heavy dowry in marriages. Dowry which used to be in lacs and even crore of rupees, both in cash and kind, jewellery, silver and gold, clothes and household things, even cooking utensils, even the pipes used for blowing on the embers of the fire, everything except items like needles and soap about which there were superstitions – took up a large part of every marriage contract and many a match foundered on the inability or the unwillingness of a potential bride's father to meet the expectations of his opposite number.[80] Originally dowry had some practical value when parents saw to it that their daughter was well provided for before she went into the *sasural* (i.e., home of her in-laws), so that she was not embarrassed to ask for every little thing. But over the centuries, its original purpose had been obscured to the point where dowry became a 'status symbol' with the practical side neglected. Moreover, the vain feeling that display of wealth at marriages, added to their dignity and rank, was also prevalent among the Rajputs. Every Rajput family, on the occasion of marriage in their family, tried to outrival the other, since it became a point of honour to perform the marriage ceremony with all grandeur and magnificence. The ruling classes, which were infatuated with family pride and importance, were unwilling to offer their daughters as wives, without a very large dowry, and in order to maintain their dignity they even took loans from the private bankers, to celebrate a marriage, even when the coffers were empty. Maharana Bhim Singh of Mewar, for example, had to take loan,[81] on the occasion of the marriages of his family members, in the first half of the 19th century. The Rajputs, considered it derogatory to restrain themselves in any kind, nor did their prestige and honour, or customs enabled them to cut on any expenses and it can be said that they resorted to this heinous practice only out of compulsion.[82] "In Shekhawati," wrote the Jaipur council of regency, to the political agent on the 20th of February, 1847, "certain *Sardars* are sharers among many and in the produce of their allotments they have not the means of subsistence – yet they assert their dignity and desire to ally their daughters with sons of the Houses of high rank, while possessing not the means of bearing the expenses attendant on such alliances(sic)."

Before the marriage was solemnized, various preliminary ceremonies were observed in the Rajputana. When the process of match-making was complete, a sort of symbolic declaration of the decision was made through the *sagai* or *tika* or engagement ceremony.[83] In some communities, negotiations of dowry were made before taking a final decision in the matter. Traditionally, the eldest male member of the girl's family or the father of the girl, put a *tilak* (*tika)* on the forehead of the boy and presented him a turban, a coconut, some silver coins, clothes, green fruits and dry fruits, sweets, a pair of *paan*, and in some cases, a gold chain and other gifts. Also, the custom of offering *milani* (cash presents) by the girl's parents to the parents of the boy and, or other important relatives was in vogue in some communities. "While the commoners hardly spent 50 to 60 rupees, over the betrothal," writes Padmaja Sharma,[84] "the upper classes and more particularly the Rajputs, offered silver and gold plated costly coconuts, dry-fruits, pearls, turbans of golden thread, *dhoti, bola-bandis, gospechs,* and pieces of costly clothes of various designs, jewelled trappings and thousands of rupees in cash". When Maharaja Man Singh of Jodhpur,[85] sent on February 16, 1823, the tika of his younger daughter to the Rao-Raja of Bundi, he sent a very costly turra along with *pag, potia,* one elephant (costing rupees 1000), two horses, four mares, and 200 gold plated coconuts, precious jewellery, consisting of a turra, gospech – all studded with jewels. In addition to this jewellery and ornaments, eight sets of costly uniforms, *gur, supari, misri, badam, pista, dhakan* and *mewa* were also presented in a huge quantity along with a cash sum of Rs 1000.[86] Then, he had to procure by paying rupees 2,00,000 (two hundred thousand or two lacs) from a banker of Kota (from whom Rao Raja also borrowed a loan for meeting the marriage expenses) and gave it to the Rao-Raja in *hathlewa* ceremony. Over and above all this, he had to feed a marriage party of four thousand persons for over a month and grant to his daughter a *jagir* worth Rs 25,000. Thus, he spent a sum of Rs 10,00,000 (ten lacs) excluding the jewellery and ornaments which had been procured from the State's *Jawahar Khana,*[87] on that single marriage.

Similarly, in the betrothal ceremony of Baiji Shri Jain Kunwar,[88] daughter of Maharaja Gaj-Singh of Bikaner (1745-1747 A.D.), with the Maharana of Udaipur in 1761 A.D., the Maharana was given coconuts of gold and silver, 14 *supari* of silver and 11 of gold, one *kilangi,* i.e., gospech, studded with 68 diamonds, 6 rubies, emeralds, etc. Besides it, one elephant, 10 horses with their riders, Rs 1000 in cash, turbans of golden threads, costly clothes, etc., were also given to the Maharana. In the marriage of princess Vallabh Kunwari,[89] daughter of Maharawat Raghunath Singh, ruler of Pratapgarh, with Maharaja Sir Ganga Singh of Bikaner, which took place on the 8th of July, 1897 A.D., Rs 5,00,000 (five lacs) were spent by the bride's father.

When this was the state of affairs of the ruling classes, the feudal lords and the ministers of the royal courts, did not lag behind and in order to have their names emblazoned by the bards and genealogists, they tried to copy their masters in the celebration of marriages with all pomp and show. Thakur Lakshman Singh, Chief of the army of Jaipur State, during Sawai Jai Singh III's rule, spent Rs 2,00,000 (two lacs) on the marriage of his daughter, Bai Jadav Kunwari, in Samvat 1904 (1847 A.D.).[90] The Rawat of Salumbar (Mewar), married his sister to the Maharaja of Idar, in 1875 A.D., in which Rs 1,00,000 (one lac) were spent on the distribution of tyag alone, while the yearly income of Salumbar was Rs 75,000 only.[91] Similarly, when the sister of the Rawat of Deogarh was married to the Raja of Delwara (both nobles of Mewar) in 1880s, Rs 1,50,000 was expended by the latter, on tyag alone, while his annual income was then considerably under a lac.[92]

The Maharaja of Bhindar, also a noble of Mewar, married his daughter to the Raja of Rutlam, of Central India (now Madhya Pradesh), in which a sum of two lac of rupees was expended on the marriage, the bulk of which fell upon the bride's father, whose annual income was about Rs 60,000.[93] The Raja of Bunera, of Mewar, married his sister to the same Raja of Rutlam, in which he spent Rs 1,50,000 (one lac and fifty thousand) on the distribution of tyag alone, while his annual income was Rs 70,000. In January, 1884, one of the chief nobles of Jaipur, Thakur Govind Singh of Chomu, betrothed his daughter to the Thakur of Pokhran of Marwar. The sum expended on the occasion of the betrothal was Rs 9,890 and when the marriage took place the Thakur of Pokhran expended half a lac of rupees on tyag alone.[94]

Thus, the lavish expenditure on various ceremonies connected with marriage, was a matter of prestige and a sort of conventional necessity, particularly for the traditional higher castes in Rajasthan. The amount of dowry taken or given in marriage was a status symbol. So much so, that a sort of exhibition of dowry, received or given, was arranged and kin and friends were invited to have a look at various articles included in the dowry. At the same time, the prestige and status and sometimes, adjustment of the newly wedded girl in her in-law's house was greatly determined by the amount of dowry she had brought with her, from her parents. It was because of dowry that birth of a daughter in certain families was looked upon with disfavour. "Marriages among Rajputs", Sleeman[95] remarked "is a matter of bargain and sale. Those who have money must pay in proportion to their means, in order to marry their girls into families a shade higher, in caste than themselves, or to get brides from them, when such families are reduced to the necessity of selling their daughters to inferiors(sic)."

The tika expenses and the *neg* (customary gifts on the occasion of joy and happiness) to be paid to the Charans and Bhats proved so taxing that daughters began to be considered as a burden on the parents, some of whom took recourse to the inhuman practice of poisoning their female children immediately after their birth.[96] Thus according to Shyamal Das,[97] "it was the heavy expenditure on the tika ceremony, which forced the Rajputs to kill their daughters." Similarly, Captain Hall,[98] the Superintendent of Merwara, remarked that, "the custom of female infanticide, had its origin in the heavy expense attending marriage ceremony contracts. The sums were payable by the male side, ever unalterable, equal to the rich and poor, without any abatement whatever in the favour of the latter. What first established the payment is unknown, but it was so sacred, inviolable and even a partial deviation so disgraceful, that the most necessitous of the tribe would not incur the imputation. Hence arose infanticide. The sums payable were beyond the means of so many, that daughters necessarily remained on hand after maturity, entailed immortal disgrace, and thus imposed a necessity on all female progeny of becoming victims to their family honour (sic)."

Apart from the excessive expenditure incurred at the marriage of a daughter, a considerable amount was spent on the Charans and the Bhats.[99] These Charans and Bhats were held in high esteem and they exerted an extraordinary influence on the minds of the people of the society. It was the custom of all the wealthy Rajputs to have as part of their household, a family-Bhat and Charan.[100] They were the faithful companions of the Rajputs, and shared their *amal* (i.e., opium) and half of their loaves in adversity and received their extravagant bounty in prosperity.[101] They presented themselves on three occasions, and the Rajputs lavishly honoured them, by giving elephants, horses, clothes, precious jewels, land, etc., apart from huge amounts of cash.[102] These three occasions were[103] : (i) while proceeding to battlefield, (ii) on the occasion of a marriage, and (iii) at the birth of a son. Initially, the payments made to them were voluntary and they remained satisfied with what they received. But with the passage of time, some of them started arguing, bargaining blackmailing and ridiculing the Rajputs, for their payments and forced them to comply with their demands.[104] Their main function became to extract as much money as possible from the Rajputs and for that aim they resorted to different practices like – *dharna* (demonstration), hunger-strike, *chaandi* or *traga*. Chaandi consisted in their readiness to mutilate, wound, starve or kill themselves. Similarly, the amount received on the occasion of marriage was known as tyag. For getting tyag, they stood in the way of the marriage procession or at the time of the departure of the marriage party, and forced the father of the bride to fulfil their demand.[105] The custom had its origin in the distribution of money among these classes at the pleasure of the bridegroom, but soon it developed into a usage and reached such heights that every Rajput who went to marry, was bound to satisfy the heavy and extraordinary demands of these people at any sacrifice. The demands of the Bhats and Charans, at times were so heavy, that few Rajput families could afford to satisfy them. If their demands were not satisfied, they wrote satires against the bride's father in particular, and would wound themselves or commit atrocities upon their own kiths and kins, in order to pressurize the marriage party.[106] The payments made to the Charans and the Bhats, sometimes amounted to 2/3rd to 3/4th of a year's income, and thus the estate felt economic hardships and became involved in debt and difficulty, which for a season threw insurmountable obstacles in the way of future marriages in the same family.[107] It was stated by the Jodhpur Vakeel, that there were about 20,000 Charans in Marwar and on occasions of the marriage ceremonies, in the families of the principle nobles of the State, as many as 4,000 or 5,000 would assemble.[108] Beside these resident Charans and Bhats, who lived in a particular territory, a large number of Charans, Bhats, Dholis, Meerasis, etc., gathered on the occasion, even from far-off regions and also from other States, i.e., if a marriage was being performed in Mewar, Marwar or any other State, the Charans, Bhats, etc., of other States besides Mewar or Marwar, were free to participate in that and collect their share of the tyag dues. One or two Charans coming from a village uniformly brought with them barbers, washermen and others numbering about 20, all of whom they got enlisted as

Charans, when tyag was distributed. It was the practice with these Charans to retain what had been received on account of these persons who in reality were entitled to partake the marriage-feast.[109]

It will be interesting here to note the origin, the historical importance and the role played by them though indirectly, in pressurizing the Rajputs to opt for the heinous crime of female infanticide in the Rajputana.

The Origin and Historical Role of Charans and Bhats in the Rajputana

Since the extortionate demands of the Charans and Bhats were one of the causes of female infanticide in Rajputana, therefore, it would be relevant here to understand the origin, the role and the historical importance of the Charans and Bhats. They (i.e., the Charans and the Bhats) were the castes, which enjoyed great respectability and exercised great influence in the courts of princely States. The specialty of these castes was that, they were devoted to the literary pursuits. In receiving gifts and composing poems and reciting genealogy, they were near to the Brahmans and in drinking wine, worshipping *Shakti* and participating in war, they resembled Rajputs.[110] Through their writings, we know about the glorious deeds and dynastic histories of various Rajput houses and families. It was they who wrote the various *Khyats, Vaartas, Raaso* and *Vanshavalis* and because of their writings many new facts have come to light. Though sometimes, their accounts are exaggerated, yet they are of vital importance in the determination of facts and dates about the chronological order of events. "The works of the native bard", observes Anil Chandra Banerji,[111] "afford many valuable data in facts, incidents, religious opinions and traits of manners; many of which, being carelessly introduced are thence to be regarded as the least suspicious kind of historical evidence."

The Charans rank as the genealogists of Rajput families and are divided into three large endogamous groups:[112]

(i) Maru (ii) Kachela (iii) Tiwaria. The first two are named after the places of their subsequent settlement. Those living in Marwar are called *Maru* Charans and those who settled in Kutch are known by the name of *Kachela* Charans. While the *Tiwarias* are named after the section of the Srimali Brahmans from whom they sprung.

They are the followers of Shakti religious sect and usually follow the manners and customs of Rajputs. They receive gifts and largess from the Rajputs on all feasts and marriages (even today) and held extensive lands and villages granted to them under *udak* or rent-free tenures.

Charans trace their ancestry to the epic age, where they figure in association with a host of other classes – the Bhats, the Magadhas, the Soots, the Nuts, etc., who performed various religious duties at the royal court, on festive and joyful occasions or at coronations.[113] They sang the glories of the ancestors of the ruling dynasties.

There are several legends, associated with the origin of Charans. One states that they were created by the Almighty God himself.[114] The legend, passed on from generation to generation, describing them to be born by Lord Shiva. It is said that Lord Shiva, was once, very much disturbed and upset, because His holy ox (Nandi) felt great difficulties in the pastures because of the fear of a lion, which was a pet animal of goddess Parvati. Lord Shiva first created the Bhat to safeguard His ox, but the guard could not prevent the lion from terrorizing the ox of the Lord. Enraged by the audacity of the lion and the failure of the Bhat, the Lord created another guard – this time the Charan, and ordered him to take His holy ox to the pastures. The new guard, before taking the ox to the pastures, praised goddess Parvati through words and verses; which made her happy and satisfied. Pacified and satisfied by the verses of the guard, the goddess assured him that her lion would never cause any harm to the ox henceforward and blessed him that "since he had pleased her (goddess Parvati) by his politeness and poetic talents, therefore his children and family members would become proficient in the art of poetry and verse-writing, without any efforts of their own." And from that day, the legend goes on, because that guard took the holy ox to the pastures for grazing (called *charaai* and *charaana* in Hindi), that guard and his family members came to be known as Charans. And this is why they worship Shakti and consider themselves as bards, poets and genealogists. In the words of Sir John Malcolm,[115] "Mahadeva first created Bhats to attend to his lion and bull; but these would not prevent the former from killing the latter, which was a source of infinite vexation and trouble, so it compelled Mahadeva to create new ones. He therefore formed the Charan, equally devout as the Bhat, but of bolder spirit, and gave him in charge of those favourite animals. From that period, no bull was ever killed by the lion." "These classes," he further says" rank as the genealogists of proud and ignorant chiefs.... It is to them that the proudest Rajput looks for solace in adversity, and for increased joy and exultation in prosperity. "John Wilson[116] believed that the Charans got their name from the feeding and rearing of cattle.

Another sacred book considers Charans as having godlike characteristics since they are well-versed in the art of poetry and are able to write verses on the spot and at the moment.[117] Maitreyi Muni told Vidur in the Shrimad Bhagvat Purana that "those who are scholars are equal to Gods, and as such, there are eight supernatural entities, who/which are equal to Gods or which have Godly element in them." These, according to Maitreyi Muni, were: (i) *Vibudha* (ii) *Pitra* (iii) *Asur* (iv) *Gandharva* and *Apsaras* (v) *Yaksha* and *Rakshas* (vi) *Bhoot, Pret* and *Pishach* (vii) *Siddha, Vidyadhar* and *Charans* (viii) and *Kinnars*.

Still another view is that those who praised their lords, or their patrons, through their poems, ballads, and their writings were called Charans, because they tried to spread the glory of their patrons, in all the four directions and thereby motivated the society to do good to everyone.[118] Thus, to glorify their lords and their families, they started keeping and singing genealogies of their patrons. As far as their original homeland is concerned it has been mentioned that they used to live in the Himalayas in ancient times and from there they migrated to other parts, when the Himalayas became over populated.[119] They are also said to have migrated from the Gangetic Plains[120] towards the Deccan with their Rajput Chiefs, when the latter were overwhelmed by foreign inroads and when their internal dissensions, during the great Mahabharata war, compelled them to leave their original habitation.

The sacred position of the Charans has been depicted at many places in the Valmiki Ramayana.[121] Similarly, in the Mahabharat,[122] it has been mentioned that, "when the Gods saw the superhuman work of the construction of bridge over the sea, at the time of the invasion of Lanka, by Lord Rama, then impressed by this majestic scene, the gods came there along with sages, siddhas and Charans and worshipped Lord Rama by sprinkling upon Him the holy water of various rivers."

Still another legend believes that some Rajputs, in order to escape the wrath of the sage Parshuram, disguised themselves as bards and later came to be known as Charans.[123] Thus by the above examples, it becomes quite clear that Charans and their sacred position has been mentioned in many works of ancient India and they were not mere 'wandering mendicants' as was thought by Lt. Col. Sutherland[124] in the 19th century.

Sir John Malcolm,[125] however believed that when the Rajputs migrated from the banks of the Ganges to Rajputana, their Brahman priests did not accompany them and hence the class of Charans arose and supplied their place; one section became their bards and genealogists and the other became merchants who travelled with the large convoys of goods.

The Charans were originally traders who supplied horses to the Rajputs and soon became intimate with them, because of their poetic talents.[126] They became esteemed and faithful companions of the Rajputs and shared their *amal* (opium) and half of their loaves in adverse situations and received their extravagant bounty in times of prosperity.[127] Besides being the bards of the Rajput chiefs, they frequently helped them and their families in times of distress and the histories of the Marwar and Jaisalmer ruling families record more than one instance of their having saved the heirs to the gaddi i.e., throne from destruction. And they were such faithful companions of the Rajputs, that in times of distress, the Rajputs used to leave their family members in the homes of their family Charans, and no enemy Rajput king had the courage and the guts to touch those members, since the Charans were considered at par with Brahmans and cow, and none had the courage to offend the sacred person, who was a bard and a genealogist too.[128] Their chief power was derived from the superstition that it was a certain ruin to shed their blood, or that of any of their family, or to cause it to be shed. "A few years back," observed Bishop Heber[129] in 1824-25, "it was usual for merchants or travellers going through Malwa and Guzerat (sic) to hire a Charan to protect them; and the sanctity of his name was generally sufficient. If robbers appeared, he stepped forward waving his long white garments and denouncing in verse, infamy and disgrace on all who should injure travellers under the protection of the holy minstrel of Shiva. If this failed he stabbed himself with his dagger, generally in the left arm, declaring that his blood was on their heads; and if all failed, he was bound in honour to stab himself to the heart, a catastrophe of which there was little danger, since the violent death of such a person was enough to devote the whole land to barrenness, and all who occasioned it, to an everlasting abode in padalon." They used this superstition to enforce the payment of debts to themselves or to those for whom they have stood security, by threatening to wound themselves if the debt was not paid.[130] The bond of a Charan, thus, was often preferred to that of a wealthy banker. Their reputation had grown to such an extent that their words were considered as surety, in the business deals, between different parties.[131] And if someone turned away from his words, then that Charan, who stood as surety, used to give *dharna* alongwith other members of his clan, on the doors of that person, and in this way forced him to respect his words. To pressurize the people, to accept their demands they used to torture themselves as well as their family members by inflicting wounds upon their bodies, by keeping indefinite hunger-strikes, by committing suicides in various ways (such as by immolating themselves or their family members, or by jumping from some building or by the blow of a sword or dragger upon their necks or stomach). Since their position was at par with Brahmans and cow, both dear and respectable to the Rajputs, therefore everybody, feared that they would be charged of *brahma-hatya* or *gau-hatya* (i.e., the murder of a Brahman or that of cow) and the sin would rest on their heads, if anything went wrong with that Charan or with his family. "Their sacred character", remarks Col. Tod,[132] "overawes the lawless Rajput chief, and even the savage Kali and Bheel, and the plundering Sahra of the desert, dread the anathema of these singular races, who conduct the caravan through the wildest and most desolate regions."

But whatever may be their origin, the Charans remained inextricably associated with various Rajput clans and were treated with greatest respect and the highest Rajput ruler would stand up, when one of his class entered or left an assembly.[133] They received *tazim* from the chiefs and when, at a social gathering, the *kasumbha* or bowl of liquid opium was handed round, a Charan, if present, was always the first to receive it from the chief. Similarly, the Charan women were also much respected and some were believed to possess the power to bring woe upon any person on whom their curse may fall.[134] The Charans were looked by the Rajputs to enshrine their heroic deeds in songs to be handed down to the posterity. Their sarcastic references to a defeat in a battle or want of courage inflamed their passions. Many rulers, who were insouciant in the administrative matters, or who cared more for their English masters and neglected their masses, or who indulged themselves in a life of pleasure, or who sat on the royal throne after murdering their kiths and kins, were sharply and openly rebuked, criticized and humiliated by the Charans and the Bhats, without any fear of the throne.[135]

Eminent historian G.N. Sharma[136] remarks that the Charan combined in himself the traits of a Brahman and that of a Rajput; he had the literary inclination of the former and received gifts from his Rajput patron for composing songs of heroic deeds of his ancestors. He resembled Rajput as a votary of Shakti (*Hinglaj Mata* being his *kula-devi* or family deity), followed his other habits and engaged in war. During the wars, they displayed their chivalry and recited the songs in praise of their patrons, to boost-up the morale of the soldiers. The names of Charan Khemraj, Naru Charan, Sandu, Ratan Mishran, etc., are famous as martyrs for the cause of their patrons.[137] The *Achaldas Khinchi Ki Vachanika* mentions the names of these Charans, who gave away their lives, while fighting against the Turkish invaders.[138] If traditions are to be believed, a saintly Charan woman, mother of Baru Charan, helped Rana Hammir from her own funds by supplying 500 horses to recover Chittor.[139]

Some of the Charan sects were styled as the *pol-paats* (poets of the door) of the different Rajput ruling races and thus enjoyed special privileges and rights at marriage and birth ceremonies.[140] The Sodas were the pol-paats of the Maharana of Mewar, the Rohariyas were the pol-paats of the Rathores of Marwar, Bikaner and Kishangarh and of the Kachwahas of Jaipur and Alwar, the Adas were the pol-paats of the Deora sect of the Chauhan clan of Sirohi, and the Ratnus were the pol-paats of the Bhatis of Jaisalmer.[141]

The Maru Charans were divided into 120 khaamps[142] or clans and in Marwar alone, out of these 120 khaamps, 53 were existent in the 19th century[143] and their number was around 20,000.[144]

Bhats

The Bhats were the genealogists of the Brahmans and Rajputs and also of many of the lower castes. The Bhats, as the hereditary guardians of history and pedigree, were held in higher estimation than even the Brahmins themselves, among the haughty and fierce nobles of the Rajputana. Sir H. Risley[145] has discussed the origin of Bhats in detail in his *Tribes and Castes of Bengal* and opines that the word 'Bhat' is derived from the Sanskrit word *Bhatta,* i.e., lord. "They are", observes Risley, "a heterogeneous group made up of

Brahmans and Rajputs welded together into one caste in virtue of their exercising similar functions." He further notes that modern opinion seems disposed to find the germ of the Brahman caste in the bards, ministers and family priests who were attached to the King's households in the Vedic times. To quote Nesfield,[146] "they are an offshoot from those secularized Brahmans who frequented the courts of princes and the camps of warriors, recited their praises in public and kept record of their genealogies.... As time went on, these courtier priests became hereditary bards, receded from the parent stem and founded a new caste." Wilson[147] derives the word from Bhata or Bhatta popularly formed from *Bhatri,* a nourisher or protector, and figuratively applied to mendicant and learned Brahmans. The Revd. M.A. Sherring[148] gives three different traditions of their origin, though he places no reliance on any of them. "They are said to have sprung" says he, "from the union of a Kshatriya with a Vaishya woman but another account is that their common ancestors were a Kshatriya father and a Brahman widow; while by a third tradition, the Bhats are said to be the progeny of a Brahman father and Shudra mother." Speaking of their mythological origin, Sir Henry Elliot[149] says "that they were produced to amuse Parvati, from the drops of sweat on Shiva's brow, but as they chose to sing his praises rather than hear, they were expelled from heaven and condemned to live a wandering life, as terrestrial bards."

R.V. Russell,[150] I.C.S., Superintendent of Ethnography, Central provinces opines that "there is no reason to doubt that Biram of Baram Bhats are an offshoot of Brahmans, their name being merely a corruption of the term Brahman. They or at least those who are the Bhats of the Brahmins and Rajputs, held a high social position and were usually addressed as Raoji. There were eleven main endogamous divisions of the Bhats: (i) Biram Bhats (ii) Kedaria (iii) Chandisa (iv) Barwa (v) Jaga (vi) Sannik (vii) Maru (viii) Ganjoria (ix) Buna (x) Bagora (xi) Kapadia. They were poets and panegyrists and recited the deeds of ancestors at large weddings. Several well known poets such as Nahar and Chand have belonged to this caste. Nahar was given by Akbar, the title of Mahapatra and Chand was the author of Prithviraj Raso – a collection of popular poems recounting the gallant deeds of Prithviraj Chauhan. The members of the other main divisions were known generally as Bahi Bhats because of the genealogy of the families which they kept. Their records were referred to when disputes arose regarding marriage contracts and adoptions. They were treated with much respect by their employers (*Jajmans*) when they visited them. They were said to be rather exacting in the respect they considered themselves entitled to and to be quick to take offence.

Forbes[151] describes the routine of a Bhat thus:

"When the rainy season closes and travelling becomes practicable, the bard sets off on his yearly tour from his residence in the *Bhatwara* or bards quarters. One by one, he visits each of the Rajput chiefs who are his patrons and from whom he has received portions of land or annual grants of money, timing his arrival if possible to suit occasions of marriage or other domestic festivals. After he has received the usual courtesies, he produces the *Wai* (i.e., *Bahi*), a book written in his own crabbed hieroglyphics or in those of his father which contains the descent of the House from its founder, interspersed with many a verse or ballad, the saying in which are chanted forth in musical cadence to a delighted audience and are than orally interpreted by the bard with many illustrative anecdotes or tales. The *Wai* (*Bahi*) is not merely a source for the qualification of the family pride or even of love of song, it is also a record by which questions of relationships are determined when a marriage is in prospect and also, disputes relating to the division of the ancestral property are divided.(sic)"

Forbes further observes that it was the duty of the bard at each periodical visit to register the births, marriages and deaths in the family of his patron since his last visit. He also chronicled all the other events worthy of remarks which had taken place affecting the fortunes of his patron. Thus, the Bhats fulfilled a very useful function as the registrar of births, deaths and marriages.

Sir John Malcolm[152] in his *A Memoir of Central India* mentions that sometimes if a Bhat was seriously offended, he fixed an effigy of the person he desired to degrade, on a long pole and appended a slipper to it as mark of disgrace and recorded the songs of infamy of the disgraced person which travelled throughout the territory of his beat and beyond also till the person concerned or his friend purchased the cessation of the curses and ridicule thus entailed. Malcolm further observes that, "it is not deemed in these countries within the power of the prince, much less than any other person, to stop a Bhat or even punish him for such a proceeding. Similarly, Bishop Heber[153] observed that, "the Bhats protect nobody, but to kill or beat one of them would be regarded as very disgraceful and ill-omened; and presuming on this immunity, and on the importance attached to that sort of renown which it confers, they are said often to extort money from their wealthy neighbours by promise of spreading their great name, and threats of making them infamous and even of blasting their prospects". "A wealthy merchant in Indore," Heber further remarks, "some years since, had a quarrel with one of these men, who made a clay image, which he called after the merchant's name, and daily in the *bazaar* and in different temples, addressed it with bitter and reproachful language, intermixed with the most frightful curses which an angry poet could invent. There was no redress, and the merchant, though a man of great power and influence at the court, was advised to bribe him into silence; this he refused to do, and the matter went on for several months, till a number of the merchant's friends subscribed a considerable sum, of which, with much submission and joining hands, they entreated the Bhat to accept. The merchant as it happened, was really overtaken by some severe calamities, and the popular faith in the powers of the minstrel character, is now more than ever confirmed (sic)."

The Biram or Brahma Bhat claim their descent from Kavi, a son of Brahma and held a considerably higher position than the other Bhats and were treated as a section of the Gaur Brahmans and were chiefly found in Uttar Pradesh and also in Gujarat, where they occupied the same position as the Charans had in Rajasthan. Their manners and customs were much like those of Brahmans and they did not marry the Bahi Bhats, as they regarded them inferior in position. They claim a very remote ancestry and reference to them frequently appears in the Mahabharata or other ancient books of Hindu mythology, where they are known under twelve different names. These names are:

(i) Brahma Rao (ii) Soot (iii) Magad (iv) Bandi (v) Saraswati-Putra (vi) Stuti-Pathak (vii) Badi (viii) Nandi-Kar (ix) Rai (x) Bhat (xi) Nandi (xii) Kani.

The Bahi Bhats inhabited Rajputana in large numbers and owe their origin to the Rajputs whose customs and manners they had adopted. They generally kept the family records of the Rajputs and recorded and updated their genealogies. Their records were referred to, if any dispute arose among them, in matters of adoption or marriage contracts. They were treated with much respect by their employers (*jajmans*) when they visited them. They were said to be rather exacting in the respect they considered themselves entitled to and were quick to take offence. "These men", remarks Col. Walter,[154] "are held in great awe in the same ways as Charans by all Hindus; they hold lands and sometimes villages rent-free, they receive great largess and wedding gifts and if it is refused, they abuse the non-givers in songs."

The Bahi Bhats were further divided into several sects.[155] They are: (i) The Brahma Bhat (ii) The Bahi Bhat (iii) The Chandisa Bhat (iv) The Bona Bhat (v) The Sasani Bhat (vi) The Barwa Bhat (vii) The Tori Bhat and (viii) the Kedari Bhat.

The Rani-Manga Bhats confined themselves to the record of the genealogies of the Ranis or females of Rajput chiefs. They were called Rani-Mangas, because they were contended to receive gifts only from the Ranis and did not attend upon the chiefs. The genealogies of the Rathore males were kept by the Kedaria Bhats, and those of the Rathore females by Chandisa Bhats. The Kedarias wrote in their records the names of the females after the names of the males, while the Chandisas wrote the name of the females first. The Buna and Gangoria Bhats dealt in salt and grain and travelled about with large numbers of pack bullocks.

The Bhats had also their own genealogists, who were called Bahi-bancha Bhats and they were found chiefly in the district of Jodhpur.

The total population of Bhats in Rajasthan in 1911 was 35,537 (18,385 were males and 17,152 were females) and those of Charans was 37,889 (19,678 were males and 18,211 were females.[156] (See Appendix I).

Methods of Female Infanticide

"Murder is the first specific crime," observes Wilson John,[157] "brought to our notice after the fall of man, and in its form of infanticide, it has been more or less practised and approved from motives of corrupted religion and mistaken social economy, by almost all the tribes and nations of the world." Among the different types of murder, the crime of infanticide is perhaps the most heinous and detestable one, which unfortunately, was prevalent in many societies of the world. The Egyptians, in the ancient times, offered the blood of men to please their gods. The Cretans observed the same custom and adhered to it a much longer time. The nations of

Arabia did the same. The people of Duma, in particular, sacrificed every year a child and buried it beneath an altar, which they made use of instead of an idol; for they did not admit of images. The Persians buried people alive. The Cyprians, the Rhodians, the Phoecians, those of Chios, Lesbos, Tenedos, all had human sacrifices. The natives of the Tauric Chersonesus offered to Diana, every stranger who perchance threw upon their coasts.

The Pelasgi in the time of scarcity, used to take an oath, that they would sacrifice one-tenth of all that would be born to them, in order to propitiate their Gods. The Romans were also accustomed to similar sacrifices. They devoted themselves to the infernal gods, and constrained others to submit to the same horrid doom. All the principal captives who graced the triumphs of the Romans were, at the close of that cruel pageantry, put to death at the altar of Jupiter Captolinus. The Gauls and the Germans were so devoted to the custom that no business was transacted among them without being prefaced by the blood of men. The sacrifices were offered to various gods, but particularly to Hesus, Taranis, and Shantates. The altars of these gods were far removed from the common resort of men, being generally situated in the depth of woods, that the gloom might add to the horror of the operation and give a reverence to the place and the proceeding. Wilson John remarked, "When the grand objects of sacrifice, the earliest prescribed rule of religion, the acknowledgement by the worshiper of a guilt deserving suffering and death, and the foreshadowing of the offering of the promised substitute and Saviour were forgotten or obscurely remembered, the maxim that the 'fruit of the body should be given for the sin of the soul' obtained a wide currency in the human family. Speedily the character of the Divinity was mistaken for that of a demon; and in the conception formed by man of God, a malevolent thirsting for blood was substituted for a love of holiness, seeking to impress on the intelligent creation, the dread of sin by pointing to the great redemption, needed for its absolution (sic)." It is important to note, that among the Israelites alone, sacrificial infanticide seems to have been absolutely forbidden.

These practices also prevailed among the Massageta, the Scythians, the Getes, the Sarmatians, and among the various nations upon the Baltic, particularly the Sueri and the Scandinavians, who believed that their happiness and security could not be obtained but at the expense of the lives of the others. Their chief gods were Thor and Woden, whom they thought they could never sufficiently glut with blood. In New Zealand, female-infants were put to death by adopting the practice of *ro-mea* or squeezing the nose, as soon as they were born, as the girl children were of no use to them in war. It was believed that where the offsprings were numerous, they made the mother work too much and therefore the mother killed the girl child but saved the male child.[158]

Among the Eskimo, conditions of life were so severe that it was sometimes a practice to kill female children shortly after birth, fearing that there may not be husbands able to support them. In Polynesia, where population often reached high density, similar practices prevailed. Infanticide was also prevalent in Japan, where it was called *mabiki* and it was adopted by those parents, who were unable to rear their children. Similarly, it was also prevalent in China and in many European countries, as late as up to the 19th century, where unwanted infants were disposed of by abandonment and exposure. In Europe, infanticide included the practice of 'over-laying' (smothering) an infant, sharing a bed with his/her parents.

The manner in which the victims were slaughtered was diverse in different nations. Some of the Gaulish nations chinned them with the stroke of an axe. The Celts placed the man, who was to be offered for a sacrifice, upon a block or an altar, with his breast upwards, and with a sword, struck forcibly across the sternum, tumbling him to the ground, from his agonies and convulsions, as well from the effusion of blood, they formed a judgement of future events. The Cimbri ripped open the bowels, and from them they pretended to divine. In Norway, they beat men's brains out with an ox-yoke. The same operation was performed in Iceland, by dashing them against an altar of stone. In many places, they transfixed them with arrows. After they were dead, they suspended them upon the trees and left them to putrefy. The same custom prevailed to a great degree in Mexico, and even under the mild government of the Peruvians, and in most parts of America. In Africa, in the inland parts, they sacrificed some of the captives taken in the war to their fetishes, in order to secure their favour. The sacrifices consisted of persons doomed by the chance of war, or assigned by lot to be offered. But among the nations of Canaan, the victims were particularly chosen. Their own children and things nearest and dearest to them, were deemed the most worthy offering to their god. The Jews, who entered the land of

Canaan, were frequently tempted to become imitators of this horrid iniquity. Manasseh actually sacrificed his son to Moloch. Even after the good king Josiah had defiled Tophet, in order to put a stop to the infantile sacrifices they practiced, the crime was revived and called forth the solemn denunctions of the prophet.

The Carthagians offered human sacrifices to several deities and especially to Kronus, whom they offered the blood of children. The Carthagians chose what they thought the most excellent and at the same time most dear to them, which made the lot fall heavy upon their children. Thus, children of tender age were offered as the price and purchase of desired good or to deprecate and avert apprehended evil. Besides these undetermined times of bloodshed, they had particular and prescribed seasons every year, when children were chosen out of the most noble and reputable families. If a person had only one child, he was more liable to be put to death, as being esteemed more acceptable to the deity, and more efficacious to the general good. Those who were sacrificed to Kronus, were thrown into the arms of a molten idol which stood in the midst of a large fire and was red with heat. The arms of the idol were stretched out with the hands turned upwards, as it were to receive them, yet sloping downwards, so that they dropped from thence into a glowing furnace below. The Carthagians, upon a great defeat of their army by Agathocles, imputed the miscarriage to the anger of Kronus – their chief god, whose services had been neglected. Touched with this, and seeing the enemy at their gates, they seized at once two hundred children of the chief nobility, and offered them in public for a sacrifice.

Such was their blind zeal that they embraced their children with great fondness and encouraged them in the gentlest terms, that they might not be appalled at the sight of this hellish process, begging of them to submit with cheerfulness to this fearful operation. If there was any appearance of a tear rising or of a cry, the mother smothered it with her kisses, that there might not be any show of weakness, backwardness or constraint, and that the whole process may appear as a free-will offering.[159]

It is remarkable that the Egyptians looked for the most handsome person to be sacrificed. Similarly, the Albanians pitched upon the best man of the community, and made him pay for the wickedness of the rest. The Preliminary Discourse of Sale's Koran affords information of the existence of these sacrifices in Arabia.[160]

."The law of Mohamed put a stop to the inhuman custom which had been long practised by Pagan Arabs, of burying their daughters alive, lest they should be reduced to poverty by providing for them or else to avoid the displeasure and disgrace which would follow, if they should be made captives, or become scandalous by their behaviour; the birth of a daughter being, for these reasons, reckoned a great misfortune, and the death of one as great a happiness." The manner of doing away with the girl child is related differently by different sources. Some say that, when an Arab had a daughter born, if he intended to bring her up, he sent her clothed in a garment of wool or hair, to keep camels or sheep in the desert, but if he wished to put her to death, he let her live till she became six years old, and then said to her mother "perfume her and adorn her, that I may carry her to her mothers" – which being done, the father led her to a well, or a pit, dug for that purpose, and having bid her to look down into it, pushed her in head long as he stood behind; and then, filling up the pit levelled it with the rest of the ground. But others say that, when a woman was ready to fall in labour, they dug a pit, on the brink whereof she was to be delivered; and if the child happened to be a daughter, they threw it into the pit, but if it was a son, they saved it alive. This custom, though not observed by all the Arabs in general, was yet very common among several of their tribes, and particularly those of Koreith and Kendeh, the former burying their daughters alive in Mount Abu Dalama, near Mecca. In Greece,[161] infanticide or the exposure of children, appears to have formed a part of the policy of those States. Solon gave permission by the law to parents to kill their children.

But in India in general and the Rajputana in particular, the nature of infanticide, was very much different from other parts of the world. Here, superstition, pride, poverty, prejudice (towards girl child) preference for sons, the existing dowry-system, the exorbitant demands of the Charans and the Bhats, the endogamous, the exogamous, the hypergamous and the isogamous marriage rules and the illicit relationships resulting in illegal pregnancy led the people to opt for the practice of foeticide and female infanticide.[162] People used to put their daughters to death without any pain or reluctance. It was believed to be the concern of the women alone and was not a part of the business of men. It was executed in the indoors of the *zenana* and the mother or other female relatives were informed about the same. When the wives of the Rajputs, delivered a daughter, the female attendants or the *dais* who were with the mother, conveyed this fact to the eldest male member of the family or to the father of the infant, and waited for his commands. A total silence on the part of the father or father-in-law was considered to imply that the child, if a daughter, should be put to death. The mother of the child was accordingly informed to act in conformity with the wishes of her in-laws. If the husband wished to preserve a daughter, his order was carried out, without any challenges, but if the mother entertained a similar desire, while the husband expressed any opposite view, then death was inevitable for the girl child.[163] Sometimes the in-laws or the male-members of the groom's side, gathered at the girl's parental home, where usually the first delivery took place, and saw to it that human emotions or human weaknesses, did not come in the way of carrying out their orders. Some of the Bidawats of Bikaner, it is said that, used to go to Shekhawati region, since their wives mostly hailed from that place, for the above mentioned purpose.[164]

Infanticide used to be committed in a very secret manner, behind the closed doors and impregnable walls of the palaces and homes, so that even the birth of the child was hardly known outside. While the birth of a son was announced by proclamation and the sounds of drums or by beating the circular metal dishes known as *thalis* with rolling pins, the birth of a daughter passed unnoticed, as if it was an insignificant incident.[165] Total silence about the birth of a daughter was maintained by all those, who either committed this crime or who knew about the commission of this crime. Even the neighbours who knew all about the fate of an innocent infant girl child, were unwilling to open their lips, on account of their camaraderie or caste or social brotherhood.

When we take into account the persons behind this horrible crime, we are startled by the fact that the mother, in many cases, used to be the executioner of her own offspring and the female slaves and attendants of the labour room helped the mother in the execution of her girl child. "Though human sympathy and generosity of the Indian women is proverbial", remarks R.K. Saxena,[166] "be they Rajputs or others, yet social factors acting in collusion with the pride of the Rajput race, made her so callous that she destroyed her own offspring, in one or the other way." As they were betrothed at an early age, they imbibed the superstitions and traditions of their families which laid down that the husbands should be regarded as gods and their commands should never be disobeyed. The disposal of the dead body was usually done by the female attendants of the family or else the same was executed by the slave-girl in well-to-do families. "As death was taken to be an infallible consequence of her birth" remarks Saxena, "and was considered to be an event of insignificance, so it was attended by no ceremony and given the least publicity." Natural affection for a daughter child was thus overcome by socio-psychological and socio-economic factors.

"In Banswara", noticed Bishop Heber,[167] "a large vessel of milk was set in the chamber of the lying in woman and if a girl was born, the infant was immediately plunged into it and before the new-born had an independent existence she was done away with life." J.C. Brown,[168] assumed that generally the Rajputs dug a hole, filled it with milk and the new born baby, if a girl, was quickly drowned in it. In Mewar,[169] the female child was kept without any nourishment till she died or was stifled by filling her mouth with ashes. Montgomery[170] believed that the practice among the Rajputs in the plains was to bury the infant alive. The body was placed in an earthen vessel and the top was covered with a thick paste. At times, according to Montgomery, the child's mouth was filled with cow-dung or the head was immersed in cow's milk.

The method of doing away with the girl child, varied from place to place, in the Rajputana. Whatever facility was available in a particular region, be it man-made or nature-made, was adopted without any hitch, to crush the life of an innocent child.[171] Some people killed their infant daughters, rather allowed them to die by denying them all sustenance from their birth. The mother was forced to withhold her milk from her female offsprings.[172] Sometimes the mother would put *amal* or opium on the nipple of her breast, which the infant would suck with the milk and die.[173] Sometimes, opium pill was put into the mouth of the child or they placed the navel string into the mouth or sometimes umbilical cord was drawn over the face of the infant to prevent its respiration and the infant died of suffocation.[174] The available records also reveal that children were put to death by mixing their food with the milky juice of the plant called *madar* (i.e., Aselepias Gigantica), *ack* or *aakra,* which is a poison.[175] The destruction of such a young and tender subject was done without any hitch or hesitation. The natural weakness of the infant, when neglected and left uncleaned caused its death, without the necessity of actual violence. Sometimes, it was laid on the ground or on a plank and left to expire.[176] But the customary practice was that the father handed over a pill of *bhang* to an attendant which was immediately placed in the roof of the infant's mouth, which the girl child rolled down with saliva and the circle was complete.[177]

Besides these, some other methods were also followed in the Rajputana, to do away with the female offsprings. At some places, they were buried alive in sand dunes while at other places, they were thrown in the dry wells. In Jaisalmer,[178] for example, the female infants were thrown in dried wells and such wells (which were used exclusively for this purpose), were called as *baiyon ka kua* (i.e., well of female children), in local parlance. Similarly, in the Shekhawati region,[179] girl children were buried alive in the nearby sand dunes, and such dunes were called *baiyon ke teebe* (i.e., sand dunes of female children) by the common men.

It is a matter of great debate, whether infanticide was practiced only in the case of first born girl child, or it was committed on every female child. But whatever the truth, this gruesome act cannot be condoned on any grounds, since it was inflicted upon the innocent infant. Eminent historian of Rajasthan, G.H. Ojha,[180] believed that the first girl child or elder girl child was killed, when the second issue or the subsequent issues again happened to be a girl child. Muhnot Naincy,[181] another court historian of eminence, believed that girls born on inauspicious days or time (for example, girls born in *mool nakshatra*) were done away with, to avert the possible calamity or to avoid the future problems related to their marriage. It is worthy to note that Naincy, though acknowledging the practice, is silent on the issue of its commitment on all or the first born girl child. Whereas, Ojha believed this practice "to be prevalent from time immemorial amongst Rajputs of the Rajputana".[182] Rani Laxmi Kumari Chundawat,[183] another eminent writer of Rajasthani tales and folklores, however, believes that "not the first one, but every female child born was put to death, by one or the other way, in certain families of Rajputs in Rajasthan".

The evil practice of female infanticide is still prevalent (even in the 21st century) in India in general and Rajasthan in particular, and has not dwindled away with the passage of time. Every now and then, we come across such incidents which present this inhuman face of our society and force us to think about the sad plight of girl children. According to the sex-ratio data of Census 1991, a large part of Rajasthan recorded a declining child sex-ratio, ranging from 850-950 girls per 1000 boys. The districts of Jaisalmer (851), Ganganagar (894), Hanumangarh (897), Bharatpur (879), Dholpur

(875), Karauli (873), Sawai Madhopur (894) and Pali (896) were specially critical. According to the sex-ratio data of Census 2001, except for three districts (viz., Banswara-972, Dungarpur-963, and Bhilwara-951), all districts in Rajasthan recorded a child sex-ratio of less than 950 girls. While the child sex-ratio has improved in Sawai Madhopur, it has worsened in the surrounding districts of Alwar, Jhunjhunun, Sikar and Jaipur, which have recorded less than 900 girls to 1000 boys. The Census of 2001 also indicates that about 5 lac girl children up to the age of 6 years, are 'missing' as compared to the number of male children in Rajasthan, which again indicates the prevalence of female infanticide as well as female foeticide in Rajasthan.[184] The number of male and female children in the total population should be nearly equal, experts say, but this has not been so in the case of Rajasthan. Experts believe that one of the possible reasons for this could be foeticide and infanticide. The Census report also reveals that the highest decline in sex-ratio is reported from Bharatpur, where 89 girls are missing per 1000 male children as compared to the last Census. For Jaipur, the figure of missing girl child stands at 29. Whereas, Ganganagar and Hanumangarh have reported a decrease of 44 females per 1000 male children. Surprisingly, in Jaisalmer, the number of females has gone up by 16. It may be a welcome sign that the number of women for every 1000 men has gone up, while it is baffling to note that the number of girls up to the age of 6 has gone down.

Similarly, according to a report published by Ankita Sharma, on 17 October 2005, p. 3, in the *Rajasthan Patrika,* about 189 'abandoned' children (both male and female) were admitted in the *Shishu Griha* (i.e., crèche run by the Department of Social Welfare of Rajasthan State), in the last three years. These unfortunate 'abandoned' children were, perhaps, the result of illicit relationships. Similarly, many parents have been caught, by the local police, in the first ten months of 2005, for willfully abandoning their girl children, in want of a son. When such parents came to know about the birth of second or third girl child, they decided to throw her or leave her at some hospital or railway station or in the train compartment or at some lonely place. According to an article published in the *Rajasthan Patrika,* on 15 May, 2000[185] (p. 8), "after a lapse of 115 years, a *barat* entered the village to marry a girl in the Devra Village of Jodhpur (Rajasthan)". For these 115 years, the villagers had not seen the marriage of any of their daughters, as there were no daughters in the whole village" the article claimed. This article again, points out towards the prevalence of female infanticide in the Devra Village of Jodhpur.

It appears from the report published in the *Hindustan Times* (Jaipur edition) on 27 April 2001,[186] (p. 1), by Anjul Tomar that female infanticide is still being practiced by the Gurjar community at Thagari Village in Karauli district. Much against the mother's wish, the village women told the reporter, their children were put to death either by feeding a grain to choke the throat or by strangulating them. The babies were also fed poisonous plant-milk, the report claimed.

In another report published in the *Hindustan Times* on 8 March 2002,[187] by K.S. Tomar it was claimed that in eastern Rajasthan, female infanticide is still prevalent in Bharatpur, Dholpur, (Rupwa and Bayana) and Karauli (Sapora). "Mrs. Zakia Inam, the State women's welfare minister, admitted that female infanticide still exists in border districts" the report said, though she felt that it was dwindling with the passage of time. The villagers in eastern and north-western belts use the traditional method of strangulating the female child after birth, the report claimed.

In another report published in the *Dainik Bhaskar*, another leading newspaper of Rajasthan, on 18 November 2002,[188] page one, it was reported that after a gap of 125 years, a *barat* appeared at the gates of the palace of Jhalawar to marry the princess of the royal family. For nearly a century and a quarter of century, no girl child was born in the royal family of Jhalawar – the report claimed. This again creates a suspicion in the minds of the readers and forces them to think about the possibility of female infanticide prevalent in the royal family of Jhalawar. Similarly, according to a report published, on 25 January 2007, p. 10, in the *Rajasthan Patrika*, female infants are still killed in some districts of Madhya Pradesh (including Bhind and Muraina) by trampling them under the leg of the cot and this has been the prevalent practice in this region for the last so many decades. The mother of the female infant is forced by the family members, to perform this gruesome act, the report claimed.

Thus, we see that female infanticide prevailed in many societies, at one time or the other, in most of the civilized and uncivilized nations of the world. In the form of female infanticide, it was (and still it is) prevalent in India in general and Rajasthan, in particular. With the growing awareness caused by the spread of education, the incidents of female infanticide have registered a decline, in comparison to the older days. In the last quarter of the 20th century and in the 21st century, because of the advancement in scientific techniques, another problem – that of female foeticide (killing of girl child or female foetus in the womb itself) has severely disturbed the sex-ratio, and as a result of it, lacs of female foetuses have been annually done away with in several countries, including India and Rajasthan. This evil aspect has been discussed in a separate chapter.

Historical Evidences of Female Infanticide

It is difficult to trace the exact period, of the emergence of the abominable practice of female infanticide in India. It is also difficult to trace the origin of female infanticide as the consequence or the fall-out of the Mohammedan invasions. It has been stated by Ferishta[189] that the practice prevailed amongst the Gakkhars "where it was the custom, as soon as, a female child was born, to carry her to the door of the house and then proclaim aloud, holding the child with one hand, that any person who wanted a wife might now take her, otherwise she was immediately put to death (sic)." According to Alexander Walker,[190] Emperor Jehangir had issued a proclamation, prohibiting female infanticide, and this has been mentioned by the author of *Ackball-Nama*. The author of the *Ackball-nama* relates that, in the route of the royal journey from Kashmir to Lahore, they came to a village, the inhabitants of which had formerly been Hindus, where number of poor people, put an end to the lives of their new-born daughters. When Jehangir came to know about this, he ordered that "this barbarous practice should be discontinued" and enacted that "whoever should commit it in future, should be put to the torture(sic)." The crime of female infanticide, was also condemned by Guru Govind Singh,[191] who in the *Rehat-Nameh* said that "... with the slayers of daughters, whoever has intercourse, him do I curse" and again "whoever takes food from the slayers of daughters, shall die un-absolved." These references, suggest that female infanticide must have existed in that age.

As discussed above, the practice of infanticide existed among the Khatris, the Gakkhars, the Khokhars, the Malhotras, the Seths, the Kakkars, the Bedis, the Kapurs, the Sodhis, the Aroras, the Suyals, the Moyal Brahmans, the Rajputs, the pure Pathans and the Mohammedans of Punjab. Maharaja Dalip Singh, son of Ranjit Singh, also presented this face of society of his times when he confessed that, "he had actually seen when he was a child at Lahore, his sisters put into a sack and thrown into the river".[192] "When several female children were born in succession," observed Mr. Coldstream,[193] Deputy Commissioner of Hoshiyarpur, Punjab, in 1881, "the destruction of the last born was carried out with the following observance – a piece of *gur* (molasses) was placed in the mouth of the child, a skein of cotton was laid on her breast and the following incantation recited two or three times: – "Eat *gur*, spin your thread we don't want you, but a brother instead(sic)."The infants were usually buried into *gharras* or water pots and buried in the ground, in Punjab, according to Mr. Coldstream.

The Burar Jats of the Cis-Sutlej States also murdered their girls. It is said that on Ranjit Singh's conquest of the country, an accidental discovery of gold under a Jat's floor, caused all the houses to be dug up, in search of treasure, where upon it was found that there was hardly a house, which did not have the bones of female children buried under the floor. It was also found to exist in the then Western Province (now Uttar Pradesh) among the Bais Rajputs of Kooba Tappa in Deogaon; the Raj Kumar Rajputs of Jaunpur; the Gautam Rajputs of Doulatabad Tappa in Nizamabad Pargana; the Raghuvanshi Rajputs of Dhobee Tappa in Kerakat Pargana in Jaunpur; the Kachawa, the Bhadauri and the Parihar Rajputs of Bara Pargana; the Chauhans and the Ahirs of Mainpuri; and the Hara, the Surajbhans, and the Kalhans of Gorakhpur. The practice of infanticide also existed in Bengal, where the infants were thrown into the Ganges, as the religious offering to the deities; and it also prevailed among the Kallars of Tamil Nadu, where girl children were put to death for social and economical reasons. Certain tribal groups like the Nagas of the North-Eastern region; the Khonds of Orissa and the Todas of Nilgiri hills also practiced it.

The practice of female infanticide also prevailed in the Rajputana, in certain clans of Rajputs like the Rathores of Marwar, the Bidawats of Bikaner, the Bhumia-Tanwars of Torawati and the Kachwaha Rajputs of Jaipur, the Bhatis of Jaisalmer, the Solanki and the Hara Rajputs of Bundi, "the low and the high Rajput classes" of Sirohi, the Rajputs of Jhalawar and also "to a considerable extent" in the Shekhawati region. The Charans and Bhats, the Minas, the Ahirs and Jats (of Bharatpur) and the Mers (of Ajmer-Merwara) also practised it. Among the lesser noteworthy royal families, it prevailed in the house of Asoph, Kuchamun and Neemuch.

The practice of infanticide, in India, was first noticed by William Carey[194] in 1794, when he witnessed "the dedication of children to the Ganges, to be devoured by crocodiles and sharks." Near his home at Ganga Sagar (Calcutta), where a grand festival was held every year, Carey saw that mothers not only threw their children into the sea, but widows and even men walked into the sea and drowned themselves, esteeming it a special act of holiness, and securing immediate heaven. Carey, at another place, "found in a basket hanging on a tree, the bones of an infant that had been exposed to be devoured by the white ants, by some mother, too poor to go on a pilgrimage to a sacred river spot." Carey represented the matter to government and the result of Carey's memorial was the publication of the Regulation for preventing the sacrifice of children. Sepoys were stationed at each gathering by the government to see that the law is observed, and consequently, this form of infanticide, soon fell into disuse.

While the practice of infanticide in Bengal Presidency was first noticed by William Carey, the practice of female infanticide in India, in general, was first noticed by Jonathan Duncan,[195] of the Bengal Civil Service and afterwards Governor of Bombay, who, while residing at Benaras, found it to be prevalent in the Rajkumars and the Raghuvanshi clans of the Rajputs of Benaras Division in, 1789. On being made the Governor of Bombay, he discovered the same practice among the Rajputs of Kathiawar and Kutch. In March 1808, Colonel Walker in a document regarding infanticide, which was addressed to the Bombay Government, wrote that "...the custom of putting their infant daughters to death has also been discovered to exist with the Rhatore (Rathore) Rajputs of Jeypore and Jhodhpur......." and "it is confirmed, by every intelligent and well informed native of the country." Walker called this custom of exclusively murdering females, "a systematical infanticide", which to him, was confined to the Rajputs of India. Col. Walker also suspected that the Jauts (i.e., the Jats) and the Mewats too practised female infanticide. Amongst the Jats in particular, the scarcity of girls led to a widespread system of polyandry. But female infanticide was only practiced by a few rich Jats of high rank. The poorer Jats got money when their daughters were married, since girls with them were at a premium. Again, in May 1812, the English officers came to know, that the Jatus (Jats) destroyed their female children as soon as they were born; but now as they were afraid of the English, they removed their pregnant women, before the time of delivery, into the district of the Raja of Bharatpur, so that they could commit female infanticide. Writing about the vastness of this cruel practice, Major Murdo, in 1818, mentioned that among the offspring of 8,000 Rajputs probably not more than thirty females were alive. Col. Walker declared this practice as "most barbarous that ever owed its existence either to the wickedness or to the weakness of human nature", and argued that, when the customs and rites of any group of people are harmless, they are entitled to toleration and protection, but they ought to be punished or amended when their evident tendency is to diminish population, and to alienate the natural affections of mankind.

In December 1819, Colonel Walker, after having retired from India, addressed a letter to the Secretary of the Court of Directors, in which he suggested ways and means to stop this inhuman practice. Persuasion and reason were the only means, according to him, through which this inhuman practice could be checked. He opined that if this could be widely applied, by the Agents of the Government, they would be found to be quite sufficient without any inquisitorial institution, and without any odious system of espionage. Walker further suggested that it was necessary to satisfy the people that the English were really sincere in their wishes to abolish this crime. But all, according to him, depended on attention to the subject for a sufficient length of time, "till the influence of custom is forgotten and the natural affections have sprung up again in the hearts of parents." In attaining the object (of abolishing female infanticide) there cannot be a doubt of our success," he suggested, "but all that is required is attention to the subject, and that too for a sufficient length of time."

The suspicion of Col. Walker (about the prevalence of the practice of female infanticide in certain Rajput clans of the Rajputana) was soon confirmed by another English officer – Sir John Malcolm – who wrote an article in this regard. In the Report of Central India, published in *Asiatic Journal*, January, 1823, Sir John Malcolm wrote that the custom of infanticide was confined to some Rajput Chiefs of high rank and small fortune, who resorted to it to prevent their daughters contracting a marriage beneath their rank, and who were keen on obtaining marriage with their equals. "The petty Thakore of Cherawul, a relation of the Amjerah family", wrote Malcolm "married a daughter of the Rawul of Banswarrah in 1821.

The tribe of the Thakore's family was so inflated by the occurrence, that it was resolved that no female should make an inferior match, and in despair of obtaining such good fortune again, they kill every female child"(sic).

The practice of female infanticide, as we have seen in the previous pages, was prevalent in the Rajputana and the rulers of different States, tried to put an end to this practice, much before the advent of Britishers in the Rajputana. In Samvat 1787 (A.D. 1731) Maharaja Sawai Jai Singh of Jaipur,[196] assembled the fifty three clans of Kachwahas and all the nobles of his Durbar and explained to them that it was a serious crime to destroy their offsprings and ordered that no parent should kill his/her daughters, within the territory of Jaipur. He also asked the foreign Vakeels, who were in his attendance, to write to their masters to formulate certain rules for the prohibition of female infanticide in their respective States. Jai Singh also tried to regulate the dowry system and asked the destitute and poor Kachwahas to come to Jaipur and celebrate the nuptials of their daughters there, and ordered that no Charan or Bhat or Rao would ask for tyag in the city of Jaipur. These rules of Sawai Jai Singh were obeyed up to the time of Maharaja Sawai Madho Singh, after whose reign, things again went wrong and many Sardars expended large sums in marriages.[197]

Similarly, Maharaja Bijai Singh (Vijay Singh) of Marwar,[198] after noticing that the extortionous demands of Charans and Bhats, was one of the factors responsible for this heinous practice in Marwar, made certain rules for the prevention of female infanticide. In 1763 A.D. he fixed (prescribed) the amount, to be paid to the Charans, Bhats, Dhooms and Dholis, on the occasion of marriages and ordered that nobody should pay, anything more than the specified amount. Any Charan or Bhat, who demanded more than the prescribed amount, was to be punished by the Raj. Maharaja Bijai Singh also ordered that whosoever commits this crime, will be banished from the State of Marwar. In 1837, Maharana Ratan Singh of Bikaner,[199] during his stay at Gaya, asked his nobles and Sardars to take an oath to give up the heinous practice of female infanticide. Perhaps he thought, that the oath taken at a religious and sacred place, would have the desired effect and that nobody would dare to break the oath on account of the fear of religion. After his return, he again, asked them to honour their oath, which they had taken at Gaya. In October 1839[200] some rules were again framed in Marwar by the combined efforts of Maharaja Man Singh, the British officers, the Jagirdars and the officials of the State. Some important aspects of these rules, specially related to Rajputs, were inscribed on marble slabs and were fixed at the district headquarters of the State.

The custom of infanticide was also prevalent among the Rajputs and Meenas of Jhalawar State.[201] In 1834, when Jhalawar State was part of Kota, Raj-Rana Madho Singh[202] welcomed the proposal of the British government to abolish the cruel evil and he issued an order in the same year to that effect. Later this order was followed by Raj-Rana Madan Singh,[203] the successor of Madho Singh. Despite their sincere efforts to crush this social evil, it could not be eradicated completely. Therefore, when Jhalawar was created in 1838, the cruel practice prevailed there. To eradicate this practice, Maharaj Rana Madan Singh issued a proclamation in 1844 declaring it illegal in the territory of Jhalawar. By this declaration, Maharaj Rana directed the Meenas to refrain from destroying their daughters and warned them against it.[204] This proclamation assured of some consideration on the part of the Durbar if they preserved their daughters. The Maharaj Rana also instructed the Patels of every village to fix up a stone in their respective villages. These instances prove beyond doubt the existence of this heinous practice in different States of the Rajputana. This also shows the enormity of the problem as it forced the rulers of different native States to issue a proclamation against it. Some of the rulers took the initiative to do away with this evil, without any outside or external pressure. This refutes the prevalent notion of historical writings, which depict the native rulers as insouciant to the administrative measures and brand them as insensitive and always indulging in war, wine and women, and has given all the credit to the efforts of British officers, to wipe out this evil. In fact, some of them, like Sawai Jai Singh of Jaipur and Maharaja Bukht Singh and Maharaja Vijay Singh of Jodhpur, took action against it, much before the arrival of British East India Company in the Rajputana.

It is interesting to note, that whereas the crime of female infanticide was noticed and reported by some English officers, some other English officers professed complete ignorance about it and even denied its existence, in their respective areas. Lt. Col. Sutherland, the A.G.G., for example, denied its existence in the district of Ajmer.[205] In a letter dated 29th of December, 1841, addressed to G. Hamilton, Esquire, Officiating Secretary to the Government, Lt. Col.

Sutherland wrote that he had no reason to believe that this crime was perpetrated to any extent in the district of Ajmer and as such according to him, it was unnecessary to issue prohibitory orders on this subject.

Similarly, Ludlow, the Political Agent in Jodhpur[206] wrote that "the secrecy with which female infants were destroyed within the recesses of the Zenana, defied detection." In a letter to Col. Sutherland,[207] A.G.G., in June 1842, he wrote that "... female infanticide has been emphatically declared by persons of all classes among the Rajputs of this country to be a crime against God and Nature." He further believed that the evil, existed by compulsion among the highest ranks, through the extortion practiced by the Charans and by force of imitation rather than of necessity among the middle ranks. Ludlow believed that the humblest orders composing the great mass of the Rajput population, preserve the lives of their female children almost invariably. Ludlow himself, was aware of the existence of daughters in many Rajput families of repute. But even then, Ludlow called female infanticide as an "unholy but a time honoured custom." And he believed it to be prevalent in the Shekhawati region "to some considerable extent."[208] Ludlow was further told by the Sardars of Marwar, that female infanticide arose from two causes "the extortionate demands of the Charans on marriages and the disgrace, which attends a family, where a daughter after having attained mature years, remains unmarried".[209]

While this was the state of affairs in other States of the Rajputana, the Jaipur council of regency, accepted the prevalence of the practice of female infanticide in its territories and sought the British help to abolish it. On 12 April, 1844,[210] the Jaipur council of regency, sent a memorandum to the Political Agent, in which they confessed that, "upon reflection, it seems that a crime of this magnitude cannot be brought home satisfactorily, through any search that can be instituted, or by any oral evidence that can be obtained." The Jaipur council of regency believed that the practice of female infanticide was the result of the heavy demands of the Charans, Bhats, Dholees, Meerasis and others of the like classes, and requested the Political Agent to restrict the movements of the Charans and Bhats and others to their respective areas. They also requested, that the presence of the Charans and Bhats of other native States should also be prohibited, on the occasion of the marriages, celebrated in the State of Jaipur.

On 5 May, 1842[211] the Jodhpur Durbar issued a memorandum prohibiting female infanticide in Marwar. In the memorandum, it was stated that infanticide prevailed to some extent amongst the inferior Rajputs of Marwar, owing to the exorbitant demands of Bhats and Charans on the celebration of marriages. It was also prevalent, according to the memorandum, in the house of Asoph. When the English officers proposed a legislative act, for the prevention of female infanticide, they were surprised to find that such an act already existed in Marwar, which by then "had fallen in disuse".[212] The heads of the Bhats and Charans were, then, called into the legislative tent and were forced to obey the orders of the Durbar and the English officers, and bound themselves to receive the sums specified in the article. The introduction of the article was much apprehended and it was believed that if the law was implemented, infanticide will come to an end. Similarly, the Maharana of Mewar declared this practice as illegal on 24 May, 1844.[213]

It is strange to note, that while some English officers considered the Rajputs as degraded race and had a very low opinion of the Rajput character and even branded them as child murderers, but as far as the prevalence of the crime of infanticide in their respective areas was considered, they professed ignorance about it. This dichotomy of labelling the whole race as child murderers and professing complete absence of female infanticide in their respective areas, is somewhat confusing. It may be the reason that their personal relations with a particular community, in a particular area, forced them to keep quiet over this sensitive issue. Or it may be because of their unfamiliarity with a particular area, because of their frequent transfers. In 1844, Lt. Col. J. Robinson,[214] Political Agent in Mewar, in a letter written to Major C. Thoresby, Offg. A.G.G. for the Rajputana, wrote that the "Rajputs are a selfish, unfeeling and remorseless race, ready to perpetrate any atrocity for the gratification of their pride or ambition" and asked that how far it would be right or expedient under any circumstances, for the British Government, to sanction a compromise with crime more especially one of so deep a dye. In all other cases, commented Robinson, crime is sought to be repressed by the dread of suitable punishment following its commission. He also asked why child murder should be allowed to form an exception. "There seems nothing in the Rajput character" opined Robinson, "which should entitle them to any particular privileges or immunities not enjoyed by the rest of their countrymen". While on the one hand, Robinson called it a crime "of so deep a dye", on the other hand, he denied any incidence of female infanticide in the States of Udaipur, Pratapgarh, Banswara and Dungarpur in last five years of his tenure.

In 1845, Lt. Col. Sutherland,[215] in a letter dated 6 June 1845, to F. Currie, Esquire, Secretary to the Government of India, reported that the practice of female infanticide was prevalent among the Rathores of Marwar, and in the house of Asoph, one of the principle chiefs of Marwar. Sutherland viewed it "with equal aversion or abhorrence with which it was viewed by the Maharaja of Jodhpur and Captain Ludlow". The Maharaja of Jodhpur told Sutherland that during the time of his illustrious predecessor Bukht Singh, there was an act prohibiting female infanticide and which also prescribed the amount, which the Charans and Bhats were to receive from a village and also the mode through which, it was to be collected. Since the legislation on the subject was enacted in Marwar, Sutherland had no doubts that "infanticide would be much less prevailing in Rajputana and that, eventually it would cease to be, one of those crimes, which darkens and degrades the character of the Rajputs". Sutherland considered it a crime and a usage, so widely spread and so inveterate as that of infanticide amongst the Rajputs.

The prevalence of the abominable practice of female infanticide in the Rajputana was also reported by the local court historians and the different census books (like *Mardum-Shumari Raj-Marwar,* 1890). Mahakavi Shyamal Das,[216] G.H. Ojha,[217] B.N. Reu,[218] Muhnot Naincy,[219] etc., all admitted that, it was prevalent amongst the Rajputs, though they differ on the cause and the extent of this practice. Shyamal Das believed that the heavy expenditure on marriage and particularly that on the tika ceremony was the main cause of female infanticide amongst Rajputs. The same reason was accepted by G.H. Ojha, who believed that the pomp and show done at the time of marriages and the consequent lavish expenditure, followed by the giving of heavy dowry, was responsible for female infanticide. Ojha believed that this evil practice had been going on "from times immemorial" and also that when more than one girl was born in a family, the previous female issue(s) were done away with. Thus according to him, the Rajputs destroyed their female-infants only when their number was more than one. Similarly, Muhnot Naincy, has accepted the prevalence of this evil practice, though he has given a different reason for its prevalence.

According to him, those female infants, who were born at some inauspicious time or muhurts (mool nakshatra for example) were killed or were thrown away, to avert the possible evil.

Rao Raja Rial Mul[220] (or Rid Mul), the Jodhpur Vakeel, believed that female infanticide had been in existence from times immemorial amongst Rajputs, and it originated in the heavy demands made upon them at marriages of their daughters, by Charans, who, if their claims remained unsatisfied, wrote satires against them and forced them to comply with their demands by wounding and sprinkling blood upon the threshold of the house where the marriage was taking place. Rao Raja Rial Mul believed that it was prevalent only among the Rajputs; and also that Mahajans, Brahmans and all other classes (except Rajputs) never destroyed their infant female children. "Among Mahajans and other classes," according to the Jodhpur Vakeel, "there is a fixed rule which can never be deviated from, and therefore they never dream of the destruction of their daughters; nor consider their existence in the light of misfortune". But at the same time, he cautioned himself by writing, that he has not, of late heard of any case of female infanticide. According to Rao Raja, it was also practised in the family of Kuchamun, Neemuch and Asoph. "In Neemuch, the widow of Sultan Singh, while mounting the pile before becoming *Sati* on the demise of her husband (which occurred in Samvat 1876 or 1820 A.D.); pronounced a curse upon her descendants, who would destroy their infant daughters and the prohibition has ever since been respected in the family" wrote the Jodhpur Vakeel.

Rao Raja Rial Mul, relates another story about the existence of female infanticide in the house of Asoph. According to him, "Nahar Singh or Nahar Khan, the Thakur of Asoph,[221] at the time of the nuptial ceremony of his daughter, made a vow that he would, during the whole year, deliver to the Charans, whatever they might demand of him. He accordingly, satisfied the claims of all comers; some obtained a horse, others article of clothing, cash, bracelets of gold, or strings of pearls. At length all was gone, and the year was not yet expired, when a Charan came, and finding the Thakur's substance exhausted, demanded of him his head – upon which Nahar Singh, in fulfilment of his vow, decapitated himself with his own hands. From this cause, the descendants of the house have, from the time in question, destroyed their daughters at the time of birth."

"Some of the *Bhatees* (Bhats) and Charans of distinction destroy their infant daughters while others preserve them, but the humbler members of these clans uniformly suffer the existence of their female children in consequence of receiving money payments from the families, into which they marry their daughters" remarked the Jodhpur Vakeel.[222] "Although it is a point which cannot be declared with certainty," wrote Rao Raja Rial Mul, "it is believed that a number averaging between 300 and 400 female infants, may have been destroyed annually in Marwar; prior to the rule prohibiting to kill them, was enacted. Since that period, however, I have not been able to ascertain that a single child has been made away with – although I have instituted enquiries upon the subject in all directions. "No person has", adds Rao Raja, "been charged with the offence – which however, it must be confessed is of such a character that no one would acknowledge its perpetration."

Though, as discussed above, female infanticide existed in many parts of the Rajputana yet in the absence of effective machinery, for the detection of the crime in different States, nothing definite could be said about the extent of the practice. As it was carried out in the interiors of the *Zenana,* and the houses of the royal people were also impregnable and as the Rajput women lived their lives as a sealed book, it was very difficult for a person, well nigh impossible for a foreigner, to get the fact. The statements made on the extent of infanticide by the Residents and Political Agents sometime appear contradictory and exaggerated. It may be the case that they depended on others for information (as they were unaware of the customs, traditions and about the people of this part of the country); but there are no means of getting at the truth, since a census had not been taken and it seemed impossible that an attempt in this direction would succeed. While many English officers believed that the Jats practiced female infanticide, Captain A.H. Bingley for example, denied its prevalence in the Jat community.[223] In 1899, he wrote that, "female infanticide, the crime which is so common among Rajputs, is practically unknown among Jats, and is rare among Gujars, as for all work in the fields, girls are almost as valuable as boys." "It is true", wrote Bingley, "that female children are not usually so well cared for and nourished as boys, and that if a lad and his sister were ill, nearly all the attention of the house would be given to the former but girls are by no means unkindly treated. They stand next in importance to, and at no great distance from the boys and if the same amount of affection is not lavished on them as on their brother, they are at any rate not neglected."

In 1844, Major Thoresby, the Officiating Agent to the Governor General reported that in Jaipur the practice was on the decline.[224] It was only confined, in his opinion, to the Bhumia Tanwar Rajputs and other inferior classes. The guilty were punished by imposing fine or imprisonment. The higher classes of the Kachwaha and Shekhawat Rajputs considered it a detestable crime, according to Thoresby. In November 1844,[225] he made a general statement for the whole of the Rajputana, that the practice was not common there and it was generally reprobated and held in abhorrence and that the offence was confined to some of the families of the poorer classes and lowest orders.

In Bundi, where it was prevalent among the Solanki and Hara Rajputs, the Political Agent reported in 1846,[226] that the Solanki Rajputs had completely discontinued the female infanticide from the time when one of them, on being found guilty of the crime, was expelled from the kingdom by the orders of the Rao Raja. Much influence was exerted on the ruler, by other chiefs for a reversal of the sentence, but Rao Raja remained firm in the decision.

The practice of female infanticide also existed among the lower ranks of the Rajputs, Puryar (or Parihar) Meenas of Jahazpur[227] (Bhilwara), Thakurs residing on the frontier tracts of the region between Bundi, Jaipur and Mewar[228] and also among the Mers of Merwara in the British territory of Ajmer.[229] The custom of offering huge sums of money to the father of the bridegroom by the girls side, was responsible for the female infanticide among the Mers. "The custom of female infanticide" wrote Captain H. Hall,[230] Superintendent of Merwara, in July 1827, "and the sale of women... were closely connected, having had their origin in the heavy expense attending marriage contracts... what first established the payment is unknown, but it was so sacred, inviolable, and even a partial deviation so disgraceful that the most necessitous of the tribe would not incur the imputation.... The sums payable were beyond the means of so many, that daughters necessarily remained on hand after maturity, entailed immortal disgrace, and thus imposed a necessity on all female progeny of becoming victims to their family honour." The Puryar Meenas inhabited the tract in the vicinity of Deolia. They were said to be a cross between the Puryar Rajputs of Mandore (in Marwar) and the aboriginal Meenas of Rajputana who were divided into 38 classes or families. The tribe claimed themselves to be of Rajput origin.[231]

Regarding the origin of infanticide among the Meenas in Rajputana, an interesting legendary tale was current among them. The traditional story reveals that in the days bygone, Shalla, descendant of Shoma, from whom Puryar Meenas sprang up, paid great reverence to god Mahadev to whom, he offered himself as a sacrifice. The Lord was so much gratified at his devotion that He asked him to ask for his reward. Shalla requested that he be granted as many sons as the hairs of his head, which was instantaneously and unhesitatingly granted by the supreme god. He severed his head in the heat of the moment, but then ill-luck began to take its toll. His daughter entered the temple and her shadow falling upon her father's headless trunk made the god so enraged that he cursed her and allowed Puryar Meenas to destroy their daughters. From that time onwards, female infanticide was practiced among the Meenas. The Puryar Meenas were said to have practised infanticide more than even the Rajputs.

"Like the Rajputs", observes R.K. Saxena,[232] "the Meenas suffered from pride and to maintain it they resorted to this practice. The family pride stood in the way to accept any match for the girl from families having inferior rank and as a natural corollary, infanticide was practised. This idle notion of superiority and pride, played the most vital role in the socio-psychological behaviour of the Puryar Meenas in favour of infanticide(sic)." Like the Rajputs, the Puryar Meenas were prejudiced in marrying a female of their own class but might marry from among the numerous aboriginal classes of Meenas. It was taken as degradation to allow one's female child to ally herself with one of inferior blood. The term 'father-in-law' was considered as one of scorn and reproach and the man who bore this relationship was looked upon with contempt and treated as inferior by the bridegroom, while it was at the same time, considered disgraceful if a girl, after attaining mature years, remained unmarried among the Puryar Meenas.

L. Wilkinson, Political Agent in Kota, obtained an accurate census of eleven villages which showed that the aggregate number of boys under 12 years of age was 369, and girls only 87, i.e., 282 or more than 3/4th of the girls were destroyed within a brief period of 12 years. In one village, there were only 4 girls to 44 boys; in another, 4 girls to 58 boys and in a third with a large population of boys, no girls were seen at all. In Paplala, a Meena village near Jahazpur, there were 22 boys and not a single girl in 1836. There were 60 girls to 103 boys in four Meena villages of Bundi. In 1860,[233] when a census of all the Meena villages in Mewar, Jaipur and Bundi was taken, it was found that the percentage of girls to boys among Meenas in Mewar was 28.88 per cent, in Jaipur, it was 29.60 per cent and in Bundi it was 53.23 per cent. They have had recourse to it in the belief, that women born in their tribe are fated to bring disgrace to their families and sect.[234] In justification of their superstitious belief they plead the authority of the *Sati*, who while ascending the pile commanded it, to its progeny and also of the goddess Bhawani herself who enjoined it. Captain Wilkinson narrates that the Meenas who had families, admitted that a few – to the extent of rare were those who did not put their daughters to death and sometimes it came to as many as three in a single family.[235] L. Wilkinson also found the existence of infanticide in Udaipur in 1821 and believed that it was more avowedly practised in Mewar, as compared to other parts of Rajasthan.[236] Wilkinson, in 1836, reported that as many as 20,000 infants were annually destroyed in Malwa and Rajputana.[237] His estimate was based upon the interviews, of the natives, with whom he met. While John Bax,[238] the Resident at Indore, came to a different conclusion. He was told by a native, Govind Rao Kantapur by name, that the number of infants put to death in Malwa and Rajputana would come to fifty cases annually. He argued that the practice of infanticide was limited to Rajput chiefs of high rank and low means. These two, diametrically opposed estimates of an average of 55 cases per day and 50 cases annually, naturally put question marks on the enormity of the crime in the Rajputana. According to the returns furnished by Wilkinson, it appears that 59 per cent of the females born were destroyed by their parents. But had it been so, the Rajputs would have faced tremendous difficulties in procuring wives for their sons, but more in procuring husbands for the few daughters brought up by them. It is also noteworthy that a great proportion of the Rajput Chiefs owing to their debauching and excessive use of opium, were denied the natural rights of procreation and were obliged to have recourse to continue their lineage. John Bax remarked that it would be unfair to infer that every female child born under a Rajput's roof whose birth has been concealed is put to death, for among Rajputs it is a common practice to give away their girls to be brought up in less noble but more wealthy families.

Thus by the above account, it becomes quite clear, that female infanticide was prevalent in many parts in India and in many sections of the society in the Rajputana. "After the murder of every infant", wrote Sleeman,[239] in his *Journey through the Kingdom of Oudh*, "the family considers itself an object of displeasure to the deity; and on the 12th day after birth they send for the *Purohit* or the family priest, and by suitable gratuities obtain absolution. It is necessary whether the family be rich or poor; but when the absolution is given, nothing more is thought or said about the matter."

Notes

1. Wilson, John, *History of Suppression of Infanticide in Western India*, London, 1855. pp. 428-29.
2. *Encyclopaedia of Religion and Ethics*, Vol. III, p. 541.
3. This barbarous practice has been criticized in the Holy Quran. It was closely linked up with their orthodox idea of becoming poor by fostering daughters or with their anxiety that their daughters may not prove to be a source of scandal by some undesirable feminine exuberances during their youth. Pakrasi, K.B., *Female Infanticide in India*, Calcutta, 1970, p. 16.
4. Malthus, T.R., *Essay on Population*, Vol. I, pp. 141-146.
5. Ibid.
6. For more information on the prevalence of infanticide (including female infanticide) in various civilizations, please refer to *The New Encyclopedia Britannica*, Vol. 6, 22 and 25, 15th edition. And also, Peggs, J., *Cries of Agony*, Delhi, 1984, pp. 113-130; and Fuller, Marcus, B., *The Wrongs of Indian Womanhood*, pp. 148-158.
7. Ibid.
8. Panigrahi, Lalita, *British Social Policy and Female Infanticide*, Delhi, 1972, pp. 5-7.
9. *The New Encyclopedia Britannica*, Vol. 6, p. 307. And also, Fuller Marcus B., *The Wrongs of Indian Womanhood*, Inter India Publications, New Delhi, 1984, pp. 151-153. Jean Baptist Tavernier (who visited India in the 16th century) has forwarded another view, regarding the prevalence of infanticide in Bengal. "When a woman is delivered," observes Tavernier, "and the infant is unwilling to take its mother's breast, it is carried outside the village and placed in a cloth, which is tied by four corners to the branches of a tree, and is thus left from morning to evening. In this way, the poor infant is exposed to the crows, which torment it.... In the evening, the infant is taken to try

whether it is willing to suckle during the following night, and should it happen that it still refuses the breast, it is taken back on the following day to the same place; this is done for three days in succession, after which, if the infant is unwilling to take the breast, in the belief that it is a demon, they cast it into the Ganges or some other river or tank which is nearer at hand."

Cf. *Jean Baptist Tavernier's Travels in India,* William Crooke, (ed.), Oriental Books Reprint Corporation, New Delhi, p. 167.

10. Krishnaswamy, S., "Female Infanticide in Contemporary India: A case study of Kallars of Tamil Nadu", in Kapur, Pramilla (ed.), *Girl Child and Family Violence,* New Delhi, 1993.
11. Risley, H.H., *The People of India,* (ed. by William Crooke) Oriental Books Reprint Corporation, Delhi, 1969, pp. 171-172.
12. Ibid.
13. Krishnaswamy, S., op. cit.
14. NAI: Translation of a note from Rao Raja Rial Mul or Rid Mal, the Jodhpur Vakeel, to John Ludlow, Pol. Ag., Ludlow to Sutherland, June 29, 1842, F. & P., Cons. No. 294-295, dt. 28 Dec. 1842, (No. 250 of 1842). And also, NAI: Sutherland to F. Currie, Esquire, Secy. to the G.O.I., 6 June 1845, F. & P., Cons. No. 70, dt. 12 Sept. 1845.
15. As told by Rani Laxmi Kumari Chundawat, the eminent writer of Rajasthan, in an interview with her.
16. The Jaipur council of regency told Major Thoresby on October 8, 1840 that they received a complaint from Torawati (a place between Shekhawati and present day Haryana, and inhabited by the Tanwar Rajputs) that one Samandar Singh son of Ranjit Singh, killed his infant daughter ten days ago. When asked by the officials of Torawati, he replied that this practice was prevalent in them "from the time of our ancestors". The Jaipur council of regency, consequently issued an *Ishtihar* (advertisement) prohibiting female infanticide in Torawati and asked the officials of Torawati to try the culprit in the *Faujdari* court.

    RSAJ: From Jaipur council of regency to Major Thoresby, dt. October 8, 1840; General, Social and Religious, Basta no. 8.
17. NAI: Trans. of a note addressed by the Jaipur Council of Regency to the Pol. Ag. dt. 27th of Oct. 1847, F.&P., Ludlow to Sutherland, Cons. No. 78 dt. 20 Nov. 1847 (Enclosure No. 227 of 1847, No. 97 of 1847).
18. As told by Rani Laxmi Kumari Chundawat, and also, Vyas, Kailash Nath and Gahlot, Devendra Singh, *Rajasthan Ki Jatiyon Ka Samajik evam Arthik Jiwan,* J.S. Gehlot Shodh Sansthan, Jodhpur, 1992, p. 106.

19. NAI: Burton to Sutherland, 12 Aug. 1846, F. & P., Cons. No. 255, 17 October 1846.
20. Kumar, Vijay, *British Paramountcy in Rajputana (A case study of relation of the Sirohi State with the British,* 1823-1905 A.D.), Books Treasure, Jodhpur, 1991, p. 154.
21. Manglani, H.J., *History, Culture and Administration of Jhalawar State*, Jaipur Publishing House, Jaipur, 1993, p. 171.
22. NAI: Ludlow, Pol. Ag. Jaipur to Major C. Thoresby, Offg. Agent to the Gov. Gen. for the States of Rajputana, dt. 12 April, 1844, F. & P., Cons. No. 152, dt. 30 Nov. 1844.
    It seems that the practice of female infanticide prevailed in Shekhawati as late as third decade of the 20th century. Thakur Chhattu Singh of village Taain, who himself hailed from a reputed Rajput family and who was an active member of Shekhawati Arya Samaj, tried to spread consciousness against this abominable crime. More information on his efforts, can be obtained from the topic "The role of Shekhawati Arya Samaj", in this book.
23. Shri Shiv Charan Das, one of the members of Charan community and the great grandson of Shyamal Das, a great historian of Rajasthan, told this in an interview with him on 30.11.2002, at Shrinathji Maharaj Ki Bagichi, Charnon Ka Mandir, Chomu Road, Jaipur.
    And also, NAI: Trans. of a note from Rao Raja Rial Mul or Rid Mal to the Political Agent., op. cit.
24. NAI: L. Wilkinson, Offg. Pol. Ag. Harauti, to A. Lockett, dt. 26 April 1833, F. & P., Cons. No. 17, dt. 23 Jan. 1834.
25. Panigrahi, Lalita, op. cit., pp. 12-13.
26. NAI: *Sketch of Merwara* (1818-1834) by Lt. Col. Hall, Superintendent Merwara, dt. 16 Dec. 1834, F. & P., Cons. No. 44, 4 May 1835.
    And also, Peggs, J., *Cries of Agony*, Delhi, 1984, p. 177.
    Col. Tod and Shyamal Das believed that the Mers of Merwara, Meds and Meos of Mewat and the Meenas of Mewar and Khairad (the place around river Banas) belonged to the same family. Cf. Rawat, Saraswat, *Meena Itihaas*, S.K. Sharma (publisher), Samvat 2057. p. 92.
27. NAI: Trans. of a note from Rao Raja Rial Mul or Rid Mal the Jodhpur Vakeel to John Ludlow, Pol. Ag., op. cit.
28. As told by Shri Shiv Charan Das.
29. Panigrahi, Lalita, op. cit.
30. Ibid.
31. Pakrasi, K.B., op. cit., p. 37.
32. NAI: Translation of a note in reply from Rao Raja Rial Mul or Ridmul, the Jodhpur Vakeel to John Ludlow, the Pol. Ag. op. cit.

33. Ibid.
34. NAI: Lt. Col. J. Robinson, Pol. Ag. Mewar to Major C. Thoresby, Offg. A.G.G., dt. 4 January, 1844; F. & P., Cons. No. 40, Enclosure No. 1 in No. 36 of 1844.
35. Altekar, A.S., op. cit., p. 7. And also, Basham, A.L., *The Wonder That Was India.*
36. "They go to the final bath; they deposit pots (called *sthalis;* the word being feminine in gender), but lift up the vessels for Vayu (called graham, the word masculine in gender); therefore they keep aside a daughter at birth, a son they lift up." *T.S.*, VI, 5, 10; *M.S.*I.145.36.
37. "The wife is indeed a friend, the daughter is distress or humiliation, the son is the light in the highest heaven." *Mahabharata,* Adi Parva, 159.11.
38. "एमा अगुर्योषितः शुम्भमाना वत्तिष्ठ नारि तवस रभस्व।
सुपत्नी पत्या प्रजया प्रजावत्या त्वागन् यज्ञः प्रति कुम्भ गृभायः।" *A.V.*, XI.1.14.
39. "शमीमश्वत्थ आरूढस्तत्र पुंसुवनं कृतम।
तद् वै पुत्रस्य वेदनं तत स्त्रीष्वा भतामसि।।" *A.V.*, VI.11.1.
And also, "पुंसवनमिति कर्मनामधेयं येन कर्मणा निमित्तेन गर्भिणी पुंमासमेव सूते सत्पुंसवनम्।" *Apastamba Griha Sutra*, 14.9, Cf. Mishra, Jai Shankar, op. cit., p. 269.
The 16 *sanskars* mentioned in the *Hindu Dharmashastras* are (i) *Garbhadhan (ii) Punsuvan (iii) Seemanto-nayan (iv) Jaatkarma (v) Naam karan (vi) Nishkraman (vii) Annaprashan (viii) Chuda karma (ix) Karna vedha (x) Vidyarambha (xi) Upanayan (xii) Vedarambha (xiii) Keshaanta (xiv) Samavartan (xv) Vivah (xvi) Anteshti.* Cf. Mishra, Jai Shankar, op. cit., p. 268.
40. "सप्त मर्यादाः कवयस्ततक्षुस्तासामिदेकामभ्यहुरो गात्। आयोह स्कम्भ उपमस्य नीडे पथां विसर्ग धरूणषु तस्थो।" A.V., V.1.6.
And also, A.V., VI.10.112.
41. Kane, P.V., *History of the Dharma-Shastras,* Vol. 5, Part-I, p. 1632.
42. Muller, Max, *Chips from a German Workshop,* Vol. II, p. 211, Cf. Crooke, W., *Tribes and Castes of the North-Western Provinces,* Vol. I, p. 10.
43. *G.D.S.*, IV, 14-17; *M.S.*, X, 5.40; *Y.S.*, 91-95.
44. The term endogamy and exogamy – *passablement barbares* – as Mr. Senart has called them, were introduced by Mr. J.F. McLennan in his well known essay on Primitive Marriage. The laws governing marriage which these terms denote were then unnamed. Endogamy is the law "which allows marriage only between persons who are recognized as being of the same blood connection or kindered; and if where it occurs, it confines marriage to the tribe or community, it is because the tribe regards itself as comprising a kindered." In short

the term endogamous division means a group from outside which its male members cannot take their wives.
Cf. *Census of India*, 1911, Vol. XXII, p. 123.

45. *Rajasthan State Gazetteer*, Vol. I, 1995, pp. 178-180.
46. "Prohibition of marriage between all persons recognized as being of the same blood, whether they form one community or part only of a community, or parts of several communities, and accordingly it may prevent marriage between persons who (though of the same blood) are of different local tribes, while it frequently happens that it leaves persons of the same local tribe (but who are not of the same blood) free to marry one another(sic)." Briefly it is the practice of marrying only outside one's own group. An exogamous division is a group from within which its male members cannot take their wives, or the inner limit within which a man may not marry. Cf. *Census of India*, 1911, Vol. XXII, p. 124.
47. The custom of hypergamy or the law of superior marriage is the rule which compels a man to wed his daughter with a member of a group which shall be equal or superior in rank than his own, while he himself may take his wife, or at any rate his second wife, from a group of inferior standing.
Cf. *Census of India*, 1911, Vol. XXII, p. 126.
48. Bingley, A.H., *History, Caste and Culture of Jats and Gujars*, New Delhi, 1978, p. 150.
49. Sleeman, W.H., Cf. Bingley, A.H., *Handbook on Rajputs*, pp. 167-168.
50. Cf. 'Chetan', Chandra Singh, *Maharao Shekha: Vansha-parampara, Khampen, aur unke Gaon*, Sahitya Kala Evam Sanskriti Parishad, Dantaramgarh, Sikar (Raj.), 2003, p. 96.
51. For a detailed study of the origin and the migration of the various clans (*khaamps*) of Rajputs, please refer to Sherring, M.A., *Hindu Tribes and Castes*, Vol. III, Cosmo Publications, Delhi-6, 1974, pp. 27-70
52. Tod, Colonel, *Annals and Antiquities of Rajasthan*, Vol. II, p. 741.
53. Report by Walker, Alexander, Resident at Baroda, 31 March, 1808, pp. Hindoo widows, 2, Part II, 33. Cf. Panigrahi, Lalita, op. cit., p. 11. Regarding the origin of female infanticide, an interesting anecdote prevailed amongst the Jahrejas. "A powerful Raja of their caste," observes Marcus Fuller, "had a daughter of singular beauty and accomplishments. He sent his family priest to search for a prince of an equal rank and wealth as a husband for her. Failing to find such an one and seeing the Raja's sorrow, he advised him to avoid the disgrace of having her remain unmarried by putting her to death.

This the Raja could not bring himself to do; but the priest volunteered to assume all the consequences of the sin, and he put her to death (sic)." Cf. Fuller, Marcus B., *The Wrongs of Indian Womanhood*, p. 154.

54. "The Sodas have less prejudice than most Rajput tribes and will drink from the same vessel and smoke out of the same hookah with a mussulman, laying aside only the tube that touches the mouth" observes Sherring. Their marriages are performed entirely in accordance with old Rajput customs, yet in their religion, they conform, for the most part, to Mohammedan rites, Sherring believed. Cf. Sherring, M.A., op. cit., p. 39.
55. "They are a very ancient tribe", remarks Sherring, "who probably contended with Alexander, before whose time they were, it is believed, established on the banks of the Sutlej.... The Johiyas are by no means extinct, as Tod imagined.... Many of them are mussulmans but some in the Sirsa district are still Hindus." Cf. Sherring, M.A., op. cit., p. 31.
56. Sherring, M.A., op. cit., p. 48.
57. Cf. *Census of India*, 1911 p. 139.
58. Cf. Ibid., p. 152. The Khanzadas, because they belonged to the Mewat region (i.e., in the present day areas of Alwar, Bharatpur and Gurgaon), were known as Mewatis before their conversion to Islam. Cf. Rawat, Saraswat, op. cit., p. 27.
59. Cf. *Census of India*, 1911, p. 156. Monier Williams believed that because of Meos, the region dominated by them, came to be known as Mewat and before their conversion to Islam they were Rajputs. Similarly, Maulvi Abu Muhammad Abdul Shakur Mewati (author of *Tarikh-i-Mewat*) believed them to be the descendants of Rajputs, while Major Powlett observed that they were the mixture of Rajputs and Meenas. Cf. Rawat, Saraswat, op. cit., pp. 27-28.
60. Cf. *Census of India*, 1911 p. 162. And also, Gahlot, S.S. and Dhar, Banshi, *Castes and Tribes of Rajasthan*, Jodhpur, 1989.
61. For more information, on this subject, please see Gahlot, S.S. and Dhar, Banshi, op. cit.
62. Tod, Colonel, op. cit., Vol. I, p. 639.
63. "जउ पहिलउ बेटी जाई, माइ बाप कालमुंहा थाइ।
जसु घर बेटी आबी, पूठि लागि चिंता आवी।
बेटी घर सम्महो पाउ चालइ, दरिद्र वाटि दिखाड़इ।
जां हुई बालि ताउं हुइ लालि पालि।
हुई बडेरी, थइ अनेरा केरी, अ वाटइ चालती, देह मरोड़इ हालती।

कुल कलंक आणई, अणहुंती कलि सामूहि ताणई।
आपणु घर सोसइ, पिरयुं घर पोसइ।
आपणु कुल ईखई, विरायुं भूखइ।
धणइ न तुसइ, थोड़लइ अपमान रुसइ।
न जाइ बेटी अनरथ खाणि भेटइ।"

And also, "बेटी जाई, जमारो हारयो।" "के जागे बेटी रो बाप।"

Cf. Rathore, V.S., *Rajasthan Ki Sanskriti mein Nari*, Rajasthani Granthagar, Jodhpur, 1994, p. 37.

Similarly, it is believed that:

Pendo Bhalo na kos ko, Beti bhali na ek
Deno Bhalo na Baap ko, Sahib Rakhe tek.

(i.e., Travelling on foot for a mile is not good, nor is the birth of a girl. Paternal indebtedness is equally bad. God may save us from these and protect our honour). Cf. Gahlot, Jagdish Singh, *Rajasthan Before Second World War, (A socio-economic study)*, Rajasthani Granthagar, Jodhpur, 1986 p. 85.

The miserable position of a girl's father is also very well depicted in the Bengali adages which say that, "he has hanging over his head a chain of shoes to strike him at every turn;" and that, "bride's father is soil and bridegroom's father is peg (*meyer baap maati, chheler baap khunti*). Cf. Risley, Herbert. H., *The People of India*, William Crooke (ed.), second edition, Oriental Books Reprint. Corporation, Delhi, 1969, p. 168.

64. Talboys, Wheeler, Cf. Bahadur, K.P., *History, Caste and Culture of Rajputs*, Delhi, 1978, p. 158.
65. Tod, Colonel James, *Annals and Antiquities of Rajasthan*, Madras edition, Vol. I, p. 123. Cf. Sherring, M.A., op. cit., p. 25.
66. Tod, Col. James, *Annals and Antiquities of Rajasthan*, Cf. Allen, Charles and Dwivedi, Sharda, Ibid., p. 253.
67. "Society at that time didn't consist of individuals but of houses and it was important for houses to maintain alliances. This applied tenfold among royal houses, where a matrimonial alliance was the next best thing to a military alliance. As the need to make political alliances diminished, so other considerations assumed great importance – economic factors, the preferences of parents and rulers, and above all, the need to marry within princely circles."

    Cf. Allen, Charles and Dwivedi, Sharda, *Lives of the Indian Princes*, Business Publications Inc., Mumbai, 1998, p. 137.
68. Gahlot, Jagdish Singh, op. cit. 57.
69. Sherring, M.A., "Hindu Tribes and Castes", Cf. Singh, K.B.K., *Marriage and Family System of Rajputs*, Delhi, 1988, p. 88.

70. Asopa, J.N., "Origin of the Rajputs", in Ratnawat, S.S., and Sharma, K.G., (ed.) *History and Culture of Rajasthan (from Earliest times up to 1956 AD)*, Jaipur, 1999, pp. 40-51.
71. Those Rajput clans, which belonged to Surya vansha were – Kachwahas, Rathores, Guhilots, Huls, Pratihars, Parihars, Chauhans, Devras, Jethwas, and Nikumbh; those which belonged to Chandra Vansha were – Chalukya, Tanwar, Guhil, Gurjar, Kalchuri, Rashtrakuta, Parmar, Chavda, Yadav (Bhati), Yaudhav, Makwana, (Jhala), Shilahar, Chandel, Gaud, and Katoch; while those which belonged to other clans were – Tank (Nagvansha), Dahiya, Dahima, Aabhir, Saindhav, Rajpal, Kotpal, Haritat, Matt, Kavinis and Anang. Cf. 'Chetan', Chandra Singh, op. cit., p. 104.
72. Asopa, J.N., op. cit., pp. 40-51.
73. Allen, Charles and Dwivedi Sharda, op. cit., p. 137.
74. Pakrasi, K.B., op. cit., p. 37.
75. Allen, Charles and Dwivedi Sharda, op. cit., pp. 137-152.
76. When the marriage proposal of Likhmi, the daughter of Kali Karna Bhati, was sent to the Rao of Pokhran, the Rao refused to accept the proposal on the pretext of the uneven teeth of the girl. Similarly, Kotechi was abandoned by her in-laws, as she used to eat "too-much". Cf. Munhata Naincy Ri Khyat, Vol., 3, p. 194 and 104.
77. NAI: Ludlow to Sutherland, dated June 2, 1842, No. 250 of 1842, F. & P., Cons. No. 294-295, dt. 28 Dec. 1842.
78. Allen, Charles and Dwivedi, Sharda, op. cit., pp. 43-56.
79. Bingley, A.H., *Handbook on Rajputs*, Delhi, 1986, pp. 167-168.
80. Allen Charles and Dwivedi Sharda, op. cit., pp. 137-152.
81. Das, Shyamal, op. cit., p. 996, pp. 1704-1705 and p. 1746. And also, Tod, Colonel, op. cit., Vol. I, p. 521.
82. Powlett, Gazetteer of the Bikaner State, p. 84, Cf. Ojha G.H., *History of the Bikaner State*, Part-II, Ajmer, 1940, p. 431.
83. *Rajasthan State Gazetteer*, Vol. 4.
84. Sharma, Padmaja, *Maharaja Man Singh of Jodhpur and his times*, Agra, 1972, p. 255.
85. *Haqiqat Bahi*, Jodhpur (V.S. 1871-80), No. 10, p. 421.
86. *Tawarikh Man Singh*, p. 263.
87. Cf. Sharma, Padmaja, op. cit., p. 263.
88. RSAB: *Bikaner Byah Bahi*, V.S. 1818, Bahi No. 32, List No. 151.
89. Ojha, G.H., *Pratapgarh Rajya Ka Itihaas*, Rajasthani Granthagar, Jodhpur, 2000, p. 325.

90. Sharma, Pt. Hanuman, *Jaipur Rajya Ka Itihaas*, Shabda Mahima Prakashan, Jaipur, 1996, p. 276.
91. RSAB: From Col. Walter, A.G.G. in Rajputana, to the Secretary to the Government of India, Foreign Department, No. 277-C, dated 23 March, 1888., Basta No. 130, File No. 1493., Ajmer Commissioner's office, p. 3.
92. Ibid.
93. Ibid.
94. Ibid.
95. Sleeman, W.H., Cf. Bahadur, K.P., *History Caste and Culture of Rajput*, Delhi, 1978, p. 158.
96. NAI: Translation of a letter from Rao Ridmul to Ludlow, op. cit. And also, *Bankidas Ki Khyat*, Vol. II, p. 361 also Bata Sangraha, p. 283.
97. Das, Shyamal, *Vir Vinod, Mewar Ka Itihaas*, Vol. 2, p. 1323.

    According to Shyamal Das, *tyag* was not distributed or given by the father of the bride; rather it was given to the Charans and Bhats from the bridegroom's side. The same view was held by Mardum Shumari Raj Marwar (1890) Vol. I, p. 32 and was also told by Shri Shiv Charan Das, who himself belongs to a reputed Charan family of Mewar. The most important cause for female infanticide in the Rajputana, according to them was the dowry system. *The Census of India*, 1911, Vol. XXII also mentions that *tyag* was given by the groom's side to the Charans and Bhats. (p. 148).
98. Cf. Peggs, op. cit., pp. 177-178.
99. Bhats and Charans were bards and genealogists of the Rajputana whose occupation was to sing in praise of eminent families.
100. गढ़, हाथी, चारण, तुरी; गढ़पतियाँ कै होयं।

    Cf. Ratnawat, S.S. and Sharma, K.G. (ed.) *Charan Sahitya Parampara, (Essays on Bardic Literature)*, Centre for Rajasthan Studies, Jaipur, 2001, p. 2.
101. Qanungo, K.R., *Studies in Rajput History*, Delhi, 1960, p. 39.
102. "कंकण बंधण, रण चढ़व, पुत्र बधाई चाव; तीन दिवस ये त्याग रा, कुण रंक, कुण राव।"

    Cf. *Mardum Shumari Raj Marwar*, 1890, Vol. I, p. 32.
103. Ibid.
104. Those Rajputs who did not fulfil the demands of the Charans and Bhats, were severely criticized by them. Until and unless their claims were satisfied, they staged *dharnas*, went on hunger-strikes and even went to the extent of sacrificing their women and old men by burning or burying them alive or by wounding themselves. After wounding

themselves, they sprinkled blood upon the threshold of the person at whose house, the marriage was being solemnized. As they refused to accept food and water, no Rajput (not even those, who were from the groom's side) could eat or drink unless the Charans were first pacified. Such was their awe. 11,000 Charans assembled at Ahuwa in Samvat 1643, at the gates of Mota Raja Udai Singh to pressurize him to come to terms with them. Cf. *Mardum Shumari Raj Marwar*, 1890, Vol. I, p. 32.

105. Ibid.
106. NAI: J. Ludlow, Pol. Agent, Jodhpur to Col. J. Sutherland, A.G.G., op. cit.
107. Ibid.
108. NAI: Translation of a note from Rao Raja Ridmul, the Jodhpur Vakeel, op. cit.
109. Ibid.
110. Sharma, Gopi Nath, *Social Life in Medieval Rajasthan*, Agra, 1968, pp. 94-95.
111. Banerji, Anil Chandra, *Aspects of Rajput State and Society*, Rajesh Publications, New Delhi, 1983, p. 194.
112. The Tiwaria Charans were originally Shrimali Brahmans who were pressed to become Charans by Raja Kanad Deo of Jalore who assigned to them 28 villages. They fought bravely for Kanad Deo against Alauddin but were defeated and had 28 of their villages taken away from them by the emperor. Subsequently, when Raja Udai Singh tried to oppress the Charans of Jodhpur they took cause with their nominal brethren and were recognized by them and had the Mataji thread placed round their necks. Cf. *Census of India*, 1911, p. 150.
113. They claim a very remote ancestry and reference to them frequently occurs in the Mahabharata or other ancient books of Hindu mythology, where they are known under twelve different names. These names are: *(i) Brahma Rao (ii) Soot (iii) Magad (iv) Bandi (v) Saraswati Putra (vi) Stuti-Pathak (vii) Badi (viii) Nandi-Kar (ix) Rai (x) Bhat (xi) Nandi (xii) Kani*, Cf. Gahlot S.S., and Dhar, Banshi, op. cit., p. 136.
114. Mardum Shumari, Raj Marwar (1890).
115. Gahlot, S.S. and Dhar, Banshi, *Castes and Tribes of Rajasthan*, Jodhpur, 1989, p. 130.
116. Ibid.

117. Valmiki Ramayana, Cf. Gadan, Badri Dan, *'Charnon Ki Utpatti'* in Ratnawat, S.S., and Sharma, K.G., op. cit., pp. 59-64.

And also

"देवसर्गष्चाष्ट विधो बिबुधाः पितरोऽसुराः।
गन्धर्वाप्सरसः सिद्धा यक्ष रक्षांसि चारणाः।।27
भूत–प्रेत पिशाचाष्च विद्याघ्राः किन्नरादयः।
दशैते विदुराख्याताः सर्गास्ते विश्वसृक्कृताः।।"28

Sri Mad Bhagvat Purana, Skandha 3, Chapter 10, Verse 27-28. Cf. *Mardum Shumari Raj Marwar* (1890), p. 330.

118. "चारयन्ति कीर्तिम इति चारणाः।"

Cf. *Mardum Shumari Raj Marwar*, 1890, p. 329.

119. "अथ गत्वा तृतीयं तु वायोः पन्थानमुत्तमम्।
नित्यं यत्र स्थिता सिद्धाश्चारणाश्च मनस्विनः।।
दशैवतु सहस्त्राणि योजनानां तथैवच।।"

(i.e., Then after Ravana went to that place, which is 10,000 *yojana* or 40,000 *kos* away from the land, and which is inhabited by the sages, Siddhas and Charans. Except Himalayas, there is no other place, which is so much above the land). Cf. *Valmiki Ramayana*, Uttar-Kand, Sarga 5, Verse No. 4.

And also

"एवमुक्तवा महातेजो गौतमौ दुष्टाचारिणीम्।
इममा श्रममुत्सृज्य सिद्ध चारण सेविते।।
हिमवच्छिखरे रम्ये तपस्तपे महातपाः।।"

(i.e., After saying this, Gautam the sage, left his ill-natured wife and also his ashram, and went on Himalaya, which was being inhabited by Siddhas and Charans, for meditation). Valmiki Ramayana, Bal Kanda, Sarga 48, Verse No. 33. Cf. Mardum Shumari, Raj Marwar, 1890, p. 330.

120. Gahlot, S.S. and Dhar, Banshi, op. cit., pp. 130-131

121. "हुंकारेण महादेवस्तम्भितोऽथ त्रिलोचनः।
देवैस्तदा समागम्य सर्षिसिद्धः स चारणैः।।"

(i.e., when Lord Vishnu stunned the three eyed god Mahadev, by his great roar, then at that time, sages and Charans came there and by their words and praises requested God Vishnu to calm down).

Valmiki Ramayana, Sundar Kanda, Sarga 55, Verse No. 29 Cf. *Mardum Shumari Raj Marwar*, 1890, p. 330.

122. "तद अदभुत राघवकर्म दुष्करं समीक्ष्य, देवा सह सिद्ध चारणैः।
उपेत्य रामं सहसा महर्षिभिः स्तम्भयषिञ्चन्सुषुभैर्जलः पृथक।।"

Mahabharata, Adi Parva, Chapter 126, Verse No. 111, Cf. *Mardum Shumari Raj Marwar*, 1890, p. 330.

123. Sharma, H.S., *Social Milieu of the Creators of Bardic Literature*, in Ratnawat, S.S., and Sharma K.G., op. cit., p. 476.

124. Lt. Col. Sutherland held that Charans were wandering mendicants, who assumed a religious character to serve their own purpose. According to Sutherland, "they were perfectly illiterate and were not properly entitled to any sacred character; yet they had gained an extra-ordinary influence over the superstitious Rajputs."

    RSAB: Ajmer Commissioner's Office, Basta No. 130, File No. 1493 (210), 1848 AD. "Exactions of Charans from Rajputs and other inhabitants". From Lt. Col. Sutherland, A.G.G. to H.M. Elliot, Esq. Secy. to G.O.I., with Gov. Gen. dated January 11, 1848.

125. Malcolm, John, *Memoirs of Central India*, Vol. I, pp. 517-18.

126. As told by Shri Shiv Charan Das.

127. Qanungo, K.R., op. cit., p. 39.

128. "मात पिता सह बीसरे , बंघु बीसा रेह ।
    सूरा पूरा बातडी , चारण चीता रेह ।।"

    And also, *Mardum Shumari Raj Marwar*, 1890, p. 342.

129. Heber, Bishop, op. cit., pp. 104-105.

130. Cf. *Census of India*, 1911, p. 148.

131. *Mardum Shumari Raj Marwar*, 1890, p. 342.

132. Tod, Col. James, op. cit.

133. "चारण छत्री भाइयां, जां घर खाग तियाग।
    खाग तियागां बाहिरा, जां रै लाग न बाग।।"

    Gadan, Badridan, *Charnon Ki Utpatti*, in Ratnawat, S.S. and Sharma, K.G., (ed.) op. cit., p. 64.

134. Cf. *Census of India*, 1911, p. 148.

135. "पत जैपर जोधाण पत, दोनूंह थाप उथाप
    कूरम मारयो डीकरो, कमधज मारयो बाप।"

    And also,

    "बो ही दिन, बो ही बखत, बा री बा तलवार
    बाप मारियो जां भुज़ां, भैंसा रो कांई भार।"

    And also

    "चापो मत कह बखत सी, कांपे छै केकाण
    अेकर फिर बापो कह्यो, तो पमंग तजैलो प्राण।"

    Gadan, Badridan, *Charnon Ki Utpatti*, in Ratnawat, S.S. and Sharma, K.G., (ed.), op. cit., p. 65.

136. Sharma, G.N., op. cit., pp. 94-95.
137. Sharma, G.N., Structure of Society and Social Life in Rajasthan (1200-1900 A.D.) in Raṭnawat, S.S. and Sharma, K.G., *History and Culture of Rajasthan from Earliest Times up to 1956 A.D.*, Jaipur, 1999, p. 291.
138. Ibid.
139. Sharma, H.S., *Social Milieu of the Creators of Bardic Literature* in Ratnawat S.S. and Sharma K.G. (ed.), op. cit., p. 478.
140. Gahlot, S.S. and Dhar, Banshi, op. cit., p. 132.
141. Ibid., "सांडू ने सीसोदिया, रोहड ने राठौड।
दुरसावत ने देवडा, जादव रतन जोड।।"
142. *Mardum Shumari Raj Marwar* (1890).
143. Ibid.
144. NAI: Trans. of a note from Rao Raja Rial Mul, op. cit.
145. Cf. Sharma, H.S. *Social Milieu of the Creators of Bardic Literature* in Ratnawat, S.S. and Sharma, K.G. (ed.), op. cit., p. 423.
146. Ibid.
147. Cf. Gehlot, S.S. and Dhar, Banshi, op. cit., p. 135.
148. Ibid.
149. Ibid.
150. Russell, R.V., *Tribes and Castes of the Central Provinces of India*, Vol. II, London, 1916, p. 252.
151. Forbes, *Rasmala*, Vol. II, pp. 261-62.
152. Malcolm, John, *Memoirs of Central India*, Vol. II, p. 132. Malcolm has described the functions and status of the Charans in his *Memoirs of Central India*, Vol. I, pp. 517-518.
153. Heber, Bishop, op. cit., pp. 104-105.
154. Cf. Malcolm, John, *Memoirs of Central India*, Vol. II, p. 136.
155. Ibid.
156. *Census of India*, 1911, Vol. XXII, Rajputana and Ajmer Merwara, Part – II, Tables, Calcutta, 1912.
157. John Wilson, *Suppression of Infanticide in Western India*, Cf. Fuller, Marcus, B., op. cit., p. 148.
158. For a detailed account of infanticide in the ancient world, please refer to Peggs, J., op. cit., pp. 113-130; *The New Encyclopedia Brittanica*, Vol. 6, 22 and 25, (15th edition); and also Fuller, Marcus, B., op. cit., pp. 148-158.
159. Peggs, J., op. cit., pp. 113-130.

160. Pakrasi, K.B., op. cit., p. 16 And also, *The New Encyclopedia Britannica*, Vol. 22, p. 8.
161. *The New Encyclopedia Britannica*, Vol. 6, p. 307.
162. A detailed account of the causes of female infanticide in Rajputana, is given in Chapter II (a).
163. *Calcutta Review*, Vol. I, 1844, p. 386, Cf. Panigrahi, Lalita, op. cit.
164. As told by Rani Laxmi Kumari Chundawat.
165. Allen, Charles and Dwivedi, Sharda, op. cit., p. 19.
166. Saxena, R.K., op. cit., p. 13.
167. Heber, Bishop, *Narrative of a Journey Through the Upper Province of India*, Vol. II, p. 88 Cf. Peggs, op. cit., p. 207.
168. Brown, J.C., *Indian Infanticide*, pp. 3-6.
169. *Friend of India*, August 1818, No. IV, p. 103, Cf. Saxena, R.K, op. cit., p. 13.
170. Minute by Montgomery, 16 June, 1853, *Selections from Public Correspondence Punjab*, 1853, Vol. I, Nos. I-IV Cf. Panigrahi, Lalita, op. cit., p. 28.
171. As told by Rani Laxmi Kumari Chundawat.
172. Allen, Charles and Dwivedi, Sharda, op. cit., p. 21.
And also, Sankaria, Badri Prasad, *Munhata Naincy Ri Khyat*, Vol. III, Rajasthan Prachya Vidya Pratishthan, Jodhpur, p. 103. Cf. Ranawat, Manohar Singh, *Itihaskar Muhnot Naincy aur uske Itihaas-Grantha*, Rajasthani Granthagar, Jodhpur, 1985, p. 218.
173. As told by Rani Laxmi Kumari Chundawat.
174. Ibid.
175. Ibid.
176. Peggs, op. cit., p. 140.
177. Saxena, R.K., op. cit., p. 13.
178. As told by Rani Laxmi Kumari Chundawat.
179. Ibid.
180. Ojha, G.H., *Dungarpur Rajya Ka Itihaas*, Rajasthani Granthagar, Jodhpur, 2000, p. 171.
181. Sankaria, Badri Prasad, op. cit., p. 103, Cf. Ranawat, Manohar Singh op. cit., p. 218.
182. Ojha, G.H., op. cit., p. 171.
183. As told by Rani Laxmi Kumari Chundawat.
184. Cf. *Hindustan Times* (Jaipur edition), 27 April, 2001, p. 1.
185. *Rajasthan Patrika*, 15th of May, 2000, p. 8.

186. *Hindustan Times* (Jaipur edition), 27 April, 2001, p. 1.
187. *Hindustan Times*, 8th of March, 2002.
188. *Dainik Bhaskar*, 18th of November, 2002, p. 1.
189. Briggs, Translation, Vol. I, p. 183. Quoted by Crooke, W., *The Tribes and Castes of the North-Western Provinces and Oudh*, Vol. I, Cf. Panigrahi, Lalita, op. cit., p. 4.
190. Parliamentary papers, 1824, p. 128, Cf. Peggs, J., op. cit., p. 169-170.
191. Cf. Cunningham, J.D., *History of the Sikhs*, First published in 1849, Rupa and Company, N. Delhi, 2002, p. 385.
192. Cf. Grover, B. L., Grover, S., *A New Look at Modern Indian* History, S. Chand and Company Ltd. New Delhi, 1992, pp. 379-80.
193. Cf. Risley, H.H., *The People of India*, op. cit., p. 174.
194. Cf. Marcus Fuller, op. cit.
195. For a detailed study of the detection of the crime of female infanticide in various parts of India, including Rajputana, in 18th and 19th century, please refer to Peggs, J., op. cit.
196. NAI: Trans. of a note addressed by the Jaipur council of regency to the Pol. Ag. Dated 27th of October 1847, Enclosure No. 227 of 1847, From Major Ludlow to Sutherland, dt. 30 October, 1847, F. & P. Cons. No. 78, date 20 Nov. 1847.
197. Ibid.
198. NAI: Trans. of a letter from Rao Raja Rid Mal, the Vakeel of Jodhpur, to Captain Ludlow, dated 4th of November, 1841. F. &P. Cons. No. 40, dated 22 June, 1842.
199. Ojha, G.H., *The History of the Bikaner State*, Part II, Ajmer, 1940. And also, *Dayal Das Ki Khyat*, Vol. II, pp. 126-132. And, Powlett, *Gazetteer of the Bikaner State*, p. 83.
200. Reu, B.N., Cf. *Har Bilas Sarda Commemoration Volume*, Vedic Yantralaya, Ajmer, 1937, pp. 522-23.
201. NAI: F. & P., Cons. No. 151-160, dt. 30 Nov., 1844.
202. NAI: Governor-General to Raj Rana Madho Singh, Jan. 23, 1834, F. & P., Jan. 23, 1834, Cons. No. 22.
203. NAI: Trans. of a *Kharita* from Raj-Rana Madan Singh to Bentinck, F. & P., dt. April 9, 1834, Cons. No. 21 dt. May 1, 1834.
204. NAI: F. & P., dt. Dec. 30, 1844, Cons. No. 151-160.
205. NAI: From Sutherland to G. Hamilton Esquire, Offg. Secy. to Govt., date 29 December, 1841. F. & P., Cons. No. 40, date 22 June, 1842.
206. NAI: From Ludlow, Political Agent at Jodhpur to Colonel Sutherland, A.G.G., dated 29 June, 1842. F.&P., Cons. No. 294-295, dt. 28 December, 1842, No. 250 of 1842.

207. Ibid.
208. NAI: From Ludlow to Thoresby, date 12 April, 1844, F. & P., Cons. No. 152, dated 30 November 1844, Enclosure No. 1 in No. 230 of 1844.
209. NAI: From Ludlow to Sutherland, date 29 June, 1842, No. 250 of 1842, F. & P., Cons. No. 294-295, date 28 December, 1842.
210. NAI: Substance translation of a memo. Furnished by the council of regency of Jaipur, to the Political Agent on 12 April, 1844. Enclosure No. 2 in number 230 of 1844, F. & P., Cons. No. 153, date 30 November, 1844.
211. NAI: Memo. regarding female infanticide in Marwar, dated 5 May, 1842, Enclosure No. 10 in No. 477 of 1842, F. & P., Cons. No. 40 dated 22 June, 1842.
212. Ibid.
213. NAI: F.& P., 7 Nov. 1844, Cons. No. 141, dt. 30 Nov. 1844, No. 160.
214. NAI: Lt. Col. J. Robinson to Major C. Thoresby, dated 4 January, 1844, Enclosure No. 1 in No. 36 of 1844, F. & P., Cons. No. 40.
215. NAI: Lt. Col. Sutherland to F.Currie, dated 6 June, 1845, F. & P., Cons. No. 70, date 12 September, 1845.
216. Das, Shyamal, op. cit., p. 1323.
217. Ojha, G.H., *History of the Bikaner State*, Part III, Ajmer 1940, p. 431. And also, Ojha, G.H., *Dungarpur Rajya Ka Itihaas*, Rajasthani Granthagar, Jodhpur, 2000, p. 171.
218. Reu, B.N., Cf. *Har Bilas Sarda Commemoration Volume*, Vedic Yantralaya, Ajmer, 1937, pp. 522-23.
219. Badriprasad Sankaria, Vol. III, p. 103 Cf. Ranawat, Manohar Singh, op. cit., p. 218.
220. NAI: Trans. of a note in reply from Rao Raja Rial Mul, the Jodhpur Vakeel, op. cit.
221. The original name of Nahar Singh or Nahar Khan was Mukund Das, who was the leader of Kumpawat clan of Rathores. He was one of the nobles of Jaswant Singh, the ruler of Marwar (who died in 1681). Aurangzeb conferred the title of Nahar Khan on Mukund Das, as he fought with a tiger without any arms, and killed it, after a challenge was given to him by Aurangzeb to do so. Cf. Mishra, Pt. Baldev Prasad, *Rajasthan Ka Itihaas*, Vol. II, Shri Venketeshawara Steam Press, Bombay, Samvat 1982 (1925 A.D.), p. 98.
222. NAI: Trans. of a note from Raja Rid Mal to Ludlow, op. cit.
223. Bingley, A.H., *History, Caste and Culture of Jats and Gujars*, New Delhi, 1978, p. 101.

224. NAI: From Major Thoresby to F. Currie, dated 7th of Nov. 1844, No. 1414 of 1844, F. & P., Cons. No. 151.
225. Ibid.
226. NAI: From Burton to Sutherland, dated 12 August 1846, F.& P., Cons. No. 255, dated 17 October, 1846.
227. NAI: L. Wilkinson, Offg. Pol. Ag., Harauti to A. Lockett, dated 26 April, 1833, F. & P., Cons. No. 17, date 23 January 1834.
228. Ibid.
229. *Sketch of Merwara* (1818-1834) by Lt. Col. Hall, Superintendent of Merwara, dt. 16 December, 1834, F. & P., Cons. No. 44, dt. 4 May 1835.
230. Peggs, J. op. cit., p. 177
231. Cf. Saxena, R.K., *Social Reforms: Infanticide and Sati,* Trimurti Publications Pvt. Ltd., New Delhi, 1975, p. 10.
232. Ibid.
233. NAI: From L. Wilkinson, Pol. Ag., Kota, to Lt. Col. Lockett., A.G.G., F.&P., Cons. No. 17, date 23 January, 1837.
234. Saxena, R.K., op. cit.
235. NAI: From L. Wilkinson, to Lt. Col. Spears, Offg. A.G.G., date 3 April, 1834, F. & P., Cons. No. 67-A.
236. Brown, J.C., op. cit., p. 59.
237. NAI: L. Wilkinson, Agent, Sehore (M.P.), to J. Bax, Resident Indore, 9 July, 1836, F. & P. Cons. No. 50, dt. 1 August 1836.
238. NAI: J. Bax to W.H. Macnaghten, Secy. to Govt. of India, 14 July, 1836, F. & P., Cons. No. 50, dt 1 Aug, 1836.
239. Cf. Bingley, A.H., op. cit., pp. 167-168.

3

Child Marriages in Rajasthan

A little girl below five years of age, dressed in colourful bridal costume and a boy, almost around the same age, in equally colourful clothes, with a sword hanging by the side on his waist, being tied into wedlock, surrounded by a horde of merry making relatives, is a common sight in some parts of the country and especially so in Rajasthan on the occasion of *Akha-Teej (Akshaya Tritiya).*

Akha Teej, or the third day of the bright fortnight of *Baishakh,* (the month of the Hindu calendar), generally falling in May every year, is a time of rejoicing in Rajasthan. This day is considered as the most auspicious day for marriages, as marriages on this day can be performed without consulting a *pundit* or astrologer (*aboojh sawa*).[1] On this day practically everywhere in Western Rajasthan, Bikaner, Tonk, Jhalawar, Jodhpur and Jaisalmer marriages including infant and child marriages are performed in large numbers, openly as well as clandestinely, even in the 21st century. According to a report published in *Dainik Bhaskar,* on 15 May, 2005, (p. 6), several child marriages were performed in Jaipur (in the villages and *dhanis* of Chaksu, Faagi, Garjeda, Didawata, Chakwara, Madhorajpura, Neemeda, Maujamabad, Sawarda, etc.); in Tonk (at Jagatpura, Niwai, Uniara, Natwara, Parana, Siras, Nala, Chironj, Duni, Todaraisingh, Peepal, etc.); in Jalore (at Kuobar village of Ummedawas, Sayala tehsil, the border areas of Jalore-Barmer) and in Alwar (Thanagazi, Rajgarh, Raini, Kotwali, etc.) According to the

Hindu of 10 May 1997, thousands of children were married in Rajasthan despite the efforts of the State administration and appeal by the-then Chief Minister of the State to refrain from child marriage. Similarly, according to the *Rajasthan Patrika* (of 10 May, 1997), hundreds of marriages took place and child brides and grooms dressed in marriage costumes touched the marriage arch (*Toran*) lifted by uncles. According to the latest report of UNFPA (The United Nations Population Fund),[2] released on 12 October 2005, 50 per cent of the girls in India are married before the age of 18. The Census report of 2001,[3] also reveals that there were 1 crore and 17 lacs boys and girls in India, who were below the age of 21 and 18, at the time of their marriage and whose marriage was not according to the minimum marriageable age as was laid down by the law, and also that there are nearly 3 lac girls, below 15 years of age, who have already given birth to at least one child. Ironically, child marriages are rampant in a State where the child marriages restraint Act, popularly known as the Sarda Act, was first conceived. Shri Har Bilas Sarda, who had given concrete shape to Sarda Act, was a native of Ajmer in Rajasthan. To understand the origin of child marriages in India (as well as in Rajasthan), it is necessary to trace the various social developments and changes, that took place in the society in the past years, and as such an attempt has been made in Chapter 1 to trace the historical situation of the status and position of women and the deterioration in her status which led to the practice of child marriages in Indian society.

The introduction of child marriages in India, as has been discussed in Chapter 1, was a result of the gradual deterioration of the position and status of women, from one of veneration and independence to sheer dependence on males, was a process that started right from the post-Vedic period.

Writers like M.N. Srinivas,[4] S. Das,[5] Prabhati Mukherjee,[6] Rama Joshi,[7] Joanne Liddle, Neera Desai,[8] Maithreyi Krishnaraj,[9] Veena Das,[10] have highlighted the role of caste system and the imposition of Brahminical austerities in the post-Vedic period, which according to them, had serious implications, with regard to the position of women. Rise of Brahmanism not only entailed caste rigidity but also emphasized the superiority of males at the expense of females. These factors restricted the social space of women and forced the people to opt for the practice of child marriage. Any caste, which wished to raise itself up the social ladder, found it necessary to conform to the marriage of girls before they reached the age of puberty and prohibition of their remarriage, even if widowed in infancy. Thus, according to them, any rise in caste hierarchy entailed numerous hardships for women.

Renowned sociologist, M.N. Srinivas has described this change of lifestyle of any upwardly mobile caste as "sanskritization". According to him, this process resulted in harshness towards women in the form of prohibition to remarry, arrangement of pre-puberty marriages and several other constraints.

Similarly, S. Das[11] has opined that during the Vedic period, when the laws which minutely regulated the rights and duties of the numerous sub-castes, as well as their interrelations with other castes, were being formulated, the Brahmins realized that there still remained one group which retained "uncertain and incalculable elements." Their greatest rival in influence and spiritual power were women and they felt, that there could be no uncontested and secure supremacy for Brahmins until women lost their revered position. Thus, according to S. Das, attempts were made to degrade them, to brand them as inferior beings, and to mould them into mindless slaves through the clever use of religious dictums.

Joanne Liddle and Rama Joshi[12] have also supported this view. According to them, the Smriti writers considered women as probable competitors and therefore to wipe out the probable competition that they might face in future, they grouped women with Shudras, considered them as private property of men and advocated "strict caste and sex orthodoxy".

Veena Das[13] has put forward another view and she believes that women were literally regarded as 'points of entrance,' as gateways to the caste system. If men of ritually low status were to get sexual access to women of higher status, then not only the purity of the women, but that of the entire group would be endangered. Since the main threat to the purity of the group, came from female sexuality, therefore it became vital to guard it and most groups solved this problem by the custom of pre-puberty marriage. Thus, according to Veena Das, marriage at an early date, marriage within the caste and even in the sub-caste, prohibition of *pratilom* marriage (where a woman of higher caste, marries a man of lower caste), marriage as a sacrament whereby a woman is tied in wedlock till she dies, were all practices which suggest the control of female sexuality. Likewise, Freidrich Engles, in his seminal work, *Origin of the Family, Private*

Property and the State, writes that "the overthrow of Mother Right was the world's historic defeat of the female sex". It was replaced by Father Right through the establishment of patriarchal families which made man the lord of the house and an absolute owner of all the movable and immovable property. It also made man as husband, the owner and proprietor of his wife. In the process, the woman was reduced from an independent human person to a mere reproductive being whose sole purpose in life was to produce legitimate heirs (obviously sons) for him. This created a structure of unilateral and stringent standards of monogamous marriages for women accompanied by the concepts of virginity of the girl and of chastity and fidelity of the wife.

Regarding the origin of infant or child marriages, Nesfield[14] has given a different opinion. He believes that the practice of infant marriages arose from the desire to protect a girl from the stain of communism within her own clan so long as she remained there and from the risk of forcible abduction into an alien clan where she became the wife slave of the man who captured her. Risley,[15] however, while conceding that this theory might account for the institution of infant marriage under certain social conditions, is of the opinion that the origin of infant marriage is to be traced to the custom of hypergamy and in illustration of the working of this custom, gives the following diagram and explanation which are reproduced *in extenso* from his *Castes and Tribes of Bengal*:

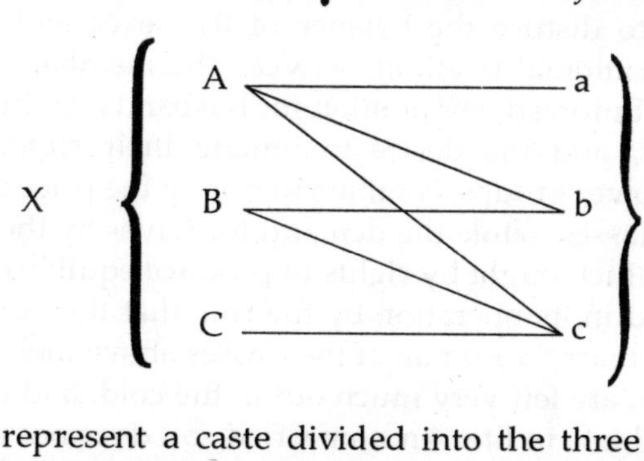

Let X represent a caste divided into the three hypergamous groups A, B and C. Within each group, the capital letters stand for the marriageable men and small letters for the marriageable women of the group. The horizontal and diagonal lines connecting the capitals with the small letters show what classes of men and women can intermarry. It will be seen that a man of the A group can marry a woman of his own group or of the two lower groups, a man of B group can marry into B or C, while a man of C is confined to his own class, and cannot marry a woman from either of the classes above him. Conversely, a woman of the C class can get a husband from A, B or C, and a woman of the B class from A or B; but a woman of the A class cannot find a husband outside her own group. Excluding polygamy or polyandry, and supposing the women to be evenly distributed among the groups they are entitled to marry into, the result of the first series of marriages would be to leave two-thirds of the women in the A-group without husbands, and two-thirds of the men in the C-group without wives. The women of all the groups, and especially those of A, will compete for husbands, and the men of C-group for wives. But the fact that the social status of a family determined not so much by the class from which it takes it wives, as by the class from which it gets its husbands, would put the men of the lowest class and the women of the highest at a great comparative disadvantage and would thus tend to produce infant marriages. For the number of possible husbands being limited, the natural tendency is to endeavour to secure them as soon as possible. Again, when the custom of infant marriage had once been started, under pressure of social necessity, by the families of the highest group, who had the largest surplus of marriageable daughters, a sort of fashion would have been set and would be blindly followed through all the grades. Two forces are thus at work in the same direction, both tending to disturb the balance of the sexes and to produce abnormal matrimonial relations between the members of different social groups. Enforced competition for husbands on the part of the higher groups, and the desire to imitate their superiors which animates the lower groups, combine to run up the price of husbands in the upper classes, while the demand for wives by the men of the lowest class, which ought by rights to produce equilibrium is artificially restricted in its operation by the rule that they can under no circumstances marry a woman of the classes above their own. These men, therefore, are left very much out in the cold, and often do not get wives until late in life. An unmarried son does not disgrace the family, but there is no greater reproach than to have a daughter unmarried at the age of puberty. Husbands are bought for the girls, and the family gets it money's worth in social estimation. Bargains, however, must be taken when they are to be had, and no father dare run the risk of waiting till his daughter is physically mature. He is bound to be on the safe side, and therefore he marries his child as she may be, whenever a good match offers."

N.K. Singhi[16] another renowned sociologist, believed that the emergence of certain social practices, customs, rites, rituals, conventions are the resultant phenomena determined by situational contextuality. According to him, the emergence of "child-marital ceremony" was the situational response to eliminate rising expenses in marriage, fulfilment of responsibilities, amidst increasing uncertainties of life due to constant battles and external invasions. Child marital ceremony, according to him, was an arrangement of group marriage leading to one-time expenses, elimination of futuristic worries, and elimination of dowry. It helped in building community ethos, and provided collective security.

Prejudices were also responsible for the origin of child marriages. Conventions and customs that accompanied the caste system made it obligatory for the parents to settle the matches for their children at the earliest, within the same caste and of equal or superior status. To the Hindus, the rules of caste rendered marriage beyond the sub-caste, almost a social sin. Along with this, factors of family connection, pedigree, religion and customs were also taken into consideration. Care was taken to marry into the families of the same status. This led to paucity of matches, making the field of selection narrower and thereby, encouraging a keener competition, resulting in child marriages. The anxiety to get the best matches left the parents no option but to marry off their daughters at an early age.

The severe standard of morality set by society for women was another contributory factor for making the system of child marriages popular among the Hindus. It was beneficial for the parents who thought it advisable to hand over their daughter to her husband, before she blossomed into her youth. Any chance of pre-marital love or sexual life, apart from her conjugal life, was thus minimized by the early marriages. Virginity and modesty of the girl were deemed to be her inalienable virtues and therefore the parents took additional care to check them.

Early marriages were further preferred by the parents, for dowry demanded at an advanced age was much more. An added impetus was given to the practice of child marriages, when it acted as an indicator of one's prestige. Moreover, the eagerness to have a son at the earliest possible moment to ensure proper performance of family ceremonies, and the belief that the son alone had the right and power to perform funeral sacrifices – strengthened the practice of child marriages.

Under the operation of these forces, child marriages became the order of the day and the practice became so widespread and compelling that nonconformity to it, came to be regarded as a matter of social disgrace.

Religious Scriptures

In the Vedic period, as discussed in Chapter 1, the practice of child marriage was not prevalent in India. A perusal of the marriage hymn, which reflects a great deal on the status and age of the bride, shows her to be fully grown and mature at the time of her marriage. Similarly, at other place in the Rig Veda, mention is made of "beautiful damsels who selected their own life partners". The tradition of imparting education to the girls and the freedom enjoyed by them in the selection of their husbands, coupled with the respect and love they enjoyed, created an atmosphere of enlightenment in the society and as such child marriages did not show their ugly face at that time. There are many hymns in the Rig Veda which clearly show that marriages were held, when both the parties were quite grown up. "With her body slim and soft, like the lines of sixteen sweet; with her youthful, budding breasts aloft, the lady like dawn, a youthful feast. With her glances glamorous, rolling her tender lips, rosy smiling. She approached her husband, pining to meet her, with fervent love, madness for her. Adept in love and household wisdom, a queen, so stately in her kingdom. With all hilarious, her youthful wine, married life she makes paradise so fine (sic)." (*R.V.*I.123.10.)[17]

R.C. Majumdar[18] observes that "the frequent mention of unmarried girls like Ghosha, who grew up in the houses of their parents (1.117.7; X.39.3; 40.5), the references to the ornaments worn by the maidens at festival occasions in order to win lovers (1.123.11; V11.2.5), to a youth's courtship of the maiden he loves (1.115.2), to the lover's gifts' (1.117.18), to their mutual love (1.167.3; 1X.32.5, etc.) and to the spell (V11.55.5.8) by which a lover hopes to lull the whole household to sleep while he visits his beloved – all this evidence speaks in favour of the custom of girls normally marrying long after they had reached puberty(sic)." The very use of different words for marriage like *udvaah* (i.e., carrying away) *parinay, upayam, pani-grahan*, etc., in Sanskrit language suggests of post-puberty marriage. In the Rig Veda, a hope is expressed that the bride would immediately take over the command, not only of the entire household, but also of the relatives. This naturally implies that the bride must be mature enough to handle all the affairs of the family, otherwise such thing would not have been said there. Likewise, there are several *mantras* in the Atharva Veda through the use of which women's hearts could be captured; also there are mantras, the recitation of which ensured a sooner marriage and there are mantras, to increase the reproductive power of both males and females, as well as to keep away the 'other' man or woman from mutual love or married life. These references again contradict the possibility of child marriages in the Vedic society.

In the Vedic age, as already discussed, women used to be well educated, well cultivated and were refined in their manners and etiquettes. Some of the hymns of the Rig Veda bear testimony to the above mentioned fact. According to the orthodox tradition recorded in Sarva-anukramnika, there are as many as twenty women among the authors of the Rig Veda;[19] this fact demonstrates a healthy tradition of imparting training to daughters, equivalent to that of sons. The initiation ceremony of girls used to take place as regularly as that of boys.[20] The Vedas unequivocally underline the indispensability and significance of education for maidens and also about marrying them at an appropriate age. Some of the verses, which present this aspect of the Vedas, are given below:

"An unmarried young learned daughter should be married to a bridegroom who, like her, is learned. Never think of giving in marriage, a daughter of very young age."[21] "A young daughter who has observed Brahmacharya, i.e., finished her studies should be married to a bridegroom who, like her, is learned."[22]

Similarly, the Atharva Veda advocates female education as well as the grown-up marriages.

"A king by observing Brahmacharya can protect his kingdom easily. An Acharya can impart education to his students, if he has himself observed his Brahmacharya. A young daughter, after the observance of Brahmacharya should be married to a young man".[23] In the famous marriage hymn of the Rig Veda, it is told that the bride was fully mature and quite grown-up at the time of marriage; there she is described as blooming with youth and craving for a husband.[24] In the same chapter, a hope is expressed that the bride would take over the reigns of the household from her parents-in-law.[25] This taking over the reigns of the household would have only become possible if the brides were mature enough to handle the responsibilities of the household.

Some scholars, in order to prove the existence of child marriage in Vedic society, have misunderstood the word *arbha* mentioned in the Rig Veda (1, 51, 13, 1) to be the indicator of minors, who were married or going to be married. But the word, according to A.S. Altekar, has been used to denote the bride and the bridegroom and the meaning of *arbha* there is tenderness rather then childhood.[26] In the same book, a hero Vimada, is described as arbha bridegroom, who has defeated his rivals and has won the hand of the bride. Thus if Vimada were a minor, then it would not have been possible for him to defeat his rivals and thereby laying his claim before the bride. Similarly, at another place in the Rig Veda,[27] mention is made of a wife, who is praying for the growth of hairs on her body. But in the same chapter it has been mentioned that the cause for this prayer was not her childhood, but a skin disease from which she was suffering. Similarly the word *amajuh*, which occurs very frequently in the Vedic literature, is also misunderstood. A.S. Altekar opines that the world amajuh, denotes an old maid of the house.[28] The usual cause that forced the maidens to remain unmarried was some serious physical defect or disease. The literature of ancient Persia[29] reveals that maidens were wedded there at the age of 15 or 16 and since the ancient Persians were related with their Aryan cousins of India, the same can be said about the age of marriage in the Vedic period.

This normative ideal of a Hindu woman, however, did not last long and from 1000 B.C. onwards, tendencies, which accelerated women's subordination, began to make their appearance. The subjugation of the non-Aryans led to the introduction of slavery, which in turn diminished the importance of women as productive members of the society. This period also witnessed the erosion of women's educational privileges, since Vedic studies was now a long and complicated process, covering a period of 12 years.[30] The introduction of non-Aryan wife into the Aryan household, the evolution of the theory of transmigration and the consequent assumption of immense religious significance by the son, considerably lowered the status of women.[31]

In the age of Sutras (i.e., the period from 500 B.C. to 100 A.D.)[32] new negations and new restrictions were further imposed on women. In the Baudhayan Dharma Sutra, it is said that, "Let him give his daughter, while she goes still naked, to a man who has not broken the vow of chastity and who possesses good qualities, or even to one destitute of good qualities; let him not keep the maiden in his house after she has reached the age of puberty. "In the same book an exhaustive list of do's and don't's has been given, which was expected to be followed by the society of the times, vis-à-vis their relationship with women.[33] The writers of other Dharma Sutras went a step further and insisted upon pre-puberty marriages and held widow remarriage in disrepute.[34] The insistence and introduction of pre-puberty marriages, soon found new supporters and slowly and gradually became the order of the day. But opinions of the scholars were divided on this issue. While Vasihstha[35] and Baudhayan[36] recommended that girls may be kept unmarried for a period of three years after their puberty, if there was some difficulty in getting proper husbands for them. But on the other hand, Gautama[37] and Vishnu recommended that marriages must be celebrated within 3 months of puberty at the most, otherwise it is better to celebrate them before the time of puberty. The Baudhayan Dharma Sutra even went to the extent of declaring that the corpse of a maiden can be burnt only after a formal marriage even after death.[38] Some thinkers pointed out that life was transitory, and if marriage was intended to ensure the continuance of the family, the bride should not be too young, when it is performed. Others contended that absolute chastity was to be most desired, and so we should select a bride, who should not have even dreamt of sexual love. In Griha Sutras,[39] it has been laid down that the bride should be a *nagnika* at the time of her marriage. The later commentators have interpreted this word, to suit their own interests. They believed that the term nagnika denotes a girl of five or six years, who has no sense of decency and who moves about, without properly covering her body. But this was not the original or real meaning of the world, for the Mahabharata describes a bride of 16 as nagnika, and the Gobhil Griha Sutra itself mentions that the nagnika bride should also be a virgin at the time of her marriage.[40] But Matridatta[41] clarified this term in the later period as he said that the term nagnika refers to a woman who is fit to welcome her husband in privacy, after her marriage.

During the period 400 B.C. to 100 A.D., the marriageable age was lowered by the scholars and it was felt that girls should be married about the time of their puberty. The period from 200 A.D. to 1000 A.D. was again a period of deterioration for the position and status of women, as the Smriti writers, who flourished at this period, imposed many new restrictions upon the body, soul and the very existence of the women of the day. Manu, for example, believed and insisted that women should never be allowed a free and independent status. In her childhood, she should remain under the control of her father, in her youth, she should remain under the control of her husband and in her old age, she should remain under the control of her sons.[42] Manu believed that women have been given birth by the Almighty to procreate and as such if suitable groom is available, they should be married, even if they have not attained the age of marriage.[43] But Manu advised that they should be allowed to remain unmarried all through their lives, in the absence of any suitable groom, but in no circumstance they should be forced to marry an unsuitable or unworthy groom.[44] It will be interesting to note that Manu respected and held women in high esteem, despite of all his negative injunctions against women. He believed that, "God dwells in, where women are loved and respected and where they are harassed, tortured, insulted or maltreated; there peace, prosperity, happiness and wealth can't remain."[45] The happiness of a man and that of the family, depends upon the happiness of women in that family; if the women are happy, then everything will be well and fine but if they are unhappy then their curse will ruin the entire family.

According to Parashar, a girl of eight is called *gauri,* of nine *rohini,* and of ten *kanya;* beyond this she is *rajaswala*. The parents and the eldest brother of a girl who is unmarried, when she becomes rajaswala, go to hell. Parashar marks the real beginning toward pre-puberty marriage because it was he who enjoined that a Brahmin who marries a rajaswala girl should not be spoken to or admitted to a dinner in the same row with other Brahmins. He becomes the husband of a *vrishali,* (वृषली) i.e., low caste woman. Parashar makes such a marriage an extremely sinful act, and consequently the husband is condemned and socially ostracized. Yajnavalkya, another Smriti writer, insisted that girls should be married before the age of puberty, otherwise every month their guardians will be guilty of the destruction of an embryo.[46] Yama, who came about four hundred years later, stated that even if a suitable match is impossible, the girl should be married before she comes of age, even to an unsuitable husband. The view of Yama was much more orthodox than Manu, as the latter was willing to allow a girl to remain unmarried even to the end of her life, if a proper husband could not be secured. Whereas the former did not mind a girl being chained to an unsuitable and undeserving husband for her whole life, if there was the least danger of the fatal line of the age of puberty being crossed before marriage. In Yama-Smriti[47] it is mentioned that if an unmarried girl of twelve years, remains in the household of father, than her father is guilty of *brahma-hatya* (i.e., the sin of murdering a Brahman).

From about 500 A.D. to 1000 A.D., Smriti writers began to encourage pre-puberty marriages and held that a girl should be regarded as having attained puberty at the age of ten and therefore her marriage must be celebrated by that time.[48] At this time, it was held that marriage of the girl, was equal to the *upanayan-sanskar* (i.e., wearing of the sacred thread ceremony) of the boy and if the appropriate age for the later was eight years then the marriage of the girl should also be celebrated at that time. A girl of eight was believed to be like gauri (goddess Parvati) and was therefore suitable for marriage. In Harit Smriti[49] it is mentioned that if a girl has her first menses in her father's home, then she becomes vrishali (वृषली) and anyone who marries a vrishali, will be held as impure and will not be allowed to participate in the religious ceremonies. Similarly, the Marichi Smriti[50] held that anybody who arranges the marriage of his *kanya* (daughter) is sure to go to *brahma-lok* (the abode of gods) and those who arrange the marriage of their rajaswala daughter (i.e., one who had her first menses in her father's home), are liable to go to *raurav-narak*. On the same lines, the Sankhya Smriti held that the elder brother, the father and the mother of the rajaswala girl are liable to go to hell[51] and that the sin that follows thereafter, can never be wiped out.[52]

Though the Smriti writers and the writers of Dharma Sutras have condemned the post puberty marriages, even then it was popular among the Brahmans alone and was not practiced by other castes or varnas in the beginning. Heroines of many of the Sanskrit dramas, written during the period AD 300 to 1200 A.D. are grown up brides at the time of their marriages. Thus, Vasavdatta of *Swapna-Vasavdatta* (written by Bhasa in the Gupta period), Kumar Devi – the wife of Chandragupta-I, Dhruvadevi – the wife of Ramgupta (son of Chandragupta), Rajya-Shri – the sister of

Harshavardhan, etc., were all of marriageable age at the time of their marriages.

Thus, from the above account, it becomes quite clear that because of the emphasis laid down by the religious scriptures of ancient India, the evil of child marriage got firm roots in the Indian social system. Later on, because of continuous foreign invasions and inter- and intra-state wars, things took a bad shape and the people in order to save their womenfolk, from being dishonoured at the hands of the invaders, took recourse to child marriages. This is the very reason, why practices like sati and jauhar developed in the Indian society. Thus, to summarize, the notions of purity and pollution, the fear and the challenge imposed by the new religions (Jainism, Buddhism and Islam), the socio-political and the economic circumstances of the age, forced the thinkers to lower the age of marriage, which slowly and gradually became the order of the day.

Social Situations and the Practice of Child Marriage in Rajasthan

Apart from the factors, discussed above, the prevalence of infant and child marriages in Rajasthan can be attributed to some other factors, which forced the people to opt for this practice. Since the various States of the Rajputana had to involve in constant wars, which ultimately made the lives of women insecure, the desire to protect girl's virginity drove many parents to force their daughters into marriage at an extremely young age. In rural communities, fetching water and firewood were usually chores undertaken by young girls, which was a cause of constant fear for the parents. In many communities (and especially among the Rajputs) indecent behaviour with a girl or rape was considered as derogatory, a humiliation for the entire family of the victim. Moreover, the unstable political condition of the various States of the Rajputana created a terror in the hearts of the parents about the safety, security and honour of their family members. It is significant to note that various States of the Rajputana had to face the onslaught of the foreign invaders, time and again, which disturbed the social, political and economic fabric of the society. The invasion of the foreign invaders and their consequent loot, plunder, mass destruction and the prevalent practice of carrying away the women of the invaded country, forced the people to opt for this heinous practice. Legend has it that the invaders raped unmarried Hindu girls or carried them off as booty, prompting Hindu communities to marry their daughters almost from birth to protect them.

The age-old belief of Hindus to marry off their children within their lifetime and the feeling of relief, the feeling of getting free from this worldly duty was one of the main reasons of infant and child marriages. Even today in the 21st century, Indian parents are bothered by the same considerations, which haunted their ancestors a thousand years ago. And when this was enjoined by some injunctions of the holy Shastras, it became a driving force. Again, the desire of the parents or some old members of the family to partake the pleasure of seeing their children united in bonds of matrimony lent support to the continuance of this practice. It was believed (and is still accepted in the traditional circles,) that one who sees his great grand children (i.e., fourth generation) and especially the male children, is very lucky and is sure to go to heaven. This desire of the great grand parents, motivated the entire family to make way for their wishes so that they may enter the land of the *pitras* (i.e., ancestors).

Moreover, in earlier days travelling to religious places and coming back safe was considered as an achievement. So, when people returned safely from pilgrimages, marriages of daughters were considered auspicious. Since friends and relatives would gather at that time, matchmaking became easier. Thus, developed the custom to celebrate marriages after returning from a pilgrimage. Similarly, it was considered auspicious to marry a girl-child on the death of some elderly person in the family.

Apart from this, many caste organizations had also prescribed certain rules and regulations regarding the age of marriage and the members of that caste had to abide by the orders of their caste panchayats. The fear of social boycott or of other punishment by these caste panchayats, forced the members to comply with them. Even today, many such incidents come to our knowledge about the social boycott of an individual or a family in the country (and especially in Rajasthan). The offenders are left to their fate and no one in the entire village or the region maintains any relation with them. They call this *hukka-pani band karna*. The offenders are denied access to public places like the village *chaupal* (i.e., meeting place of the villagers), the village-well, the local mandi, etc. Rules regarding marriage (endogamous, exogamous, hypergamous, isogamous) made the field of selection narrower and encouraged competition which ultimately resulted in infant or child marriages. The difficulty of finding a suitable match, with regard to age and position, became all the more difficult in proportion to the growing age of the girl, which left the parents with no other option but to select a match at the earliest.

Further, the belief that to save the family name, it was better to tie the daughter into the marriage knot, before she blossomed into womanhood gave support to the practice of child marriages. For the husband, the pre-puberty marriage was a guarantee of the virginity of his wife and for the bride's side this was a guarantee that the early marriage of the girl, would save their family honour from any scandals, which may arise in future.

Economic reasons also motivated the people for early marriages, since early marriage provided one more member to the family to work in the fields, and early marriage ensured early motherhood. In order to curtail the marriage expenses, the guardians and parents were (and are still) keen to marry all their children on the same day or in the same *mandap*. This curtailment of marriage expenses, forced them to opt for child marriages, as it was convenient for them as well as for their relatives. This is the very cause for the prevalence of child marriages amongst many castes, and is specially so amongst Gujars[53] and Rebaris[54] (or Raikas, as they are known in Marwar) in Rajasthan. On the occasion of *baavanni* or *mausar* (i.e., feast given by the family members to the community members, after the death of someone), when the community members belonging to the Gurjar caste of 52 villages gathered, child marriages were (and are still) performed by them. On such occasions, it was compulsory for them to tie their children in the marriage knot, even if they were one or two months old. Moreover, the dowry demanded at the time of early marriages was very less, as compared to marriages at the later stage because certain factors like qualification of the groom, income, education, etc., were not taken into consideration in infant or child marriages, which later on could possibly create hindrances in the process of selection of bride or groom. The dread of famines or the hope of good harvest also motivated the parents to seek alliances for their sons or daughters. "It is probable", observes Abbe, J.A. Dubois,[55] "that the original reason why the Hindus selected these four months (March, April, May and June) as most auspicious for marriages, is that during these months all agricultural work is either finished or suspended on account of the great heat, and also because the crops, which have just been gathered in, help to defray the expenses of the wedding(sic)."

Moreover, the prevalence of joint family system, where three or four generations lived together, under one roof, and where the eldest male member of the family took all the important decisions related to marriage, education, job, etc., of his children or of his grand children, also favoured child marriages. The unquestioning obedience to the head of the family, who enjoyed complete powers, enormous responsibilities and who controlled the financial matters, indirectly worsened the independent position of the woman. The joint family system, still prevalent in the Indian society, assured the family members of their daily bread and provided them shelter as well. When two or three or four generations lived together in a house, it was the duty of the elders to meet out the demands as well as needs of each and every member of the family. Thus the younger ones, whether they were married or unmarried, were looked after by their elders, and they were free from any worldly tensions. The elder members were of the view that they need not labour, as long as there were other family members to shoulder the responsibilities of the household. Writing about this aspect of Hindu family, P. Thomas[56] observes "A Hindu gentleman's household is a miniature state of fifty to hundred men and women.... As regards property, a sort of communism prevails in the joint family. Every member of the household whatever his calling or occupation, is required to hand over his income to the head of the family and it goes into the common pool...It is the economic structure of the joint family that makes the Hindus marry young, regardless of the question whether or not they are able to support wives and children."

The family traditions and the examples of child marriages, within the family, motivated the members of the family to advocate child marriage. If some marriage occurred in the family or in the village, wherein the bride or the groom was minor, then such examples are cited by the elder members of the family, to support their views.

Beside these factors, having an unmarried daughter at home, was considered as an anathema by the people, for they were very much concerned about the safety and security of the virgin girl. Any scandal could bring disgrace to the entire family and to rule out this possibility, people resorted to child marriages. "Under these circumstances", observed Risley,[57] "when in the case of a daughter, parents see that, unless they marry her at once, the one or two bridegrooms that are open for their selection would be availed of by others, and that they would be disabled from marrying her before the eleventh year, and that they would thereby incur a religious sin and social degradation as regards the caste, they would seize the opportunity to marry their daughter, quite disregardful of the evil effects of infant marriages."

Child Marriages as Reflected in Census Reports

According to the *Census of 1901,*[58] the highest proportion of both married males and married females of under 10 years of age, in the Rajputana and in the British administered territory of Ajmer-Merwara, was found in Marwar, where out of every 10,000 boys and girls, 580 boys (5.8%) and 1,118 girls (11.18%) respectively were married. The State of Kishangarh showed the next highest ratio with 249 married boys (2.49%) and 901 married girls (9.01%); then came Dholpur, Lawa and Shahpura. In each of these States and Estates there were a large proportion of the higher classes which practised early marriage. In the Bhil States of Banswara and Dungarpur, and in Jaisalmer, Bikaner, Alwar, Karauli, Bundi, and Kota the ratios were low. Pratapgarh had only a small number of married boys at this age but its ratio of young married girls was higher than those of Bundi and Kota. For the period 10 to 15, Dholpur with 2,184 (21.84%) had the highest proportion of married males; Marwar was next with 2,126 (21.26%) and then came Bharatpur, Kishangarh, Shahpura, and Karauli. The States with the lowest ratios were Jaisalmer (351), Banswara (428), and Dungarpur (472). Bundi, Bikaner and Kota had also low ratios. Among girls at this period, the states of Dholpur, Bharatpur, Jaipur, Jhalawar, Karauli and Kishangarh (all in Eastern Division) showed the highest proportion of wives: their ratios varied from 6,575 in Dholpur to 4,329 in Kishangarh. The lowest ratio of the wives between the age of 10 and 15 was found in Banswara (1,426), Dungarpur (1,777) and Jaisalmer (1,926).

The *Census of 1901*[59] also reveals that the marriage of children under 10, among both sexes was more common in the Western Rajputana than in any of the other Divisions, and especially among the Hindus. It is noteworthy that this practice was not common in both sexes in the Southern Division, which was greatly due to the very large proportion of Animists and Jains in the population, among whom, the average age of marriage was much higher than among the Hindus or the Muslims. There were only four units, including the Ajmer District, where the proportion of married females, under 10 years, was as high as that of Marwar; while on the other hand, the other two States in the Eastern Division – Jaisalmer and Bikaner, were among the first eight with the least tendency to child marriage. The proportion of married women under 5 years of age in Marwar was 17 per 1000, and in the age group of 5-9, 90 per 1000, compared to 13 and 77 respectively for the whole of the Western Division. The State of Jhalawar had the largest proportion of married females in 1911, i.e., out of every 1000 girls, 83 were married which was strikingly opposite to the lowest figure of only 3 in Kushalgarh. It is, however, not so striking as the Marwar figures of 1901, where there were 123 out of every 1000 girls of this age who had been married. It is noticeable that both in 1901 and 1911 Shahpura, Marwar, Dholpur, Kishangarh and Jhalawar have been the five States with the highest proportion of child wives. In both years, Kushalgarh and Banswara had the smallest proportion and Alwar and Dungarpur were among the first five in both the years. In 1911, Kota, Bundi and Jhalawar alone showed a larger proportion of child-wives than they did in 1901. Of the two British Districts, Merwara ranked among the 6 units with the least and Ajmer among the 4 units with the greatest tendency to child marriage, despite the fact that it was administered by the British Government and despite the fact that it was the centre of higher education, as well as the centre of Arya-Samaj movement in the Rajputana. In their relative position to other units as regards absence of child marriage, Dungarpur, Jaisalmer, Merwara, Mewar, Tonk, Shahpura, Marwar, showed a better state of affairs and Alwar, Kota, Bundi, Karauli, Pratapgarh, Bharatpur, Ajmer, Dholpur, Kishangarh and Jhalawar as worse ones; the remaining five showed a stable condition.

Prevalence of the Practice of Child Marriage amongst Certain Castes

According to the *Census of 1911*,[60] in the Provinces of the Rajputana and in the British administered territory of Ajmer-Merwara, the highest proportion of married males under 5 years, was in the Gujars, Jats and Balais of Ajmer-Merwara and the Bhambhis and Rebaris of Rajputana; and that of females, among the Rebaris, Bhambhis, Kasais, and Jats in the Rajputana, and the Jats, Gujars and Kumhars in Ajmer-Merwara. Between the age of 5 and 11 period, the

Jats, Gujars, Kumhars, Balais, Charmakars, Nais and Malis of Ajmer-Merwara, and the Rebaris, Kasais and Bhambhis of Rajputana had the highest proportion of married males; and the Jats, Gujars, Malis, Kumhars, and Charmakars of Ajmer-Merwara, and Kasais, Rebaris, Jats, Gujars and Rangrez of the Rajputana, that of married females. Excluding Christians, the Bhils, Meos, Mahajans, Rajputs, Kayamkhanis and Rawats were among those who showed the least tendency to childhood marriage in the Rajputana among both sexes, and the Saiyads among females. In Ajmer-Merwara, Mers, Rawats, Merat Kathats, and Mahajans had the lowest proportions of married and widowed children of either sex.

Caste	*Locality (Rajputana/ Ajmer-Merwara)*	*Number of married and widowed per 1000 of same age*			
		0-4		*5-11*	
		Males	*Females*	*Males*	*Females*
Balai	Ajmer Merwara	8	18	58	138
Bhambhi	Rajputana	9	25	61	134
Charmakar	Ajmer Merwara	5	12	55	161
Gurjar	Rajputana	2	5	40	156
	Ajmer Merwara	10	34	109	229
Jat	Rajputana	3	11	50	160
	Ajmer Merwara	10	41	138	257
Kasai	Rajputana	3	21	91	242
Kumhar	Ajmer Merwara	3	20	72	209
Mali	Ajmer Merwara	-	17	50	216
Nai	Rajputana	1	4	26	105
	Ajmer Merwara	2	13	55	147
Rangrez	Rajputana	2	7	57	147
Rebari	Rajputana	6	30	93	196

Source: Census of India 1911, *Rajputana and Ajmer-Merwara*, pp. 161-162.

Prevalence of Baby Marriage and Pre-Natal Betrothal in Certain Communities

According to the *Census of 1911*,[61] out of every 1000 children in the Rajputana among those under 1 year of age, there were 52 married and 2 widowed males and 135 married and 2 widowed females. Nearly all of these were among the Hindus. In Ajmer-Merwara there were only 10 females and 1 male of this age returned as married, and none as widowed.

It is significant to note that the practice of infant marriage was prevalent among the Kunbis (Kurmis) of Jhalawar, Kota and Marwar; the Chaubes of Karauli; the Bhambhis, Jats, Kumhars, Malis, Nais, Rebaris and very occasionally among the Brahmans and Maheshwaris and others of the higher castes, in Marwar; and, in Ajmer-Merwara, it was prevalent among these same castes as well as Rawats and Mers. In most of these cases the custom meant nothing more than this, that in two families of great intimacy, should the wives become pregnant, an agreement was made between the parents that should the children be of opposite sexes, they would be betrothed to each other. In one caste in certain parts of Gujarat it was said that the practice had its origin in the custom of celebrating marriages in the whole caste on one day only, once in every ten or twelve years; the unborn babies were, therefore, trapped into the marriage net. This, however, did not apply to the Rajputana. But among the Chaubes in Karauli the practice was said to be due to a system of exchange which had grown up from scarcity of females. Accordingly, when A married his daughter to B's son, B promised to give his daughter in return to A's son. But, should B have no daughter at the time, he promises to give one when born. Should no daughter be born to him, he must find a wife for A's son from among his nearest relatives.

Number of Married Children (under 1 year of age) in the Rajputana: Religionwise

Religion	*Married*		*Widowed*	
	Males	*Females*	*Males*	*Females*
All religions	52	135	2	2
Animists	1	2	-	-
Hindus	46	123	2	2
Jains	-	2	-	-
Muslims	5	8	-	-

Source: Census of India, Rajputana and Ajmer-Merwara 1911, pp. 161-162.

It is striking to note that the practice of child marriage was prevalent in almost all of the native States of the Rajputana, but it had firm roots in Marwar, Mewar, Sirohi, Jaipur, Kishangarh, Bikaner, Jhalawar, and Tonk and in the British-administered territory of Ajmer-Merwara. According to the *Census of 1911*, in Marwar there were 3,299 children (780 were male and 2,519 were female), in the age group of 0-4 years, who were found married and out of them 91 (45 were male and 46 were female) were child widows and child-widowers. In Mewar, in the same age-group, there were 666 children (212 were male and 454 were female) who were married and out of them 30 children (7 male and 23 female) were widowed. Similarly in Jaipur, 566 children (159 male and 407 female) were married and out of them 20 children (3 male and 17 female) were widowed in this age group. While in Kishangarh, 187 children (44 male and 143 female) were married and out of them 10 children (7 male and 3 female) were widowed. The same is the case with Sirohi, Tonk and Ajmer. In Sirohi, 343 children (70 male and 273 female) were married and 7 children (1 male and 6 female) were widowed. In Tonk, 413 children (130 were male and 283 were female) were found married in the age group of 0-4 years and out of them 26 children (11 male and 15 female) were widowed. It is remarkable that this practice was also prevalent in the British administered territory of Ajmer-Merwara, despite the works of Christian missionaries and Arya Samaj and despite the fact that it was a centre of higher education in those days. *The Census of 1911* reveals that there were 489 children (98 male and 391 female) who were married in the age group of 0-4 years and out of them 15 children (4 male and 11 female) were widowed. Similarly, in Merwara, 79 children (32 male and 47 female) were married and there were no child-widows and child-widowers in this age group. According to the *Census of 1911*, none was found married in the age group of 0-4 in the states of Bundi, Karauli and in the Chiefship of Kushalgarh (See Appendix V).

If we take into account the *Census of 1921*, the same picture emerges. The States of Marwar, Mewar, Jaipur, Bikaner, Kishangarh, Kota, Sirohi and the British administered territory of Ajmer-Merwara figure prominently as the places, where child marriage was widely practiced while in Kushalgarh, Lawa Estate, Bharatpur, Karauli, Jaisalmer, Dungarpur, Abu, Bundi, it was less prevalent. In Marwar, in the age group of 0-1, there were 20 children

(13 male and 7 female) who were married. While in the age group of 1-5, there were 700 children (130 male and 570 female) who were married. Similarly, in the age group of 5-10, there were 16,982 children (4,432 male and 12,550 female) who were married. The number of widowed children in Marwar, in the age group of 0-10 years, was 968 (383 male and 585 female), which was highest in all the native States of the Rajputana. In contrast to it, in the states of Bundi, Dholpur, Dungarpur, Bharatpur Jaisalmer, Jhalawar and Karauli; and in the Chiefships of Kushalgarh and Lawa, there was not a single incident of marriage in the age-group of 0-1 years. Similarly, only 40 cases of marriage were registered in Banswara, 5 in Bharatpur, 2 in Abu, 8 in Bundi, 8 in Dholpur, 13 in Dungarpur, 16 in Jaisalmer, 5 in Kushalgarh and 6 in Lawa Estate in the age-group of 1-5 year; which was in sharp contrast to 700 in Marwar, 2,280 in Mewar, 321 in Sirohi, 380 in Tonk, 683 in Ajmer-Merwara, 118 in Shahpura, 195 in Kishangarh, 641 in Alwar, 459 in Bikaner and 1,352 marriages in Jaipur in the age group of 1-5 years (See Appendix VI).

These Census reports reveal that female children were married earlier than most of their male counterparts and also that the number of child-widows was much more than child widowers, in most of the States. It also forces us to think about the sad plight of child-widows, as the society at that time allowed only the male-members to remarry and felt uneasy at the mere thought of widow-marriage. The deplorable condition of the widows and the various restrictions imposed on her regarding eating, dressing, social intercourse, as well as the feeling of inauspiciousness attached with her, perhaps forced some of them to opt for Sati, in the medieval periods.

The Custom of Gauna or Muklawa

As discussed above, the practice of pre-natal or infant or child marriage was prevalent in the erstwhile States of the Rajputana, but the marriage was not consummated till the ceremony of gauna or muklawa was performed.[62] If the parties were of a mature age at the time of the wedding, the ceremony of gauna was performed at once and the marriage was then consummated. But if the bride and bride-groom were of tender age, the gauna ceremony was not performed until the 1st, 3rd, 5th or 7th year (i.e., an odd year) after the marriage.[63] The gauna ceremony usually, but not always, marked the commencement of married life. In some parts of the country and among some castes, it was performed only in order to remove the restriction against the bride going to her husband's house and had nothing to do with the commencement of conjugal relations, the date of which was determined by the parents of the bride, when she had attained maturity, after consultation with the astrologers.

According to S.G. Kabra,[64] the State of Rajasthan has been needlessly denigrated for child marriages and the media (especially foreign media) has flaunted this visual to project how backward Rajasthan is amongst the States of India. According to him, the central point that is missed out in this sensitive and emotive issue is the fact that, unlike Bengal, where the child bride after marriage goes to the husband's place, and the marriage is consummated, in Rajasthan, child bride never goes to the husband's place after the marriage ritual. The husband has to wait for the ceremony of gauna or muklawa, only after which she is allowed to go to the husband's place. The present prevalent age of gauna or muklawa is 17 to 19 years and the real age of marriage, that is the age at which the marriage is consummated, according to S.G. Kabra.

He believes that the singulate mean age at marriage of females in Rajasthan was 15.07 in 1971 and 16.09 in 1981. And this mean age at marriage, according to him, is on the basis of Census records where the age of marriage entered is the age at the time of ceremony and not the age at the time of gauna. If the age at gauna were taken into consideration, the mean age at marriage of females will be no different than in other States and perhaps better than several States.

Similarly, N.K. Singhi[65] believed that the colonial cognitive construction of India was part of politics of knowledge aimed at perpetuation of hegemonic rule. They aimed at negativated construction of Indian society and packed up themes and issues out of context for hammering the notion of historical backwardness. Sati, child marriage, purdah, widowhood were used as illustrations of disabled and fractured society. These illustrations, according to him, were fitted into a cognitive mould to declare India as a backward society which needed to be reformed and changed. Thus, orientalism and later on cognitive imperialism led to denigrated construction of India and Indians. The arguments forwarded by S.G. Kabra and N.K. Singhi seems convincing as the age of consummation of marriage is not quite as low, as is generally believed by the people. *The Census Record of 1911* (p. 164) regarding the Rajputana and Ajmer-Merwara, has given details regarding the age of consummation among certain selected castes of the Rajputana. According to it, the average age at which consummation took place amongst the Ahirs was from 15-20 for boys and from puberty to 16 among girls. Amongst the Bhils, it was 14 or 15 for girls and 18 or 20 for males. The age of consummation, amongst Gujars, was from 13 to 15 for the girl and 16 to 18 for males. Similarly, in Jats, it varied from 13 to 16 for girls and 16 to 20 for boys. Amongst Minas, consummation took place about the age of 12 or 14 with girls and 15 to 18 with boys; in Rajputs it was 13 to 18 among girls and 16 to 20 among males; and in Rawats of Ajmer-Merwara, it varied from 12 to 15 with girls and 17 to 21 with males.

Interrelation of Child Marriages with other Social Evils

As discussed above, the practice of child marriage is widely prevalent in Rajasthan, not only in communities which are considered as backward and underprivileged but also in upper castes. On the very day of Akha-Teej (Akshaya-Tritiya), thousands of child marriages are performed every year in different parts of Rajasthan. According to a report published in the *Hindustan* in 1990, in Rajasthan alone 1,30,000 girl children are married off each year in a day.

Child marriage puts forth another challenge to a bride who is physically and psychologically ill-prepared for responsibilities. By getting married as a child, she is denied her right to be a child and enjoy her childhood, as her brothers do. The very experience of being uprooted from her parental home and going and living in her in-laws home is a traumatic experience for her, as various kinds of duties, obligations, negations, etc., are imposed on her, which causes strain and frustrations in her personality. Marriage at an early age, denies children (and especially the girl child), the opportunities to have education, training and income-generating skills and thus creates difficulties in their way in attaining maturity, self-confidence and an all round development of personality. The joint family system, in which three or four generations of the family lived together under the same roof, also undermined the position of wives, including child wives. Such joint living involves the need for tremendous discipline, conformity and self-effacement and greatly lessens a woman's chance of developing any sense of independence or responsibility. As a child bride, she is totally dependent on her husband and her in-laws, and thus her whole existence merges with that of her family, and her wishes, her desires become secondary. The denial of the opportunities mentioned above, indirectly deprives her of her right to utilize her potentialities and to live healthily, which in turn affects her whole life adversely.

(i) *Child Mothers*: The first and foremost ill-effect of child marriage is the rise in the number of child mothers, in the society. It has been observed that in many rural areas, girls become mothers between the age of 12 and 16 years. Researches point out that child mothers tend to suffer from ignorance, maternal malnutrition, severe anaemia, a shorter gestation period and antenatal hyper-tension, all of which pose formidable challenges for a "safe motherhood".[66] The major life threatening complications for very young mothers are pregnancy induced high blood-pressure, anaemia and difficulty in delivery, due to disproportion between the preview size and the head of the baby. Pregnancy induced high blood pressure is a special hazard. It occurs more often during the first pregnancy and the incidence is five times higher in the age group below 15 years than in the age group of 20-24 years. This can cause serious complications and even death. Iron deficiency is another risk for the young mother. Adolescents who become pregnant within four years of menarche (which is between 10-14 years in India) are physically and psychologically immature and since they are still growing they have greater nutritional require-ments than adult women.

Birth of the baby becomes more hazardous amongst child mothers because the pelvic growth is not usually complete until several years after menarche. Malnutrition during childhood results in stunted growth and these factors result in a higher proportion of abnormal presentations and prolonged labour, and the need for intervention like forceps, vacuum or Cesarean section. Some of the reasons of high rate of material mortality are malnutrition, weak health, and early marriage. Child marriage increases many folds the risks of becoming a child mother and child-widow with all the resultant ills, agonies, oppression and violence on her.

(ii) *Child Widows*: The second ill-effect of child marriage is the presence of child-widows in the society. The following observation, made in *Indian Social Reform,* Part I, p. 171, describes the number of child widows and child widowers in the then society and presents its ugly face. "In 1819, there were amongst Hindus, Sikhs, Jains and Buddhists 89,051 boys below the age of four who were married and

223,560 married girls of the same age. The number of widows below the age of four was 10,644. The number of married boys between five and nine years of age was nearly six lacs and two thousand and that of girls over 18.5 lacs. The total number of married males below the age of fourteen was 2,725,124 and that of girls was 6,871,999. The number of widows between five and six years of age was 52,759 and of those between ten and fourteen years of age was 143,100. Of these, two lacs and more of widows below the age of fourteen, all but some 4000 were Hindus proper"(sic). Similarly, according to the *Census of India, 2001*, there are 64 lac children, who were found to be married before the age of 18, and there were one lac and thirty thousand widows, who were below the age of 18 years. Moreover there, were 56,000 girls, below the age of 18, who were left or deserted by their in-laws or who were leading a divorced life.

A child widow often faced (or may face) tremendous torture at the hands of the family members. She was cursed and blamed for the death of her husband and was looked down upon as inauspicious for the family. Discrimination was made between restriction imposed upon the child widow and child widower. Child widower was married off again while child widow was expected to spend all her life in penance and was at the mercy of her family-members. In the medieval times, some of them were compelled to commit sati which can be equated with forcing her to commit suicide. Thus, a child widow was forced to lead a life facing deep-rooted stigma, frustrations and hatred as also to tolerate silently physical, social, economic and emotional hardships and exploitation at the hands of even the family members, who indulged into different types of oppression, violence or could even sexually abuse the child wife, child mother or child widow.

Though, it is true that in many families child widows were cared and looked after very well and no distinction was made between a child widow and other members but it is also true that there were (and still there are) families who exploited such helpless creatures, for petty and selfish motives. As has been discussed above, the system of pre-natal marriage or baby marriage was in vogue in certain communities of Rajasthan and the plight of the girl child whose betrothal ceremony was performed when she was in the womb and who lost her husband or fiancée when she came out in this world was really miserable. It is significant to note that the Brahmans, the Rajputs and the Mahajans had the highest number of child-widows in the Rajputana society, according to the *Census of 1911*.

In the Rajputana, the highest number of widowed children, according to the *Census of 1911*, was in the State of Marwar. In the age-group of 0-4 years there were 91 children, (out of them 45 were male children and 46 were female children) who were widowed. Similarly, in the age-group of 5-9, there were 556 children (221 male and 335 female children) who were widowed. After Marwar, the State of Jaipur had the highest number of widowed children. In the age-group of 0-4 years, there were 20 widowed children and out of these 3 were male and 17 were female. Similarly, in the age-group of 5-9 years, there were 285 children (75 were male and 210 were female children) who were registered as widowed children. While in Mewar, in the age-group of 0-4 years, 23 female children and 7 male children were registered as widowed children; and in the age-group of 5-9, 188 children (79 males and 109 female children) were widowed. It is strange to note that in the British administered territory of Ajmer, the number of widowed children was higher than other States and Chiefships (except Marwar, Mewar and Jaipur). Around 11 female children and 4 male children were registered as widowed in Ajmer, in the age-group of 0-4 years; while 123 widowed children (58 male and 65 female children) were in the age-group of 5-9 years.

It is also strange to note that while the number of widows was higher in the Southern Division, in comparison to other States and Chiefships, it was not so in the age-group of 0-4 and 5-9 years, (except Mewar). In Banswara, Jhalawar, Kushalgarh and Lawa, there was not a single widowed child (male or female) in the age-group of 0-4 years. While in Pratapgarh, there was one child widow in this age group; in Sirohi there were 6 child widows and 1 widower and in Dungarpur, 2 child widows were present in the age-group of 0-4 years.

In the States of Bundi, Dholpur, Bharatpur, Karauli, Kota and in Shahpura and Merwara, there was not a single child widow or widower in the age-group of 0-4 years, though there were married children in this age-group in the above mentioned States and *Thikanas*.

While in the age-group of 5-9 years, 117 widowed children (45 male and 72 females) were there in Bharatpur; 79 widowed children (26 male and 53 female) were in Alwar; 71 widowed children (10 male and 61 female) were in Bikaner; 50 widowed children (18 male and 32 female) were in Bundi; 40 (23 male and 17 female) were in Dholpur; 65 (25 male and 40 female) were in Kota; 40 (20 male and 20 female children) were in Kishangarh; and 67 widowed children (18 were male and 49 were female) were in Tonk in the Rajputana in 1911. These figures clearly reveal that the number of child widows was higher, than the number of child widowers in almost all the States of the Rajputana in 1911 (See Appendix V and VI).

Prohibition of Widow Remarriage among Certain Castes

The practice of child marriage as well as that of prohibition of remarriage of widows, developed under the pressure of peculiar social conditions, exercised a powerful influence on the social status of the castes. The prohibition of widow marriage is traced to the primitive belief that the dead chief or the head of the family will require companionship and service in the world to which he has gone. "The closer contact with more barbarous races", observes Sir Henry Maine,[67] "the growth of the sacerdotal spirit and the desire to get rid of the inconvenient lien which the widow held over her husband's property resulted in the prohibition of remarriage of widows". The causes which have tended to favour the growth of the custom prohibiting widow remarriage, according to him, are as follows:

(i) The anxiety of the early Hindu law givers to circumscribe a woman's rights to property which would unquestionably tend to forbid her to join her lot, to a man whose interest it would be to assert and extend those rights, as against the members of her husband's family.

(ii) The growth of the doctrine of spiritual benefit, which would require her to devote her life, to the annual performance of her husband's *shraadha*.

(iii) The Brahminical theory of marriage, which regards as the essential part of the ceremony, the gift of the woman by her father to her husband's – the effect of which is to transfer her from her own gotra or exogamous group into that of her husband's; the idea underlying the theory is, that the right of ownership over her, which was vested in her father having been transferred to the husband, and he being no more, there is no one to give her away; and since Hindu marriage must take the form of a gift her marriage is therefore impossible.

(iv) The custom of hypergamy or the law of superior marriage – the rule which compels a man to wed his daughter with a member of a group which shall be equal or superior in rank to his own, while he himself may take his wife, or at any rate his second wife, from a group of inferior standing.

Risley[68] believes that this custom which "clearly may have arisen wherever great pride of blood coexisted with a mode of life demanding the continual maintenance of a high standard of ceremonial purity, appears to owe its form to the passages in the early texts which admit of the marriage of a man of a higher caste to a woman of a lower caste, but condemn the converse practice in the strongest terms". He points out that, "the first consequence of the restriction would be a surplus of marriageable women in the superior groups; for the men of a given superior group might, and presumably in some instances would, marry women of an inferior group, while men of this group would be barred for the women of the superior group. Competition for husbands would follow; the bride price of early usage would disappear and would be replaced by the bridegroom price ... widows would certainly be the first to be excluded from the marriage market for in their case the interests of the individual families would be identical with those of the group. The family would already have paid a bridegroom price to get their daughter or sister married, and would naturally be indisposed to pay a second, and probably higher price to get her married again. The group, in its turn, would be equally adverse to an arrangement which tended to increase the number of marriageable women."

It is significant to note that in the Brahmans, the Rajputs, the Mahajans and the Kayasthas, widow remarriage (be it that of child widow) was strictly forbidden. According to the Census of 1911, the castes in which the proportion of widowers was the highest were the Gola Purabs, Kayasthas, Mahajans and Brahmans in the Rajputana and the Mahajans, the Jats, the Brahmans and the Gujars in Ajmer-Merwara. In the Table 1, mentioned below, the castes which had the largest proportion of widows have been mentioned. It is evident from this Table, that in the Rajputana and Ajmer-Merwara the Brahmans, the Rajputs, and the Mahajans, among whom the prohibition against widow-remarriage was strict, the number of child widows was the highest. Of the other castes in the Rajputana with a proportion of over 200 widows, it is noticeable that the Sadhus and Bairagis were devotee castes, and the Darogas, Chakars, and Gola Purabs were the hand-maiden castes. Of the two remaining ones, the Kayasthas forbade widow remarriage, and the Kayam Khanis were Rajputs converted to Muslim faith, who had retained most of the Hindu customs; and evidently the Rajput prejudice against widow remarriage lingered among them. In this connection it is curious to note that the Meos or Mewatis, the other large Rajput tribes converted to Islam, had a very low proportion of widows, only 136 per 1000.

Table 1

Castes with more than 200 widows per 1000 females

Rajputana		*Ajmer-Merwara*	
Brahman	263	Brahman	281
Rajput	261	Mahajan	276
Mahajan	259	Rajput	274
Sadhu	246	Nai	217
Daroga	220	Mali	210
Chakar	216		
Gola Purab	214		
Kayam-Khani	214		
Kayastha	212		
Bairagi	203		

Source: Census of India 1911, Rajputana & Ajmer-Merwara, chapter VII, p. 161.

The Practice of *Naata* or *Karewa*

In Rajputana, the practice of *naata* or *karewa* (re-marriage) was prevalent amongst certain Hindu castes[69(a)] like the Sodhias, the Bishnois, the Malis, the Patwas, the Thatharas or the Kansaras, the Pinjaras, the Gadris, the Bandharas, the Chitaras, the Ghanchas, the Keers, the Kalals, the Lohars, the Ghanchis, the Suthar Beesotara Khatis, the Darogas (Ravana Rajputs), the Mers or Cheetas, the Rebaris, the Bhadbhunjas, the Baridars, the Beldars, the Mogiyas, the Dhadis, the Bhats, the Pitalyas, the Jogis (the Kalbeliya Jogis and the Nath Jogis), the Ramawat Sadhus, the Meghwals, the Raigars, the Khateeks, the Kolis or the Koris, the Ganwariyas, the Teergars, the Mehars, the Nats, the Bavris, the Thoris, the Kanjars, the Bediyas, the Dhankas, the Gurda or the Gurudas, the Harijans, the Meenas and the Bhils. While amongst the Muslim castes[69(b)], naata or karewa was prevalent amongst the Saiyyads, the Shekhs, the Makranis, the

Sindhi Muslims, the Chadwas, the Gadits, the Kheradi or the Kharradi, the Bhishtis, the Neelgars, the Jalali Fakirs, the Chhipas, the Silawats, the Bhatyars, the Bhadbhunjias and the Julahas. There was practically no difference in the various States in the form of ceremonies followed by the widow marrying castes; and the ritual observed by them, was much the same. As a rule no Brahman or priest officiated and the ceremonies were for the most part restricted to the new husband giving the woman *chure* (bracelets) and new clothes and taking her into his house generally after dark on Saturday night. The custody of the children (by the first marriage) remained with the deceased husband's family, and the widow forfeited all share in her late husband's property. Among the higher classes, which permitted widow marriage, the deceased husband's family could not interfere in the matter of the widow's second marriage, nor could they claim any compensation for the bride price paid for her on her first marriage; but among many of the lower castes the widow was expected to marry her late husband's younger brother (*devar*) and if she was unwilling to do so and married some other man, then the new husband had to pay *zagda* or compensation to the younger brother of the deceased husband. The forms observed by the Jats, the Gujars, the Kumhars, the Bhils and the Charmakars, who were representatives of the higher, middle and lower classes of the castes and of the Bhils, who permitted widow marriage, are briefly as follows:[70]

(i) *Jats*: Among the Jats a widow was permitted to marry anyone outside the prohibited degrees of relationship. In some parts of the country, marriage with the deceased husband's younger brother was allowed but this was prohibited among the most important subdivisions such as the Sinsinwar, the Khuntela, the Saboria and the Chahar. The *panchas* (i.e., village elder men) were informed and the widow after changing bangles entered her new husband's home. Some local customs required the widow to take a load of grass from the new husband's head and then enter the house followed by the bridegroom, or the bride-groom to take a pot of water from the widow's head and enter the house followed by the widow. If the parties belonged to different villages the widow was usually conducted to her new husband's house at night. There was a superstition in some parts, that if any person sees the face of the widow when going to be remarried before she reaches her new husband's house, that person will die within six months.

(ii) *Gujars*: Among the Gujars, the widow could marry her deceased husband's younger brother or even his elder brother which was very rare among the Hindus. If she married some one else, *jhagra* or zagda (compensation) was paid to the deceased husband's relatives.

(iii) *Kumhars*: Amongst the Kumhars, a widow could marry, whom she pleased, outside the prohibited degrees of relationship. The form of ceremony usually followed, was taking off the vessel of water from the widow's head by the bridegroom. The woman then used to put on the bracelets, which the man gave her and then entered his house.

(iv) *Bhils*: A widow was supposed to marry her deceased husband's younger brother, amongst the Bhils. If she objected, the younger brother was entitled to have zagda from the man who contracted *nata* or *natra* with the widow. The bridegroom gave the woman bracelets and provided a feast to his relatives and members of the tribe.

(v) *Charmakars*: Amongst the Charmakars a widow was expected to marry her deceased husband's younger brother but was not bound to do so. If she married any other man – who used to be outside the prohibited degrees of relationship – zagda was usually paid to the deceased husband's relatives. The panchas were informed and new bangles were given to the widow by the bridegroom.

(vi) *Bishnois*: Widows were allowed to contract *nata* or *natra* amongst them. They could marry their deceased husband's younger brother but were not obliged to do so. The husband gave the widow a new suit of clothes and white lac bracelets and took her home on Saturday night after dining at her parent's house and paying the *reet* money.

Table 2 presents some of the important castes which allowed widow remarriage, generally, by the *nata* or *dhareja* ceremony. Though this was not such an honourable ceremony as that of an ordinary marriage, yet the issue from such marriages was recognized as legitimate. This custom however, did not reduce the proportion of widows very much, so far as the Jats, the Malis, the Kumhars and the Gujars were concerned. Perhaps they were influenced by the example of higher castes which discouraged this practice.

Table 2

Selected Hindu castes which allowed widow remarriage

Caste in order of social precedence	*Proportion of widows per 1000 females*	
	Rajputana	*(Hindus) Ajmer Merwara*
Jat	169	199
Gurjar	158	160
Ahir	146	200
Mali	166	211
Mina	157	150
Rawat	121	138
Kumhar	162	184
Bhil	102	109
Mer	142	145
Merat Gorat	100	58
Koli	154	145
Charmakar	146	154

Source: Census of India, 1911, *Rajputana and Ajmer Merwara,* p. 161.

(iii) *Sexual abuse of the child-wife, child-mother or child-widow*: The third ill-effect of child marriage is or can be the sexual abusement of the girl child. The word sexual abuse may be described as any sexual behaviour or activity:

(a) that targets the body of a girl child, by way of any gesture, symbol, song or words, which disturbs her or is harmful to her emotionally and psychologically;

(b) which physically exploits a girl child, with or without her consent.

These are some of the ways through which a child-wife or a child mother or a child-widow can be harassed. As she is not mature enough to protest the sexual onslaughts of her in-laws, therefore she is forced to accept it, as her destiny. In a family, if the elder brother or brothers of the groom are leading a single life or if they are widowers, then the plight of the child-wife is even worse. Similarly, if the groom is himself younger than his wife, in the case of an uneven or ill-matched marriage, then also chances are that his wife can be physically assaulted or mishandled by his own kiths and kins. The actual incidence of sexual abuse of girl-child or of child-wife is not known and cannot be known exactly, as the feeling of shame or the fear of character-assassination or the fear of bringing disrepute to the family's name prevents the victim, to bring it to the notice of family or that of the society. Moreover, the emotional black-mailing by the offender, or by the family of the victim, obstructs her way to get justice and to bring the culprits to book. Many cases go unreported in India, as like elsewhere, because most of the victims and their family members do not want to talk openly about their trauma because of social pressure. Moreover, the family members of the victims have no faith in the law. As rightly stated by the eminent sociologist M.N. Srinivas[71] that "the sexual abuse of children is rampant, yet it has escaped the researcher, as the fear of stigma is a major hurdle" especially among the middle and upper class families. This was corroborated by the findings of a study conducted by the BBC in which "one out of every 10 women reported some kind of sexual abuse during childhood by known persons, ranging from father, uncles, cousins, doctors and counsellors."

As reported in *India Today*, in its issue of October 31, 1992, for every reported case, at least 100 would go unreported, more so if the assailant is father, brother, brother-in-law, cousin or any other close relative.

(iv) *Polygamy*: The practice of child marriage had helped in the prevalence of another social evil polygamy, equally pernicious to the status and position of women, in the ancient and medieval period. As described earlier, a child mother faces many physical and emotional problems, which can be injurious to her health. As her body is not fully fit to deliver a baby, therefore, thousands of child mothers perish. In each maternal death, according to Vanava Pendse, (ex-head of the department of Obstetrics and Gynaecology, Udaipur Medical College) illiteracy, lack of awareness, irresponsible attitude of the health staff and non-availability of proper health care and obstetrics services, play a vital role. A report of the White Ribbon Alliance for Safe Motherhood (WRASM) too confirms this. It says that 15 per cent the deaths of young women in India occur from complications related to child birth and unsafe abortions and over 80 per cent of pregnancy and child birth deaths occur due to one of the six causes: haemorrhage, eclampsia, obstructed labour, sepsis, unsafe abortions and pre-existing conditions (such as amnesia and malarial or tubercular infections). The death of the young mother doubles or even triples the threat to the life of children below five years of age, thus furthering the already high infant mortality rate. This gives birth to the practice of polygamy, as the child husband, after the death of his child wife, marries again. According to the *Census of India 1901*, (p. 90), there were in the Rajputana 1,046 wives to 1,000 husbands. The proportions in the three Divisions were – in Western Division 1,103, in Eastern Division 1,029 and in Southern Division 1,023. The Census data also reveals that polygamy was more common amongst the Jains, the Hindus and the Animists.

It is apparent that child marriages and the practice of female foeticide are linked to various other social abuses and for the abolition of these social practices more determined effort is required. Despite the efforts of various social and caste organizations and enlightened individuals and even that of the Government of India, these two problems are still in existence, even in the 21st century.

Notes

1. The other *aboojh sawas,* according to Hindu astrology are, *Chaitra Shukla – Ramnavmi; JyeshthaShukla – Nirjala Ekadashi, Gangadashmi; Asadh Shukla – Bhadlya Navmi; Kartik Shukla – Dev uthani Ekadashi; Magh Shukla – Suraj saten, Basant Panchami;* and *Falgun Shukla – Fulera doj.*
2. Cf. *Hindustan Times,* 13 October, 2005.
3. Cf. *Rajasthan Patrika,* 31 March 2005, p. 8.
4. Cf. Joshi, Rama and Liddle, Joanne, *Daughters of Independence: Gender, Caste and Class in India,* p. 60.
5. Das, S., Purdah, *The Status of Indian Women,* pp. 52-53.
6. Mukherjee, Prabhati, *Hindu Women,: Normative Models.*
7. Joshi, Rama and Liddle, Joanne, op. cit., p. 60.
8. Desai, Neera and Maithreyi, Krishnaraj, *Women and Society in India.*
9. Ibid
10. Cf. Bakshi, S.R. and Bala, Kiran, op. cit., p. 186.
11. Das, S., op. cit., pp. 52-53.
12. Joshi, Rama and Liddle, Joanne, op. cit., pp. 59-60.
13. Cf. Bakshi, S.R. and Bala, Kiran, op. cit., p. 186.
14. Cf. *Census of India, 1911,* Vol. XXII, p. 128.
15. Ibid.

16. Singhi, N.K. 'Child Marriage in Rajasthan: A myth', Paper presented in 1995 in *Rajasthan Voluntary Health Association*, Jaipur.
17. Cf. Kapoor, Devendra Kumar, op. cit., pp. 49-50.
18. Majumdar, R.C., Pusalkar, A.D., Majumdar, A.K., op. cit., pp. 392-394.
19. Altekar, A.S., op. cit., p. 10.
20. Ibid., pp. 9-10.
21. *R.V.*, III. 55.16, Cf. Upadhyaya, B.S., op. cit., pp. 179-180.
22. *Y.V.*, VIII.1, Cf. Upadhyaya, B.S., op. cit., p. 180.
23. *A.V.*, XII3.17; 18; XI.5.8; Cf. Upadhyaya, B.S., op. cit., p. 180.
24. *R.V.*, X.85.9-22
    "अन्यामिच्छ प्रफर्व्य संजायां पत्या सृज।।"
    "सूर्या यत्पत्यें शंसंती मनसा सविताददात् ।। "
25. *A.V.*, X.85.46.
26. Altekar, A.S., op. cit.
27. *R.V.*, VII. 91.5, 6.
28. Altekar, A.S., op. cit., p. 32
29. *Vendidad*, 14, 15.
30. Altekar, A.S., op. cit., p. 348.
31. Ibid., pp. 340-348.
32. Altekar, op. cit., pp. vii & viii.
33. *B.D.S.*, I.1.19.
34. Altekar, op. cit., pp. vii & viii.
35. *V.D.S.*, XVII.59.
    "ऊर्ध्वं त्रिभ्यो वर्षेभ्यःपतिं विन्दत्तुल्यम।
    त्रीणि वर्षाणयुदीक्षेत कुमारी ऋतुमती सती।।"
36. *B.D.S.*, IV.1.14.
    "त्रीणि वर्षाणयुदीक्षेत कुमारी ऋतुमती सती।
    कुमारी ऋतुमती त्रीणि वर्षाणयुदीक्षेत।।"
    and also,
    B.D.S., IV.1.12-14
    "माता चैव पिता चैव ज्येष्ठो भ्राता तथैव च
    त्रयस्ते नरकं यान्ति दृष्टवा कन्यां रजस्वलाम।।"
37. *G.D.S.*, XVIII.20.
    "त्रीन्कुमारी ऋतूनतीत्य स्वयं युज्येतानिन्दितेन उत्सृज्य पिञयानलंकारान।"
38. *B.D.S.*, V.9.
    "तथैव कन्यां च मृतां प्राप्त यौवनां तुल्येन पुंसा प्राप्तगृहवत्तां दहेत्।"

39. *V.M.S.*, p. 766.
"त्रिंशद्वर्षः षोडशवर्षा भार्यां विन्देत नग्निकाम्।।"
and also,
Gobhil Griha Sutra, 3.4.6.
"नग्निकांतु वहेत्कन्यां यावन्नर्तुमती भवेत।।"
and, *Hiranyakeshi Griha Sutra*, I.19.2 Cf. Mishra, Jai Shankar, *Prachin Bharat Ka Samajik Itihaas*, p. 360.
40. *Gobhil Griha Sutra* III.4.6,
and also
Hiranyakeshi Griha Sutra, I.19.2.
"नग्निका सजाता ब्रह्मचारिणी।"
41. Matridatta, Cf. Altekar, A.S., op. cit., p. 52
"तस्माद्वस्त्राविक्षेपणार्हा नग्निका मैथुनार्हेत्यर्थ :।"
42. *Manu Smriti*, V.150, p. 167.
43. Ibid., IX.87, p. 288.
44. Ibid., IX.88, p. 288.
45. Ibid., III.56, 57, 58, 59, 60, 61, 62, p. 78.
46. Cf. Altekar, A.S., op. cit., pp. 56-57.
47. RSAB: MKJR., *Yama Smriti*, Cf. File No. C2/10, Prevention of marriages of children and persons of incompatible ages etc.
"कन्या द्वादश वर्षाणि याऽ प्रदत्ता वसेदगृहे। ब्रह्महत्या पितुस्यस्या :।।"
48. RSAB: *Yama Smriti*, III.21, 22 Cf. File No. C 2/10, Mehkama Khas, Jodhpur Records.
"अष्टवर्षा भवेद गौरी, नववर्षा तु रोहिणी
दशवर्षा भवेत्कन्या अत.ऊर्ध्व रजस्वला।
प्राप्ते तु दशमे वर्षे यस्तु कन्यां न यच्छति
मासि–मासि रजस्तस्याः पिता पिबति शोणितम्।।"
49. RSAB: MKJR., *Harit Smriti*, Cf. File No. C2/10.
"पितुर्गेहेतु या कन्या रजः पश्चत्यसंस्कृता।
साकन्या वृषलीज्ञेया तत्पतिर्वृषली पतिः।।"
50. RSAB: MKJR., *Marichi Smriti*, Cf. File No. C2/10.
"गौरीं ददन्नाक पृष्ठे बैकुंठं रोहिणी ददत्।
कन्यांददद ब्रह्मलोकं, रौरवन्तु रजस्वलाम्।।"
51. RSAB: MKJR., *Sankhya Smriti*, Cf. File No. C2/10.
"माता चैव पिता चैव ज्येष्ठ भ्राता तथैव च
त्रयस्ते नरकं यान्ति दृष्टवा कन्यां रजस्वलाम।।"
52. RSAB: MKJR., *Sankhya Smriti*, Cf. File No. C2/10.

"पितृ वेश्मनी या कन्या रजः पश्चत्य संस्कृताः।
तस्यां मृतायां नाशौचं कदाचिदपि शाम्यति।।"

53. Cf. *Rajasthan Patrika*, 28 June, 2000, p. 1; and 19 Nov. 2004, p. 12.
54. Vyas, Kailash Nath, Gehlot, Devendra Singh, op. cit., pp. 165-166.
55. Dubois, Abbe, J.A., *Hindu Manners, Customs and Ceremonies*, translated by Henry K. Beauchamp, III edition, Oxford, 1906, p. 214.
56. Thomas, P., *Hindu Religion, Customs and Manners*, D.B. Taraporewala Sons and Company Pvt. Ltd., Bombay, 1960, p. 62.
57. Papers relating to Infant Marriage and Enforced Widowhood in India, p. 178. Cf. Risley, *The People Of India*, p. 190.
58. *Census of India, 1901*, Vol. XXV, p. 89.
59. *Census of India, 1911*, p. 158.
60. Ibid; pp. 161-162.
61. Ibid.
62. *Census of India, 1911*, p. 164.
63. Ibid.
64. Kabra, S.G., "Child marriage in Rajasthan: a Myth", a paper presented in *Rajasthan Voluntary Health Association*.
65. Singhi, N.K., "Child marriage in Rajasthan: a Myth", a paper presented in *Rajasthan Voluntary Health Association*.
66. Kapur, Promilla, "Family Violence Against Girl Child" in *Girl Child and Family Violence*, op. cit, p. 18.
67. *Census of India*, 1911, p. 125.
68. Ibid.
69. For more details on this subject, please see Vyas, Kailash Nath and Gehlot, Devendra Singh, *Rajasthan ki Jation Ka Samajik evam Arthik Jiwan* op. cit.
70. Cf. *Census of India*, 1911.
71. Cf. Ibid.

4

Indigenous Reform Efforts

The history of social reforms in India, during the 19th century, is the history of contradictions and paradoxes, of liberalism and orthodox tendencies. A section of the educated Indians (mostly in English schools and colleges), impressed by the western ways, and infuriated by the constant criticism of Indian culture and social institutions by the Christian missionaries, wanted to do away with the social evils through active propaganda, demonstrations, newspaper columns and through government machinery. The other section, equally educated and proud of their motherland and believing in the cultural traditions, was totally against government's interference in the social affairs of their country. The first group was represented by Raja Ram Mohan Roy, Ishwar Chandra Vidyasagar, Keshab Chandra Sen, and many others; and the second group was led by Dayanand Saraswati and Lokmanya Bal Gangadhar Tilak. But it must be noted here, as the next pages will reveal, that Tilak was not against social reforms, but he was against the government's interference and believed that for a reform to be durable, it must grow from within. Tilak wanted political freedom first and opposed government's intervention in socio-religious institutions.

Apart from these developments going on in other parts of the country, the voices against the social evils, were raised in the Rajputana too. It is surprising as well as pleasant to note, that here in the Rajputana, reforms were initiated by reform organizations, e.g.,

Arya Samaj, the native rulers as well as various caste panchayats. This is in contrast to the established view of historiography, which depicts the native rulers as always indulging in war, wine and women and blames them to be insensitive and insouciant to the administration as well as social cause.

It is true that the works of Arya Samaj, Desh Hitaishini Sabha, Walterkrit Rajputra Hitkarini Sabha motivated the people as well as native rulers for further reforms, but much before the birth of these social organizations or their founders, the process of social reforms in northern India was started by Emperor Akbar and in the Rajputana by the caste organizations (for example the Pareek Brahmins of Jaipur) as well as its native rulers (like Sawai Jai Singh of Jaipur, Maharaja Bukht Singh and Vijay Singh of Jodhpur). The significance of these reform efforts, prior to the British period, lies in the fact that they were the result of a mature and well-thought-out policy, inspired by the spontaneous reformative zeal and free from any outside or external pressure or influence. Following is a record of the reform process, carried out in British India as well as in the various native States of Rajputana.

In the recorded annals of Indian history, the earliest individual effort, to do away with certain prevalent social evils like infanticide, child and unequal marriages, polygamy, sati, excessive indulgence in intoxicating drinks, etc., was perhaps made by Emperor Akbar[1], who issued orders against these malpractices as early as the 16th century. This is a lesser known fact, that in addition to his conquests and administrative organization, Akbar also aimed at, what Abul Fazal, his court historian, calls "the reformation of the manners of the people". Perhaps he was aware of the enormity of these problems and also the consequences which greatly undermined the position of women, in particular and therefore he tried to eradicate them. One of the aspects of his *Din-i-illahi*, which started in 1582, was that "members should not cohabit with pregnant, old and barren women; nor with girls under the age of puberty". This, clearly, was an attempt to restrict unequal or mismatched marriages, which were in vogue in India, from the ancient time. Similarly, to check the child and infant marriages and to discourage polygamy, he passed a regulation in 990 A.H.(Allahi Hizri), which stated that "boys were not to marry, before the age of 16, nor girls before 14, because the offsprings of early marriage were weak...no one was to marry more than one wife, except in cases of barrenness, but in all other cases the rule was, "one man and one wife...." It is surprising as well as pleasant to note that Akbar was also aware of the deplorable conditions of the widows and especially the child widows and therefore he ordered that "if widows like to remarry, they might do so", though this was against the ideas of the Hindus. In the same manner, to check the prevalent practice of sati, he ordered that, "a Hindu girl, whose husband had died before the marriage was consummated should not be burnt. If a Hindu woman wished to be burnt with her husband, they should not prevent her, but she should not be forced". These examples clearly reveal that Akbar was a far-sighted ruler, who for the benefit of his subjects, and more particularly for the women of the country, tried to make regulations to do away with certain prevalent social evils. This also shows that he had the courage to oppose as well as to stand against the popular practices, however old and however well-established they may be. In the absence of relevant historical records, it is difficult to ascertain what effect it had upon the lives of the widows, how many widows felt motivated to remarry and how many actually remarried, how many widows (and particularly the child widows) were thus saved from the funeral pyre, how far it was successful in checking the problems of polygamy and child and infant marriages, and how many lives of the female infants were thus saved by his kind-hearted and benevolent orders. But even then, the above mentioned orders of Akbar are of special significance to the students of history, as they bring out the humanitarian but hidden face of the Mughal monarch and prove that he took interest in the social affairs of his day and seriously thought about removing some of the glaring defects of the society of his times, much before the birth of Sawai Jai Singh of Jaipur, William Carey (the British missionary, who noticed infanticide in India first of all and raised his voice against it in 1794 A.D.), Raja Ram Mohan Roy, William Bentinck, Ishwar Chandra Vidyasagar, Keshab Chandra Sen, B.M. Malabari, Swami Dayanand Saraswati, etc. It is really pitiable that such drastic reform efforts of this noble monarch, could not find supporters, as the age in which he lived was ruled by conservative and orthodox tendencies and the people were not prepared to shed their age old inhibitions and taboos. These reforms, which he conceived, were far ahead of his times and consequently failed to capture public attention and imagination. But, it must be admitted here, that this noble gesture of Akbar – the great monarch, paved the way for future reforms. After full 257 years of the birth of his *Din-i-illahi,* the voice against child marriage and unequal marriage was raised once again in India, but this time it was started by the educated section of the Bengali society in Bengal.

In January 1839, Mahesh Chandra Deb,[2] a Bengali intellectual, presented a paper entitled 'A Sketch of the condition of the Hindoo Women' in the *Derozian Society for Acquisition of General Knowledge,* in which he presented the deplorable condition of the Indian women and talked about the ills of arranged marriage, child marriage, polygamy, seclusion and the ban on widow remarriage. "It is much to be regretted and no less to be wondered at," he observed, "that a subject of so much vital importance, so intimately connected with the welfare and regeneration of fallen unhappy India, should have so long remained untouched. It is equally a matter of great sorrow and astonishment that no powerful impulse has yet been given to the cause of these miserable and unhappy creatures; that no efficient project has yet been set on foot to ameliorate the condition of the Hindoo women...."Regarding child marriage, Deb remarked that, "we are married at an age when neither the graces of the mind nor of the body are sufficiently developed," and, "which entails the heaviest evils, moral and physical, upon the Hindoo women and crowns their unhappy situation."

The movement against child marriages, started first of all in Bengal, from the second half of the 19th century, though individual voices against it (as mentioned above) could be heard much before. The educated and the liberal section of Bengali society started the crusade against it and tried to awaken the masses by pointing out the abuses, caused by the child marriages. In 1850, *The Sarva-Shubhakari Patrika*[3] published first of all an article, in which the sad plight of child widows and child-mothers was dealt in detail and it asked its readers to ponder over their pitiable condition and pleaded for its abolition. In January, 1856, when the Hindu Widow's Remarriage Bill was on the anvil, more than four hundred enlightened citizens of Bengal, presented a petition to the Government praying for 'a General Marriage Law for the Natives' of comprehensive nature.[4] But no Act for a general reform of the system of marriage was then passed except the Hindu Widow's Remarriage Act and the government passed the matter in total silence. To bring this matter again into the public notice, Shyama Charan Shiromonee wrote *Balyavibaha Natak* in 1860.[5]

This cause was again taken by Ishwar Chandra Vidyasagar (1820-91), who strongly protested against consummation of child marriages. Vidyasagar, who believed not merely in the preaching of reforms but in putting them into practice, formulated a pledge to which he committed himself and which he expected his supporters and admirers to implement. One of the aspects of the pledge was that he would not allow his son to marry before he was eighteen or his daughter before she was eleven. He also proposed that it should be an offence for a man, to consummate marriage before his wife had had her first menses and as majority of the girls did not exhibit that symptom before they were thirteen, fourteen or fifteen years of age, the measure as suggested by him, would give larger, more real and more extensive protection than the Bill. At the same time, he believed such a measure could not be objected to on the ground of interfering with a religious observance.[6] The efforts of these reformers bore fruits and in 1846, a Law Commission was persuaded to make intercourse between husband and wife, below a given age, an offence. Accordingly, the Indian Penal Code of 1860, declared consummation, when the wife was below ten years of age, as rape and prescribed punishment extending to transportation for life.[7] The law as it ultimately came to be enacted, sought to prevent the sexual abuse of both married and unmarried women below a legally determined age. By raising the minimum age of consent (i.e., the legal age at which sexual relationships were deemed to have been consummated with the concurrence of the female), the Act marginally increased the scope of criminal law to punish the male sexual offender and at least theoretically sounded a warning to the protagonists of early marriage.

But this could not improve the lot of child-wives since they were trained from their childhood, by solemn precepts and overt examples to revere their husbands, to obey them meekly and to stand by them always and with such conditioned mindsets, they could not have thought of availing themselves of this law, despite whatever cruelty was perpetrated on them. In a society where female literary rates were quite low and where the traditional social structure had become too ossified to permit a reordering of gender relations, such amendments in law alone could not be expected to produce very satisfactory results. Thus, the above mentioned legislation was ineffectual, but it paved the way for fixing the age of marriage at a later stage.

In November 1870, Keshab Chandra Sen, another social reformer of Bengal and the President of the Indian Reform Association, decided to refer the question of marriageable age to the eminent medical-men of the country, for their opinion.[8] The medical authorities in Calcutta unanimously declared that 16 should be the minimum marriageable age of girls in India. Following is the opinion of doctors on this point:[9]

Name of the Doctor	*Min. Age*	*Proper Age*
Dr. C.C. Dey	14	-
Dr. T.E. Charles	14	-
Dr. A.V. White	15 or 16	-
Dr. M.L. Sircar	16	18
Dr. T.K. Bahadur	16	-
Dr. Norman Chevers	16	-
Dr. D.B. Smith	16	18 or 19
Dr. J. Evart	16	18 or 19
Dr. J. Fayrur	16	18 or 20
Dr. S.G. Chuckarbatty	16	21
Dr. A.R. Panduranga	20	-

Keshab Chandra Sen summed up the conclusion of the committee in these words, "the medical authorities in Calcutta almost unanimously declared that 16 is the minimum marriageable age of girls in India...but for the present at least it would be expedient to follow the provision in the Bill which makes 14 the minimum marriageable age of girls in this country; leaving it in the hands of time to develop this reform shortly and gradually into maturity and fullness".[10]

In July 1871, Dr. Mahendra Lal Sircar,[11] noted physician and founder of the Indian Science Association, published a paper on the earliest marriageable age of Indian girls in the *Calcutta Journal of Medicine* and strongly denounced child marriages 'on true physiological grounds'. He emphasized that at least on the basis of medical science it was possible to say that early signs of puberty in the female did not necessarily demand prompt marriage. On the contrary, it was premature marriage which in many cases, might hasten to produce an unnaturally early puberty and perhaps to moral laxness.

"We would deem it a misfortune to the country," he observed, "if the agitation inaugurated by Babu Keshab Chunder Sen, be allowed to subside without it's producing the desired effect upon the mind of the community, if the note of warning unanimously given by leading medical gentlemen of Calcutta be unheeded. We know the disastrous effect the custom has produced in the shape of deterioration of race and it will be culpable perversity on our part, if informed on the remedy we fail to apply it, through prejudice or pride". The works of Brahmo-Samajis under Keshab Chandra Sen, brought good results and in the Bill introduced by Sir James Stephen in the Legislative Council on 16 January 1872, 14 was laid down as the minimum marriageable age for girls. The Bill became an Act as Act III of 1872 or the Native Marriage Act (popularly known as the Civil Marriage Act) and forbade the marriage of girls below the age of 14 and boys below the age of 18.[12] This Act "abolished early marriage, made polygamy penal, sanctioned widow marriages and inter caste marriages for parties not coming under any of the existing marriage laws and not professing any of the current faiths". However, this Act was not applicable on the Hindus, the Muslims and other recognized faiths and as such had very limited impact on the Indian Society.[13] Inspired and influenced by the thoughts of Keshab, in 1873, a batch of youngmen, under the leadership of Nishikanto and Nabakanto Chattopadhyay[14] of Dacca, formed Balyabibaha Nibarini Sabha (Society for the prevention of child marriages) to oppose child marriages and also began the publication of a monthly journal called *Mahapap Balya Bibaha* or the great sin of child marriage. In 1877, some young progressive Brahmos organized a secret league, one of their pledges being "never to encourage marriage between young men below twenty-one and girls below sixteen".[15] In the same manner, the Mymensingh and Faridpur Education Committees[16] seriously considered the idea of debarring married men from taking the Entrance Examinations in 1878. But inspite of all these efforts, majority of the people remained indifferent, orthodox and conservative in their approach and attitude. However, one positive result that emanated from the early debate on marriage reform was perhaps a greater awareness of the evils attendant on premature marriage.

The question of child marriage again came in the forefront in the eighties of the nineteenth century, when on 15 August, 1884 Behramji M. Malabari (1853-1912),[17] a Parsee journalist, poet and philanthropist, published his famous notes on *Infant Marriage in India* and *Enforced Widowhood*. Malabari considered them to be allied social evils.[18] These 'notes' which were circulated among officials and private persons, British and Indian, marked the beginning of the All India social reform movement. Malabari believed that early marriage was sapping the vigour of the Hindu 'race'.[19] For the removal of early marriages, Malabari suggested that:[20]

(a) After five years, universities should not allow married students to appear at examinations.

(b) Heads of Government departments should give preference to unmarried men in making appointments.

(c) Materials, describing the evils of early marriage, be inserted in school text books by the Education department.

(d) A National Association for Social Reforms be created with the existing societies as branches and it should include most of the prominent members of the government from the Viceroy and Governors and beyond.

Malabari, on 18 August 1884, submitted a memorandum to the Government, in which he pointed out that infant marriage was the cause of many social grievances, including enforced widowhood.[21] According to him, it forbade the exercise of free will of the parties and resulted in physical defects and moral taints. Even in happy marriages, he believed, early consummation breaks down the constitution resulting into many diseases. The giving up of studies on the part of a boy husband, the birth of sickly children, the necessity of feeding too many mouths, poverty and dependence, a disorganized household, perhaps leading to sin on the early death of the husband, were some of its evident results. But its culmination was, he said, the addition of one more widow to the forty million already existing, and two or three orphans to the fraternity of unprotected infants. Social and economic evils apart, Malabari referred to a very obnoxious aspect of infant marriage, namely, the marriage of a girl of twelve or fifteen with a boy of eight or ten. Marriage was generally brought about by the father or the elder brother of the boy. Malabari argued that if the guardian happened to be a widower, one can guess the evil designs of such a marriage. "It is a criminal arrangement, leading to sin all round much to the suffering of the unfortunate girl who must in name remain the wife of the boy" – he remarked. To improve the conditions of life for widows, he asked the government to assure that all widows learn of their rights to remarry under the Widow Remarriage Act of 1856; to use its authority to protect widows from involuntary seclusion and "social ill-usage": and to prohibit priests from excommunicating anyone who assisted in a widow remarriage. Lacking the scholarly attainments of a Bhandarkar, the personal following and organizational skill of a Ranade, and the religious enthusiasm of a Keshab Chandra Sen, Malabari nevertheless knew what publicity and public opinion on behalf of reform could accomplish in India and in England. Most Indians, at that time, lacked the information about the injustices committed in the name of social and religious practices and Malabari provided them the details.

Malabari's 'notes' exploded like a bomb and virtually every social reformer in the country (whether known or unknown), supporters of orthodoxy of all descriptions, medical men, lawyers, princes, government servants, British administrators and public bodies (some long established and some created for the purpose of supporting or attacking his proposals) replied in favour or against his 'notes'. Some pointed to the ineffectiveness of Malabari's proposal to restrict college education to unmarried boys, others to the injustices of penalizing a boy for what his parents had arranged; some wanted to make early marriages illegal; others urged a law against premature consummation of the marriage. Many respondents took up related issues, such as ill-assorted or ill-matched or uneven marriages and polygamy and urged legislation in those areas. Thus, Malabari was successful in drawing the attention of the masses, towards some of the ills of the society and in creating a wave in favour of the social reforms. Majority of Indians who replied to the notes, favoured legislation or other government action of some sort to restrict infant marriages. The most thoughtful replies pointed to connections between widowhood and child marriage. For the first time the social reform movement attracted truly national attention, than did the once-a-year meetings of the Indian National Congress.

Through his prolific writing, through his passionate arguments, Malabari impressed eminent persons like M.G. Ranade, K.T. Tellang (Judge of the Bombay High Court), Dayaram Gidumal (an Assistant Judge at Ahmedabad), Sir R.G. Bhandarkar, Bipin Chandra Pal, and many others.[22] Regarding child marriage, M.G. Ranade expressed his opinion in the followings words:[23]

"After making all allowances it cannot be denied that Hindu society contracts very unfavourably with all other civilized races in both the points noted so prominently by Mr. Malabari. It is also not denied that early marriage leads to early consummation, and thence to the physical deterioration of the race, that it sits as a heavy weight on our rising generation, enchains their aspirations, denies them the romance and freedom of youth, cools their love of study, checks enterprise, and generally dwarfs their growth and fills the country with pauperism, bred of over population by weaklings, and sickly people and lastly it leads in many cases to all the horrors of early widowhood."

When the Government asked for Ranade's views on Malabari's Notes, he observed that "in the absence of a self-regulating power in the Hindu society, the only way to secure the emancipation of the Hindu community from this bondage to past ideas is to withdraw one by one those fetters of so-called religious injunctions and turn them into civil restraints, which are more amenable to change and adaptation".[24] To remove the evil of child marriage, Ranade suggested State action on the following lines:

(a) That minimum marriageable age both for boys and girls be fixed by law, not compulsory in the sense of annulling marriages contracted before attaining the said limits, but only permissive in the sense of leaving the parties concerned, freedom to question the binding character of the marriage so contracted – the age limit to be 16 to 18 for boys, and 10 to 12 for girls, subject to exception in particular castes and localities.

(b) That municipal and local boards should be empowered to certify ages and that the parties concerned should be required to obtain licenses from these boards, before marriages are to be solemnized.

(c) That the universities should, after a reasonable notice confine their honours and distinctions to those who, in addition to the other qualifications, submit the condition of remaining single during their college or school course.

(d) That the Penal Code be amended so far as to declare sexual intercourse with a girl under 14 to be rape.

(e) That men of 45 upwards should be prohibited by law from marrying young virgins, so also the marriage of young men with girls older than themselves should be prohibited as being unnatural and mischievous.

(f) That a second marriage during the lifetime of the first wife should be allowed only if there be in the first wife one of the defects in view of which the *Shastras* sanctioned such a marriage. These defects were quarrelsomeness, addiction to such vices as drink, or opium or adultery, existence of a contagious disease, barrenness or giving birth only to female children.

M.G. Ranade advocated the policy of invoking the assistance of the State to raise the age of consent from 10 to 12. But there was considerable opposition to this proposal from the orthodox quarters and particularly from persons of the school of thought who were coming to the forefront under the leadership of Bal Gangadhar Tilak. Tilak attacked it vehemently in his papers, the *Kesari* and the *Mahratta*. Tilak, while emphatically not unfriendly to social reform, believed in the imperative necessity of checking, from the larger national stand-point, the disintegrating forces, by fostering a due sense of pride in and respect for the social and religious institutions of the people. Tilak was for the blending of the old culture and the new. He strongly resented State interference for the simple reason that reform to be durable, must be a growth from within.[25] He insisted that social reforms should come from within by the education of public opinion and should not be imposed upon the people by any act of coercion.

In contrast to Tilak's views, Ranade held that regulation of the age of marriage was in every country "a part of its national jurisprudence". He rejected the arguement that the State could not interfere with the victimized party, that is widows or infant brides, as they did not complain. "Perhaps the worst effect of injustice," he wrote, "is that it depresses the downtrodden victims to such an extent that they lick the hand of the oppressors". In his lecture on 'State Legislation in Social Matters',[26] delivered in 1885, Ranade defended his position by stating that "the State in its collective capacity represents the power, the wisdom, the mercy and charity of its best citizens. What a single man, or a combination of men, can best do on their own account, that the State may not do, but the State cannot shirk its duty if it sees its way to remedy evils, which no private combinations of men can check adequately or which it can deal with more speedily and effectively than any private combination of men can do". And as far as Tilak's objection against "external help in internal matters" is concerned, Ranade believed that "the initiation is to be our own, and based chiefly upon the example of our venerated past, and dictated by the sense of the most representative and enlightened men in the community, and all that is sought at the hands of the foreigners is to give to this responsible sense, as embodied in the practices and usages of the respectable classes, the force and the sanction of law".

Against Tilak's stand on the revival of old institutions, Ranade said, "when we are asked to revive old institutions, people are very vague as to the time that they have in view". "What shall we revive?" Ranade asked.[27] "Shall we revive the old habits of our people when the most sacred of our caste indulged in all the abominations as we now understand them, of animal food and drink which exhausted every section of our country's zoology and botany? The god of those days ate and drank forbidden things to excess, in a way no revivalist now will venture to recommend. Shall we revive the twelve forms of sons or eight forms of marriage which included capture and recognized mixed and illegitimate intercourse? Shall we revive the *niyoga* system of procreating sons on our brothers' wives when widowed?... Shall we revive the *sati* and infanticide customs or the flinging of living men into the rivers or over rocks or hook swinging or the crushing beneath Jagannath's car? Shall we revive the custom of many husbands to one wife or many wives to one husband?" Ranade aptly remarked that "in a living organization as society is, no revival is possible. The dead and the buried or burnt are dead, buried and burnt once for all and the dead past cannot, therefore, be revived except by a reformation of the old materials into new organized beings. If revival is impossible reformation is the only alternative open to sensible people." Thus, adaptation to new conditions of life and renunciation of old practices, revision of many traditional ways and time honoured conventions were considered by Ranade as of immediate importance in order to bring about healthy progress. While there was nothing wrong in seeking inspiration from the past to sustain self-confidence, our reverence for the past must not blind us to present deficiencies in our character – that was his insistence.

The reform of early marriages was also considered by the Indian National Social Conference. The Conference which came in existence in 1887, focused the attention of the leading Indian intellectuals on matters relating to social reforms. In its third annual session at Bombay in 1889, the Conference passed the following resolution:[28]

"That in the opinion of this Conference, the distinction made by the penal code, between the general age of consent (12 years) laid down in section 90 and the special age prescribed in clause 5 and the exception in section 375, is both unnecessary and indefensible, and that with a view to prevent early completion of marriages which leads to the impairment of physical health of both husband and wife, and to the growth of a weakly progeny, cohabitation before the wife is twelve years old should be punishable as a criminal offence and that every effort should be made by awakening public conscience to the grave dangers incurred to postpone the completion of marriage till the age of 14 at least, as being in accordance with the dictates of our ancient medical works and modern science and countenanced by the approved sentiment and practice of the country. That every member joining any of the Social Reform Associations connected with this Conference should be asked to pledge himself not to complete in his own case or in the case of his children, who are minors, any marriages before the bride completes her 14th year."

In its fourth session held in 1890, the Indian National Social Conference passed the following resolution:[29]

".... That this conference is of the opinion that the well-being of the community demands that the practice of child marriage be discouraged by the public sentiment, and that within the sphere of various castes and communities, strenuous efforts be made to postpone the celebration of marriage rites till 12 in the case of girls and 18 in the case of boys and the consummation of the marriage till after they attain the age of 14 and 20, respectively, and the members of the various social associations in the country should pledge themselves to see that these limits of age are realized in actual practice and public opinion educated to advance these limits still higher."

To evoke public opinion in support of the movement for abolition of early marriage some reform associations were also formed in different parts of India.[30] Such organizations were the Poona Social Reform Association, Indian Reform Association (in Calcutta), Social Reform Association, Chikurde (in Satara), Indian Friends Association (Social Reform Branch) in Sholapur, Hindu Social Reform Association and Social Reform Association (in Bangalore), Hindu Social Reform Association (in Chikakol), Hindu Social Reform Association (in Gulbarga), Hindu Marriage Association (in Madras) Hindu Social Reform Association in Sindh, Madras Reform Association, Hindu Social Reformer (in Mangalore),

Hindu Social Reform Association (in Secundarabad), The Sanmarga Samaj at Bellary and the Berar Social Reform Association.

The efforts of the early reformers brought good results and soon many other enlightened scholars like Sir R.G. Bhandarkar, K.T. Tellang, G.G. Agarkar, Sir T. Madhava Rao, J.R. Phule, Deewan Bahadur R. Raghunath Rao, etc., supported the Bill.

But the policy of the British Government in India at that time was to move with great caution. Lord Ripon, in 1884,[31] wrote to Malabari that the Government would have to move slowly in connection with his appeal. Similarly, the official inquiry (in 1886) under Lord Dufferin's[32] administration, to determine whether legislation should be introduced or not expressed that "the reforms of Malabari, must be left to the improving influences of time, and to the gradual operation of the mental and moral development of the people by the spread of education". The reasoning behind the decision not to act was that the 'evils', which Malabari described did not fall under existing civil or criminal law, nor were the courts being asked to enforce the social customs productive of those evils. Moreover, it was also felt that nothing could be done within the "ordinary machinery" at the government's disposal; and the legislature should refrain from enacting new laws and thereby "place itself in direct antagonism to social opinion".

In view of the attitude of non-interference in matters of social reform by the Government of India, Malabari, in accordance with the suggestion of Prof. Max Muller,[33] decided to appeal to the people of England, particularly its women. He went there thrice and by his speeches and writings tried his best to arouse public sympathy. He was actively helped there by the National Indian Association in Aid of Social Progress and Female Education in India', established in 1871 by Miss Marry Carpenter.[34] It arranged for his public appearance and its Journal *The Indian Magazine and Review* brought to public notice the discussions which Malabari had started on the question of early marriage and reform. To arouse the conscience of the educated class of England, Malabari, in 1890, published *An Appeal on Behalf of the Daughters of India* and succeeded in creating a strong public opinion in England. Influenced by his writing skills, his arguments, his untiring zeal, a committee was formed in England, under the auspices of the Association, which included eminent persons like Lord North-brook, Lord Dufferin, Lord Tennyson, Herbert Spencer, Max Muller, James Bryce, etc.

While Malabari was in England, K.T. Tellang, one of the reformers, kept the fire burning and sought to translate the growing national interest in social legislation into proposals more realistic and workable than those of the "notes". He believed that "reform is most urgently called for in regard to the time of consummation and not so much in regard to the time of marriage(sic)."[35] Taking a cue from this, Dayaram Gidumal published a pamphlet which concentrated attention on the Indian Penal Code instead of on caste and family customs. The code incorporated an earlier Age of Consent Act, passed without much opposition in 1860 at the urging of Ishwar Chandra Vidyasagar, which established ten as the age of a girl below which sexual intercourse with her was regarded as rape. Gidumal proposed that there be enacted an amendment to the Penal Code raising the age of consent to 12, for married and unmarried girls.

In 1890, fifty-five lady doctors practicing in different parts of India, appealed to the Viceroy to pass an Act prohibiting the consummation of marriage with girls under fourteen.[36] A petition, on similar lines, from two-thousand Indian women was also sent to Queen Victoria.[37] Supporters of the age of consent Bill, belonging to different parts of the country and various walks of life, gradually grew in numbers. On 15 February 1891 a committee was formed in Calcutta to work for the Bill.[38] The committee sent a memorial to the Government of India signed by 8,000 persons, amongst whom were priests, landlords, lawyers, medical men, engineers, architects, traders, merchants, manufacturers, public and private servants.

In Calcutta, 151 educated ladies of different faiths, Hindus, Brahmos, Muslims, Christians and Buddhists, acted together to support the Bill. In Bihar, Raja Har Ballabh Narayan Singh of Sonbarsa took the lead in supporting this measure and there were many leading families of Patna, Bhagalpur and some other places in favour of it. Half a dozen professors of the Ravenshaw College, Cuttack, supported the Bill.

In Bombay, 514 ladies of the Arya Mahila Samaj supported the Bill. It was also supported by Anjuman-I-Islam of Bombay, Aryan Ladies Association of Poona and Nagpur. In the North-western provinces and in Oudh, the Bill was supported by Sir Syed Ahmed Khan and many prominent persons of Benaras, Agra and Aligarh. In Lahore, representatives of important religious organizations like the Singh-Sabha, the Sanatan Dharma Sabha, and the Arya Samaj expressed views in favour of this measure.

The growing public opinion in support of the Age of Consent Bill helped the Government to place it before the Viceroy's Council in 1891. Several factors were responsible for this shift in policy, which had not existed five years before, when Malabari presented his proposals in his famous "notes". First, the attitude of the British government had changed as it was now ready to take a pro-reform stand, under pressure from enlightened individuals, social organizations and newspapers interested in welfare of the Indians. Second, the fact that the Bill was not a major innovation in the law but was an amendment in the existing Code, made the official stand easier to defend. Third, the Indian opinion favouring the legislation had gained strength from 1886 (i.e., after the Rukhmabai case)[39] and the moderate leaders were also demanding government intervention. Sir Andrew Scoble, who introduced the Bill in the council, held that it was the right and duty of the State to interfere for the protection of any class of its subjects.[40] "It is said," he remarked,[41] "that the offence (of premature sexual intercourse with child brides) when committed by a husband against the wife, ought not to be classed as rape and should be visited by a limited punishment. I do not think it is desirable that the gravity of the offence should be minimized in this way... It is an offence affecting the wife not as wife but as human creature..." When the Bill was presented in the Viceroy's council, it was supported by the majority of the Indian members, on grounds of humanitarianism. The enlightened Indian members believed that "that the Proposed Act was not a measure of social reform but merely seeks to remove a glaring defect in the criminal law(sic)".[42]

When this was the state of affairs in British India, the Native States could not keep themselves aloof from the main current and it is interesting to note, that some of them, like the Maharaja of Travancore and that of Bhinga, gave their moral support to the Age of Consent Bill.[43] This is in contrast to the prevalent notion that the native rulers were apathetic, insouciant or insensitive to the social cause, as was depicted by the records of the English officers. On the other hand, a strong urge for social reforms, was seen in them, for the Bill was greatly supported by the Raja of Bhinga and the Maharaja of Travancore.

The Maharaja of Travancore, expressed his views in these words "no Hindu who has at heart the real welfare of his community will expect the government to shut their eyes to the grossest outrages on humanity. That the Bill, if passed, may be felt as an outrage on orthodox susceptibilities of the Hindus, is an imaginary anxiety, with no real ground to stand on". Similarly, the Raja of Bhinga observed that "the sooner a stop is put to these gross outrages on humanity, the better for the country".

Supported by the educated section and some of the native States, on 19 March 1891, the Bill was passed as Act X of 1891 and by it the age of consent of marriage of girls was raised from ten to twelve. This Act boosted the spirits of the enlightened persons and was a signal for them to better the lot of womenfolk by saving them from oppressive social customs. This also infused a spirit of liberalism in many royal courts of British India. In 1893, the Government of Mysore (GoM) rejected the will of majority of representatives of the Mysore Assembly who opposed the Infant Marriage Regulation, declaring that "the regulation is in some quarters regarded as an undue interference with the liberty of the subjects, but [general sentiment] demands the abolition under the authority of law of certain usages which are as much opposed to the spirit of the Hindu *Shastras* as to the best interests of society". The Maharaja of Mysore, passed an Act in 1894, which "intended to put a stop to marriages of girls below eight years of age and ill-assorted marriages of young girls below fourteen with old men above fifty".[44] Thus a person who brought about the marriage of an infant girl, that is a girl who had not completed eight years, or aided or abetted such a marriage, or any man over eighteen years of age who married an infant girl was liable to a prosecution sanctioned by the government, to be punished with simple imprisonment up to six months. Similarly in 1904, the Baroda Early Marriage Prevention Act was passed, which went a step further by laying down twelve as the minimum age of a girl at the time of marriage.[45] In order to respect public sentiment on the subject and to avoid unnecessary inconvenience and embarrassment to the public, this Act provided that if the guardians of a minor girl (i.e., one who had not completed her twelfth year) whose age was above nine desired to get her married, they might do so with the permission of a tribunal consisting of the local sub-judge and three assessors of the petitioner's caste. The parents had to satisfy the tribunal that if the marriage of the minor girl was not allowed, it would probably not take place at all or not within one year of the bride attaining maturity, or that the parents and guardians of the girl were not likely, owing to old age or infirmity, to survive until she came of age and that she had no other guardian, or that inevitable difficulties of a similar nature were likely to occur. The tribunal if satisfied could grant permission for the celebration of marriage before the girl was twelve. In order that this concession might not be abused, it was provided that if the sub-judge disagreed with the assessors the case should be referred to the district judge and his decision was to be final. Encouraged by the works of other States, Indore State legally regulated the age at marriage in 1918 by prescribing fourteen years and twelve years as minimum marriageable ages for a boy and a girl respectively.[46]

By the beginning of the 20th century, public conscience had been aroused more strongly than before, against the ills of early marriage. In the Census Report of 1911,[47] it was observed that "the practice has been denounced by many social reformers since Malabari opened the campaign a quarter of a century ago; and the Social Conference which holds its meetings annually in connection with the National Congress has made the abolition of child marriage one of the leading plants in its platform. It is... strongly discouraged by the Brahmos in Bengal and the *Aryas* in Northern India. The more enlightened members of the higher castes, who do not allow widows to remarry, are beginning to realize how wrong it is to expose their daughters to the risk of lifelong widowhood, and a feeling against infant marriage is thus springing up amongst them."

The problem of child marriage was again projected for British India, by Lala Girdhari Lal in 1921.[48] As earlier, government expressed the view that, due to backward social conditions in the country, initiative in the matter should come from a private individual, rather than from the government. In February 1922, Rai Bahadur Bakshi Sohanlal moved a Bill in the Assembly to raise the age of consent in both marital and extra-marital cases to fourteen.[49] When the Bill was referred to the provincial governments for opinion some were lukewarm, other governments like that of Bihar and Orissa, the Central Province, Berar and Bengal were against it and only the Bombay and the U.P. governments hailed the proposition with enthusiasm.

The Government of India accordingly did not allow the Bill in the next session (September, 1922). The matter was again taken up in the Assembly in 1924; this time by Sir Hari Singh Gour. The select committee to which the Bill was referred allowed the age to be raised to fourteen in extra-marital cases but reduced it to thirteen for marital consummation.[50] The legislators were not satisfied by the

Bill as it emerged from the select committee, and in spite of strong governmental opposition, raised the age to sixteen in extra-marital and fourteen in marital cases.[51] The government did not allow the Bill to go through; instead it presented a new Bill in September 1925, fixing fourteen as the age in extra-marital cases and thirteen in marital cases. The House was not however satisfied, and Sir Hari Singh Gour again pleaded in 1927, as the Bill was thrown out in 1924. An Age of Consent Committee, popularly known as the Joshi Committee, was thereupon appointed to go into the matter in detail. The committee recommended that the age be raised to fifteen in marital cases. Consummation before fifteen was to be known as "marital misbehaviour" and the offender was to be punished with imprisonment of either description for ten years and a fine when the wife was under twelve years of age, and for one year or a fine or both when she was between twelve and fifteen. In extra-marital cases the age was to be raised to eighteen. In the case of any sex relation with a girl under sixteen, the offender was to be punished with transportation or imprisonment for ten years. If the girl was above sixteen and if she consented, the imprisonment could be extended to two years with or without a fine. To prevent premature consummation the committee further recommended that the marriage of a girl under fourteen should be prohibited and penalized. The Government did not revise the age of consent, but steps were taken to fix the minimum age for marriages.

In pursuance of this, the 'Child Marriage Restraint Act' was passed in 1929. Har Bilas Sarda, whose contribution has been discussed in next pages, played a significant role in the passing of this Act and because of the efforts of Sarda, this Act is popularly known as Sarda Act. According to this Act a male under 18 years of age or a female under 14 was considered a child.[52] "Whoever being a male above 18 years of age and below 21, contracts the child marriage shall be punishable with fine which may extend to 1000 rupees". And if he was above 21 he could be punished with simple imprisonment extending to one month, or fine, of Rs 1,000 or both. Likewise, "whoever performs, conducts or directs any child marriage shall be punishable with simple imprisonment which may extend to one month, or with fine which may extend to 1,000 rupees or with both, unless he proves that he had reasons to believe that the marriage was not a child marriage. The inherent defects of the Act for its successful operation were that it did not make child marriage a cognizable offence and no action could be taken by the government. for its breach unless a complaint was made within one year of the solemnization of the marriage". Secondly, such a complaint had to be lodged in a Court of a Presidency Magistrate or a District Magistrate, and, "at any time after examining the complaint and before issuing process for compelling the attendance of the accused, the Court shall, except for reasons to be recorded in writing, require the complaint to execute a bond, with or without securities, for a sum not exceeding one hundred rupees, as security for the payment of any compensation which the complaint may be directed to pay; ... and if such security is not furnished within such reasonable time as the court may fix, the complaint shall be dismissed. According to the Amended Act of 1938 the court may, if satisfied from information laid before it through a complaint or otherwise, that child marriage in contravention of this Act has been arranged or is about to be solemnized, issue an injunction against any of the persons prohibiting such marriage, after giving notice to such a person to appear in person or by a pleader and to show cause against the issue of the injunction". "Whoever disobeys such injunction . shall be punished with imprisonment of either description for a term which may extend to three months, or with a fine which may extend to 1,000 rupees or with both".

In spite of shortcomings, the Child Marriage Restraint Act of 1929, more popularly known as Sarda Act, became a milestone in the social history of India. It not only provided solace to hundreds and thousands of child-brides, but it also became a landmark, which motivated and guided the reform efforts in the Princely States of India as well as that of Rajasthan. In different corners of the country, this Act was presented as a *nazeer*, as an example and the people requested their rulers to frame rules on the same lines, and made child marriages a penal offence. In the next pages, an effort is made to study the reform process as carried out by the rulers as well as various social and caste organizations in the Rajputana, to put a stop to the practice of child marriages and female infanticide.

II
Role of Desh Hitaishini Sabha

Social development and reform efforts in British India deeply influenced the native States of the Rajputana. It is significant here to note that the efforts to purge the society from social evils, started much before the commencement of social reform movement in Bengal, much before the arrival of British East India company in India and much before the birth of the reformative spirit of Sawai Jai Singh III of Jaipur. As we shall see in the next pages, the earliest of the efforts to put an end to certain social evils was undertaken by the Pareek Brahmins of Sanganer (Jaipur), who, as early as Samvat 1600, framed certain rules to check the practice of spending heavily on the occasions of marriages. The Pareek Brahmins of Sanganer (Jaipur), fixed a *maryada* i.e., limit on the marriage-expenses and made it very clear by writing it in black and white and distributing the copies of the agreement among Pareeks of other regions. But it must also be made clear here, that the reform efforts of the Pareeks of Jaipur were directed towards their own betterment and were made obligatory on Pareek community alone.

Moreover, the efforts of certain enlightened rulers of the Rajputana (like Sawai Jai Singh III of Jaipur, Maharaja Bukht Singh and Vijay Singh of Jodhpur), created an atmosphere which was conducive to the social reform process. The examples set up by them paved the way for future reforms, as the cue was picked up by the native rulers and different social or caste organizations.

The first step in this direction, was taken up by the State of Mewar when in 1877, Maharana Sajjan Singh convened a meeting at Udaipur with the intention of adopting rules to regulate marriage expenses in Mewar.[53] It was attended by 32 Chiefs and State officials and resulted in the formation of the Desh Hitaishini Sabha (now onwards Sabha) on the 2nd of July, 1877. The aim of the Sabha, as specified at its inception, was to regulate marriage expenses of the Rajputs, and to fix the tyag amounts, given to Charans and Bhats on the occasions of marriages, and to restrict the practice of polygamy prevalent in the upper sections of the society.

As we have seen in Chapter II that the system of dowry, the pressure of performing marriages with grandeur, coupled with other socio-political and economic factors, forced the parents to kill their new born babies. Some of the enlightened rulers of the Rajputana, understanding the gravity of the situation, tried to put an end to these social evils, though it is a matter of debate as to how far their efforts were successful in curbing these evils. The efforts of Sawai Jai Singh III of Jaipur, Maharaja Bukht Singh and Vijay Singh of Jodhpur as well as the efforts of British officers have been discussed in detail in Chapter 2 and Chapter 5, to have a clear picture of the-then social conditions as well as of their reformative zeal. In order to put an end to this heinous practice, they tried to regulate the marriage expenditure and also restrict the movements of Charans and Bhats to their respective territories besides prescribing other harsh punishments. Their efforts had the desired effect and slowly and gradually the incidents of female infanticide started declining.

The Sabha also worked on the same lines and framed rules, limiting the expenditure done on the occasions of marriages, to facilitate the parents to make arrangements for the marriage of their sons and daughters, without any difficulty. Similarly, the Sabha also framed rules for restricting the practice of polygamy, prevailing amongst Rajputs, Brahmans and Mahajans.[54] It was laid down that only those Rajputs, whose annual income exceeded Rs 500 were to give tyag to the Charans, Bhats, etc., and even in that circumstance, the amount given as tyag, was not to exceed 10 per cent of the total annual income. On the occasion of the marriage of the eldest son or daughter, a Rajput would spend only 25 per cent of the total annual income. On the marriage of other sons, other than the eldest, a Rajput would spend 10 per cent of the total annual income and 1 per cent of the total expenditure on tyag.

According to the rules laid down by the Sabha, tyag was to be given to only those Charans and Bhats, who were the residents of the State, in which the marriage was being solemnized and not to those who gathered from outside the State. It was also laid down that the Brahmans and the Mahajans could spend 25 per cent of their annual income on the occasions of marriages. They could also marry up to the age of 40, provided that they did not have any issue from the first wife. Permission of a third wife was given to the Rajputs, till they were 45 years of age and if they had no issues from the previous marriages. Those who wished to remarry, after the prescribed age limit, were to take prior permission from the Sabha.

In 1879, the Udaipur Durbar asked the Political Agent to issue orders to other native States, to restrict the movements of Charans and Bhats, living in their territories and stop them from entering into Mewar, for the purpose of getting tyag from there.[55] The Udaipur Durbar also told the Political Agent that they have ordered their Charans and Bhats, not to go to foreign territories, for the above mentioned purpose. The Political Agent, issued orders for it asking the native States and the British officers to do the needful; but the

British government did not show much interest in it, as it considered it to be a problem of the Rajput rulers.

The importance of Sabha lies in the fact that the need to curtail the expenditure on marriages among Rajputs and its relation with the evil of female infanticide, was also felt by it and an attempt was made to regulate it. Similarly, those Rajputs who were poor, were exempted from giving tyag to Charans and Bhats. It is difficult to say, whether these reforms were self-inspired or were influenced by the British officers as there are no records available. M.S. Jain, however opined that, Shyamal Das, the court historian of Mewar Durbar, had deliberately kept quiet on the birth, the functions and the rules of the Sabha, even after being a member of it.[56] His loyalty, according to Jain, towards his British masters, stopped him from giving much information in that respect. Had he written much about the Sabha, the truth about the originality of Walterkrit Rajputra Hitkarini Sabha, as far as its rules were concerned, would have appeared before the public and could possibly belittle the aura of Walter, observes Jain.

It is significant to note that much before the birth of Sabha, some of the rulers of different States, did try to do away with the practice of female infanticide and feeling that the extortionous demands of Charans and Bhats was one of the main causes of it, tried to restrict their movements within the territory, to which they belonged. They also tried to regulate the heavy expenditure incurred on the occasion of marriage and also fixed the amount of tyag, which was to be given to Charans and Bhats on joyful occasions. But none of them tried to put an end to the prevalent practice of polygamy, which was widely in practice in the upper classes of the society. Here lies the real significance of Sabha, as its efforts to put restrictions upon polygamy, were first of its kind in the written history of the Rajputana. Though Arya Samaj denounced polygamy much before the Sabha and did not support it under any circumstance, yet it must be noted here that the efforts of Arya Samaj did not have the legal force behind them, as they were not empowered by the authority of the State, whereas the Sabha was an official body and its rules were made obligatory on the upper sections of the society. The Sabha allowed polygamy, only in case, where a male issue could not be begot from the previous marriage or marriages. If seen from the eyes of the feminists and social activists of the 20th and the 21st century, this restriction could look disturbing, insulting and offensive, as it puts the entire blame of being barren or of producing "daughters only" on the mothers and allows the father to enter into a new matrimonial relationship. But if we take into consideration the socio- political, religious and economic situations, it would appear as revolutionary, and a far-sighted effort to put an end to the practice of polygamy.

The formation of the Sabha proved to be crucial to the reform movement in the Rajputana, as it was another attempt from the side of the rulers, to set things right and to put an end to certain social evils. It generated another wave of reform, and inspired the enlightened people to activate themselves for the development of their communities. The establishment of the Sabha was an important move and almost after a decade, it was followed by the Walter Krit Rajputra Hitkarini Sabha (now onwards, WKRHS), which was established by a British Officer. The WKRHS was formulated by Col. Walter, who was the Officiating Agent to the Governor General for the States of the Rajputana in 1888; and in the second meeting of the committee members, which commenced from 15th to 24th of February, 1889 at Ajmer,[57] this organization came to be known as WKRHS.

Col. Walter, who had spent almost the whole of his official life in the Rajputana, also felt that there was an urgent necessity for framing rules, whereby the expenses of marriages and funerals among Rajputs could be curtailed. His long experience had convinced him that one of the evils resulting from the unnecessary heavy expenditure in marriages was female infanticide and that the adoption of rules whereby such expenses were regulated would result in the abolition of this evil. Though attempts were made from time to time in the Rajputana yet they had been ineffective as there was no uniformity of the rules, in different States.

In October 1887, Col. Walter, addressed a circular to all political officers, on the subject of the adoption of a set of rules for regulating the expenses of marriages amongst Rajputs and suggested that a large representative committee should assemble at Ajmer, for the settlement of the above mentioned issue. The members of this committee were to consist of one official, one leading Jagirdar and one Charan from each State. His suggestion met with the "heartiest approval" of every ruling chief in the Rajputana, with the exception of the Maharawal of Banswara, who informed Lieutenant Pinhey that he was unable to find any suitable person either to represent the Durbar or the Charans of Banswara.

During his winter tour, Col. Walter, personally discussed this and many other questions, with the chiefs of the States and they expressed a wish that some measure for curtailing excessive expenditure at funerals as well as marriages should be considered at the meeting. The Maharao Raja of Bundi showed great interest in the proposals of Walter and was the first to suggest of determining the minimum age for marriages of boys and girls in order to impose a check on child marriages. The Maharao Raja of Bundi in 1888, in his communications to Col. Walter, suggested desirable marriageable ages of bride and bridegroom as 14 and 18 years respectively. Col. Walter took up the cue and incorporated it in his speech at a State Banquet given by His Highness, the Maharaja of Jaipur. He also stated the importance of a voluntary suggestion by a native prince and described it as "the greatest social reform that could be introduced into the Hindu Society in India".

The representatives of the States met at Ajmer and formed a committee, which began its proceedings on Monday, the 5th of March, 1888, and continued its sittings throughout the week. Col. Walter was especially anxious that whatever decision was arrived at, should be unanimous, and that the various questions should be settled by the delegates themselves untrammeled by the presence of a British officer. At the same time, he assured them that whenever they desired, he was willing and ready to help them with his advice, and on several occasions, deputants waited on him to discuss matters in which they needed his help.

On the morning of Saturday the 10th of March, 1888, Col. Walter and Col. Trevor, the Commissioner of Ajmer, proceeded to the Daulat Bagh, where 40 delegates, had assembled.[58] The important document, "which was drawn up entirely by the representatives themselves" was read out and the representatives told Col. Walter that it was a unanimous decision of all and that they accept every rule, mentioned in the document.

When this part of the ceremony was over, Kavi Raj Shyamal Das, the historian, genealogist and bard of Mewar, who was respected all over the Rajputana, thanked Col. Walter and the British government on behalf of all the delegates, for the meeting and for settling once and for all the vexed question of tyag[59] and expressed his disappointment over Col. Walter's leaving for England and prayed the British government to give an extension to his service in India. In all, twenty-two (22) rules were made by the committee, which are as follows:[60]

Rule No. 1: If the marriage is that of the Thakur himself, or an eldest son, or a daughter, the amount to be spent was fixed as under:

(a) When the value of the Estate was above Rs 20,000; not more than 1/4th of the annual income was to be spent.

(b) When the rental was below Rs 20,000 but was not less than Rs 10,000 not more than 1/3rd of the annual income was to be spent.

(c) When the rental was below Rs 10,000 but was not less than Rs 1000; not more than ½ (half) of the annual income was to be spent.

(d) When the income was below Rs 1000; not more than 2/3rd of the annual income was to be spent.

It was laid down that the above limits were in no case to be exceeded, but one could spend less if he so wished.

Rule No. 2: Seeing that the disputes arise regarding the gifts, which the girl's father sends to the father of the groom; it was laid down that the sending of *tika* (i.e., presents given on engagements) should be altogether stopped. However, the customary presents of opium, betel leaves, etc., which were sent on the occasion of the betrothal, were to continue, but the engagement itself was to be arranged by the groom's father.

Rule No. 3: Of the sum to be spent on tyag under Rule 1, Rs 9, local currency per cent, on the annual income of the Estate, was to be distributed as present, by the father of the bridegroom, among the Charans, Raos, Dholis, etc., in the proportions fixed by the custom prevailing in each State. The share of this payment which the Dholis would receive, was inclusive of the amount given on account of *ghur-charhi*. Except the above percentage, the fathers of the young couple were not to give any other item to Charans, Raos, and Dholis, on account of marriage.

Rule No. 4: Persons who held property valued at less than Rs 500 would pay nothing. When the property was worth Rs 500 to Rs 1000, the amounts to be given as tyag or presents to the Charans, etc., would be half of those specified in Rule 3.

Rule No. 5: A list would be made of the Charans, Raos, Dholis etc., attending the celebrations, and the day after the completion of the marriage rite, they would be paid their shares, and would be dismissed to their homes.

Rule No. 6: Only the Charans, Raos, Dholis, etc., who were residents of the territory in which the marriage was taking place, were entitled to the receipts of presents. Those of foreign territory were forbidden to come. It was also laid down that only the father of the bridegroom would make the payment; the father of the bride was liable to pay nothing.

Rule No. 7: In the case of the marriage of sons other than the eldest, and of brothers of the Thakur, who were dependent for support on the latter, the expenditure would be 1/10th of that specified in Rule 1, and the amount to be distributed as tyag, one per cent on the income of the Estate.

Rule No. 8: If sons and brothers were allowed separate maintenance, the expense would be calculated on what the Estate allowed them, according to the usual proportions above fixed.

Rule No. 9: The scale of tyag set forth in the preceding rules applied to the first marriage only. If a second or third marriage was contracted, the payment would be at the rate of Rs 2 local currency per cent. When the income was less than Rs 5000, no tyag was to be distributed on the occasion of second or third marriage, while in the case of a younger son or brother no tyag was to be disbursed if the marriage was other than the first, when as already settled, 1 per cent would be distributed as tyag on second or third marriage. It is the eldest son only who would be liable for tyag according to the rate above stated.

Rule No. 10: In the capital of the State itself, no Sardar was at liberty to distribute tyag.

Rule No. 11: Tyag would be distributed strictly in accordance with the scale laid down: no enhancement or reduction was to be made. If some people, regardless of their reputation, have never given tyag, they need not do so in future.

Rule No. 12: The amount of presents fixed, was to be accepted with thanks and distributed before witnesses. The recipients were not to go to foreign territory, nor could they use abusive language. Charans, Raos, Dholis, etc., were to be guided by the intention of the rules, which was drawn up and each State was to see that it is enforced.

Rule No. 13: It was also laid down that five years hence, a committee would assemble to reconsider the rules, which were fixed to regulate marriage expenses, and the distribution of presents; and after another interval of five years, a similar committee would be convened to report on the advantages or drawbacks of the arrangements.

Rule No. 14: In every State a committee would be appointed, which would consist of a Sardar, an official and a member of the

Charan and Rao caste or with such modifications in the constitution as the Durbar might be in favour of. It would be the duty of this committee to make arrangements for carrying out the regulations, regarding the expenditure to be incurred on marriages and deaths and on tyag, as well as the other instructions embodied in these rules. When a marriage was to be celebrated, one month's previous notice was to be given by the head of the Estate concerned to this committee, which would be required to see that the regulations prescribed are conformed to. The committee would be empowered to permit at their discretion, the attendance of those of their territory who were privileged to be present or to make such other arrangements as they might deem expedient. The provisions of Rule 5 would remain in force for two years, after which it would be considered whether it was better to disburse the tyag to the assembled Charans, etc., or to have the money remitted to the committee for distribution.

Rule No. 15: The fathers of some girls owing to their not possessing the means, could obtain the necessary funds for their daughters' marriage from the bridegroom's fathers. This was considered as a most objectionable practice and one that was opposed to the Dharmashastras. Many fathers, although without adequate means shun such impropriety and adjust the marriage expenditure to their present circumstances. There are others again, who have neither land nor maintenance, and are practically without any means, and only earn livelihood as cultivators. If such as these who elect to do so, take Rs 100 and spend the lot on the marriage it matters little, but no greater sum should be taken, and they should as far as possible strive not to take anything. Should it be proved that the girl's father accepts, or the boy's father gives any sum contrary to this rule, the delinquents will be suitably punished.

Rule No. 16: It laid down that boys and girls should not be married before the age of 18 and 14 respectively. It was also laid down that as regards engagements concluded before this date, the marriage could take place, as soon as the girl completes 14 years, irrespective of the boy's age.

Rule No. 17: When a widower has attained the age of 45 years, and has a son living, he should not contract another marriage.

Rule No. 18: The expenses on the occasion of death would be on the following scale:

(a) When the value of the property owned was less than Rs 1000; 2/3rd of the income was to be spent.
(b) When the property was worth from Rs 1000 to 5000, 1/4th of the income was to be spent.
(c) When the property was worth from Rs 5000 to Rs 10000, 1/5th of the income was to be spent.
(d) When the property was worth above Rs 10,000, 1/8th of the income was to be spent

It was also specified, that one could spend less than the amount specified, but not more.

Rule No. 19: The sums to be spent on marriages and deaths have been set forth above, but should the proportion which has been fixed, calculated on the value of the property, yields a very insignificant sum, or if there be no property, then notwithstanding what is contained in the preceding rules, the party concerned was at liberty to spend upto a limit of Rs 100 on a marriage and Rs 75 on death.

Rule No. 20: Besides the committee in each State, the premier Sardar of each clan would superintend the arrangements for giving effect to these regulations.

Rule No. 21: It was urged to give widest publicity to these rules and for this, each State might have copies printed off and distributed amongst all classes of Nobles, Jagirdars & Others.

Rule No. 22: It was laid down that as there were no Charans in Karauli, those from the adjoining States of Jaipur and Alwar could go there.

Thus, these were the twenty-two rules, which were framed by the committee.

On the 16 January 1889, Col. Walter asked Col. Trevor, the Commissioner of Ajmer to make necessary arrangements for a second meeting of the Committee members at Ajmer.[61] Col. Walter expressed his satisfaction on the working of the rules in all the States but even then he felt the necessity of a second meeting, of the "Original Committee", Hence, on 15 February 1889 a meeting of the committee was held at Ajmer which commenced from 15 to 24 of February 1889.[62] The members from all the States attended the meeting with the exception of Jaisalmer and Dungarpur. The following resolutions were passed in the second meeting of WKRHS:

1. It was resolved in the second meeting that this committee shall be known as the Walter Krit Rajputra Hitkarini Sabha, and the Agent to the Governor General was elected as the President and the Commissioner of Ajmer, as the Vice-President.

2. All the measures taken in the different States with regard to these rules were to be published in the government press of each State and circulated among the various sub-committees.
3. At the betrothal the bride's father would make the usual mark or *tika* on the bridegroom's forehead and would give him beetel-leaves to eat, and a plain coconut, together with cash not exceeding one *mohar* and not less than one rupee. The lower classes of people such as servant's etc., entitled to receive gifts, were to be paid according to the rates fixed below, which must not be exceeded:
   (a) Estates valued above Rs 50,000 annually were to pay Rs 100.
   (b) Estates valued between Rs 50,000 and 20,000 annually were to pay Rs 50.
   (c) Estates valued between Rs 20,000 and 10,000 annually were to pay Rs 20.
   (d) Estates valued between Rs 10,000 and Rs 5,000 annually were to pay Rs 15.
   (e) Estates valued between Rs 5,000 and 1,000 annually were to pay Rs 10.
   (f) Estates valued below Rs 1,000 annually were to pay Rs 5.
4. It was resolved that as a general rule twenty people might be taken, but in the case of marriages on a large scale, the number should be fixed at the rate of two men for every hundred rupees allowed to be spent by the girl's father. It was further laid down that the marriage procession should arrive at the house of the bride's father on the day fixed for the marriage, stay there for two days and take leave on the fourth or on the fifth day at the latest, if the fourth was considered inauspicious for departure. Further it was laid down that the persons who attend weddings could bring servants with them in accordance with the following scale:
   (a) A person whose scale is valued above Rs 50,000 can bring 25 servants.
   (b) From Rs 50,000 to Rs 20,000 can bring 15 servants.
   (c) From Rs 20,000 to Rs 10,000 can bring 10 servants.
   (d) From Rs 10,000 to Rs 5,000 can bring 5 servants.
   (e) Below Rs 5,000 can bring 2 servants.

It was also resolved that no one should bring more than the numbers fixed, though any one could bring less if he liked.

5. The sum received from the master or landlord, was to be spent in addition to the amount fixed by the rules, but not the sum received in *neota*.
6. It was also specified in the second meeting of the committee, that in case anyone was guilty of breach of the rules, the special committee in the State, to which he belonged would deal with such offence and convey such warning or award such punishment as was deemed proper.
7. It was also specified that the ratio of expenditure to income should be fixed according to the schedule to be prepared.
8. It was also decided that it was very necessary that a half-yearly register of births, deaths and marriages be submitted to the special committees at the capitals of different States through the district officials or *Nizamuts*.
9. Whenever a party would go to a State or district other than his own to get his son married it was laid down that he should obtain a document from the State Nizamut or tehsil to which he belonged, mentioning the amount of his annual income and the sum he could spend.
10. The meeting of the committee was to be held annually at Ajmer for the next three years.
11. It was also resolved that the following papers be printed and supplied to the capital towns and districts of all the States for the information of the people at large:
    (a) General Report submitted by this committee to the President.
    (b) General Statement giving the details and numbers of marriage and funeral ceremonies performed in each State.
    (c) Statement showing the amount of expenditure at Marriages and deaths and the distribution of tyag, etc., referred to above in Rule IX.

The WKRHS was organized to promote a scheme of social reforms pertaining to Rajputs, especially to curb the practice of female infanticide but, gradually, it extended and included within its fold, issues like polygamy, child and unmatched marriages, minimum age of marriage, expenses incurred in marriages and funeral ceremonies, tyag and also included in its sphere castes other than Rajputs. Though attempts had been made to check female infanticide much before the birth of WKRHS, therefore it cannot be said that it was the pioneer in the abolition of female infanticide in the Rajputana. But the relation of female infanticide with the practice of spending large amounts in the marriage ceremonies as well as in the ceremonies related to death and the impoverishment which arose side by side with these practices, which ultimately forced the people (and especially Rajputs) to opt for female infanticide, was understood by him. It is difficult to ascertain what led Colonel Walter to formulate this organization, as the records available presents a contradictory picture. Whether it was his ardent desire to reform the society of the Rajputana or whether he undertook this work, in order to have an extension of his tenure, as M.S. Jain has pointed out,[63] is difficult to tell. It is true that he desired an extension and tried to have it by writing and requesting his senior officers and ultimately succeeded in getting it. It is also true, that in the very year of its formation Lord Northbrook, Lord Kimberley and the Bishop of Carlisle in the House of Lords expressed their warmest appreciation of the reforms introduced by the Rajputana princes under the guidance of Col. Walter.

It is significant to note that the WKRHS combined in itself the good principles and points of all the previous reform efforts, and thus clubbed them under its own roof. The principles of WKRHS, were almost the same as those of Desh Hitaishini Sabha but differed in few respects. Firstly, not only the giving of tika by the bride's father but also taking of money from the groom's father for the bride i.e., *reet* was prohibited by the WKRHS, which was much prevalent in the then society.[64] Moreover it was laid down that the expenditure incurred at the time of engagement was to be incurred by the groom's family and not by the bride's side as was customary in those days. Another difference between the Desh Hitaishini Sabha and WKRHS was the prescription of minimum age limit for marriages of boys and girls. The WKRHS prescribed 14 as the minimum marriageable age for girls and 18 for the boys, which was somewhat higher than what was being prescribed by various caste panchayats and other social organizations in the Rajputana as well as in British India. It also asked the parents to marry their daughters, before the age of 25 and enjoined that the Local Sabhas, should endeavour to find a suitable match for a girl who remains unmarried after this age. It is significant to note here, that Emperor Akbar too, in order to check child marriages, prescribed 14 and 16 as the minimum marriageable age for girls and boys[65] but his orders did not produce the desired effect. The same was the case with WKRHS as it could not root out the age old social beliefs regarding child marriages. The real significant thing about the WKRHS was, that for the first time in the history of the Rajputana, an attempt was made to raise the age limit of marriage. As late as 1924, the caste organizations prescribed 8, 10, 11 or 12 as the minimum marriageable age for girls.

It also fixed the amount to be spent on the occasion of marriage of the Rajputs and laid down that the prescribed limits were not to be exceeded in any case, though one could spend less, if one so wished. Similarly, the amount of tyag, was also fixed according to the categories of the landholders and the Charans and Bhats were also forced to accept what was prescribed in the rules of WKRHS Moreover, they were forbidden to enter into foreign territories for the purpose of getting tyag. It was also laid down that only the father of the bridegroom would make the payments, i.e., tyag to the Charans and Bhats and the father of the bride was liable not to pay anything. These provisions of WKRHS reminds one, of the provisions of the proclamations of Sawai Jai Singh III, and Maharaja Bukht Singh and Vijay Singh of Jodhpur who in the 18th century, worked on the same lines and prescribed the same remedy for the above mentioned evils. The role of these enlightened rulers, who purged the society of the prevalent social evils, will be dealt in the next chapters in detail.

To check these evils, it suggested the appointment of a committee (or local Sabha) in every native State of the Rajputana and Malwa, which was to consist of a Sardar, an official and a member of the Charan and Rao castes. It was the duty of this committee to make arrangements for carrying out the regulations, regarding the expenditure to be incurred on marriages and deaths and on tyag, as well as other provisions of the WKRHS. It also forbade the marriage of a widower, who was above the age of 45 and who had a living son, to contract another marriage. Besides the committee in each State, the premier Sardar of each clan was given the power to superintend the arrangements. A half yearly register of births, deaths and marriages was to be kept by the local Sabhas, to keep a record of the above mentioned particulars and also the infringements, if any happened.

It published yearly reports to review the effects of the rules. Each of the local committees in different States of the Rajputana submitted its report and a comparative analysis was drawn on the basis that report. The WKRHS also gave a comparative analysis of the breaches of laws amongst Rajputs and Charans of various native

States of the Rajputana. According to the report of 1905,[66] 4,198 marriages and 1,589 funerals were performed amongst the Rajputs and 220 marriages and 129 funerals amongst the Charans. Of the 4,198 marriages and 1,589 funerals ceremonies performed amongst the Rajputs, 3,894 marriages and 1,499 funerals were in accordance with the rules; and out of 220 marriages and 129 funerals amongst the Charans, the rules of the WKRHS were observed in 198 marriages and 126 funerals. The report also presented the fact that the progress was not satisfactory in the States of Bharatpur and Dholpur while the local Sabhas of other States did a commendable work. Not only this, it also examined the causes which resulted in violation of laws. As in the case of Dholpur, a large number of delinquencies were associated with the fact that intermarriages were performed between the inhabitants of the Dholpur State and those of the adjoining British and Gwalior territories, where these rules were not in vogue. Similarly, the WKRHS warned those local Sabhas, who used to send incomplete reports to the central body and asked them not to commit mistakes next time. This report of 1905 also shows the progress of the WKRHS in comparison to 1900, and 1904.[67] While in 1900, 2,743 marriages were performed amongst the Rajputs of the Rajputana, 240 marriages were against the rule regarding age; and 147 marriages were against the rule regarding number of wedding party. Similarly, in 1904, 3,837 marriages were performed amongst the Rajputs and out of them 90 were against the rule concerning age and 91 were against the rule concerning number of wedding party.

According to the General Statement of Marriages and Funerals performed amongst Rajputs during the year 1909,[68] 328 marriages were performed in Jaipur and out of them 327 were according to the rules and one was against it, as far as the age of marriage was concerned. According to the Statement, no cases of infringement were reported, in 1909, as far as the rules related to marriage expenses, tyag and tika were concerned. In Jodhpur, 239 marriages were solemnized and out of them 3 were against the rule, related to the age of marriage. No cases of infringement were reported as far as tyag, tika or marriage expenses were concerned. Similarly in Jaisalmer, 246 marriages were performed amongst Rajputs in 1909 and 2 were against the age of marriage, while 30 were performed against the rule related to marriage expenses and 1 was against the tyag rules. In the State of Bikaner, 108 marriages were solemnized in 1909, and out of them 3 were against the prescribed age of marriage,

1 was against the rule regarding marriage expenses and no case of infringement was reported as far as rule related to tyag was concerned. In 1909, 1,170 marriages took place amongst the Rajput community, residing in 19 native States of the Rajputana and out of these 1,158 marriages were performed according to the rules and 12 against it, as far as the age of marriage, fixed by WKRHS is concerned; in 1,139 marriages, the rules regarding marriage expenses were obeyed and in 31 cases they were violated; in 1,169 cases, the tyag rules were obeyed and in 1 case, it was disobeyed; in 1,104 cases the rules regarding tika were followed and in 2 cases they were violated.

According to the General Statement of Marriages and Funerals amongst Rajputs during the year 1912-13,[69] 322 marriages were performed in Dholpur and out of them 309 were in consonance with the rules regarding age of marriage of the WKRHS, while 13 were against it. No cases of infringement were reported in Dholpur, as far as the expenses incurred in marriages and tyag were concerned. In Ajmer-Merwara, 151 marriages were solemnized in 1912-13 and out of them 144 were according to the rule and 7 were against the rule regarding the age of marriage. No cases of violation, as far as rules for limiting the marriage expenses, tyag and tika were concerned, were reported. Thus, in short, 5,216 marriages were performed amongst the Rajputs of the Rajputana (of all the 19 States) in 1912-13 and out of them 48 were performed against the prescribed age of marriage; 15 were performed against the rule regarding marriage expenses; 3 were performed against the tyag rules and no incident, in which tika rules were violated, were brought to the notice of the Central Committee of WKRHS.

It is remarkable that the drawbacks of the Sabha were not overlooked and it was observed that, at times, the rules framed could not be carried out satisfactorily, as the various rules framed by different communities differed in each State. It could give rise to controversies, if the two parties engaged in a marriage, belonged to two different States, out of which one might have no rules or the rules of two States (although community is same) might differ. The rules which were in force in the Rajputana differed from those in Malwa, and hence it created confusion.[70] In Malwa, for example, the practice of taking money for the marriage of a daughter, from the groom's side (called as reet) was strictly prohibited, whereas in the Rajputana, one could accept upto Rs 100, on account of his incapability to marry his daughter, from the groom's side. Moreover, the Malwa-rules allowed more followers in the barat than the Rajputana rules. Similarly, the maximum age of marriage for a man, prescribed in the Rajputana by WKRHS was 45 while in the case of Malwa it was 55. To solve this anomaly, it was resolved in 1909 that, the rules of WKRHS Malwa would be applicable on all the barats (marriage processions) of Malwa, which would come in the Rajputana, for the purpose of marriage and those which would go from the Rajputana to Malwa, would be bound by the rules of WKRHS Rajputana. Similarly, tyag was calculated in the Rajputana on the income of a landholder, whereas in Malwa it was calculated on the total expenditure of marriage. Moreover, in the Rajputana, tyag was to be distributed on the marriages of younger brothers and sisters, while this was not so in Malwa. To resolve the disputes arising thereby, it was laid down in Resolution XI of 1905, that when a Rajput would go to Malwa for a marriage, he would distribute tyag according to the rules laid down by the Malwa Sabha and when he would come from Malwa to Rajputana he would be governed by the Rajputana rules. It also laid down that in case of a marriage procession proceeding to British India or any place outside the Rajputana, where these rules were not in force, the distribution of tyag would depend upon the wish of the bridegroom's father. To avoid situations/conflicts, it encouraged framing of uniform laws for each community. Consequently a widower above 45 years of age was allowed later on, (by Resolution V of 1896), to remarry, if he was healthy and strong. But the bride was to be above the age prescribed by the rules. In case a widower of 45 years, had an infant child, by his deceased wife and if it was difficult for him to bring up the child as well as to look after his household affairs, the State Committee could make a special exception to the rule, after satisfying itself that it was proper to do so.

The report of September, 1909 is significant as it incorporates the salient features of the rules framed at its meetings in 1888 and in subsequent years. Another factor which stands out is that its preamble clearly stated the rules to be "binding on Rajputs of all ranks except ruling chiefs". This can be considered as an impediment as the practice was widely prevalent amongst the ruling families. In the socio-religious set-up of the Rajputana, where the ruling family set examples for others, any reform which did not include them could not be expected to be thoroughly successful.

To put a further check on the breaches, Resolution II of 1893 provided for half-yearly registration of births, deaths and marriages to the special committees at the capitals of the different States through the district official or Nizamuts. Exceptions could be made only when marriage had been arranged before these rules came into force and the girl was 14 years of age. But it was advisable that girls were to be married before the age of 20. It was also provided that no second marriage shall take place during the lifetime of the first wife, unless she (first wife) is afflicted by an incurable disease or has no offspring. Resolution V of 1895 laid down that if any person agrees to give his girl in marriage to a man, knowing that the latter is already married to another woman, commits the same offence as the person proposing the marriage. Thus, this resolution brought both the parties on a single footing and held them responsible and made it punishable before the committee. Similarly, to put a check on the *tika* expenses, resolution V of 1907 provided that the entire amount of *tika* should be forfeited and the acceptor of the tika should be fined to the extent of one-half of the amount of tika.

Moreover, it also laid down that any person who informs the committee of cases in which giving and acceptance of tika have really taken place, shall be given as reward one-fourth of the forfeited tika amount. The local Sabhas were asked not to disclose the name of the informer if he so desired and should the information thus received turned out to be incorrect, the local Sabhas were empowered to award a suitable punishment to the person giving the false information.

The WKRHS was formed to deal only with the problems of the Rajputs but later on, it included the Charans and gradually, by 1890, extended to other communities like the Brahmins, the Vaishyas, the Kayasthas, and the Mahajans in the States like Bikaner, Jodhpur, Karauli, Kishangarh, Kota and Alwar and the Jats of Bharatpur and Dholpur.[71] Members of 12 castes, other than the Charans and the Rajputs, framed rules for the guidance of their ceremonies and submitted to the Durbar. The report of 1894[72] points out that rules had been made for castes other than the Rajputs and the Charans in Bikaner, Jodhpur, Karauli, Kishangarh, Kota and Alwar and also that the Jat States of Bharatpur and Dholpur had formed local committees for the introduction of its rules. In 1909-10, the barbers of Karauli also framed rules for themselves, on similar lines. Similarly, the Khati, Dhimar and Khandelwal Communities of Bharatpur framed rules for themselves in 1918-19. The main achievement of WKRHS lies not only in making modest reforms among the Rajputs but in the fact that it made others adopt them. Col. Walter's scheme involved no legislation and did not call for any action on the part of the police.[73] It was a gentlemen's agreement and it worked in creating a public opinion. This created an impression that the method of Walter could be adopted for other castes too. Soon, the Aggarwal community adopted the lines of the Rajputs and in 1889, the Mers and the Merats of Merwara framed rules fixing the age of marriage for girls at 11 years, which was introduced in 1891.[74] Similarly, in 1890-91, the Rajguru Purohits of Jodhpur and the Pushkarna Brahmins of Bikaner framed rules providing that no marriage should take place in which the prospective bridegroom and the bride did not attain the age of 15 and 11 years respectively.[75] The other sects of Brahmans also agreed that no marriage be solemnized where either party was under 11 years.[76] In 1891, the Malis of Jodhpur and the Sidhs of Bikaner followed the example of Rajguru Purohits. There was so much enthusiasm that as many as thirty-six communities framed rules with regard to the age limits of the bride and the bridegroom.[77]

Despite the efforts of WKRHS (beside others), it was not successful in completely eradicating the practice. In fact, the Sabha lost its hold and became almost non-functional and no annual meeting of the Sabha was convened for almost a decade since 1924. Perhaps the passing of the post of Secretary to the Rajputs had something to do with its being non-functional. It is remarkable here to note, that for the first 14 years, persons other than the Rajputs held the post of Secretary of the central committee and worked for the social upliftment with great zeal. Kayastha Durga Prasad, Munshi Nand Lal Bhargava and Pandita Shankar Nath were the Secretaries of WKRHS who carried on the reform process in the initial years.[78] But when this post was passed on to Kishan Singh of Gangwana, who himself was a Rajput noble, the WKRHS lost its vitality and much of its earlier reformative spirit. The same thing happened with the State committees, which ultimately made it a decorative piece. It may also be the reason that after Walter, none other British Officer, cared for social reforms with as much zeal and enthusiasm as Walter did. The cause of its being non-functional may also be ascribed to the growing consciousness among the various castes, regarding social reforms, which made the British officers feel that the time had come to limit their influence and interference in the social matters and allow the things to happen in their own way.

It is significant to note that on August 11, 1934, Thakur Bachan Singh of Dervala (Jhunjhunun),[79] who was the Secretary of WKRHS, Jaipur and Rajasthan Kshatriya Mahasabha, Ajmer, wrote a letter to the H.H., Jaipur in which he lamented the fact that the WKRHS had become an instrument of oppression and had ceased to be of any help to the ordinary Rajputs. According to him, the poor and illiterate Rajputs were put to a lot of inconvenience on account of the WKRHS and they were forced to give tips and bribes to the Tehsildars and the Nazims to get the necessary permission for performing marriages and nuktas. He also told that he had obtained the signatures of thousands of Rajputs, who agreed with him and who wished to do away with this Sabha. He also reported that he had written several letters, in this regard, to Rao Bahadur Thakur Narendra Singh, who was a member-in-charge of the WKRHS, but nothing had happened and no action was taken on his letters.

On the 15 March, 1935, Thakur Bachan Singh again appealed to the H.H. Jaipur[80] to put an end to this body, as he believed that it was of no use and had become non-functional. But nothing came out of this letter and consequently, he sent a copy of the letter to the Resident at Jaipur, who took this matter seriously. H. Burton, the Resident at Jaipur,[81] admitted that the last recorded meeting of WKRHS was held in 1924 and since then "there does not appear to have been any meeting nor has there been any demand on the part of any of the States for such a meeting." However, he opined that the mere existence of the Sabha (i.e., WKRHS), even in its present unsatisfactory condition, could exercise some check on extravagance at marriages and funerals and that on these grounds its continued existence could be justified. Col. George Ogilvie,[82] A.G.G., remarked that a contributory cause for its inactivity lied in the fact that its Secretary absented himself, which had brought this body to a "stage of inactivity and inanition".

Consequently, in 1935,[83] the A.G.G. wrote a letter to all States asking them whether they were prepared to resuscitate the activities of the WKRHS or wished it to be closed down. The replies received showed that 9 States were in favour of abolition and 9 States were in favour of continuance. The Jaipur Durbar offered the suggestion that a Conference should be called in order to decide as to whether the Sabha (i.e., WKRHS) should cease to exist or whether its rules should undergo revision. At the same time the Jaipur Durbar considered that the Sabha, even in its present unsatisfactory condition, served a useful purpose and opined that for that reason it would be inadvisable to abolish it.

As a result, a Conference was held on the 19-21, May 1936 at Ajmer to decide the fate of this body, and Raja Amar Singh of Bunera (Mewar) was nominated as its Chairman.[84] In the Conference, all the representatives of native States agreed that the rules that were made nearly half a century ago had outgrown their usefulness and it was high time that drastic changes be made in them.[85] "Eradication of social evils", Raja Amar Singh of Bunera, in his closing speech as the Chairman, observed, "largely depends on the education of the people to the realization of their disastrous effects rather than on the enforcement on rigid rules and regulations."

"On account of the heavy penalties", he further observed, "that have been from time to time inflicted in several States for technical infringements of the rules and the difficulties that are sometimes experienced by the poor Rajputs in obtaining certificates for marriages and nuktas, many of the Rajputs have begun to look upon it, as an institution that checks them at every stage of their ordinary life." "The Sabha (i.e., WKRHS) has therefore," he remarked, "suffered to a great extent in its usefulness for lack of interest and cooperation on the part of those for whose sole benefit it was inaugurated."

Seeing the difficulties, it was decided by the members that a sub-committee should be appointed to look into the matter carefully.[86] Consequently, Thakur Madho Singh of Sankhwas (Jodhpur), Rawul Sangram Singh of Samode (Jaipur), Raja Chandrasen of Kunadi (Kota), Thakur Anand Pal of Karauli and Kunwar Ganpati Singh of Kharwa (Ajmer) were appointed as members of the sub-committee.

It was also decided in the Conference, that in order to make WKRHS more useful and to create greater interest in its activities, its aims and objects should be extended so as to include other social reforms of the Rajput Community as well. The question of freeing the Rajputra (Central) Sabha (i.e., WKRHS) from official tutelage was also raised by the Resident for the Rajputana and in view of the observations made by him in the opening speech at the Conference held at Ajmer on 23 September, 1940, it was decided that in future the President and the Vice President of the Central Sabha be drawn from among the Princes, and their election be held accordingly (vide

Resolution no. 4).[87] In accordance with the said resolution H.H. the Maharaja of Jodhpur and H.H. the Maharawal of Dungarpur were elected President and the Vice President respectively.[88]

Seeing the great anomalies in the present rules, the central body of WKRHS, repealed all the existing rules and framed another set of rules, which came into force from the 1 January, 1941.[89] According to the new rules, the name of WKRHS was changed to Rajputana Walterkrit Rajputra Hitkarini Sabha and its rules were made applicable on all the Rajputs of the Rajputana, except the ruling princes and chiefs. It was decided that the President and the Vice President of the Rajputana Sabha would be elected every third year from amongst the princes by the representatives of the States. Each State in the Rajputana became entitled to nominate one Rajput member to the Rajputana Sabha, whose term "was for at least three years". Any person who informed the Sabha of the cases in which tika money was given or taken, was to be given a reward not exceeding one-fourth of the tika amount. The amount thus received was to go to the Rajput Fund, which was to be used for marriages of the daughters of the poor Rajputs, for providing scholarships to the needy and deserving Rajput students, for donations to private Rajput educational institutions and recognized boarding houses, etc., and for helping the needy Rajput widows. In the annual conference of Rajputana Walterkrit Rajputra Hitkarini Sabha in December 1943, it was resolved that the Sabha was for the benefit of both the Rajputs and the Charans and its rules should continue to apply to both the communities, therefore the following amendments were made in 1943: (i) In section 2, "all Charans" was added after Rajputs and before "of Rajputs" (ii) In section 16, "or Charans" was added after the words "as far as possible be Rajputs", (iii) In section 17, "or a Charan" was added after "be a Rajput," (iv) in section 8, "or Charan" was added after "one Rajput." The amount realized by fines and forfeitures from Charans, under these rules, was to be credited to the Charan Fund and spent for the benefit of Charans on the same lines as provided for the Rajputs.

Arya Samaj: Crusade Against Child and Unequal Marriages

One of the most important and extensive social reform movements was initiated by Swami Dayanand Saraswati (1824-1883), who was one of the few great men of the world, who sacrificed everything for emancipation of mankind. He was a great scholar, a yogi, a social reformer, a philosopher and a political thinker. Swami Dayanand was one of the most powerful figures of modern India, who spread the Vedic religion and through the Arya Samaj, played an important part in the Indian renaissance. "He had taken a long and deep draught," observed *The Hindu Patriot* of 17 January 1870, "at the perennial spring-head which had quenched his thirst and filled his soul with indescribable peace. He had wandered long and far in the gloom before he received the light – the light of true and pure Dharma, the religion of the Vedas. With insight born of this light, he saw clearly through the vast and enveloping mist of error, delusion and superstition which was bedimming the vision of the inhabitants of India and of other parts of the globe. He did not hug this new-found treasure to his bosom like a miser lest others might come to know of it and snatch it away from him; but, like a generous prince he made a free gift of it to his people".

During his travels to various parts of India, he found the condition of his country and that of the Hindu society deplorable and depressing. Many superstitions, dogmas and undesirable rituals were propounded in the name of religion. They included untouchability, prohibition on education and remarriage of women (even if widowed in infancy or childhood), sati (self immolation by a wife upon the death of her husband) and child and unequal or unmatched marriage. Swami Dayanand resolved to awaken India and the Hindu society. In his famous book, *Satyartha Prakash* (The Light of Truth), he sought to dispel rituals, dogmas and superstitions among all Indians.

He, in order to preach his social and religious philosophy visited the different natives States of the Rajputana like Karauli, Gangapur, Bharatpur, Chittaurgarh, Beawar, Jodhpur, Dholpur, Jaipur, Udaipur, Shahpura, Kishangarh, Kushalgarh, Mount Abu, and *thikanas* of Raipur, Bagru, Dudu, Sardargarh, Achrol and Benara and the British administered territory of Ajmer-Merwara from 1865 to 1883 and impressed the masses as well as the native rulers and nobles.[90] He believed that if rulers could be involved in the social reform process then things would become much easier as the people still considered them in high esteem. Therefore, initially, he concentrated upon impressing the native rulers and Chiefs the need to identify with the cause and undertake due steps to bring about a social change. His charismatic personality and his versatility dazzled and impressed the native rulers and Jagirdars of Rajputana.

For the first time, he came to the Rajputana in 1865, and visited the British-dominated territory of Ajmer, and observed with great interests, the pomp and show of the priests at Pushkar. He had his first shastrartha (i.e., religious debate) at Ajmer in 1865, with Christian priest John Tobson.[91] On 14th November, 1878 he had a great shastrartha with Dr. Husband—the Christian priest of Ajmer and by his forceful arguments and eloquent speech, he created a great dent on the minds of the ordinary as well as elite people of Ajmer. After the discourse, Rao Bahadur Singh I, Istimrardar of Ajmer, invited him to come to Masooda (Ajmer) and Swamiji stayed there from 2nd of December to 10th of December 1878.

Before discussing the role of Arya Samaj in the eradication of social vices in the Rajputana, it will be relevant here to understand the views of Dayanand Saraswati on different social issues pertaining to women, viz., marriage, proper age of marriage, child and unequal marriages, widow remarriage, education of boys and girls, etc.[92]

Dayanand's Views on Education

On April 10, 1875, Swami Dayanand established the Arya Samaj as a permanent organization to continue to educate the Hindus of their rich heritage and to reform the social structure within India, largely through the spread of education, especially that of women. He held ignorance as the root cause of all the miseries and felt that emancipation depended on removal of this ignorance and also that there is no emancipation as long as ignorance persists. "The world is fettered by the chain forged by superstition and ignorance", he declared,[93] "and I have come to snap asunder that chain and to set slaves at liberty. It is contrary to my mission to have people deprived of their freedom". "The purpose of my life", he said once,[94] "is the extirpation of evils; introduction of truth in thought, speech, and deeds; the preservation of unity of religion; the expulsion of mutual enmity; the extension of friendly intercourse; and the advancement of public happiness by reciprocal subservience of the human family."

He recommended various multifarious activities for the betterment of women in Indian society. He not only emphasized upon the abolition of abhorrent practices and customs pertaining to them, but also, advocated women's upliftment through provision for their education. He also motivated them to come out of their purdah or veil and fight for their own cause. He revolted against the abuses from which they suffered, recalling that in the heroic age they occupied in the home and in the society a position at least equal to men. They ought to have equal education, according to him, and supreme control in marriage, over household matters including the finances. He strongly recommended women's education and their participation in all religious ceremonies including the performance of yajnas.

Dayanand was a staunch supporter of education and believed that the chief duty of the father, preceptor, and kinsmen is to adorn the offspring with the ornaments of the best education, the sense of duties and the attainment of good qualities, morality and nature. "Those fathers and mothers are great enemies of their own children", he cited a sloka from Chanakya Niti,[95] "who have not taught them any kind of knowledge...It is the imperative duty, the highest virtue, the cause of fame of the parents to make their children learned, virtuous, civilized and well educated at the expense of their own comfort, thought and wealth." He believed that the soul of man can never be adorned with the ornaments made of gold, silver, rubies, pearls, corals, and other gems (but by education). He believed in the universality of education and as such considered that it was the duty of the State to see that no children are left behind in getting school education. In support of his contention, he cited the following verse from Manu Samhita,[96] which said that "there should be a government order and national custom," he remarked, "that persons must not keep their sons and daughters at home after they are 8 years of age. They must send them to schools at the pain of penalty". Similarly, addressing the native kings, he said,[97] "The king should order the enforcement of the vow of chastity among all the girls and boys of his dominions for a definite period of their age, and have them acquire knowledge to be civilized. If it be not obeyed by any young person, its mother and father should be punished. In plain words, it should be a standing order of the king that none should keep their sons or daughters at home after their eight years of age"(sic).

He believed that just as boys should be taught religion, grammar, and other sciences of practical utility, similarly girls should be taught grammar, religion, medicine, mathematics and other household works, so that they themselves may handle the problems of the day –today life and not become the shadows of their husbands. "A girl, who has followed the Brahmacharya for 24 years," he remarked,[98] "and who has read the *vedangs* (i.e., *shiksha, kalpa, vyakarana, nirukta, chhanda* and *jyotish*) and *upanga* (i.e., *mimansa, vaisheshik, nyaya, yoga, sankhya, vedant* and *ayurveda*) is a boon for the mankind and is respected everywhere." He believed in having separate schools or gurukuls for girls, which were to be run exclusively by women staff only. Their marriage should not be allowed to take place until the time they return from their academy on the termination of their educational training.

He was also against the age old prejudices, which were prevalent in his times, about the education of women and Shudras (स्त्रीशूद्रौ नाधीयातामिति श्रुतेः) and as such, he declared in unambiguous terms that all human beings, whether men or women have a right to study. "Blessed are the men and women", he observed,[99] "whose mind is engaged in the pursuit of knowledge, who are of amiable disposition and polite manners, who observe the rules of veracity and other virtues, who are free from pride and impurity, who destroy others' vices, who are adorned with the jewels of the advocacy of truth, who alleviate the sufferings of humanity in the world by the inculcation of knowledge and who do good to others by means of works ordained by the Vedas".

"Like boys who acquire perfect Knowledge, and good training by observing the vow of chastity and, when of age, marry maidens, youthful, educated, lovely, suitable, equal to them; let girls also acquire perfect knowledge and the best training by studying the Vedas and other scriptures during their vow of chastity and, attaining puberty and full majority, marry bachelors, youthful, handsome, educated and equal to them.(sic)"[100] On the question of what should women learn, he believed[101] that the Brahmin and warrior class women should learn all branches of knowledge, the merchant class women should acquire commercial knowledge, and the servile class women should know the culinary art and the duties of service. Like men, who must at least learn something of grammar, religion, and ethics, women should also learn grammar, religion, medicine, arithmetic, handicraft, as a matter, of course. "For without the knowledge of these arts," he further said, "they cannot distinguish right from wrong, behave themselves agreeably towards the husbands and other relatives, beget children properly, nurture them, bring them up and train them well, perform the domestic chores done as they ought to be done, cook or superintend the cooking of food, and prepare drink like medicine according to the method prescribed by the medical art, so that disease may not attack the household, and all the inmates live happily". Dayanand also wished that the students, whether male or female, should take an oath, to marry only after completing their studies.[102]

He was also aware of the frequent quarrels and other unhappy situations encountered by the uneducated wives and educated husbands in their day today lives and the incongruities that crept in such marriages. Commenting on these situations, Dayanand remarked that,[103] "if the master of a house be educated and his wife uneducated or vice versa, there will every day be a war between gods and devils in the house. How can there be joy in it ? Without knowledge a woman cannot discharge the domestic duties properly, such as the management of the household, just treatment of all, duties of married life, mutual satisfaction of husband and wife, domestic work under the control of the mistress of a house, and similar other duties".

His deep concern for the deplorable position of women, motivated the members of the Samaj to open up new schools, libraries, Vanita ashrams, beside opposing vehemently the prevalent social abuses like child marriages, ill-matched or uneven marriages, polygamy, etc.

Dayanand's Views on Marriage

The institution of marriage attracted Dayanand's attention as it had become one of the main tools for limiting the movement and social space of the women, which confined them within the four walls of the home and one of the causes of the subservient and inferior position of the Indian women. Such a noble institution, designed by the Aryans in the Vedic times, for the all round development of the human personality and for the fulfilment of religious duties, became a tool of oppression, suppression and repression in the later ages and consequently Dayanand paid greater attention towards this institution as well as the social evils associated with it. He claimed equal rights in marriage for men and women, and though he regarded marriage as indissoluble, he admitted the remarriage of widows and went so far as to envisage a temporary union (*niyoga*) for women as well as men for the purpose of having children, if none had resulted from the first marriage.

Beginning with *Satyartha Prakash* in 1875, his first major literary attempt at comprehending social, religious and theological issues, he conveyed to the masses, his perception of the institution of marriage in his subsequent publications. In *Satyartha Prakash* he deals with the more practical aspects of the institution, its aims, implications, and its relevance in society. In his *Ved Bhashyas*, he has written about his conception of an ideal marriage. In *Sanskar Vidhi*, Dayanand deals with the importance of 16 *sanskars* including the ceremonial and ritualistic aspects of marriage and also reflects on the goals and ideals of the holy wedlock. Similarly, his *Vyavahar Bhanu* (published in March 1880, from Vedic Yantralaya, Varanasi) deals with the inter-personal relations of husband and wife in the form of conduct and duties towards each other. Apart from these publications, in many of his lectures and letters, he has given his perception about the institution of marriage, in unequivocal terms. He believed in the necessity of marriage since "marriage safeguards the basic structure of family and thereby society, checks adultery, makes available the owners of property and there is commitment to inter personal relations and that young and old are properly cared for."[104] He believed that if marriage were abolished, there would be a fatal increase in adultery and sensuality and it would then erode the sense of moral values, leading to a weakening and destruction of the race. "No individual should flee away", wrote Dayanand in connection with the necessity of marriage, "from Grihastha ashram for it is this ashram which forms the pivot, which sustains all good behaviour as well as other ashrams in society. The smooth functioning of all human and state affairs depends on the Grihastha ashram."

But at the same time, while professing the necessity of marriage, Dayanand was of the opinion that it was better to remain unmarried, rather than to marry some unsuitable person. "It is better that youths and damsels remain unmarried till death," he observed,[105] "than that unequals in qualification should be matched, that is, the bride and bridegroom should not be of mutually repellent qualities, tendencies and natures." "The parents of girl", he said, "should never marry their daughter to a man who is inferior, unmatched and wicked, might she remain in the house of her father un-married till death." Dayanand was not in favour of child marriages and unequal marriages. He urged the people to marry at the right age, i.e., after observance of Brahmacharya and completion of Vedic studies. "Incompatibility of temperaments and qualities in marriage", according to him, "do not lead to happiness in married life, nor does it lead to the procreation of good and healthy children".

Dayanand Saraswati denounced the practice of child marriage on biological, religious and educational grounds. He believed that marriage before puberty ruins the constitution of women more than that of men. He recommended 25 and 16 years as the minimum age for marriage for men and women. The girl should be at least 16 years, he believed, on the occasion of her marriage and three years should have passed since she had her first menses.[106] According to Dayanand, the husband's age should be at least one and a half times more than the age of his bride, which is a requirement and the maximum difference ought not to exceed the double of the age of bride. The ideal marriage for Dayanand, was between a man and a woman of 48 and 24 years, respectively. He considered marriage of a girl of sixteen years with a man of twenty-five years as 'inferior'; of a girl of eighteen or twenty with a man of thirty-five or forty years as 'medium'; and of a girl of twenty four with a man of forty eight years as 'superior' marriage. "That country is happy," he observed,[107] "in which this best custom of marriage, the observance of chastity, and the vigorous pursuit of knowledge exist to a great extent; but that country sinks into misery in which there is no enforcement of chastity, no light of knowledge, and which has the custom of the marriage of infants at an early age, or of unworthy and discordant couples. For the amelioration of society depends on the perfection of chastity and acquisition of knowledge, and the deterioration of it, on their disuse and decline".

Dayanand believed that child marriages created an obstacle in the physical and mental development of the girl child and created hindrance in the way of her getting education. He believed that child marriages spoil and ruin those, who without observing the rule of chastity and without acquiring knowledge and proficiency in the best moral culture, marry in early life. To support his views, he cited the following verse from the Rig Veda:[108]

"Like the cows that have never been milked before by anybody, let those perfectly youthful women undertake the responsibility of maternity, who have passed infancy, who are able to accomplish all human works in the best way possible, who have passed girlhood or immaturity, who have attained perfect youth and acquired sound moral training, who derive intellectual pleasure from the teaching of the great scriptures of wisdom written by eminent scholars noted for success in their vow of studentship and observance of its rules, and who have married youthful husbands."

Dayanand considered the children from early marriages as 'children of children', and believed that early marriage hampered the development of the intellectual faculties of women and was also injurious for them physiologically. He believed that, the best children are the fruits of the marriage of women between 16 and 24 years old, when their uterus is perfectly developed and the body has grown strong, and of men at 25 to 48, when their semen is mature and the body has grown stout and strong.[109]

Dayanand Saraswati was also against unequal marriages, that were widely prevalent in his times. To stop the unequal marriages, one method according to him, was the acceptance and observance of strict monogamy. "When the marriage is performed," he observed,[110] "man and wife are, as it were, sold to each other; that is whatever is in their body from head to foot...belongs to them in common. They should never do any act without each other's approval... Not even the remotest thoughts (of adultery, whoring, prostitution, etc.) should ever be entertained in their minds. A man should always be content with his wife, and a woman with her husband." According to his philosophy, strict monogamy should be observed by anyone and everyone and it should not be imposed on widows alone. Neither the widow nor the widower should be allowed, to contract another marriage, as it would disturb the social equations of the society. While the Hindu Shastras imposed monogamy only on widows, Dayanand pleaded for its universal application. He rejected remarriage on the following grounds. First, as he believed, remarriage diminished love between husband and wife; second, this could give rise to disputes regarding property, third, widow remarriage would destroy many noble families and their property by constant alienation; and fourth, remarriage would destroy all love and bring infraction of duty towards the departed consort.[111]

Commendable Form of Marriage

Dayanand believed that marriages should not be imposed or thrusted upon the girl or the boy; rather they should be married at an age, when they are physically and mentally alert to understand the significance of marriage. "It is better that marriage should be in the power of the marrying parties. If the parents ever take it into their head to bring about their sons and daughters' matches, they should not be made without their consent; for, the marriage contracted with their mutual consent is seldom attended with displeasure and variance, and it brings forth splendid children. Marriage without consent of the bride and bridegroom is always attended with trouble. The chief concern in marriage is of the bride and bridegroom and not of their parents; for if they are pleased with each other, they become happy; but if not pleased, they suffer trouble.[112]

He believed that *swayamvara* marriage was the best form of marriage, as it was totally based on the choice of the bride and as, daughters were not given away in marriage like goats and animals. In this type of marriage, the bride and the prospective groom saw to it that they suited each other in point of knowledge, disposition, character, beauty, age, vigour, stature, modesty, manners, strength, family-status and built of the body, etc. There is no happiness in marriage so long as there is no harmony in the character of the marrying parties. "When the time of the marriage of youth and damsels approaches, that is to say, when it is a year or six months to the completion of the terms of studentship and of the course of educational training, the likenesses or photographs of the bachelors should be sent to the schoolmistresses of girls' schools, and those of the maids to the schoolmasters of boys' schools. The couples for marriage being selected, their biographies from birth up-to-date should be obtained for comparing their merits, habits and tempers. When their characters harmonies with each other, the photographs and memoirs of the couples to be matched, should be handed over to the marrying parties with the request, that they should inform their masters and mistresses of their intention. When the marriageable parties have come to the determination to be united in wedlock they should be simultaneously sent home from their respective schools. If they want to marry before their teachers, their marriage should be celebrated there and then. If not, it is better to hold their marriage at the house of the girl's parents. When the youth and the maiden are brought together, the teachers, the girl's parents should have them hold conversation or discussion on some subject between them in the presence of a number of good people. If they have to ask each other of some private matter, they should put it down on paper before the assembly and place it in each other's hand asking questions if needed".[113]

"This country of *Aryavarta* ever enjoyed prosperity and progress, "he remarked,[114] "so long as all the sages, philosophers, princes, emperors, and people acquired knowledge during the time of their vow of bachelorship and observed the custom of marriage in which a maid selected her husband (*swayamvara*: self-choice). But when the acquisition of knowledge during studentship ceased to be and the contraction of marriage became the duty of parents, national degeneracy and physical deterioration set in, and it has been coming down gradually and steadily all over the country ever since. Hence, the evil customs of early marriage should be given up by sensible people, who should adopt the aforesaid custom of marriage, in which a maid selects her husband (*swayamvara*). It should be done in the class to which the marrying parties belong. The determination of classes should be based upon the principles of similarity in qualifications, habits, and tempers".

Dayanand's Views on Remarriage

Dayanand suggested that those men and women whose marriage ceremony had only been performed, but who had not seen their consort, i.e., women being virgins and men innocent of sex work, should marry again. The men and women of the sacerdotal, military and mercantile class, who have had conjugal intercourse, should not marry again after the death of their consort.[115] He discarded the notion of remarriage, on the following grounds:

(i) There will be little love between man and wife; for, they will leave their consort whenever they like and will form connection with another. (ii) When they marry after the death of their spouse, they will carry off the property of their predecessors, whose family members will cry foul. (iii) Many noble families will disappear and altogether be effaced, and their property will be gone to the winds. (iv) The virtue of the chastity of men and women will be destroyed. Hence, it should never be adopted by the regenerates of the upper classes.

On the question that "will the abolition of remarriage, not lead to the cessation of line and destroy a family and will not men and women fall into adultery and other vices, and commit abortion and other heinous sins", Dayanand replied, "If men and women wish to live a chaste life there will be no evil. To continue their line of descent on the failure of issue, they can adopt a son of their own caste, if they like. It will prevent the occurrence of adultery. If they cannot keep up their chastity, they can beget children by the niyoga form of marriage (temporary nuptial compact)".[116]

Niyoga: He believed that it was rather sinful to prevent the celebration of niyoga.[117] For, according to the laws of nature in God's creation, natural attraction, between men and women cannot be checked except in the case of those persons who have renounced the world, who are eminently learned, and who are clairvoyants or yogis. "Do you not regard abortion the destruction of foetus and the great misery of widows and widowers to be a great sin ?", he asked." For, as long as they are young, they naturally wish to beget children and to enjoy the life of the senses; but due to hindrance in meeting due to government or caste obstructions, they have recourse to evil practices and sinful acts in secret". The best way to prevent this adultery and wickedness, according to him, is to exercise control over the senses, nay, to avoid contracting remarriage or niyoga. If it be possible, it is well and good. But if there is no such person of moral courage, they should be remarried and allowed to enter into the niyoga compact in time of dire necessity. This will diminish adultery and secure the increase of mankind by proper course of love and procreation of the best children. It will completely put an end to the sin of abortion.

He believed that a niyoga should be celebrated like a marriage. Like marriage the tie of niyoga should have the approval of good men and the mutual consent of the marrying parties. When a man and a woman wish to be united by niyoga, they should make a solemn declaration before the members of their families that they make a mutual covenant of niyoga, for the purpose of raising up issues, and that they will separate on the accomplishment of the object. If they continue their connection after it they should be considered as sinners and liable for punishment by the people of the same class and government. They should see each other once a month for fecundation. After conception they should live their years apart from each other.

He reiterated that men and women of the twice-born classes are permitted by the Vedas and other scriptures to marry but once, and not twice. The marriage of bachelors and maids is founded on justice; but there is injustice or unrighteousness in a marriage between a widow and a bachelor, or between a maid and a widower. As a man does not wish to marry a widow, so does woman. When a maid does not take a married man for her husband, nor does a bachelor like to accept the hand of a widow. Men and women will be under the necessity of making the compact of niyoga. It is right that like should be united with like in matrimonial relations.

In support of his views, he cited the following verse from the Rig Veda,[118] which said that "a widow can take in the alliance of niyoga a younger or elder brother of her deceased husband within 6 degrees of descent, a man of her tribe, or one of superior class. But the connection of niyoga is permitted when a widower and a widow have a desire for raising up issue in the event of utter failure of progeny. In other words, on the failure of issue, the alliance of niyoga may be formed between a woman and her husband's younger or elder brother for the purpose of procreating offspring. But if these allied parties have intercourse from carnal desire after the birth of children, it would be degrading. The time of the alliance of niyoga expires with the sign of the second conception. They should not amorously meet afterwards. If the niyoga compact is formed for the interests of both parties, it should cease with the fourth pregnancy. In fine, 10 children can be begotten by the above mentioned compact. Afterwards the conjugal intercourse between men and women is regarded as sensuality, and they are looked upon as fallen people. Also if married men and women cohabit after the 10th conception, they are thought to be lecherous and censurable.... Marriage and niyoga are for the purpose of procreating children not for carnal sports like those of beasts". He believed that the practice of niyoga should be adopted by both wives and husbands, who have lost their partners and who have not begotten any children. "When a man finds himself unable to beget children, he should suffer his wife to go to another...in like manner, a woman afflicted with disease and other defects, and finding herself incapable of bearing children, should allow her husband to raise issue upon another."

To propagate his philosophy in the native States of the Rajputana, Dayanand Saraswati selected Ajmer, as the centre of his socio-religious activities as it was the centre of higher education in those days, and also to counter the missionary influence and consequently opened a Branch of Arya Samaj at Ajmer on 13th of February 1881,[119] and from this date a new chapter opened in the social history of the Rajputana. The Samaj, in order to give a multidimensional aspect to its activities, opened Dayanand Ashram in 1887, Dayanand Anglo-Vedic School in 1888, Arya Anathashram (orphanage) in 1895, Arya-Kanya-Vidyalaya in 1898, school for the untouchables in 1900, Arya-Ratri Pathshala (i.e., Night Schools) in 1904, Dayanand Vaachanalaya and Dayanand Library in 1905, Vidhwa-Ashram (a place for the widows) in 1908, Arya Seva Dal and Arya Veer Dal in 1915, Sadhu-Ashram in 1925, Vanita Ashram in 1926, and also established Dalit-Uddhar Hitkarini Sabha in 1934.[120] The Arya Samaj thus became the first national organization, which was successful in acquiring a stronghold in the Rajputana. By 1911, Arya Samaj had 47 branches in the Rajputana, which was an indicator of Swami Dayanand's immense popularity and his untiring efforts.

To give a provincial character to the Arya-Samaj, Ajmer, in December 1888 Arya-Pratinidhi Sabha, Rajasthan-Malwa was established by Ram Bilas Sarda, Har Bilas Sarda, Lala Har Bakshi Chandak, Dr. Krishna Lal, Master Vazir Chand and Thakur Pancham Singh Verma. This Sabha was the Sabha or conference of nominated members of 12 branches of Arya Samaj, which were in the provinces of the Rajputana and Malwa. In December 1889, the members of the Arya-Samaj, Ajmer, in order to give a wider publicity to the philosophy of Dayanand, started preaching his tenets in different local, regional and inter-regional fairs like Pushkar, Teej, Tejaji, Ramdev Peer, Sheetala Mata, etc., a method which was later on copied by many of the caste organizations, especially the Jats, to arouse consciousness amongst their fellow brethrens to do away with the prevalent social evils. The importance of print media, as a mode of social change, was also understood by the Samaj and consequently it published a number of magazines and journals like *Arya Martand, Arya Mahila, Arya Bhumi, Tyag Bhumi, Desh Hitaishi,* etc.

To educate the people about the social and religious philosophy of Dayanand, Arya Samaj opened its branches at Beawar in 1884, at Masooda in 1885, at Nasirabad in 1890, and after 1901 it opened its branches at Kadel, Pushkar, Pisangan, Lad-Pura, and Saradhna.[121] On 10th of February 1888, the Arya Samaj opened its first school at Kesarganj, Ajmer.[122] In April 1889, its name was changed from Dayanand Ashram School to Dayanand Ashram Anglo-Vedic School (DAVV). To spread education and to fight against orthodox traditions, schools were opened at Vijaynagar in 1915, Nasirabad in 1923, Kesarganj (Ajmer) in 1940.[123]

From 1922 to 1947, Arya Samaj started giving co-education and many co-educational schools were opened at Ajmer, viz., Arya Bal

Mandir and Arya Bal Niketan (at Ramganj, Ajmer), Dayanand Bal Mandir (at Ghee Mandi, Naya Bazar, Ajmer), Arya Public School (at Lakhan-Kotri), Arya Shishushala (at Kumhar Basti), Arya Vedic School (at Sansi Basti), Vedic Shishu Mandir and Dayanand Pathshala (at Kayastha Mohalla), Arya Achoot Pathshala (at Diggi Mohalla), and Arya Nagari Pathshala (Usari Gate, Ajmer).[124] Those students who hailed from poor families and consequently could not afford school education at other places, were given admissions in these schools. The above mentioned schools, were deliberately opened at densely populated areas, so that maximum number of poor students could be benefitted. Beside these schools, the Upadeshaks or the preachers of the Samaj also imparted education in the distant areas. The names of Swami Nityanand Brahmachari, Swami Vishvesharanand, Pt. Ganpati Sharma, Pt. Ram Sahay Sharma, Pt. Prakash Chandra Kaviratna, Pt. Sheetal Chandra Sharma, Swami Lakshmanand, Swami Satchidanand, Swami Shantanand, Swami Karunanand, Pt. Parmanand, Pt. Mahendra, Shri Amar Singh Verma, Pt. Chogalal Pragyachakshu, Dr. Suryadev Sharma, Sh. Onkar Lal, Sh. Kanhaiya Lal, Th. Yograj Singh, Pt. Surendra Sharma etc. will always be remembered for their untiring efforts in the awakening of the masses.[125] Some of these Upadeshaks also opened primary schools at Pushkar, Ladpura, Saradhana, Badkchyawas, Alyanawas, Mangaliwas and Pisangan.[126] By quoting the examples, anecdotes and tales from the religious scriptures and by their devotional songs or bhajans, these Upadeshaks tried to make education interesting as well as pleasure giving and in this way contributed in the social reform movement in Rajasthan.

Similarly, the Jaipur branch of Arya Samaj (called as Vedic Dharma Sabha) was established by Pt. Kaluram, (at Krishnapole Bazar) on 16 June, 1877.[127] He, in order to preach the philosophy of Swami Dayanand, visited Fatehpur, Rajiyasar, Dujyar (Nagaur), Sujangarh, Bissau, Churu, Jhunjhunun, Nagaur etc. and established the branches of Arya Samaj in nearly 30 villages of Shekhawati including Dumkor, Jujhar, Fatehpur, Sujangarh etc.[128] On 1 January, 1939,[129] the committee members of Jaipur Arya Samaj decided to open a DAV school at Jaipur and made Mr. Firaya Lal the coordinator of the committee. Consequently, on the 14th of January 1939, a Harijan school at Heeda ki Mori was adopted by the Jaipur Arya Samaj. On the 13th of February 1940, a branch of Arya Samaj was opened at Dausa by Master Sundarlal and his son Vijay Bihari Lal.[130]

On 23rd of July 1939, the members of Jaipur Arya Samaj decided to open branches of Arya Samaj at other places of Jaipur State.[131] Consequently, a branch was opened at Chomu in 1941. The Krishna pole Arya Samaj, in order to awaken the masses of Jaipur State against the prevalent social vices like child marriage, unequal marriage, nukta or mausar etc., sent Pt. Surya Narayan on a tour of nearby areas and Pt. Surya Narayan toured 14 places in ten days and asked the people and social institutions to discard these evils and send their requests and appeals to the ruler of Jaipur, for the introduction of an Act against these evils. On the 29 November, 1942,[132] the Jaipur Arya Samaj, on behalf of "all the Hindu subjects of Jaipur State", sent a petition to the H.H. Maharaja of Jaipur, and asked him to "immediately introduce an act against child marriage in the Jaipur State, as is prevalent in British India and other native States." This was perhaps the first time, when the general public asked the Maharaja of Jaipur to introduce an act similar to the ones prevalent in British India and other Indian States. The Upadeshaks of Jaipur Arya Samaj like, Gokul Das Bhajanopdeshak, Pt. Gokul Chandra, Pt. Ganpati Sharma, Somanand Saraswati, Sh. Bhagwan Sahay Vidyavachaspati, etc. also created awareness amongst masses, through their bhajans and sermons. Similarly, Swami Narsingh Dev Saraswati of Jaipur, had a shastrartha with Pt. Devi Prasad Vidyavachaspati of Churu on *Striyon ko Veda padhne ka adhikar hai* (women have the right to study the Vedas), in which by his forceful arguments, he won the day and thus proved the importance of education for women.[133] Thus, by the above account, it becomes clear that the members of Jaipur Arya Samaj also played a significant role in the social reform movement. It is important to note that beside these male members, the wives and the daughters of these Arya Samajis also contributed in their own way and shared responsibility. On the 18 December, 1937,[134] the Jaipur Arya Samaj decided to start the women branch and therefore entrusted its work on Smt. Gopal Devi, Smt. Kamla Mahajan, Smt. Shanti Devi, Smt. Satyawati, Smt. Priyamvada Chaturvedi, Smt. Rampyari Devi, Smt. Vidyawati Bhatnagar, Smt. Shakuntala 'Vijay', Smt. Kamla Sharma, Smt. Savitri Devi Sharma, Smt. Ramawati Devi, Smt. Keshar Devi, Smt. Gopal Devi, Smt. Damyanti, Smt. Manorama etc. The names of these ladies will always be remembered for their zeal and untiring commitment towards social development.

The efforts of Pt. Kaluram produced good results and his forceful arguments in favour of Vedic religion and against social vices impressed the people of Shekhawati. Influenced by his thoughts, Seth Devi Bax of Mandawa, started the first branch of Arya Samaj in Shekhawati, in 1927, at Mandawa.[135] In accordance with the principles of Dayanand, regarding education of females, he also started a girls' school at Sahon Ki Haveli in Mandawa, in which the girls of rural as well as urban areas came to study. Seth Devi Bax, with the help of Th. Chhattu Singh of Taain village,[136] Th. Vishal Singh of Patode village, Chaudhry Govind Ram and his grand-sons-Harlal Singh and Chimnaram of village Hanumanpura, Babu Jagannath Sah, Pt. Kalicharan, Pt. Bhaniram Nai, Bastiram Darzi, Gindaram Darzi, Bastiram Thalia, Pt. Khemraj master and Bhoodaram and Ram Singh carried out the works of Arya Samaj in Mandawa, despite the heavy opposition from the Thikanedars of Shekhawati, including that of the Mandawa. Their efforts influenced the families of Mahajan community of Mandawa like Khemani, Newatia, Saunthalia and Sarafs and also some of the Brahmans like Ramratan Joshi, Biharilal Purohit, Makkhanlal Khandelwal etc.[137] In May, 1929, Arya Samaj of Mandawa opened schools not only for the students of upper castes but also for the students of lower castes.[138] Nearly 50 students of downtrodden classes were studying in this school, who were given the school uniforms and other necessary items by this Samaj. The Samaj also opened a library and reading room in the Arya Samaj Bhawan of Mandawa.

This motivated some of the local youths like Gurudev Khemani, Rameshwar Ramgarhia, Jankilal Newatia, Baluram Ladiya, Hanuman Goyanka etc. to start Shri Yuvak Sabha, for the spread of education and for the opposition of social evils.[139] The Arya Samaj of Mandawa, beside opposing the evil practices of child marriages, mausar, casteism and supporting the issues like widow marriages, female education etc., also invited the Upadeshaks and Bhajanopdeshaks from other parts of the country, to preach the philosophy of Dayanand and to give their lectures and sermons in Mandawa.[140] Radhamohan Gokul, Pt. Jeevram Dwivedi (of Bhartiya Hindu Shuddhi Sabha, Delhi), Pt. Devendra Shastri (Acharya, Gurukul of Sikandara), Swami Atmanand and Swami Chetanand were some of the few, who were invited by the Samaj of Mandawa. Seth Devi Bax was also in favour of widow marriages and consequently, he arranged the marriage of Laduram with a widow named Lachchi.

It is a lesser known fact that Th. Chhattu Singh of Taain Village, (who himself was a Rajput and who became a member of Arya Samaj, Mandawa in 1904 A.D.), also worked against the practice of female infanticide.[141] Despite the serious efforts of the native rulers and that of the British officers, this practice could not come to an end, and it seems that it was prevalent amongst the Rajputs of Shekhawati region even in the early decades of the 20th century. He, along with Pt. Khemraj, tried hard to create awakening amongst his community members, against female infanticide, by discussions and by dialogues. Since, it was carried out in the Zenana, behind closed doors, and since it was done with the consent of the father (of the child) or father-in-law, therefore, it was decided that Th. Chhattu Singh would discuss this horrible crime with the male members of the Rajput community, while Smt. Chandrawati (wife of Pt. Khemraj) would meet and ask the ladies of the Rajput families, to protest against this inhuman practice and motivate them to shun this age old evil custom. This campaign, continued for many months and slowly and gradually, the incidents of female infanticide in Shekhawati region, diminished.

Arya Samaj and the Role of Stree Arya Samaj

In the society of the times, there were many social and religious evils which were sapping the society from within. Polygamy, child-marriages, unequal marriages, marriages of the old people, *mausar, chandni,* dances of the *bhagtans* (i.e., prostitutes) etc. were some of the few.[142] These practices were undermining the status and position of the women restricting their space and freedom of movement and consequently, to create awareness among the women the Arya Samaj established different Stree Arya Samaj in the Rajputana. As far as the birth and objectives of Stree Arya Samaj is concerned, J. Reid Graham[143] has observed that there were constant complaints in the journals of the Samaj that the "Arya Samaj consisted of men who can talk in terms of social reform but women in the homes still held the orthodox ideas and insisted on the orthodox ceremonies. Therefore the Arya Samaj efforts at reform were not able to go forward." "It was evidently to help meet this situation that the Stree Samaj was founded" according to J. Reid Graham. On the other hand, J.N. Farquhar,[144] believes that Stree

Samaj was just another attempt of the Arya Samaj to copy Christian missionaries' methods of preaching and conversion. Other forms of imitation, according to Farquhar, were their being the tract society, Arya Kumar Sabha, their working among and for the orphans and depressed classes. Thus, he believes that the Arya Samaj was greatly influenced by Christianity and it was fashioned on the same lines.

On the 26 December, 1904, the First Stree Arya Samaj was established at Ajmer by Smt. Gulab Devi Maheshwari.[145] By 1912, the Arya Stree Samaj gained wide publicity and there were as many as 60 Stree Samaj.[146] The Stree Samaj primarily came into existence for those women who because of their illiteracy and of their confinement to their homes, were unable to listen to the lectures, given by the male members of the Arya Samaj.[147] The primary function of the Stree-Samaj was to spread the social and religious philosophy of the Master. The meetings of the Stree-Samaj were held every fortnight on Friday from 12 a.m. to 4 p.m. to facilitate women members to attend them.[148] The Stree-Samaj also organized regular lectures to enlighten the women of the Rajputana on different social issues like women's education, boycott of purdah, abolition of child and unequal marriages, encouragement to widow remarriages, etc.

At Ajmer, the women from the business community and especially from the Oswal community played a remarkable role for the upliftment of the downtrodden women, and also for those who were living in their *havelis*. Smt. Gulab Devi, Nathi Bai, Satyavati Devi, Siddh-Kunwar Bai Oswal, Sukhda Devi Sarda, Badami Devi Jain, Gheesi Bai Maheshwari, Krishna Devi, Kaushalya Devi, Shyam Devi, Ganga Devi, etc., were some of the prominent names of the Arya Stree Samaj, Ajmer. These women leaders, in order to inculcate the philosophy and tenets of the master as well as to spread social awareness, also formed Stree-Samaj of their castes, e.g., Jain Stree Samaj, Maheshwari Stree Samaj, Oswal Stree Samaj, Aggarwal Stree Samaj, Bhargava Stree Samaj, Kayastha Stree Samaj. etc., which comprised the women members of their caste alone.[149] The Jain Women's Conference held at Ajmer under the chairmanship of Kiran Devi Chordiya denounced child marriages[150] and so did the Kayastha Mahila Mandal, which was established in Jaipur, to impart education to women. Similarly, Parvati Devi Didwania, daughter of Sh. Jagannath of Jhunjhunun, organized Mahila Shakti Vardhini Sabha.[151]

The Arya Samaj, started an educational movement, to ameliorate the condition of women. At Ajmer-Beawar, to develop confidence, self-honour and to make women dependent, three Arya-Kanya Pathshalas were established, in which arrangements were made to give free education to women. On the 27 February, 1898, the first Arya-Putri Pathshala was started at Purani-Mandi, Ajmer. It was the first Girls School in Ajmer, which was run exclusively by the donations of the local people; and which was not managed by the British Government.[152] From 1898 to 1947 A.D. not even a single pie was taken from the girls and they were even provided school-dress, books and other requisite material. This school started with 9 girls and in 1947-48, the number of students went upto 224.[153]

Not contented with preaching alone, the leaders of the Stree Samaj made substantial contribution by devoting their life, energies and money, for the cause of women's' upliftment. In 1898, Smt. Gulab Devi, wife of Shri Mathura Prasad Maheshwari, (one of the leaders of Ajmer Arya Samaj) started a girls school at her residence at Kesarganj, Ajmer on the 10 April, 1898. She was aware of the utility and the importance of female education and therefore she made it her mission to wage crusade for the cause, at a time when the society of Rajputana had various prejudices against the education of girl-children. She also set up Rajasthan Stri Shiksha Nidhi, to promote and facilitate women's education in the whole province. Free education was given in this school and by 1947, the number of students of this school rose to 364.[154] Similarly, Godavari Devi of Stree Samaj Beawar, had such a commitment towards the amelioration of women, that she donated her property for the sake of spread of education among them. On 6 March, 1913, Smt. Godavari Devi, started Shrimati Godavari Arya Kanya Pathshala at her residence, with nearly 15 girls. Embroidery, sewing, knitting, house-keeping, child-rearing, performance of religious sacraments, etc. were also taught in the above mentioned schools, besides the government syllabus.[155] The curriculum of this institution reveals that the aim of education was to make girls better wives and mothers beside widening their mental horizons.

In July 1928, Kaushalya Devi, Subhadra Devi, Sukhda Devi and Manorama Devi of the Stree Samaj established Purdah Niwarak Mandali, Ajmer.[156] In January 1930, Smt. Parvati Devi Sarda (wife of Shri Har Bilas Sarda), Sukhda Sarda (wife of Shri Chand Karan

Sarda), Savitri Devi and Gulab Devi participated in the sessions of All India Women's Conference, held at Delhi and represented the women of Ajmer.[157]

Thus, by the above description, it becomes quite clear that Arya Samaj did a commendable work for the amelioration of the condition, position and status of the women of Indian society, by encouraging them to come out of their veils and by opening schools for their convenience. The Arya Samaj gave the voice to the unvoiced, cried for the uncried, wept for the unwept and made strong those who were considered as weak siblings. The words and philosophy of Dayanand Saraswati became the cry of the nation and whosoever heard that, with a balanced and impartial heart, was logically convinced by the forceful arguments of Dayanand Saraswati. Some of the followers of Dayanand, also published pamphlets describing the evil consequences of the child and unequal marriages. In 1893, Munshi Chatar Biharilal published his *Risala-e-Dharma Mitra,* Bawa Chhajju Singh published his *Brahmacharya Versus Child Marriage, Tract No. 1* 1893, *A well-wisher of the Hindus, Claims of the Arya Samaj on the Hindus,* and Swami Shraddhanand wrote a number of articles describing the evil consequences of child marriages and unequal marriages on the Hindu society.[158] Swami Shraddhanand suggested that boys should be married at the age of 25 and the girls should be married at the age of 18.[159] Similarly, Pundit Din Dayal, one of the members of Arya Samaj, through his eloquent speeches, started a wave (mass-movement) against the child and unequal marriages and he himself set an example by marrying his daughter at the age of 13 with a boy who was 19 at that time.[160] Pandit Chuttanlal Swami published his *Vivah-Vayo Vichar* in 1927 and quoted several verses from different religious scriptures, which were against child marriage and thereby told his readers that child marriages were not in existence in the early Vedic times, rather they were a very late addition in the Hindu society. To educate the masses about the harmful effects of child marriages, the Arya Pratinidhi Sabha, Rajasthan, sent its Baal Vivah Nishedhak Mandal[161] to various native States of Rajasthan, who held discussions and debates with the local people. The Samaj, after deliberating on the pitiable condition of the widows and specially child widows, also focused its attention on widow remarriages. Satyadev Vidyalankar, one of the members of the Samaj, started a monthly newspaper – *Rajasthan* – from Akola,

Maharashtra, in which he published articles in favour of widow remarriages, and condemned child and unequal marriages.[162] The Stree Arya Samaj, Ajmer, conducted the remarriage of Maan Kanwari, a child widow of the Khandelwal community of Ajmer, with Gopilal of Udaipur, who was also a widower, on 3 March, 1935. Similarly on the 28 December, 1936, the remarriage of Hansa Bai, a child widow of Maheshwari community, was conducted with Madholal.[163] The Arya Stree Samaj, Ajmer, performed remarriage of child widows of 17 different communities. Similarly, the Vanita Ashram, Ajmer, conducted 7 widow remarriages in 1926-27, 37 in 1928-34, and 64 widow remarriages in 1936-47.[164] In the same manner, Lala Gangaram Agrawal, one of the members of Arya Samaj and the leader of widow remarriage movement in Lahore, established a branch of Gangaram Vidhwa Sahayak Sabha at Ajmer on 19 March, 1927,[165] to discard child and unequal marriages as well as marriage of the old people, and to popularize widow remarriages. Gangaram Vidhwa Sahayak Sabha was established at Lahore on 1 December, 1914 and by 1927, it had over 600 branches all over the country.[166] In the various native States of Rajasthan, it had 17 branches and some of them were in Jodhpur, Bikaner, Dholpur, Jaipur, Bharatpur, Beawar, Kekri, Phulera, Nathdwara, Chittaur, etc.

But the name of Shri Har Bilas Sarda, one of the members of the Arya Samaj, will never fade from the social history of India. Sarda, through his writings, through his speeches, through his passionate arguments created a revolution in the hearts and minds of the people, and ultimately was successful in passing an Act, which is known as the Child Marriage Restraint Act or Sarda Act. The name of the Arya Samaj, of its members; of its contribution and that of Har Bilas Sarda is a glorious chapter in the amelioration of the condition, position and status of the women of India. After the Bill passed by Shri Har Bilas Sarda, became an Act of 1929; the Arya Samaj started protesting the child marriages with a new zeal. They appealed to the people to boycott such marriages and to bring such cases to the notice of the courts and the government. The Arya Samaj also requested the different Native States, to frame rules and enact law, on the lines of the British Indian Provinces. Various local leaders of Arya Samaj wrote open letters to the masses, to the Native Durbars requesting them to enforce the Child Marriage Restraint Act in their respective States. When the Maharaja of Jodhpur, proposed a law, for the eradication of child and unequal marriages and got it published in the *Marwar Gazette* of 16 September, 1939, it was greatly welcomed by the Arya Samaj besides other enlightened social and caste organizations. Similarly, the Arya Samaj in Jaipur appealed from time to time, the Maharaja of Jaipur to enforce the Child Marriage Restraint Act in their State; and were successful in 1945, when the Maharaja of Jaipur made a legislation on the lines of the Child Marriage Restraint Act.

By the above account it becomes quite clear that the Arya Samaj played a commendable role in the upliftment of women. The Samaj opened a large number of schools, colleges and public libraries in various States of the Rajputana. The need and the importance of education as a tool for personality development and also as a mode of social change was understood and emphasized by the Arya Samaj, much before any other social organization in Rajputana. Infact, the Desh Hitaishini Sabha and the WKRHS did not advocate education as an important vehicle of social change, and here lies the real significance of Arya Samaj.

Similarly, the Arya Samaj prescribed 25 and 16 as the minimum marriageable age for boys and girls which was much higher than the WKRHS (as it laid 18 and 14 for boys and girls). In fact, Dayanand was the only reformer in the whole of the 19th century, who prescribed such higher limits for the marriages of boys and girls. Ishwarchandra Vidyasagar laid down 18 and 11 years as the minimum marriageable age for boys and girls, Keshab Chandra Sen advocated 14 or 16 years as the right age of marriage for girls, Mahadev Govind Ranade laid down 16 or 18 for boys and 10 or 12 for girls and the Indian National Social Conference prescribed 18 years for boys and 12 years for girls.

Dayanand also held a rational approach towards the settlement of marriages as he recommended that wedding arrangements should be preceded by enquiries about the candidates and not by means of deceitful and meaningless horoscopes (or sorrow-scopes as he called them), but by proper investigations. These are the two unique contributions of Arya Samaj which reflect upon the originality of ideas as well as the liberal personality of Swami Dayanand.

He denounced child marriages on biological, emotional, educational and religious grounds. To have greater accessibility among the masses, Dayanand's citation of the Shastras, on issue of child marriages, was also a unique thing in the social history of the Rajputana. This is true that reformers like Vidyasagar, Keshab Chandra Sen, M.G. Ranade, cited the Shastrik injunctions to prove that child marriage was not in vogue in Vedic times, much before Dayanand, their influence was however, restricted to Bengal or Maharashtra only. On the insistence of Keshab Chandra Sen, Swami Dayanand accepted Hindi as the language of communication and started giving his lectures in Hindi, so that the ordinary men could also understand him and his philosophy.

Swamiji considered swayamvara form of marriage as the best marriage as it gave full authority to the women to select husband for herself after taking due consideration of the health, qualities, physical built-up, beauty and intelligence of the prospective groom. After the demise of Dayanand, Swami Shraddhanand one of the disciples of Dayanand, prescribed the marriageable age for girls and boys as 18 and 25. It is difficult to say that how many people in the Rajputana, accepted the prescribed age limits of Arya Samaj, as far as marriage of their sons and daughters was concerned, as there are no records available on this matter. It seems that the society at that time, if we take into consideration the religious and economic condition of the period, was not too broad-minded and progressive to accept such radical social changes, as was proposed by the Arya Samaj. Further, Dayanand's prescription that an ideal marriage is one, where the husband was one and a half times more than the age of bride, found little favour with the tradition-bound society, as this thought was much ahead of his times. Similarly, Dayanand's perception about inferior, medium and superior types of marriages and its advocacy is difficult to understand. It would have been much more convincing if he had contemplated 48 as the maximum limit of marriage rather than prescribing it as the proper age for marriage. This notion contradicts his own theory of the observance of four ashrams, as it would place domestic responsibilities on the shoulder of a person, when he should actually start withdrawing himself from them. Moreover this difference of ages between husband and wives would, reflect in their relationships and would not allow them to intermingle on equal grounds. Dayanand's views both on minimum marriageable age and right type of marriage reflects originality and individuality of his personality, which was free from narrow considerations.

As a social reformer, Dayanand in his early life, denounced polygamy in harsh words and allowed it under no circumstance, but later on, after thinking over the deplorable condition of widows and especially child widows, allowed it. The Arya Samaj, in order to preach the philosophy of the master, tried a new method of social intercourse through the use of fairs and festivals like that of Pushkar fair of Ajmer, Seetlamata fair at Karauli, Fair of Baba Ramdev, Mallinath, Goga Peer, and even used the platform of cattle fairs to enlighten the rural masses. On these occasions, the responsibility of the programmes rested upon the local bodies of Arya Samaj. This again was a unique step, as no other organization before Arya Samaj, had taken such a farsighted step and tried to reach out the common masses.

While the Desh Hitaishini Sabha and the WKRHS relied heavily upon the support of rulers and nobles for their existence, the Arya Samaj made the common men its target group and focused all of its attention to have their involvement in the social reform process. This fact alone creates a sharp distinction between the Arya Samaj and other social organizations and speaks volumes about the organizational and managerial skills of the leaders of Arya Samaj. Because of this factor, the Arya Samaj is still vibrant, energetic and active even in the 21st century, as it became a (and still is) people's movement, over the years.

Its true that some of the rulers and nobles were influenced by the philosophy of Dayanand Saraswati and provided him necessary monetary support as well as hospitality to enable him to carry out his work in the Rajputana. Maharana Sajjan Singh of Mewar, Rajrana Fateh Singh and Rajrana Jalim Singh of Delwara, Rao Takht Singh of Bedala, Rawat Arjun Singh of Asind, Th. Manohar Singh of Sardargarh, Th. Govind Singh of Badnore, Rao Sawai Krishna Singh of Bijolia, Raja Fateh Singh of Bhilwara, Rawat Ummed Singh of Kanod, Raja Raj Singh of Shavadi, Th. Ranjit Singh and his son Th. Lakshman Singh, Th. Nand Kishore Singh of Jaipur, Th. Rawul Karna Singh and his son Rawul Narendra Singh of Jobner, Th. Govind Singh of Chomu, Thakur Govind Singh of Bunera, Thakur Nahar Singh of Shahpura, Kaviraja Shyamal Das, (who later on became one of the founding members of Walter Krit Rajputra Hitkarini Sabha) and Mohanlal Vishnulal Pandya of Mewar, were some of the influential persons, who also helped him in his mission.[167] Similarly Maharana Sajjan Singh of Mewar gave him Rs 1200.00 for the publication of his *Ved-Bhashya*. It is remarkable to note that Swamiji revised his *Satyartha Prakash,* completed the commentaries on the Vedas and found the Paropkarini Sabha at Udaipur, under the patronage of the Maharana of Mewar. The

Paropkarini Sabha was established at Meerut on August 16, 1880 A.D., but it was reconstituted by Swamiji and was registered at Udaipur on February 27, 1883 and Maharana Sajjan Singh of Mewar was nominated as its President. These examples suggest that the influence of Samaj was limited to some of the ruling families.

Another important aspect of the Arya Samaj was the network of Arya Stree Samaj, which was established to create an awakening among them and to motivate and enable them to fight against the prevalent social abuses. These Arya Stree Samajs established schools, exclusively for women and made special efforts to impart education to those, who were married and who because of their domestic responsibilities were confined to the four-walls of their homes and havelis. To ameliorate the condition of women, the efforts done by Arya Samaj can very well be compared with the process of gently hitting the nail, as its purpose was to change the mindset of the people slowly and gradually and to make them think over the whole social scenario once again.

He was a Luther fighting against his own misled and misguided Church of Rome; and his first care was to throw open the wells of the holy books, so that for the first time his people could come to them and drink for themselves. He translated and wrote commentaries on the Vedas in the vernacular – it was in truth an epoch-making date for India when a Brahmin not only acknowledged that all human beings have the right to know the Vedas, whose study had been previously prohibited by orthodox Brahmins, but insisted that their study and propaganda was the duty of every Arya man and woman, He presented the Vedas with new interpretations, which were more humanist, more rational, and which were in consonance with the changing times.

The works of Arya Samaj and its vehement arguments for the emancipation of women led to counter-reformation in the Hindus and perhaps, influenced some of the caste organizations as well as caste leaders to undertake reform activities within their own castes. The Arya Samaj showed them the path and provided them the light of reason and logic and thereby motivated them to take the Herculean task of cleaning their own stables.

Role of Har Bilas Sarda

In the history of social reforms Har Bilas Sarda's contribution is of seminal significance. His entire family was closely associated with the movement, led by the Arya Samaj in Ajmer. It is interesting to note that not only men but also women of the Sarda family, took active part in the Arya Samaj movement and worked actively for the amelioration of women. The greatest contribution of Har Bilas Sarda is in the field of social legislation. He was a vehement spokesman against the social evils and his social agenda included urgent need of determining the minimum age for marriage.

Har Bilas Sarda was born on 3 June, 1867 in a reputed Maheshwari family of Ajmer.[168] He was the only son of Har Narayan Sarda, who was the librarian of Government College, Ajmer. Young Sarda delighted to assist his father in the annual stock taking of the college library, and in this way had ample opportunities of familiarizing himself with many important books. When quite a young man he together with a few friends, opened a debating club in Ajmer, and there he took part in discussions of a social and semi-political nature, thus equipping himself for his future brilliant career as a judge and a reformer. In 1888, he participated in third annual session of All India Congress Committee, held at Allahabad. Here he came in contact with the leaders of Congress.

Har Bilas Sarda, when he was only eight years old, went to see Swami Dayanand Saraswati, who came to Ajmer in 1875.[169] The thoughts of Dayanand Saraswati greatly impressed young Sarda and he became member of the Arya Samaj. In 1888, he was made the President of the Arya Samaj of Ajmer and was also appointed as President of the representative body of Rajputana Arya Samaj. In 1890, he became a member of the Paropkarini Sabha, which was formed according to the wishes of Dayanand Saraswati. Sarda became the Joint-Secretary of this Sabha in 1894 and when Mohanlal Pandya resigned from the post of Secretary, he was selected for that post.

Sarda was the key-man in the opening of DAV School in Ajmer and later on he became the President of DAV Committee of Ajmer.

From 1924 to 1930, he was thrice nominated as the representative of Ajmer-Merwara region in the Central Legislative Assembly. During this time, he became a member and office bearer of many committees. In 1930, he was selected by the Government of India, as the member of Primary Education Committee.[170] This committee was to give its report on the level of education, given in the British administered provinces.

In the annual meeting of All India Vaishya Conference which was held in 1925, Har Bilas Sarda was appointed as its president and in 1930, he presided over the 42nd Conference of National Social Reforms Committee, an organization which was started by M.G. Ranade, and which was held at Lahore.

Sarda was an active member, and he had the credit of passing three non-official Bills in the Central Legislative Assembly. One of them was Child Marriage Restraint Act, which is better known as Sarda Act. In 1927, he presented the Child Marriage Restraint Act in the Legislative Assembly. In support of his Bill, he gave a memorable speech on the 15 September, 1927, at Shimla. By his fiery arguments, his eloquent wordings, and citation of passages from the religious scriptures of the Hindus, he told the masses that child marriage was not sanctioned by the earlier religious scriptures and that it was a later addition. He cited the works of Manu and Dhanvantari especially, whose works were regarded as old, as well as supportive.[171] Sarda urged the people that his Bill was not in opposition to any caste or religion, but was in consonance with them. He told that his Bill was a modest attempt for the acceptance of 'Inalienable Rights' of women.[172]

Sarda was very much moved by the pathetic condition of the child widows. According to the Census of 1921, there were 612 Hindu widows, who were less than one year. The number of child-widows between 5 to 10 years was 85,580; and the number of child-widows, who were less than 15 years was 3,32,472.[173] Quoting the Census data of 1921, Sarda told that 11 per cent of the women of Hindu society were married at the ages of 10 and 11 years and 44 per cent were married even before reaching the 15th year. He described in detail the moral, social and physical consequences of child marriages. He quoted the excerpts from Dr. Lanchaster's book *Tuberculosis in India* and observed that there was a direct relationship between early marriages and tuberculosis and told his audience that because of child marriages, many brides and grooms suffer an ultimately death from tuberculosis.[174] Sarda appealed to the masses to shun this social evil on social, psychological, biological and nationalistic grounds. He told the gathering at Shimla that for the sake of the mother land, and for its liberation and emancipation, it was necessary to free women from the chains of early marriage as well as other social negations. Thus, he linked the evil of child marriage with the bondage of the country and tried to appeal to their nationalistic sentiments, which was a unique thing in itself.

The Government of India, at the time of passing of Sarda's Bill, showed a luke-warm attitude. The Home Secretary announced that he would oppose the Bill. Sarda severely criticized the Government's lukewarm attitude and urged it to frame laws on the lines of progressive States like Baroda, Indore and Mysore. He called the so-called humanitarian attitude of the government, a farce, a sham and told it in uncompromising words that a government, which claims itself to be progressive and the motto of which is equality, liberty, justice and public welfare opposes the bill is ridiculous. He disapproved the policy of Government of India and said that his was not a lone voice rather he represented the voice of lacs of Indians and also that if it was unable to pass an Act on its own then at least it should keep neutral and allow its government members to vote according to their conscience.

The bill was introduced in the Assembly on 15 September, 1927.[175] In his speech in the Legislative Assembly at Shimla, he remarked that the primary object of the Bill was to put a stop to child widowhood, which was a result of child marriage. The secondary aim of the Bill, he remarked, was to remove the principal impediment to the physical and mental growth of the youth of both sexes and the chief cause of their premature decay and death. He considered the Bill as a modest attempt "to recognize that female children even amongst the Hindus, have certain inalienable rights and that the State with any pretensions to civilization will deem its duty to protect them, without heeding to the vagaries that masquerade in the guise of social customs".[176]

From September 1927 to January 1928 this Bill was presented before the public for their support. During this period Sarda kept on addressing the masses and requested them to give their unflinching support to the Bill.[177] He also appealed to the wives of the British officers and in addition even wrote to the women members of the House of Commons in Britain.[178] On the 29 January, 1928, the meeting of Legislative Assembly was called at Delhi in which again Sarda gave a historic speech to the members. Because of his sincere efforts all the national organizations and caste-organizations requested the Government of India to accept the Bill proposed by Sarda. On 19 Nov. 1928, the Marwari women of the Rajputana asked the government to pass the bill. In the same way the local and the provincial government too requested the Government of India to pass the Bill of Mr. Har Bilas Sarda. The Brahmin community of

Madras province, the Governors of Central Province, U.P., Punjab, Bombay, Bihar and Orissa and the Commissioners of Coorg and Ajmer-Merwara gave their vote in favour of the Bill. Similarly, the judges of different High Courts gave their unconditional support to the Bill of Har Bilas Sarda. Sarda told the Legislative Assembly that his Bill was not only a measure for social reform, rather it was a measure to stop the crimes committed for centuries against the women. He enlightened the members of the Assembly by quoting the findings of Dr. Campbell, principal of Lady Hardinge College, Delhi according to the research of whom the first issue of 40 per cent of child-mothers died because of being physically weak. He told that not only the eyes of all the Indians but also those of the citizens of United Kingdom and the United States of America were watching them. He quoted an English poem in which it was said that "Hear Senates, hear this truth sublime, He who allows oppression shares the crime."[179]

The next meeting of the Legislative Assembly was held on the 23 September, 1928 at Shimla in which final discussions were held. Sarda's moving appeal and repeated reminders resulted in the constitution of an Age of Consent Committee, which laid emphasis on the necessity of an Act prohibiting child marriages, in its report, and asked Government of India to consider this matter seriously.[180] Sarda once again gave an eloquent speech in favour of the Bill and thus succeeded in passing of the Bill, which came to be known as Child Marriage Restraint Act of 1929. The main provisions of the Act were as follows:[181]

(1) The marriage of the boy or girl married in minor age is prohibited and liable to punishment.
(2) The guardians of such a boy or girl married in minor age would be deemed responsible for it and subject to be penalized.
(3) Within one year of marriage the case can be filed.
(4) No Magistrate other than the first class one can hear such cases.
(5) The sponsorer of such a case shall have to deposit Rs 100 as security so that in case of default the other party may demand the loss.

After his Bill became an Act, thousands and thousands of people wrote congratulatory letters to him and expressed their thanks and gratitude. Thus, the Child Marriage Act of 1929 was a great leap forward in the amelioration of the condition of child brides. This Act came into force on April 1, 1930.[182]

Though the Child Marriage Restraint Act or the Sarda Act, as it is popularly called, because of the contribution of Har Bilas Sarda in getting it passed, declared 18 as the minimum age for marriage for boys and 14 for girls, it was fraught with certain limitations. First, the provisions number 4 and 5 of the Sarda Act, proved more a block in the way rather than of help, as it allowed only First Class Magistrates to hear the cases of child marriages. There were no First Class Magistrates in the villages to prevent such marriages and this helped the parents or the guardians to perform the marriages of their sons and daughters, without any fear. Second, provision number 5 laid down that the sponsorer of the case (i.e., the informer of child marriages), was to deposit a sum of Rs 100 as security, which made it difficult for an ordinary man to arrange rupees hundred, to inform. At times, the parents eager to marry off their children at an early age, simply ignored the Act, and considered the fine of Rs 100 as an additional expense on the occasion of marriage. Third, this Act was made applicable only on British India and not on the native States. This gave the people a narrow lane, to bye-pass the Act. Many people, in order to save themselves from the jurisdiction of the Act started going to the Indian States to perform child or unmatched marriages, and thus defied the very purpose of the Act. Further, the Sarda Act contained no provisions to deal with unmatched marriages, which were widely prevalent in the society then. In fact, this matter was passed in perfect silence. Many questions, regarding unmatched marriages, were left unanswered by this Act. If a girl of 14 years was married to a man of much higher age say 50, 70 or 80, her marriage was valid according to the Act, but this marriage neglected other social, psychological, biological and emotional factors, which was a great drawback on the part of the Act.

But all said and done, the significance of this Act lies in the fact that it set 18 and 14 as the minimum marriageable ages for boys and girls respectively and made it a penal offence to commit child marriages and paved the way for future reforms in other native States. Soon, voices were raised and demands were made for a similar Act in the native States. But despite the efforts of these enlightened individuals and social organizations the practice of child marriage is still prevalent in India (and especially in the State of Rajasthan) where it takes place in large numbers on auspicious days like Akha-Teej and Basant-Panchami, even in the 21st century.

Notes

1. Cf. Sharma, S.R., *Mughal Empire in India,* Lakshmi Narain Agarwal, Agra, 11th edition (year not mentioned), pp. 177-182.
2. Mahesh Chandra Deb believed that Mohammedan invasions and Hindu sacred scriptures were mainly responsible for this deterioration in the position of women in India. "It is these religious codes of our country men," he remarked, "which render their wives literally slaves both in body and mind to their will and caprice…. I abhor from the very core of my heart, those abominable principles, the inculcation of which makes women emphatically called the better half of our species merely 'the slaves of a tyrant's will…." Cf. Sen, Amiya P. (ed.) *Social and Religious Reform – The Hindus of British India,* Oxford University Press, New Delhi, 2005, pp. 138-141.
3. Ghosh, Benoy, *Samajik Patre Banglar Samaj-Chitra,* Part III, pp. 62-63. (Extract published in *Ananda Bazar Patrika,* 9 October, 1971).
4. Sen, Prosanto Kumar, *Biography of a New Faith,* Vol. II, pp. 60-61.
5. Sen, Amiya P., *Hindu Revivalism in Bengal (1872-1905), Some Essays in Interpretation,* Oxford University Press, New Delhi, p. 370.
6. Datta, Kali Kinkar, *A Social History of Modern India,* MacMillan, New Delhi, 1975, p. 313.
7. Kapadia, K.M., *Marriage and Family in India,* Oxford University Press, Bombay, 1958, p. 146.
8. Shastri, Sivanath, *History of the Brahmo Samaj,* Vol. I, 1911, p. 249. And also, Chintamani, C.V., *Indian Social Reform,* Part IV, pp. 260-291.
9. Ibid.
10. Shastri, Sivanath, op. cit., p. 250.
11. Cf. Y. S. Chintamani (ed.) *Indian Social Reform, Part IV,* Madras, 1901, pp. 255-56. And also, Datta, Kali Kinkar, op. cit., p. 317.
12. Sivanath Shastri, op. cit., pp. 246-248.
13. Grover, B.L. and Grover, S., *A New Look at Modern Indian History,* S. Chand and Company Ltd., New Delhi, 1992, pp. 380-381.
14. Shastri, Sivanath, op. cit., p. 328. And also, Sen, Amiya P., *Hindu Revivalism in Bengal (1872-1905),* p. 369.
15. Datta, Kali Kinkar, op. cit., p. 314.
16. Sen, Amiya P., *Hindu Revivalism in Bengal (1872-1905),* p. 369.
17. Heimsath, Charles, H., *Indian Nationalism and Hindu Social Reform,* Oxford University Press, Bombay, 1964, p. 151.
18. Ibid., p. 152.
19. Ibid., p. 154.

20. Ibid., p. 152.
21. Kapadia, K.M., op. cit., p. 149.
22. His newspaper *Indian Spectator* was a major organ for the spread of social reform ideas. Later in 1901, Malabari founded *East and West* – a journal, which was dedicated to the cause of social reforms. To evoke sympathy and support for his crusade, Malabari visited different places and addressed meetings at Lahore on 7 October, 1885; at Agra on 10 February, 1886; at Aligarh on 14 February, 1886; at Lucknow on 17 February, 1886; at Allahabad on 19 February, at Mathura on 25 February, 1886. In all these meetings, resolutions were passed against, what Malabari referred to in his speech at Allahabad as "the scourge of child marriages". Cf. Datta, Kali Kinkar, op. cit., p. 319.
23. Gidumal, Dayaram, *Status of Women in India,* Cf. Parvate, T.V., *Mahadev Govind Ranade: A Biography,* Asia Publishing House, Bombay, 1963, p. 153.
24. Parvate, T.V., op. cit., p. 153.
25. "यामुलें सामाजिक सुधारणा नको अस्ते आम्हीं मृणतों असें कोणीही समजूं नये। आमचें एवढेंच मृणणें कीं। डॉ. भण्डारकर यानीं सामाजिक सुधारणेचा व राजकीय हक्कांचा ओ हा संबंध जोड़ला आहे तो अगदीं भ्रान्तिमूलक व निराधार आहे।।

    'Samajik Sudharneche Marg', Kesari 21 January, 1896. Cf. Verma, V.P., *Lokmanya Tilak: Jiwan aur Darshan,* Lakshmi Narayan Agarwal Prakashak, Agra, 1982, p. 39.
26. Parvate, T.V., op. cit., p. 152.
27. Ibid., pp. 147-148.
28. Datta, Kali Kinkar, op. cit., p. 323.
29. Ibid.
30. Sen, Amiya P. (ed.) *Social and Religious Reform – The Hindus of British India,* pp. 212-218.
31. "I shall rejoice if the results of your inquiries should show that there exists an opening for the Government to mark in some public manner the view which it entertains of the Great importance of reform in these matters..." Cf. Gidumal, Dayaram, op. cit., p. cxii.
32. Heimsath, Charles, op. cit., p. 158.

    A. P. McDonell, Off. Secy. to the Government of India, on this question remarked that, "In dealing with such subjects as those raised in Mr. Malabari's 'Notes', the British government in India has usually been guided by certain general principles...When caste or custom enjoins a practice which involves a breach of principles which involves a breach of criminal law, the state will enforce the law. When caste or custom lays down a rule which is of its nature enforceable in civil courts but is clearly opposed to morality or public policy, the state will decline to accept it. When caste or custom lays down a rule which deals with such matters as is usually left to the option of citizens, which does not need the help of civil or criminal courts for its enforcement, state enforcement is not considered either desirable or expedient...There is one common sense test which may often be applied with advantage in considering whether the state should or should not interfere in its legislative or executive capacity with social or religious questions...The test is can the state give effect to its command by the ordinary machinery at its disposal? If not, it is desirable that the state should abstain from making a rule which it cannot enforce without a departure from it's usual practice or procedure...The Governor General Council, as at present advised, would prefer not to interfere..." Cf. Sen, Amiya P. (ed.) *Social and Religious Reform – The Hindus of British India* p. 104.

33. Max Muller had earlier written to Malabari to suggest that he should appeal to the women of England to offset the government's decision not to intervene with legislation.

    Gidumal, *The Life of Malabari*, p. 204. Cf. Heimsath, Charles, op. cit., p. 160.
34. Ibid.
35. Excerpted from K.T. Tellang's letter to B. M. Malabari, 16 September, 1884. Cf. Sen, Amiya p. *Social and Religious Reform – The Hindus of British India*, p. 151.
36. *The Times*, Oct. 8, Nov. 7, 1890. Cf. Heimsath, Charles, op. cit., p. 168.
37. Ibid.
38. *Journal of Indian History*, April, August and December, 1971. Cf. Datta, op. cit., p. 330.
39. Rukhmabai was the wife of Dadaji, who brought suit to force his young wife to live with him; when she refused, the court (following the British precedents) ordered her imprisonment.
40. Sir Andrew Scoble considered this Bill as necessary "to protect female children from immature prostitution and from premature co-habitation," while introducing this Bill in the Indian Legislative Council.

    Cf. *Har Bilas Sarda Commemoration Volume*, Vedic Yantralaya, Ajmer, 1937, p. 196.
41. Cf. Sen, Amiya P. *Social and Religious Reform*, pp. 105-109.
42. Cf. Datta, Kali Kinkar, op. cit., p. 332.
43. Ibid.

44. Kapadia, K.M., op. cit., pp. 150-152.
45. Ibid.
46. Ibid.
47. *Census Report, 1911*, part I, p. 271.
48. Kapadia, K.M., op. cit., p. 153.
49. Cf. *Har Bilas Sarda Commemoration Volume*, op. cit., p. 197.
50. Ibid.
51. Kapadia, K.M., op. cit., pp. 152-153.
52. Ibid.
53. Barhat, Krishna Singh, *Rajputana Ka Itihaas*, Vol. I, p. 84.
54. Jain, M.S., op. cit., p. 240.
55. RSAB: Ajmer Records, Commissioner's Office, File number-2 (1886); Cf. Jain, M.S., op. cit., p. 240.
56. Ibid.
57. RSAB: From Col. Walter, A.G.G. in Rajputana to the Secretary to the G.O.I., Foreign Department; No. 277-C, dated 23 March, 1888; Basta No. 130, File No. 1493; Ajmer Commissioner's office.
58. Though Col. Walter has mentioned the names of 41 representatives, who took part in the meeting, yet in the original list of representatives, the name of Kavi Raj Buldeo Raj of Khetree, was found to be deleted by hand. Therefore the number 40 is mentioned here.

    RSAB: Proceedings of a committee of Sardars, officials and Charans, from all the States of Rajputana, held at Ajmer, for the purpose of regulating the expenditure connected with ceremonies at marriages and deaths among Rajputs. Basta No. 130, File No. 1493, Commissioner's Office, Ajmer.
59. RSAB: From Walter to Secretary, G.O.I., Foreign Department, no. 277-C, dated 23 March, 1888; Basta No. 130, File No. 1493, Commissioner's Office, Ajmer.
60. Ibid.
61. RSAB: From Col. Walter to Col. Trevor, dated 16 January, 1889, Basta No. 130, File no. 1493, Commissioner's Office, Ajmer.
62. RSAB: Supplementary rules framed by the general committee of Rajput Sardars and Charans, assembled at Ajmer from 15 to 24 February, 1889; Basta No. 130, File No. 1493, Commissioner's Office, Ajmer.
63. Jain, M.S., op. cit., pp. 240-247.
64. However in December 1943, the permission of accepting or taking of *reet* was given to those parents, who because of their financial diffi-

culties were unable to perform their daughter's marriage. They were allowed to accept a sum not exceeding Rs 100, from the groom's side and were asked not to spend more than this amount on the marriage.

RSAJ: Proceedings of the meeting (of WKRHS) held on 25 December, 1943, General, Social and Religious, Basta No. 12.

65. Sharma, S.R., op. cit., p. 182.
66. RSAJ: Annual General Report from the members of the General Committee of the WKRHS to E.G. Colvin, A.G.G., Rajputana, and the President and Chairman of the WKRHS.
67. Ibid.
68. RSAJ: General Statement of marriages and funerals performed amongst the Rajputs, during the year 1909. Appendix-A. Annual General Report to E.G. Colvin, A.G.G., for 1909.
69. RSAJ: Annual General Report to E.G. Colvin, A.G.G., for the year 1912-13.
70. RSAJ: Annual General Report of Walterkrit Rajputra Hitkarini Sabha, Jaipur, 1909.
71. NAI: For. Intl. B, June, 1894, No. 391.
72. Ibid.
73. Lawrence, W.R., *The India We Served*, pp. 278-279.
74. R.A.R. Bikaner State, 1895-96, p. 76.
75. Singh, S.R., *Nationalism and Social Reform in India*, 1885-1920, p. 158.
76. *Indian Social Reformer*, p. 209.
77. *The Indian Spectator and the Voice of India*, Aug. 9, 1896.
78. (a) Kayastha Durga Prasad was appointed as the Secretary of the WKRHS on 1 September, 1889.

    RSAJ: General, Appointment of a Secretary of WKRHS, Record no. 015 (Part IV), 1890/401, Residency.

    (b) Munshi Nand Lal Bhargava, became Secretary in 1900 and left this post in 1905, as he got a new and higher job in the Government.

    (c) Pundit Shankar Nath, became Secretary of WKRHS, in 1905 in place of Munshi Nand Lal Bhargava.

    RSAJ: Annual General Report of WKRHS, 1905, p. 51.
79. RSAJ: From Bachan Singh of Dervala to the Vice President, Council of State, Jaipur, dated 11th of August, 1934. General-20 current, proposed abolition and reconstitution of WKRHS, File No. 150.
80. Ibid.

81. RSAJ: From H. Burton, the Resident at Jaipur, to the Vice President, Council of State, Jaipur, dt. 22 May, 1935; General-20-current, proposed abolition and reconstitution of WKRHS, File no. 150.
82. RSAJ: Speech made by Col. George Ogilvie, A.G.G., as the President of WKRHS, in its Conference on 19th May, 1936. General-20-current, File No. 150.
83. Ibid.
84. Ibid.
85. RSAJ: Speech made by Raja Amar Singh of Bunera (Mewar), on 21 May, 1936, as the Chairman of WKRHS General-20-current, proposed abolition and reconstitution of WKRHS, File No. 150.
86. RSAJ: From Rawul Sangram Singh of Samode to Education member, Council of State, Jaipur, dt. 26 May, 1936. General-20-current, proposed abolition and reconstitution of WKRHS, File No. 150.
87. RSAJ: Copy of note, recorded by Rawul Sangram Singh of Samode, dated 14 October, 1943. General-20-current, File No. 58.
88. Ibid.
89. RSAJ: Revised rules of WKRHS, General, Social & Religious, Basta No. 9.
90. For a detailed study of Swami Dayanand's stay and work in the States of Rajputana, please refer to Vidyalankar, Satyaketu, *Arya Samaj ka Itihaas,* Vol. I and II, Arya Swadhyaya Kendra, N. Delhi, 1984; and Bawa, Chhajju Singh, *Life and Teachings of Swami Dayanand,* Dayanand Sansthan, Delhi, 1997.
91. It appears that there is some confusion about the date and year of Dayanand's first shastrartha, in the Rajputana. According to Bawa Chhajju Singh (*The Life and Teachings...,* p. 164), the first shastrartha that Dayanand held was with Rev. Mr. Grey, Rev. Mr. Robinson, and Rev. Mr. Schoolbred of Beawar (Ajmer), on 28 Nov. 1878, at Ajmer. While, Satyaketu Vidyalankar (*Arya Samaj ka Itihaas,* Vol. II, p. 405) has written that it was held at Ajmer, in 1865, with John Tobson.
92. For a detailed study of Swami Dayanand's social philosophy regarding these subjects, please see the English translation of *Satyartha Prakash,* written by Durga Prasad and entitled *Satyartha Prakash: The Light of Truth,* published by Dayanand Sansthan, Ved Mandir, Delhi-36.
93. Ibid., p. viii.
94. Ibid.
95. *Chanakya Niti,* Cf. Ibid., p. 38.
96. *Manu Samhita,* VII. 152.
97. Prasad, Durga, op. cit., pp. 74-75.

98. Ibid.
99. "युवा सुवासाः परिवीत आगात्स उ श्रेयान भवति जायमानः।
तं धीरासः कवय उन्नयन्ति स्वाध्यो मनसा देवयंतः ।।"
100. "ब्रह्मचर्य्येण कन्या युवानं विन्दते पतिं।।" *Atharva Veda*, K. 11, pt. 24, Ad. 3, verse 18. Ibid., p. 73.
101. Ibid., pp. 74-75. "In intellectual education," he remarked, "their study should satisfy the five great canons, namely, the laws of spirits, the laws of nature, the wisdom of sages, the eight-fold evidence of logic, and the voice of conscience. The eight-fold evidence of logic consists of perception, inference, analogy, Holy Writ, history, the converse, possibility, and non-existence. In other words, their study should include both physics and metaphysics, as relating to the six categories of existence, namely, substance, quality, action, agreement, difference, and causation". To raise the educational standard to the ancient greatness of *Aryavarta*, the scheme of Studies, as desired by him, should consist of *Ashtadhyayi, Nighantu, Nirukta*, selections from *Manu, Ramayana, Mahabharata,* six schools of philosophy, (viz. *Mimansa, Yoga, Nyaya, Vaishesik, Sankhya, and Vedant*), ten Upanishads, (viz. *Isha, Kena, Katha, Prashna, Mundak, Mandukya, Aitareya, Tatireya, Chhandogya, and Brahdaranyak*), four Vedas (*Rig, Yajur, Sama, and Atharva*), four *Brahmanas*, Astronomy, *Suryasiddhanta*, Music, *Narad Samhita, Arthaveda* or politics and 4 Military Art."
102. "पूर्वीरहं शरदः शश्रमाणा दोषा वस्तोरूषसो जरयन्तीः।
मिनाति श्रियं जरिमा तनुनामप्यू नु पत्नीर्वृषणों जगम्युः।।"
i.e., "I shall marry after having attained full growth and vigour of mind and body, and acquired perfect knowledge and moral training in accordance with rules of studentship, so as to obtain good old age when days and nights mar the beauty and weaken the strength of the body by pushing it on to decline of life just as they deprive previous autumns and fading twilights of their charm." Cf. Ibid., p. 83.
103. Ibid., p. 73.
104. Ibid., p. 116.
105. "काममामरणात्तिष्ठेद गृहे कन्यर्तुमत्यपि।
न चैवैनां प्रयच्छेतु गुणहीनाय कर्हिचित।।" Ibid., p. 81.
106. "The best time for a girl's marriage is when she is from 16 to 24 years of age, and for a youth when he is 25 to 48 years of age. The marriage of a girl of 16 and youth of 25 years is of the lowest order; of a girl of 18 or 20 years and a youth of 30, 35 or 40 years is of the middle order; of a maid of 24 and a bachelor of 48 years of the best kind." Cf. Ibid., p. 79.

107. Ibid., p. 79.
108. "आ धेनवो धुतयन्तामशिश्वी : सवर्दुघाः शशया अप्रदुग्धाः ।
नव्यानव्या युवतयो भवन्तीर्महद्देवानामसुरत्वमेकम् ।।" Cf. Ibid., p. 82.
109. Ibid., p. 80.
110. Ibid., p. 105.
111. Ibid., p. 109.
112. Ibid., pp. 81-82.
113. Ibid., p. 90. "सन्तुष्टो भार्यया भर्त्ता भर्त्रा भार्या तथैव च ।
यस्मिन्नेव कुले नित्यं कल्याणं तत्र वै ध्रुवम् ।।"
-*Manu Samhita* III, 60. Happiness, fortune, and fame dwell in that family in which the wife is ever contented with the husband, and vice versa; and misery, poverty, and reproach overtake that family in which discord and quarrel reign. Therefore, the custom of a woman's choosing her husband (*swayamvara*), which has been in vogue in *Aryavarta* from time immemorial, is best calculated to meet the end of matrimony.
114. Ibid., p. 83.
115. "सा चेदक्षतयोनिः स्याद् गतप्रत्यागतापि वा ।
पौनर्भवेन भर्त्रा सा पुनः संस्कारमर्हति ।।" *Manu Samhita*, IX, 178. Cf. Ibid., p. 109.
116. Ibid., p. 109.
117. Ibid., p. 111.
118. "कुह स्विद्दोषा कुह वस्तोरश्विना कुहाभिपित्वं करतः कुहोषतुः ।
को वां शयुत्रा विधवेव देवरं मर्यं न योषा कृणुते सधस्थ आ ।।" *R.V.*, X, 40.2.
119. Vidyalankar, Satyaketu, op. cit., Vol. I, p. 594.
120. For a detailed study of the social and educational role of Arya Samaj in Ajmer, please see Goyal, Lata, *Rajasthan mein Arya Samaj aur uske Karya* (1883-1940), unpublished.
121. *Arya Pratinidhi Sabha*, Rajasthan Reports, 1890-91, 1902-1903, p. 3; 1904-05, pp. 3-5.
122. DAV School Annual Report, 1901-02, Vedic Yantralaya, Ajmer, 1903, p. 14.
123. *Arya Martand*, 1 Feb. 1941, p. 12.
124. *Arya Martand*, 2 March, 1947, p. 3.
125. Vidyalankar, Satyaketu, op. cit., Vol. II, pp. 424-426.
126. Arya Pratinidhi Sabha Rajputana Annual Report, 1949-50, pp. 13-14.
127. For a detailed study of the works of Jaipur Arya Samaj, please refer to Vijay, Om Sharan, *Krishna pole Bazar Jaipur Arya Samaj Ka Itihaas* and

Arya Samaj Jaipur Ke Samaj Sewi, published by Shiv Kumar Kurmi Patidar (former Head, Arya Samaj Krishna pole Bazar Jaipur), 1990.

128. Kurmi, Shiv Kumar Patidar, *Arya Samaj Jaipur Ke Samaj Sewi*, published by Kurmi, Shiv Kumar Patidar (former Head, Arya Samaj Krishna pole Bazar Jaipur), 1990, pp. 1-2. For a detailed study of the works of Arya Samaj Jaipur, please see Vijay, Om Sharan, *Krishna pole Bazar Jaipur Arya Samaj Ka Itihaas*. And also, Mishra, Ratan Lal and Mahavir Prasad Sharma, *Shekhawati Arya Samaj Ke Chaar Stambha*, published by Dr. Ghasi Ram Verma, Kingston America, year not mentioned.
129. Vijay, Om Sharan, *Krishna pole Bazar Jaipur Arya Samaj Ka Itihaas*, p. 50.
130. Ibid., p. 52.
131. Ibid., p. 51.
132. Ibid., pp. 52-53.
133. Kurmi, Shiv Kumar Patidar, *Arya Samaj Jaipur Ke Samaj Sewi*, op. cit., p. 19.
134. Vijay, Om Sharan, *Krishna pole Bazar Jaipur Arya Samaj Ka Itihaas*, p. 46.
135. For a detailed study of the works of *Shekhawati Arya Samaj*, please refer to Mishra, Ratan Lal and Mahavir Prasad Sharma, *Shekhawati Arya Samaj Ke Chaar Stambha*, published by Dr. Ghasi Ram Verma, Kingston America, year not mentioned.
136. Ibid., p. 34.
137. Ibid., p. 39.
138. Ibid., p. 43.
139. Ibid., p. 44.
140. Ibid., p. 45.
141. Ibid., pp. 109-110.
142. *Chandni* was a practice prevalent in certain upper sections of society and especially in the Oswal Community of Rajasthan. Whenever a woman moved outside her home, she was covered with a cloth of silver colour, which used to be 8 feet long and 5 feet wide. The four corners of that cloth were held by four maid servants, each holding one of the corners, so that none could see the face of that woman. Cf. Bhutodiya, Mangilal, op. cit., p. 346.
143. Graham, Reid.
144. Farquhar, J.N., *Modern Religious Movements in India*, pp. 124-125. "The causes which have combined to create the movements are many. The stimulating forces are almost exclusively Western,

namely, The British government, English education and literature, Christianity, Oriental research, European science and philosophy, and the material elements of Western civilization; but the beliefs and the organization of the ancient faiths have been the moulding forces of great potency. The Arya Samaj is an interesting example of the interaction of rationalism and modern inventions with belief in transmigration and the inerrancy of Vedic hymns." And also, "Christianity has ruled the development throughout. Christianity has been, as it were, a great searchlight flung across the expanse of the religions; and in its blaze, all the coarse, unclean, and superstitious elements of the old faiths stood out quite early in painful vividness." Cf. The Alien Roots of Indian Awakening, in *Debates in History, Debates on History: Situating Renaissance, Reform and Social Change in Modern India, Social And Religious Reform*, Amiya P. Sen, op. cit., pp. 202-205.

145. *Report of Arya Stree Samaj*, Ajmer, 1906-13, Vedic Yantralaya, Ajmer, 1914, p. 3.
146. Shastri, Vishnu Lal, *Handbook of Arya Samaj*, p. 88.
147. *Arya Stree Samaj, Ajmer Ka Vivran*, 1906 A.D. to 1913 A.D., p. 2.
148. Ibid.
149. (a) *Report of Arya Stree Samaj*, Ajmer, 1934-35, p. 3-14.
(b) *Report of the Jain Samaj*, Ajmer, 1915-16, Vedic Yantralaya, Ajmer, 1917, pp. 4-5.
(c) *Report of Agrawal Sabha*, 1917-18, Rajputana Press, Ajmer, 1919 p. 2.
150. Koṭhari Rita, op. cit., p. 184.
151. *Arya Mahila*, April, 1932, pp. 831-32.
152. *Annual Report of Arya Putri Pathshala*, 1898-99, Vedic Yantralaya, Ajmer, 1899, pp. 1-2.
153. *Annual Report of Arya Putri Pathshala*, 1947-48, pp. 3-4.
154. *Report of S.M.A. Kanya Pathshala*, 1948-49, p. 16.
155. Report sent to Asst. Supdt. of Female Education, Delhi and Ajmer-Merwara, by Smt. Godavari Devi Kanya Pathshala, Report No. 3, dt. 28 March, 1948.
156. *Report of Arya Stree Samaj*, Ajmer for 1928-29, p. 12.
157. *The Hindustan Times*, 5th of Feb. 1930.
158. Kiran, Devendra, *Status and Position of women in India, with special reference to women in contemporary India*, Shakti Books, Vikas Publishing House, New Delhi, 1985, p. 28.
159. Shraddhanand, Swami, *Hindu Sangathan*, p. 131.

160. Shastri, Vishnulal, op. cit., p. 103.
161. Vidyalankar, Satyaketu, op. cit., And, Mishra, Ratan Lal and Mahavir Prasad Sharma, *Shekhawati Arya Samaj Ke Chaar Stambha*. And also, Pemaram and Vikramaditya, *Jaton Ki Gaurav gatha*, Rajasthani Granthagar, Jodhpur, 2004.
162. *Rajasthan*, 1 March 1925, *The Hindustan Times*, 1 Nov. 1932.
163. Arya Stree Samaj Ajmer, Vivah File no. 3, 1936-37, Vedic Yantralaya, Ajmer, 1938, pp. 2-3.
164. Report of Vanita Ashram Ajmer for April 1934 to March 1947, p. 23, 24, 27.
165. *Vidhwa Bandhu*, 1 Nov.1927, pp. 32-38.
166. Ibid.
167. Vidyalankar, Satyaketu, op. cit., Vol. II, pp. 405-426.
168. *Har Bilas Sarda Commemoration Volume*, Vedic Yantralaya, Ajmer, 1937, p. 196.
169. Bhati, Narayan Singh, Samaj Ratna Har Bilas Sarda in *Parampara* (ed.), Rajasthani Shodh Sansthan, Jodhpur, 1985-86, p. 17.
170. Ibid., p. 21.
171. "My Bill does not go against the spirit or the letter of any religious behest; for no Shastras, ancient or modern enjoin that a girl must be married before she attains puberty."

     Har Bilas Sarda, *Speeches and Writings*, p. 34.
172. Sarda remarked that the primary aim of the Bill he proposed, was to put a stop to child widowhood and the secondary was to remove the principal impediment to the physical and mental growth of the youth of both sexes and the chief cause of their premature death and decay.

     Har Bilas Sarda, *Speeches and Writings*, p. 35.
173. Cf. Narayan Singh Bhati, op. cit., p. 26.
174. Ibid., p. 27.
175. Har Bilas Sarda, *Speeches and Writings*, p. 33.
176. Ibid., p. 34.
177. Bhati, Narayan Singh, op. cit., p. 28.
178. Sarda, Har Bilas: *Recollections and Reminiscence*, p. 68 Cf. Pareek, R.S., *The Contribution of Arya Samaj in the Making of Modern India*, p. 147.
179. Ibid., p. 32.
180. The Age of Consent Committee appointed by the Government of India in 1928, made the following remarks:

Cases of Sati were few and far between. They compelled attention by the enormity of the evil in individual cases, by the intense agony of the burning widow, and the terrible shock they gave to human feelings. In the case of early maternity (following child marriages) however, the evil is so widespread and affects such a large number of women both among Hindus and Muslims, as to necessitate redress. The evil is so insidious in all the manifold aspects of social life that people have ceased to think of its shocking effects on the whole social fabric.... If legislation was justified for preventing Sati, there is ample jurisdiction for legislation to prevent early maternity both on grounds of humanity and in furtherance of social justice."

Cf. *Har Bilas Sarda Commemoration Volume*, op. cit., p. 177.

181. Pareek, R.S., op. cit., p. 147.
182. In 1933, Rai Bahadur Seth Champalal of Beawar arranged the marriage of his 16 years old son with a girl of 13 years; it was stopped by the interference of police. Similarly, on 28 July, 1933, Har Bilas Sarda himself requested one Mr. Madho Singh of Ajmer, who was marrying his 13 years old daughter, and ultimately succeeded in stopping that.

    RSAB: Ajmer Record Police File no. 21 dt. 7 December, 1937, p. 31.

5

Role of Caste Organizations in the Eradication of Child Marriages

The castes were groups with a well-developed life of their own, the membership of which was determined not by selection, but by birth and, the status of a person depended not on the wealth of a person, but on the traditional importance of the caste in which he was born. The earliest account of the institution of caste in India, was given by Megasthenese, in the third century B.C.[1] "It is not permitted to contract marriage with a person of another caste, nor to change from one profession or trade to another, nor for the same person to undertake more than one, except if he is of the caste of philosophers, when permission is given on account of his dignity" wrote Megasthenese.

The traditional caste system of India came into existence, when the Aryan race of North India migrated to other parts of the country and as a result of this expansion, had to fight long and continuous battles with the non-Aryan tribes. When these tribes were defeated, after a passage of time, they were incorporated into the Aryan social system and thus the society at that time, witnessed two different social systems working side by side – the Aryan culture and the non-Aryan culture. Slowly and gradually, intermarriages started occurring between them, and as a result of this, new castes emerged on the Indian social scenario besides the four established Varnas (i.e., Brahmin, Kshatriya, Vaishya, Shudra).[2] The characteristics of an Indian caste include rigid, hereditary membership in the caste into which one is born, the practice of marrying only members of the same caste, restrictions on the choice of occupation and on personal contact with members of other castes, and the acceptance by each individual of a fixed place in society. The caste system has been perpetuated by the Hindu ideas of samsara, punar-janma (reincarnation) and karma (i.e., quality of action). According to these religious beliefs, all people are reincarnated on earth, at which time they have a chance to be born into another higher caste, but only if they have been obedient to the rules of their varna-dharma (i.e., caste) in their previous life on earth. In this way, karma has encouraged people to rise to a higher caste.

The four original varnas (i.e., Brahmin, Kshatriya, Vaishya and Shudra) have been divided and subdivided again and again over many centuries, and today it is impossible to tell their exact number. Estimates range from 2,000 to 3,000 different castes established by the Brahmanical law throughout India, each region having its own distinct groups defined by profession and fixed by custom. These castes have regulated the lives of its members, right from its inception, and have framed rules regarding various social institutions. It was the duty of the elder men to look after the policy matters of the caste and to force people to obey those rules, which they thought were, made for the betterment of the community.

The governing body of a caste is called the caste panchayat, the authority, the domination of which is approved and accepted by all the members of a caste. Some of the offences dealt by the caste panchayats are:[3]

(a) eating, drinking or having similar dealings with a caste or sub-caste, with which such social intercourse is held to be forbidden;
(b) keeping as concubine a woman of another caste;
(c) seduction of or adultery with a married woman;
(d) fornication;
(e) refusal to fulfil the promise of marriage;
(f) refusing to send a wife to her husband, when old enough;
(g) refusing to maintain a wife;
(h) non-payment of debt;
(i) petty assaults;
(j) breaches of the customs of trade peculiar to the caste;

(k) encroaching on another's clientele, and raising or lowering prices;
(l) killing a cow or any other forbidden animals;
(m) insulting a Brahmin;
(n) defying the customs of the caste regarding feasts, etc., during the marriage and other ceremonies.

The caste panchayats, since they were the governing body of a caste, awarded punishments to those, who defied the supremacy of the panchayat or who violated the rules, framed by it. The punishments that these bodies awarded were:[4]

(a) outcasting, either temporary or permanent;
(b) fines;
(c) feasts to be given to the castemen;
(d) corporal punishment and
(e) sometimes religious expiation.

G.S. Ghurye[5] has rightly remarked that castes are small and complete social worlds in themselves, marked off definitely from one another, though subsisting within the larger society.

Though a great deal has been said about the negative role of the panchas or caste panchayats in curbing the independent and free thinking of the community members and the various negations imposed and punishments given to offenders, it is striking to note that these very caste panchayats were the torch-bearers of reform in the Rajputana in the 19th and the 20th century. These caste panchayats and caste conferences, influenced and inspired by the works of social reformers of British India, the works and the teachings of the Arya Samaj, the efforts of the Walter Krit Rajputra Hitkarini Sabha, tried to mitigate the sufferings of the people, through their annual/monthly/weekly conferences or meetings. Various social problems were discussed in such meetings, and attempts were made to purge the community from such evils.

By caste conferences, we mean those bodies of persons who met together annually to think over the best methods for the amelioration of a particular community, confined to social matters alone. These caste organizations drew their leadership from the indigenous educated section of the society and dealt with those issues, which were considered to be of utmost importance, to the welfare of that community of that caste alone. It is significant to note that almost all such organizations pondered upon abolishing the abhorrent practices and customs pertaining to women like child and unmatched marriages, enforced widowhood, purdah, etc. These organizations played an important role in educating the public mind towards the necessity of legislations and, on the other hand, requested and motivated the native rulers to issue legislations to that effect.

It is also important to note, that whereas the prohibition of practices like Sati and female infanticide were dealt upon by the native rulers and the British officers and proclamations were issued, owing to their (sometimes self-inspired) reformative zeal, the crusade for the legal prohibition of child and unmatched marriages centred round indigenous reformers.

Following is an account of the efforts of various caste organizations, to do away with the various social evils, prevalent in the-then society.

Efforts of the Pareek Community

In the history of the Rajputana and also that of the caste organizations, the earliest effort to do away with the social evils was perhaps done by the Pareek Brahmins of Sanganer (Jaipur). And the incident, which motivated them to think over the social problems, is of great significance, as it is related to the pomp and show in a marriage ceremony.[6] In Samvat 1600, on the occasion of the marriage of the daughter of Joshi Jogaji, a rich businessman of Sanganer (Jaipur), the father of the bride spent Rupees ninety lacs and eighty thousand on that marriage.[7] This marriage was performed in such a grand manner that gold and silver mohurs (coins) were served in the food, beside other dishes. What happened there was, that seeing the beautiful design and make-up of the *pattal* (plate made by paper or leaves), one of the members of the groom's side remarked that will gold and silver mohurs be served in these pattals and when this was brought to the notice of Joshi Jogaji, he answered in the affirmative, and thus the mohurs were served with other dishes. But since, these mohurs were served with other dishes, it was considered by the members of the Pareek community, as impure and *joothi* and as such nobody accepted them and they were given to the sweeper, who later on, constructed a bavadi (i.e., water tank) in Sanganer, with that money, for the use of the lower classes. Seeing this extravagance and pomp and show, and feeling that this display of wealth would lead others to follow and thereby put pressure on the poor parents, the members of the Pareek community gathered and decided to frame certain rules, which were made obligatory on all the caste members, of whichever place they belonged to. Rules regarding marriage ceremonies, the number of persons to be taken and the number of days of the stay of the *barat* (marriage party), the articles to be given in dowry, the *neg* to be given to the lower sections, and the presents to be given by bride's father, to the groom's family, on different occasions (like Holi, Gangaur, Deepawali, after the birth of a son, etc.) were determined by the community members. It was also laid down, that nobody would give anything in excess to what has been determined and nobody would ask for more then the prescribed limits. Anyone found guilty, was to be ostracized by the community members. Social ostracism was a severe punishment in those days and it is significant to note that the use of it, to curb the tendency of doing heavy expenditure on marriages, was first of its kind in the history of caste-organizations in erstwhile Rajputana or present day Rajasthan. The step taken by the Pareek community members, to fix a maryada or limitation, on the expenditure incurred on marriages, paved the way for future reforms.

In Samvat 1940 (1883 A.D.), the Pareek community issued a Mahzar, in which, once again, rules were framed regarding different social problems and social practices. In all 56 rules (called chhappan kalam in the document) were made obligatory for the community-members.[8] But for the purpose of our study, only those rules are being discussed, which have a direct relation with child and unequal marriages. Rule number 10, bound the members not to marry their wards, to a bride or a groom, other than that, which was previously settled by the parents. It was felt that some parents, in lieu of money or some other expectation, used to break the marriage-contract and marry their wards, in some other families. To put a stop to this tendency, it was laid down, therefore, that those who will do such a thing will be ostracized for a period of four years and nobody will keep any relation with that person.

Rule number 11 laid down that after the sagai (i.e., engagement) contract has been entered upon, if someone breaks the contract without assigning any sufficient cause, the matter would immediately be put before the panchas (i.e., elder men) and it will be their duty to develop understanding between the two parties and force them to respect their prior decision. If any one, without assigning any sufficient cause, breaks the sagai contract and defies the order of the panchas, then he would be turned out from the caste.

The panchas would, then request the Raj or the State to take necessary action against him and force him to respect his prior commitment. If the offender wished to re-enter the caste, after some time, then he could do so after paying a fine of Rs 11. Rule number 11 also specified the words 'without assigning any sufficient cause' and this included any major infectious disease in bride or groom, his or her's physical incapability or characterlessness.

Similarly, rule number 45 tried to control the prevalent practice of selling or purchasing of the bride or the groom by the parties concerned. It read as "anyone who will marry his son or daughter in lieu of money or helps in the performance of such a marriage, will be thrown out from the caste, for a period of 6 months. If the party concerned gives back or takes back the money and then requests the panchas, expressing their feeling of shame and guilt for their fault, then they could be taken back in the community after paying a fine of Rs 11 each".

In Samvat 1978 (1924 A.D.), Sri Pareek Sanskrit Pathshala, Merta City, organized a three days meeting to discuss various social problems, which was attended by the Pareek members of Jodhpur region. In all, 36 rules (kalams) were made in the Sabha. Rule number 4 laid down that no body should marry after the age of 40. Rule number 5 again asked the members not to break-off the *sagai*-contract. Rule number 6 put further restrictions on the presents or the cash offering given to the groom's side by the bride's side. It laid down that at the time of the sagai or the betrothal, Rs 1 and a coconut was only to be given to the groom's side as dastur or tradition. After the sagai, ornaments, dresses and gold worth Rs 300 could be given; and nothing more than this amount should be given. Rule number 27 asked the members to refrain from taking the bride-price. If someone was unable to perform the marriage of his daughter, on account of poverty, he could, according to the rule, request the Pareek Pathshala of Merta for financial help and the institution would then provide Rs 51 from its own account and would help in the performance of marriage.

Rule 31 laid specific instructions against child marriages and enjoined upon the members not to marry their daughters before they attained the age of 10 and their sons before the age of 15. If because of some unforeseen circumstances, her marriage could not be performed at the age of ten, then the father of the girl should try to marry her before the age of 15, and in no circumstance he should keep her unmarried after the age of 15. If he is arranging the marriage of two or more than two daughters, on the same day or at the same time; he could do so, provided that the age of the younger girl was not less than 8 years.

The reform efforts of the Pareek community spread to other places of Rajasthan and soon the community members residing in different places of Rajasthan, started pondering over social issues. In Samvat 1982 (A.D. 1925), around 400 people gathered at Gogasar village in Bikaner and framed rules for themselves. Almost 11 rules were framed in Gogasar. Rule number 2 laid down that if anyone breaks the marriage contract of his/her daughter, without any sufficient cause, he would be fined Rs 2100 by the panchas. This provision was made to check the prevalent practice of taking bride-price and marrying her to unsuitable grooms. Rule number 3 laid down that nobody should take or accept bride-price and if any one, was found doing so, he will be thrown out of the caste. Similarly, rule number 5 tried to put a check on the marriage of old people as well as ill-matched or uneven marriages. It enjoined that nobody should marry after the age of 40.

The Pareek community residing in the Kota State also framed certain rules, which were approved by the Mehkama Khas on 4 June 1927 and came into force from July 1, 1927. Rule number 1, laid down that the marriage of a girl below 12 years and that of a boy below 16 years should not be performed. Rule number 2 laid down that the marriage of a girl below 18 years, should not be performed with a man who is more than twice the age of the girl. Rule number 5 laid down that the parents or the guardians of a girl, who is 18 or more than 18 years old, could marry her to the person of their choice but even in that circumstance a man above 45 years was forbidden to marry a virgin girl. If someone violates this rule, then according to rule number 6, a first class Magistrate would hear the case and could give punishment of six months imprisonment (simple or rigorous) and/or a fine upto Rs 1000. He was also empowered to stop the performance of marriage. Rule number 8 made these rules obligatory on all the citizens of Kota State and stated that whosoever commits this offence outside the territory of the State will be punished after his arrival in the State. Relaxation from certain clauses of these rules, was given to those castes in which the practice of naata (i.e., remarriage) was prevalent. Similarly, the Walter Krit

Rajputra Hitkarini Sabha was also excluded from these rules, as it had its own set of rules.

In the State of Bundi, Maharao Raja Raghuvir Singh gave approval to certain rules, framed by the Pareek community, which were registered by the State Council – Aliya on the 3rd of July, 1926. According to these, taking or accepting of bride-price or marrying her to any unsuitable groom in lieu of money or performing un-even or ill-matched marriages or forcing a virgin girl to marry an old person was made punishable by the State. Both the parties (the groom's as well as bride's) were to be punished for violation of the rule. The State empowered the Nazims and the Thanedars to take necessary action against such marriages and also ordered that if any govt. servant helps in the performance of such marriages or conceals it will also be punished. The wave of reforms soon spread to other parts of the State, and in 1928, the Pareeks residing in Khinchiwara, Mauthara, Harauti, Umat-wara also framed rules on the same lines. Minimum marriageable age of a girl was fixed at 10 years and it was laid down that the marriage of a girl should be performed between the ages of 10 to 13. Similarly the minimum marriageable age of boys was fixed at 15 years. It also forbade a second marriage of the males; a male could marry for the second time only if he was between the age group of 30 to 35 years and if his first wife was not alive. The rules also criticized the practice of accepting bride price by the parents, and the selling of the girl, to a wealthy but unsuitable groom.

Not contented with the framing of rules for themselves alone, some enlightened members of the Pareek community wrote letters and petitions to the rulers of their respective States and requested them to intervene and frame rules for other castes also for the prevention of child and unmatched marriages. Joshi Devi Chandra Visharad,[9] a resident of Jodhpur, e.g., on 5 November 1929 wrote and distributed a pamphlet among the masses in which he asked them to give their moral support to the Child Marriage Restraint Act, passed in British India in 1929. He urged the masses to request the Maharaja of Jodhpur to issue a similar Act for the State of Marwar. In his pamphlet Joshi Devi Chandra described in detail the effects of child marriage on the mental and physical health of child brides. The distribution of this pamphlet ignited the hearts and minds of the people and motivated other individuals as well as organizations to write similar letters to the Durbar.

The necessity of education as well as its importance as a tool of social change was also understood by these enlightened individuals and soon appeals were made from different quarters, for the promotion of education in their respective States. On 5 September, 1931, Joshi Devi Chandra again wrote a letter to the Vice President of Jodhpur and requested him to make necessary arrangements for the education of the females of their State. He expressed his resentment on the paucity of educational institutions in Jodhpur and lamented about the various obstacles, which came in the way of females, for getting education. He questioned the very purpose and the justification of the existence of schools "when the girls cannot go there and get a chance to enrol themselves in the schools." He believed that the most suitable time for girls for getting knowledge was from 10 to 20 years and until and unless these years of their age were not given totally for education it was a dream to see the females well educated and the nation advanced and healthy. He deplored that the girls in Marwar were generally married in the age group of 3 to 10 years and because of their poor physique thousands of girl-mothers died in Marwar. "Thousands of poor souls," he wrote, "born by such immature mothers die as soon as they leave the wombs of their mothers and come out." He along with other educated people of Marwar, appealed to the youths to come forward for the welfare of their mothers, sisters and daughters and to request the Maharaja to protect the people of Marwar from the evil custom of child marriage by promulgating a Child Marriage Restriction Act, similar to the one enacted in British India.

The youths of Marwar also composed several songs relating to the evil consequences of child and unmatched marriages. When the Maharaja of Jodhpur published the Child Marriage Restriction Bill in the Marwar gazette of August 16, 1930, many enlightened persons expressed their satisfaction and happiness. But when this Bill failed to see the light of the day, because of the opposition of certain communities, they were disappointed. "This was not the suspension of the Bill," wrote Joshi Devi Chandra, "but it was the suspension of the progress of the poor women. The women are after all human beings and when there is a law in Marwar for the protection of hay, why should there not be a law for the protection of the women is difficult to understand." He asked the Durbar that when whole of the world has brought the protection of the women under law, what plea can there be for the exception of Marwar then. He urged that to make the girl a mother in her immature age and thus to put a restriction upon her development is a severe crime and it is the main duty of an administrator to eradicate this.

Similarly in 1945, Pareek-Parishad of Jaipur, encouraged by the previous works of the community members, raised the minimum marriageable age of girls to 14 and that of the boys to 18. It also forbade the second marriage of the males after the age of 40. If someone contracted or entered upon a second marriage, when his first wife was already alive, he was to be ostracized by the community members.

The above account highlights the significant contribution of the Pareek-Brahmin Community, as they were the first, in the recorded annals of Rajasthan, who pondered over the social problems and tried to do away with them, as early as second half of the 16th century. The grand marriage at Sanganer (Jaipur), in which gold and silver mohurs (i.e., coins) were served in the food, forced the members to put a stop to such pomp and show in the marriages and thus opened a new chapter of reforms, in the history of Rajasthan. This episode and the consequent reactions, which followed later on in the shape of various reforms were done without any outside or external influence. This contradicts the prevalent notion in historiography, as it has given great emphasis on the works and efforts of the British officers and sidelined or bye-passed the efforts of the various caste-organizations. Much before the birth of reformative spirit of Sawai Jai Singh of Jaipur, who issued proclamation against female infanticide in 1731; much before the arrival of British East India Company in the Rajputana and much before the birth of Desh Hitaishini Sabha and Walterkrit Rajputra Hitkarini Sabha, the effort to control and to put a stop on certain social problems was done by the Pareek Brahmins of Rajasthan.

While this was the affairs of the Pareek community of the Rajputana, the efforts to generate community-consciousness against the prevalent evils, amongst its own members, were also witnessed in the Kayastha community. In January, 1872,[10] Munshi Kali Prasad Kul Bhaskar, one of the enlightened members of Kayastha community, started a Kayastha school at Bahadurganj Mohalla, Allahabad. He also started a monthly newspaper – *Kayastha Samachar*, on 30 November, 1872.[11] It is significant to note that this newspaper was the first of its own kind, which was exclusively dedicated to the cause and the upliftment of a particular caste. This example perhaps influenced and motivated other castes to start their own newspapers, later on. In the same year (1872), Munshi Har Govind Dayal Shrivastav established Kayastha Sadar Sabha Hind at Lucknow.[12] The call given by the Kayastha Samachar to its own caste-brethrens, to work for the cause of the community and to highlight the contribution of Kayasthas, did not go in vain and soon in 1884,[13] three other newspapers and magazines – *Kayastha Vyavahar, Gaur Kayastha* (published by Babulal from Satyaprakash Press, Prayag) and *Kulshreshtha Samachar* (published from Mathura in Hindi and Urdu), were published by some of the enlightened members of the Kayastha community, with the above mentioned objective. These magazines, to ponder over the prevalent social scenario and to wipe certain social evils, emphasized upon the need of an All-India Kayastha organization. This motivated Munshi Har Govind Dayal Shrivastav and Babu Jayanti Prasad Mathur (Deputy Collector), to establish an All India. Kayastha Conference at Lucknow, which held it's first annual meeting at Lucknow on 27 and 28 November, 1887, in which the Kayastha members, residing in Rajasthan, also took part.[14] Thrilled by the enthusiasm and the warm reception of the community members, the second Kayastha Conference was held at Allahabad in 1888. A provincial Sabha of that caste was formed in the Rajputana and Lala Gopinath was made its secretary.[15] The fifth session of this Sabha was held at Ajmer in 1892.[16]

The Kayastha Sabhas were irregularly convened and discussed the eradication of evils like child-marriage, unequal marriage, minimum marriageable age, etc. In the Rajputana, there were as many as 36 Kayastha Sabhas working for the advancement of the community, under the direction of the Provincial Sabhas, with its head quarters at Ajmer. A Kayastha Club's Association on an All-India level was also formed and a branch of it was opened at Udaipur in 1891-92, with Mathura Prasad Shrivastav as its President.[17]

Krishna Vidyalankar (a Kayastha writer of Badayun, U.P. and a member of Arya Samaj), in order to spread the ideas of Swami Dayanand Saraswati, amongst his own people, regarding abolition of child marriage wrote books entitled *Baal Vivah* and *Vedic Sambhog Maryada.*[18]

The method of the Kayasthas for spreading social reforms was by working through local Sabhas and by propaganda often carried out through some journals of the Kayasthas, which were published in English and vernaculars. *Kayastha Shubhachintak*, (published in 1888, from Allahabad), *Kayastha* and *Kayastha Upadesh* (published in 1889, from Lucknow), *Kayastha Upkarak* (in 1889, from Agra), *Kayastha Pancha* (in 1890 from Prayag), *Kayastha Hitaishi* (in 1890, from Darbhanga), *Kayastha Conference* (in 1883, from Kanpur), *Kayastha Hitkari* (in 1894, from Prayag), *Kayastha Kaumudi* (in 1894, from Muzzafarpur), *Kayastha Kulbhaskar* (in 1903, from Itawa), *Kulshreshtha* (in 1910, from Aligarh), *Kayastha Kul Sewak* (in 1918, from Jodhpur, under the editorship of Chiranji Lal Mathur) were some of the few magazines and newspapers, which played a commendable role.[19] *The Hindustan Review of Allahabad* (in English) and the *Kayastha Hitkari* of Gwalior (Vernacular) were widely in circulation in the Rajputana. They strongly supported the social reform approach for the advancement of the caste development.[20]

In 1889, the Mers and the Merats of Merwara framed rules fixing the marriageable age for girls at 11 years. It was introduced in 1891. Similarly, in 1890-91, the Rajguru Purohits of Jodhpur and Pushkar, Brahmins of Bikaner framed rules, providing age of marriage for boys and girls as 15 years and 11 years, respectively. Other sects of Brahmins also expressed similar views and in Jodhpur, almost 36 communities framed rules pertaining to the age limit of the bride and the bridegroom.[21] The example of these castes, was followed by the Malis of the Rajputana, who participated in their caste conferences held every year to provide education for their children and frame rules against the performance of early marriages.[22]

By 1891-92, these developments spread over to other places and communities and soon the Jains decided to purge their community from the social evils, and consequently the Jain Sabhas or Reform Associations emerged at Ajmer, Jaipur, Kekri, Alwar and Jhalawar.[23] One of the objects of their associations was social reform through liberal education.

In order to educate the people and to make them think over the social issues, the Jain community started various magazines and newspapers. The tradition of the Jain newspapers, in Hindi, started from 1880, when *Jain Patrika* was published from Prayag.[24] Till 1895, as many as six newspapers were being published by the Jain community, from different places. The name of these newspapers were *Jiyalal Prakash*, *Jain*, *Jain Bodhak* (published from Sholapur,

Maharashtra), *Jain Prabhakar* (published from Ajmer), *The Jain Hitaishi,* (published from Muradabad, U.P.) and *The Jain Gazette* (published from Ajmer). *Jain Bhaskar* and *Jain Mitra* were started in 1897 and 1900 respectively by the Jain community. The founder of *Jain Mitra* was Mool Chand Kisandas Kapadia, who used this newspaper as a platform, to raise his voice against the various social evils, prevalent in their community. From January, 1901, the *Jain Mitra* became the mouth piece of Bombay Digambar Jain Prantik Sabha. Gulab Chand Dhadda started *Shri Jain Shvetambar Conference Herald* from Mumbai, in 1905. In the issue of March, 1906, Dhadda published his article, in which various social evils including the practice of selling of the brides, in lieu of money, were discussed in detail. To generate awareness among the women of the community, Babu Jyoti Prasad started *Jain Nari Hitkari,* which was published from Saharanpur (U.P.). In this magazine various articles related with the deplorable condition of women appeared. *The Jain Nari Hitkari* urged the people to come forward and shun the prevalent practices of purdah (or chandni), polygamy, ill-matched or unequal marriages, etc. In April 1917, *Jain Samaj* was started from Bombay, under the editorship of Tekchand Singhi. The main objective of this newspaper was "to rouse the Jain people, of the Rajputana and Malwa, from the deep slumber of ignorance".

In 1920, Rai Sahab Krishna Lal Bafna started a monthly newspaper from Jodhpur, the name of which was *Oswal*. Prithvi Raj Daga of Sujangarh and Padam Singh Surana of Agra edited this newspaper.[25] Articles related with the evils of child and unmatched marriages, polygamy, marriage of the old people, mausar, etc. were published in it, to educate the people. In 1934, another newspaper – *Oswal Sudharak* was published from Agra, under the editorship of Akshaya Singh Dangi. In 1937, the name of this newspaper was changed from *Oswal Sudharak* to *Oswal* and Vijay Singh Nahar was made its editor. Under the editorship of Govardhan Singh Mahnot, in 1939, various articles which sharply criticized the prevalent social evils, appeared in this newspaper, which infuriated the orthodox segment of the society.

The Oswal Nav-Yuvak Samiti was established in 1926 in Calcutta, to spread the wave of reforms amongst the Marwari community, residing in Calcutta. The members of this organization also started a hand-written magazine, the name of which was *Oswal Nav-Yuvak* and Siddha Raj Dhadda of Jaipur was made its first editor. Later on, V.S. Nahar and Bhanwar Mal Singhi took the task of editing and consequently under their editorship, this magazine took a more revolutionary turn and various mind-boggling and heart-penetrating articles regarding social evils, were published in it. Because of the critical approach of the magazine, the orthodox segment of the society got offended and consequently the editors were forced to resign. In 1940, Bhanwar Mal Singhi, started *Tarun Oswal* from Calcutta, through which he continued his struggle against the prevalent malpractices.

It is significant to note, that against the various prevalent social malpractices, the women of the Jain community did not keep mum and they fought neck and neck with their male counterparts. Coming out of the Purdah and shunning other social negations, they expressed their grievances as well as their suggestions, through their writing talents. In May, 1921, the Bharat Varshiya Digambar Jain Mahila Parishad, started Jain-Mahiladarsha, under the editorship of Pandita Chandaa Bai.[26] This magazine played an important role in spreading knowledge and creating awareness among the Jain women. The specialty of this magazine was that it was edited by a lady and articles of women only were published in it, which focused mainly on issues related to women. While all other magazines and newspapers were run and edited by the male members of the society, this was the only magazine which was of the ladies, by the ladies and for the ladies. Pandita Chandaa Bai edited this magazine for almost 52 years, which is an ample proof of her commitment towards the betterment of women.

Similarly, *The Marwar Jain Sudharak* – a monthly magazine was published from Abu Road in 1924 and *Jain Jagat* was published by Fateh Chand Sethi, from Ajmer, in 1925.[27] In the *Jain Jagat*, the articles published by Darbari Lal Nyayatirtha were considered as the most revolutionary in nature, as he sharply criticized the prevalent social malpractices.

In 1932, *Sudharak* was published by Rai Sahab Kesarlal Ajmera from Jaipur.[28] From February, 1935 *Jain Shikshan Sandesh* was started by the *Jain Shikshan Parishad of Beawar*, under the editorship of Shobha Chandra Bharilla and Shanti Lal Vanmali Sheth.[29] It was a "friend of the educational institutes and a guide of the parents." Its main aim was to spread the light of knowledge and to put off the darkness of ignorance. These newspapers and magazines tried to educate the masses against the prevalent social vices. In the issue of

April 1917, p. 5, *Jain Samaj*[30] wrote that "the child and unequal marriages, marriages of the old people and ignorance were destroying the very fabric of the Jain Society" and asked its readers to shun these social vices and motivate others to do so. It urged the parents not to marry their minor children, and not to take the institution of marriage so lightly.

Similarly, Tara Chand Dosi,[31] in his article, published in *Jain Samaj,* in May 1917, expressed his discontentment against the practice of child marriage. His article dealt in detail with the sufferings of child mothers. Poorna Chand Jain, in his article *Ek Sulagta Sawaal,* published in *Tarun Oswal,* in June 1940,[32] lampooned the very idea of the marriage of the old people. He urged the readers to destroy the existing society and create a new one in its place, which was to be free from all these social evils.

Babu Anokhelal Sidakat,[33] made fun of ill-matched marriages in his articles, which were published in various newspapers. In one of his articles in *Jain Yuwak* in the issue of October 1928, he ridiculed the notion of ill-matched marriages, in the following words:

"अस्सी बरस के खुद हैं, दुल्हन है दस के अंदर।
गोदी में ले के बाबा पोती को, बस खिलायें।।
भारत की बदनसीबी, गर ये नहीं तो क्या है?
मरने के जिनके दिन हैं, वो ब्याहने को जायें।।
मूए सफेद सिर पर, दाँतों से मुंह है खाली।
फिर भी हवस है कोई कमसिन गले लगायें।।"

Babu Anokhelal Sidakat, in the same article urged the people to take strict action against those who perform or who help in or who attend a child or ill-matched marriage and challenged the society in the following words.[34]

"ऐ कौम के सुधारक, ऐ रहनुमाये मजहब।
देखा करोगे कब तक, ये आह–दुर्दशायें।।
होता रहेगा यों ही, क्या जुल्म स्त्रियों पर।
सोती रहेगी यों ही, क्या आपकी सभायें।।"

The efforts of these enlightened individuals, bore fruit and soon their voices became the voices of common men and an attempt was made by the members of the Jain Community, to answer the questions raised by them, from time to time. This resulted in All-India conferences of the Oswal community, which were held in different parts of the country.[35]

First All-India Oswal Conference (*Akhil Bharat-Varshiya Pratham Oswal Maha-Sammelan*)

To create awareness among the Oswals, who were spread all over the country, against the prevalent social evils and to create a feeling of brotherhood among the different gotras, an All-India Oswal Conference was convened at Ajmer in 1932, by the efforts of Rai Sahab Krishna Lal Bafna of Jodhpur and Dayal Singh Johari of Agra. This conference was attended by many socio-political and business luminaries of the Oswal community, who came from all parts of India. Poorna Chandra Nahar, scholar and archeologist from Calcutta, was appointed its President. Many resolutions were passed in the conference which included the boycott of purdah, restriction on child marriage, and on the marriages of people over 40 years of age, restriction on polygamy, mausar, sale of bride as well as that of groom and restrictions on various outdated social and religious ceremonies, which were done at the time of marriage. In this conference, Gulab Chand Dhadda of Jaipur, proposed to raise the age limit of marriage, from 40 to 45; which was opposed by a group of members, headed by his own son Siddha Raj Dhadda. As a result of the opposition of these persons, the proposal was turned down.

The importance of this conference lies in the fact that for the first time, persons from all parts of country, assembled at Ajmer to discuss the social problems of their community and tried to form certain rules, for the betterment of their community.

Pragyachakshu Pundit Sukh Lal, Kundan Mal Firodiya, Rajmal Lalwaani, Gulab Chand Dhadda and Nathmal Chordiya were some of the people, who dominated the conference.

Second All-India Oswal Conference

The second conference was held again, at Ajmer, in 1934. This conference was presided over by Shri Achal Singh, Congress-Leader of Agra, and Dayal Singh Chordiya, famous jeweller from Agra. In this conference, 15 resolutions were passed in all, most important of which was the abolition of mausar. Because of the progressive attitude of the enlightened members of the community, who wished to make rigid rules against child marriages and other vices, controversy started up and the conference found itself in direct opposition, with the orthodox and conservative members. However, the view of the progressive members prevailed, and many resolutions against child and unequal marriages, mausar, sale of brides and grooms were passed in the conference. In accordance with the resolutions of the conference, the youths of the conference, by way of dharnas and *anshans* tried to persuade people not to marry their sons and daughters in their childhood and were successful in stopping some child marriages. This use of dharnas and anshans was perhaps inspired by the dynamic leadership of Mohan Das K. Gandhi, who successfully used these techniques in the freedom struggle of India. The association and the presence of congress leaders gave a boost to the morale of reformers. Whenever and wherever a child or an unmatched marriage took place in their community, the progressive members tried to stop them, through the use of Gandhian ways. Through their petitions to the various native rulers, through their open letters, addressed to the masses, they tried to create awakening against these social evils. They also requested the native rulers to put a check on such practices by introducing an Act, similar to that of Sarda Act, in their States for the betterment of the society.

Third All-India Oswal Conference

In 1935, the third conference of the Oswal community was held at Mandsaur (Malwa) and was presided by Rajmal Lalwani of Jamner. It was attended by more than one thousand members of the community, who came from all quarters of the country. This itself was an indicator of the changing times and mindsets of the community members and also reflected the reformative zeal among them. In the third conference, resolutions were again passed against child marriages, unequal marriages, selling of bride and that of groom, mausar, etc. "On the one hand", one of the resolutions stated, "because of the paucity of resources, the youths of the community are not getting brides befitting their age, health and status; on the other hand, the old but rich people, because of the glamour of their wealth, are able to marry a number of times. As a result of this, the number of widows and the cases of unchastity are rising in the society. The conference therefore passes a resolution, that henceforward all such marriages of unequal nature should be prohibited." In this conference, a new resolution was passed which laid emphasis on the marriage of unmarried girls with unmarried boys only. This resolution was passed because many parents sold their daughters or their sons, in lieu of money, to the parties which gave them money for marrying them to a much elder girl or boy, of their own. In 1934-35, a businessman of Oswal community, married his 15 years old daughter to a rich businessman of Calcutta, who was 60 years old. Because of such incidents, which were general in nature, the Oswal community passed the above mentioned resolution and this was greatly appreciated by the progressive section of the community.

Fourth All-India Oswal Conference

It was held in Calcutta in 1937 and was presided over by Shri Gulab Chand Dhadda a social worker of Jaipur State. The speciality of this conference was that for the first time, enlightened people from different castes (other than the Oswals) were also invited, to take part in the discussions regarding social reform. The Maharaja of Bhavnagar, the Maharaja of Tripura, Laxmi Niwas Birla, Bhagirath Kanoria, Ram Kumar Bhuvalka, Vinay Kumar Sarkar, Veni Shankar Sharma, etc., were some of the notable persons who attended this conference.

In this conference, resolutions were once again passed against the above mentioned social evils and also against the hegemony of caste-panchayats. In 1935, the marriage of an Oswal girl of Sadree was fixed with a boy of Jhabua. At the time of marriage the actual age of the girl was 18 years and that of the boy was 15 years. When the parents of the girl, came to know about the actual age of the boy, they refused to marry their girl as the boy was lower in age and their contention was that they were kept in dark about the actual age of the boy. When this matter was taken to the caste panchayat, the members of the panchayat forced the parents of the girl, to marry her with that boy, as he belonged to an influential and wealthy family. Despite the stiff opposition from the girl's side, the panchayat was ultimately successful in getting her married to the same boy. The threat of social ostracism, given by the panchayat, forced the girl's parents to comply with the orders. This incident of the dominating role of panchas started a debate on the hegemony of the caste- panchayats and therefore it was decided in the fourth conference that the right of the caste-panchayats to boycott someone from the caste, should be taken from them.

Fifth All-India Oswal Conference

It was held at Pushkar (Ajmer) in 1939, and Moti Lal Bhoora of Jabalpur presided over this conference. Bhoora drew the attention of the members on the problems of child marriages, unequal marriages, sale of brides and grooms, marriages of the old people, which were still prevalent in the Oswal community, even after the commendable works of the conference. Bhoora urged the members to take a clear stand on the different social issues and do what they preach. 'Charity begins at home' was his message to the members.

The work done by these caste-organizations soon motivated other castes, to take appropriate actions against the prevalent social maladies. The fear of lagging behind from others, loomed large at their faces and became a driving force for their future reforms. At the third session of the Vaish conference held at Saharanpur in 1894, two delegates from Rajasthan took active part in getting a resolution passed in which the minimum marriageable age of girls and boys was fixed as 11 and 15 respectively.[36]

In 1896, the Agrawal community of Rajasthan could not keep itself unmoved by the currents of the reformative zeal, and consequently a Sabha, by the name of Agrawal Sabha of Ajmer was constituted, to awaken the women and to put a check on the expenditure incurred on the occasion of nukta and mausar.[37] Certain rules were made by this Sabha, for the above mentioned purpose, but as there was no one to enforce them, these rules proved to be of no help.[38] But despite this weakness, its significance lies in the fact that an effort was made by them to ponder over some of the social problems and the wave of social reform overtook them. In 1901, the Agrawal Sabha of Ajmer, started a monthly newspaper in Hindi, by the name of *Agrawal-Upkarak*, in which articles regarding the social abuses, appeared.[39] On 2 September, 1904, Agrawal Youngmen Association was formed by some of the enlightened members of Agrawal community, to impart education to the community members.[40] Chunni Lal Agrawal of the Sabha proposed to open an Agrawal Pathshala for the boys of the caste and it was decided that Hindi, vocational education, and matters of day-to-day knowledge would be taught to the students. On 5 November, 1904, this school was opened in the Kadakka Chowk of Ajmer, with 96 students. This school provided education up to class VIII. In the second and third decades of the 20th century, Raghunath Vakeel, Ram Charan Mittal, Mangal Chand, Gograj, Kanhaiya Lal Agrawal Lohe-wale and Daulat Ram Goyal started creating awareness in the Ajmer-Beawar region, in favour of widow remarriages and for the prevention of child marriages.[41] These enlightened individuals also worked for the promotion of female education. To unite the Marwaris, under one roof, an All India Marwari Conference was set up at Calcutta in 1935, which discussed different political and social issues.[42]

In February, 1907, Maheshwari Sabha was established in Beawar, by Ram Chandra Jaju, L.C. Nahar and Har Lal Tapadia to inform the community members about the progress done by other castes in social matters and thereby to create an atmosphere, in favour of social reforms.[43] In the very next year i.e., in 1908, the Maheshwari Sabha opened a day school and also a night school to educate the girls and boys of their caste.[44] Efforts were also made by the *Sabha,* to impart vocational training to the students, by the schools. In order to educate the people about the ill-effects of child and un-matched marriages, and to put a stop to the practice of purchasing brides (for the wealthy but unsuitable grooms), the Maheshwari Youths of Ajmer formed a committee by the name of Vidhwa-Sahayak Samiti.[45] Kunwar Chand Karan Sarda of this committee, believed that the remarriage of widows was necessary for the betterment of the society.[46] Har Bilas Sarda, a member of the Maheshwari Sabha, created awakening in the country, in favour of Child Marriage Restraint Act and ultimately got it passed. It was because of his sincere efforts, that child marriage came to be regarded as an offence.[47]

The efforts of these caste and social organizations did not merely revolve around the opening of schools or publication of newspapers and magazines. Rather they tried to achieve their aims through continuous petitions to the native rulers. On the 26 April, 1931, Sumer Mal Jain,[48] the Secretary of Lonkashah Jain Mission, Jodhpur, made a representation to the Jodhpur Durbar in which it was stated that an unmatched marriage was going to be celebrated on the 1 May, 1931 at a village named Teori in Jodhpur, between a boy named Nemi Chand, son of Keshrimal Sankhlecha, who was 11 years old and a girl named Suwa, daughter of Ghewar Chand Parakh, who was 14 years old. According to the representation, the poor physique of the boy and the robust health of the girl were itself improper for this marriage-tie. "The evil effects of such ties", according to Sumer Mal Jain, "were told to the parents and the caste panchayat despite distributing leaflets and getting into active propaganda but it could not produce any favourable results". Sumer Mal Jain wrote in the representation that his Mission boldly asserts that unless an Act is passed by the State, the assurances of the panchas are paper-assurances and he requested on behalf of Lonkashah Jain

Mission to issue injunctions against such marriages and asked the Jodhpur Durbar to introduce an Act to eradicate the social evil of child marriage and unequal marriage.

Similarly, on the 4 June, 1931, Dadhich Mitra Mandal,[49] requested the Jodhpur Durbar, that Pandita Nityanand Shastri of Jodhpur who was not less than 45 years, was going to marry a little girl of 12 years. The Mandal represented that Nityanand Shastri belonged to their caste and this was going to be his third marriage. This marriage was going to be conducted on 9 June, 1931 and the Mandal told the Durbar that the intending couple was planning to leave Jodhpur for the performance of the marriage ceremony. Thus, they requested the Durbar to intervene in the matter and stop this marriage in the State. On the 20 March, 1933, Keshri Mal Bhandawat[50] of Shri Jain Sudharak Press, Ajmer wrote a letter to the Mehkama Khas of Jodhpur asking about the action taken by the State in an unequal marriage held in Porwal community of the Oswals, in the territory of Jodhpur. On 31 January, 1934, R.C. Aggarwal, the Assistant Secretary of All India Aggarwal Mahasabha wrote a letter to the private secretary of the Maharaja of Jodhpur, in which he requested His Highness and the State Council to adopt some stringent measures on the lines of the Child Marriage Restraint Act of 1929 of the Government of India. In his letter, he wrote that the child marriages are the root cause of many social evils which are sapping the vitals of the society. He requested the Jodhpur Durbar to take effective measures for eradicating these evils from the society as was done in Baroda, Mysore, Indore and other states.

In 1939, Kunwar Sardar Mal Thanvi, Secretary of Shri Pushkarna Nav-Yuvak Mandal,[51] wrote an open letter to the general masses and requested them to pressurize the Jodhpur Maharaja to enact a legislation similar to that of British India regarding child marriage. He criticized those who stood in the way of formation of rules for the prevention of child marriage, unequal marriage and sale of bride. Pushkarna Nav-Yuvak Mandal also suggested the Maharaja that the practice of child marriage was not supported by the Shastras and in support of this contention, the Mandal representatives quoted that the Pushti-margiya Vaishnav Sampradaya headed by the Goswami mahant of Nathdwara peeth, followed the practice of marrying their daughters, not before the age of 14. The Mandal suggested the Jodhpur Maharaja that:

(i) The marriage of a girl below 13 years and that of a boy below 21 years, should be made a penal offence and the party concerned should be fined upto Rs 1000.
(ii) If any person marries a girl who is less than 27 years of the age of man, then he should be fined upto Rs 1000 and should be given three months imprisonment.
(iii) Anybody who motivates others to perform child marriages un-equal marriages should also be fined and should be sent to jail.
(iv) This Act should be known as Child Marriage and ill-matched Marriage Restraint Act and should be made applicable on all the citizens of Marwar as well as all other Marwari people, who are living outside the territory of Marwar.

Similarly, the Shwetambhari Thanakwasi passed a resolution, banning child and unequal marriages.[52] The Jain Women's Conference, held at Ajmer, also discouraged infant marriages.[53] At Churu and Sardar-Shahar, there were requests to prevent pre-puberty marriages and the Jain's at Bhimasar also made a request to that effect.[54]

The submission of petitions for stopping early marriages was not confined to the frontiers of the Rajputana alone. The efforts of the various caste and social organizations bore fruit and many educated persons sent their applications, petitions to the native rulers to put a stop to the prevalent nefarious practices. On 25 January 1936, Shri Marwar Nav Yuvak Jain Mandal, Bombay[55] published an open letter in their magazine *Jain Jyoti,* in which they requested the subjects of Marwar to write applications to the Maharaja of Jodhpur, requesting him to make law for the prevention of child and unequal marriage and issue an Act prohibiting the sale of girls. The Jain Mandal also suggested different ways to eradicate these evils. Some of their suggestions were:

(i) There should be an Act, the name of which should be Kanyavikraya Act or Sale of Girls Act.
(ii) It should be applicable on all the communities living in Marwar. It should be made applicable also on all the subjects living outside the territory of Marwar.
(iii) Child marriage, sale of girls, marriage of old persons should be made an offence.
(iv) If anybody is found to take money in lieu of the marriage of his daughter or of other female member, that amount should be forfeited by the government.

(v) If anybody marries his daughter, before the age of 14 years or/and his boy before 17-18 years of age, (s)he should be punished by the Raj.
(vi) The amount of tika should not be more than 500 rupees.
(vii) A marriage register should be maintained in which the ages of boys and girls should be registered.
(viii)If any person feels difficulty in getting his daughter married on account of financial problems, the deficit should be made good by the Raj.

Chunnilal Faujmal Chajed, a resident of Pune,[56] wrote a pamphlet on the 10 January 1934, requesting the Jodhpur Durbar to put an end to the child marriages, unequal marriages and the sale of bride. He requested the Maharaja to enact an Act, similar to that, which is prevalent in Baroda, Indore and the British India. He also gave the following suggestions:

(i) That a law should be made, in which the marriage of a girl below 14 years of age and that of a boy under 18 years of age, should be declared as child marriage and as such should be made illegal.
(ii) That the bridegroom should not be more than two and a half times the age of bride and he should be more than one and half times the age of the bride, at the time of marriage.
(iii) Sale of bride, i.e., marrying the girl for the sake of money, should be prohibited at once.
(iv) Proper arrangements should be made by the government, for the education of girls and also for the females.
(v) A register should be maintained in which the ages of the bride and the groom should be entered, as this would put a check on child marriages.

Similarly, Aasu Ram Roop Chand Ramniyawala,[57] a resident of Hubli, sent a pamphlet to Maharaja Ummed Singh of Jodhpur in which, after writing in detail about the evils of child marriages and unequal marriages and their effects on the individual and society, he requested the Maharaja to issue orders for the abolition of the above mentioned maladies.

The Marwari youngmen, residing in Poona, submitted a request signed by nearly 170 persons, requesting the Maharaja of Jodhpur, for the prevention of early marriages.[58] The minimum marriageable age for the girls and the boys proposed by them was 14 and 18 years respectively. These Marwari youngmen from Poona, requested the Maharaja to maintain a marriage-register, in which the ages of boys and girls should be registered at the time of betrothals.

The Rajputana Provincial Hindu Conference[59] unanimously adopted a resolution in its session at Pushkar (Ajmer) in November 1928, that the marriage of girls and boys below 14 and 18 years of age, be made a penal offence. Similarly, the Third Ajmer Women's Conference emphasized that child marriages in the Rajputana should be banned.[60] On the same lines, the Rajputana Ladies Conference (held in 1928) impressed upon the various governments of the Rajputana to effect legislation prohibiting marriages of boys below 18 years and girls below 14 years of age.[61]

A number of organizations had been established to deal with the issues related to Kshatriyas. The All India Kshatriya Mahasabha had been established with the purpose of social upliftment of the Kshatriyas. On 5 November 1934 a meeting was held at Jeena-Mata (Sikar),[62] by the local Rajputs and those of the adjoining territories and also included some members from the British India of the Kshatriya Mahasabha. It was convened for the purpose of social upliftment. It was also resolved that a branch of the aforesaid body be opened in Jaipur to accelerate the work of eradicating the social evils. Virendra Shah, the General Secretary of this Mahasabha, highlighted the importance of the role of the "thinking section of the community" and "all those who have been guiding and controlling the destiny of the Kshatriyas and the country, since time immemorial",[63] that is, the educated section of the society and the rulers respectively, in initiating social reforms. To discuss the social problems, the Rajputs again organized a Sabha in the Ringus Station Railway Dharmashala on the 20 November, 1934.[64] This Sabha was attended by 400 villages. Some of the prominent persons which attended this Sabha, were Rao Gopal Singh of Chowkri, Thakur Jiwan Singh, the Kamdar of Thikana-Akhoor, Kunwar Bachan Singh of Mandawa, Thakur Chhajju Singh Taain, Thakur Kalyan Singh Balreya, Thakur Sampat Singh Gangyasar, Rajaji Sahib of Ranoli, Upadeshaks Vishwanath Singh, Shivnath Singh of Akhil Bharat Youth League and Satyapal Vidyalankar of the Gurukul School. The Khandelwati Rajputs also attended this Sabha.

The opening ceremony of this meeting was performed by Thakur Vishwanath Singh and Shivnath Singh on the subject of Jati-Sudhar and the duties of the Thakurs for which they were legally bound. In this Sabha, Thakur of Mehroli and Raja Amar Singh of Sisua were elected as President and Secretary respectively for the same. The following aims were determined by the Sabha:

(a) That fullest opportunity be given to talented Kshatriyas of the poor or middle classes, to hold all the important offices in the Mahasabha in order that the confidence of the Kshatriya masses may be restored in the Mahasabha and that it may render the poorer members of the community, the utmost help which they may need.

(b) That the Mahasabha may be able to help all the deserving Kshatriyas to play a prominent part in the administrative, political, economic and social fields of the country's life in future, like their ancestors did in the past.

The laws of Kshatriyas, which were framed in 1944,[65] brought forth the prevalence of Gandharva and Swayamvara form of marriages in their community since the Vedic times. This was used as an example to prove non-existence of child marriages amongst them, as only a girl who had attained maturity could judge the pros and cons of the matrimonial proposals of the two forms, as mentioned above. Similarly, the All India Kshatriya Yuwak Sangha[66] passed a resolution against child marriages, at its annual meeting, held at Ajmer.

These developments in the social milieu inspired and motivated other castes too. But rather than taking direct action against the prevalent social evils, it was thought that education was the best remedy and it would, slowly and gradually, change the mindset of the people and thereby make them ready for any future social changes. Thus an attempt was made by other sects, to open schools for the education of boys and girls. In 1899, Seth Hirachand Sancheti, Seth Dhanraj Luniya, and Kasturi Mal Bhadtiya of Oswal community, started an Oswal Pathshala in Ajmer, to educate the children of their community.[67] The Oswal Samaj, in its urge to broaden the narrow mindsets of the community people, established libraries, to make them aware of the various social developments in and out of the State. Thus, Sthanak Jain Pustakalaya was established in 1918 A.D., Jain Gurukul on the other hand in 1928 was established by the Oswal Samaj.[68] In 1929, a gurukul was established by Mishri Lal Muhnot of Bagri village of Beawar, with the sole aim of spreading the light of knowledge. Muhnot, in order to awaken the masses against the ills of child marriage, unequal marriage and to create sympathy in the hearts of the people against the sad plight of widows and child widows, started a monthly magazine – *Kusum* in Hindi.[69]

In 1922, the Oswal-youths of Jodhpur established Akhil Bharat-Varshiya Nav-Yuvak Mahamandal,[70] to discuss the social problems and to think over the best possible methods for social upliftment. Similarly, in 1929, Anand Lal Surana and Rishabh Das Ranka organized Oswal Nav-Yuvak Mandal in Ajmer. In order to make people aware about the various social developments, and to arise consciousness, about the Gandhian ideas and philosophy, The Sasta-Sahitya Mandal was established in 1925, by Jeet Mal Luniya and Jawahar Mal Luniya. They also started *Tyag-Bhumi* – a newspaper was started in 1927, and *Seva-Bhawan* – a magazine was started, in 1930 in Ajmer.[71]

The works of these caste-organizations and conferences went a long way in the awakening of the masses and motivated others to take action against the social problems. On the 28 December, 1924 the annual meeting of All India Vaishya Conference was conducted at Bareilly (U.P.) and was presided over by Har Bilas Sarda, one of the community members and also a member of the Arya Samaj, who later on became popular on account of his works against child marriage.[72] Sarda, urged the caste members to work for the upliftment of the women, to encourage widow-remarriages, to denounce the child and unequal marriages, the practice of purdah and laid emphasis on the importance of education among the masses and especially among the women of the community. He warned the people against the ill effects of these nefarious practices and urged that until and unless their community freed itself from these social evils, they would not be able to create a place for themselves in the history.

The All India Vaishya Mahasabha had been established for the social, moral and educational upliftment of the Vaishya community. On 2 April, 1936, a request was made to the Jaipur Durbar to take action, as it deemed fit, to restrain early marriages in the State of Jaipur.[73] Resolution number 5 was passed by the Maha Sabha, at its conference at Jaipur. As per the resolution, whole hearted support was extended to the Sarda Act and an appeal was made to the Vaishya community to fix the marriageable age for boys and girls at 18 years and 14 years, respectively. A significant feature of the resolution was that it attributed the mental, moral and physical degeneration of the society to the practice of child marriage. And it appealed to the rulers of Jodhpur, Jaipur and Kishangarh to legally prohibit the practice and frame Child Marriage Restraint Act similar to that of the British India as well as that of the States of Udaipur, Travancore, Mysore, Baroda, Indore, Gwalior, Alwar, Bharatpur and Kota. The Maha Sabha also requested the Agent to the Governor General in Central India to bring into force the Child Marriage Restraint Act 1929 in the Chavnis, i.e., military cantonments of the British India, under his jurisdiction as well. Certain members of the Maha Sabha, favoured the adoption of stringent measures to curb the practice. J.M. Seetla Prasad Bajpai made a direct attack on the double standards of those, who on the one hand condemned child marriage, and on the other hand, made no direct or genuine efforts to curb it. He even suggested social excommunication as a mode of punishment for those, who indulged in the practice. He tried to bring out the fact that the legislations could be effective only when the people were prepared for it.

Raghubar Dayal, the Joint Secretary of All India Vaishya Mahasabha forwarded a copy of the resolution, passed at the conference, and it was issued to the I.G. of police, Jaipur.[74] Though the I.G. of Police expressed his sympathy with the cause and believed that "early marriages will not be discouraged without some form of legislation"(sic) and expressed his happiness over the recent regulation, introduced by the Education Department of Jaipur to the effect that no student below the 10th class or under 18 years of age should be married yet he believed that this measure, was insufficient to deal with the evil of child marriage. But the Central Advisory Board rejected the proposal, as it considered the enactment of any proclamation on the matter as an interference with the religious and social liberty of the people.

In Samvat 1945 or 1888 A.D., the Gaur-Brahmins of Jaipur[75] issued a Mahzarnama, in which rules were made regarding the age of marriage, remarriage and about the expenditure incurred at auspicious and inauspicious occasions. Rule No. 29 laid down that if anybody asks the groom's side for money, for the marriage or betrothal of his girl, his invitation in the caste-programmes would be stopped. The money thus forfeited would be returned to the groom's side. But if, on account of poverty or difficult circumstances, someone was unable to perform the marriage of his daughter, then the marriage and all the expenses would be performed by the panchayat. Similarly, Rule No. 31 laid down that nobody should marry after the age of 45 and laid down that "if any one violates this rule and performs the marriage, then he as well as the father of the girl will be ostracised". Rule No. 32 fixed the minimum age of marriage for girls and boys as 10 years and 16 years respectively. The offender was to be punished by the panchas and they would punish "in whatever manner they deemed fit". This Mahzarnama also tried to check the prevalent practice of polygamy and laid down, according to Rule No. 30, that, "nobody should remarry, if his first wife was alive and healthy". If the wife suffered from some incurable disease or if she was barren or was characterless, then only second marriage was allowed.

The Rajasthaniya Gaur Brahmin Sabha[76] took a crucial step in the direction of social legislation, when in its 3rd annual session, held at Jaipur on the 29 December, 1934, it passed a resolution to abolish marriages of boys and girls, less than 18 and 11 years respectively. The Sabha also expressed its disinclination towards un-matched marriages. Besides, the Sabha requested Sawai Man Singh, the Maharaja of Jaipur, to legislate against child marriages in the Jaipur State.

On the 6 March 1938, Pt. Kundanlal Gaur,[77] the President of Jaipur Rajya Yuvak Parishad, sent a letter to the Maharaja of Jaipur in which he asked the Durbar to consider the evil effects of child marriages on the society and requested him to enact Children's Restraint Marriage Act in Jaipur, under which the marriage of a boy below 16 years and that of a girl below 12 years of age be made an offence.

The Rajputana-Central India State's People Conference[78] at Ajmer issued a memorandum to the rulers of the Rajputana and Central Indian States for preventing child and unequal marriages, extravagance on funerals and untouchability. On the 31 October 1938, K.L. Kalyantri, President of the Rajputana Central India States Peoples Conference-Ajmer, requested the Maharaja of Jodhpur to give serious consideration to the matter of child and unequal marriages in his State. He told the Maharaja that the effects of child marriage were even more serious and devastating than dangerous epidemics like cholera and plague. "While the latter affects the happiness of some families for the time they are prevalent but like a swarm of locusts, this ugly veil of this system plunges several families in inexplicable horror"(sic) he wrote. He also called the child marriages as "latent cancer in the body of the society" and asked the Maharaja that "a criminal is given capital punishment for murder of a single individual but unfortunately this system – a cannibal of millions of souls is allowed to silently perpetrate devouring crime everyday" and urged the Maharaja that "it is high time for all the enlightened rulers to come forward and purge this evil, which has taken a firm root in the society". K.L. Kalyantri also submitted a copy of the Child Marriage Restraint Act entitled Sarda Act by Kunwar Chand Karan Sarda, to the Maharaja of Jodhpur, in which was given an illuminating survey of the evils that followed the system of child marriage.

The Rajputana Provincial Hindu Conference,[79] held at Pushkar in November, 1928, adopted a resolution against marriages under 18 and 14 years, for boys and girls respectively. The staggering data in the census report of 1931 of child marriages, which resulted into evils like child widows, induced the Sabha "to rouse the conscience of the people and the princes of the Rajputana". The Sabha directed its energies towards drawing support to abolish the practice.

To create awareness among the Meenas, against the various social malpractices prevalent in their society, some educated Meenas formed Meena Jati Sudhar Samiti[80] in1924. Chhotu Ram Jharwal and his colleagues, Mahadev Ram Pabdiwal and Jawahar Ram Manotal, who had formed this Association, undertook tour of the neighbouring areas of Jaipur State for this purpose and for spreading literacy among them. Among the reforms which they aimed to introduce were giving up of liquor, singing of vulgar songs, and obscene dances. The members of the Sudhar Samiti went from village to village in the Dhundar region, and started chatshalas (i.e., schools) in the villages. On the same lines, the Meena Rajput Maha Sabha, Jaipur was established with a view to regulate reforms, related to marriageable age and marriage ceremonies amongst the Meena Rajputs of Jaipur. The first meeting of the Sabha was convened at Jamva-Ramgarh on 3 June, 1935.[81] They endeavoured to pressurize the Jaipur State to enforce laws pertaining to the above mentioned issues on the lines of the laws promulgated in the Indore State, amongst the Meena community. In the general meeting held at Indore on the 4 January, 1936,[82] the Meena community decided that henceforward they would not marry their daughters below the age of 13 and also fixed certain rules regarding the nukta ceremony prevalent in their community. It was decided that only those, who had no loans to pay, would perform the *nukta* ceremony. This was to be decided by the Patels and other gentlemen of the village that whether one was in debt or not. It was also decided that the rich persons could perform nuktas, in which not more than 101 persons were to be invited. Nobody was allowed to cross the limit thereby fixed by the Sabha and if someone violated the rules, it was laid down that, he would be tried by the law in force.

On the 27 January, 1936[83] Dhanna-Ram Engineer, President and Rambux Patel, Vice President of the Sabha requested the Vice-President of the Council of State of Jaipur to enforce the same regulations in the State of Jaipur and urged that this would "save the community from ruins and very many evil ways and customs." They also told that the efforts for their upliftment were going on since 1931 and that, they had branches of the Sabha at Jaipur, Bharatpur, Alwar, Karauli, Kota, Bundi, Marwar, Mewar, Jhalawar, Indore, Bikaner and Shekhawati.

It is significant to note that the Jaipur Durbar had issued an official notice to the effect that the State did not deem it expedient to interfere in the social matters of the various communities "any more" as it felt that the people could themselves look after their interests.[84] This was conveyed by the Vice-President to the Meena community in the form that no official help could be provided to them, although the Durbar agreed and sympathized with the objectives of the Sabha.[85] In 1942, at the Delhi session of the Akhil Bhartiya Meena Kshatriya Mahasabha, which was presided by Surajbhan Bairwa, twenty thousand Meenas from different parts of the country, assembled to discuss the social and political condition of their community.[86] Shri Bhanwarlal Chaandwal, Birdhichand Khoda, and Jhuntharam Nandla were the representatives of the *Meenas* of Jaipur State. Besides condemning the prevalent social evils, the infamous Criminal Act, which branded the whole of the Meena community as criminals, was also discussed and condemned. To raise consciousness amongst the Meena community about their 'glorious past', Muni Magansagar (who belonged to Meena community, but who later on adopted Jainism) wrote *Meena-Purana*. Under his guidance and leadership, the first caste conference of the Meena community was held on 16 and 17 April, 1944 at Neem-Ka-Thana, Sikar and later on at Shahjahanpur, Alwar. Muni Magan Sagar noticed that the consciousness towards social reforms was increasing amongst the Meenas of Dhundar region (Jaipur), but no such attempts were made amongst the Meenas of Merwara, Khairad, Mewar etc. Therefore, he organized a conference of Padihar (Parihar) Meenas, in June 1944, under his presidentship and asked them to shun away from the prevalent social evils. In 1944-45, Jaipur Rajya Meena Kshatriya Mahasabha organized a caste conference, under the presidentship of Shri Ramvriksha Seehra. In this conference, discussions were held about the removal of prevalent social abuses and about methods of the upliftment of their caste. Similarly, in December 1945, under the presidentship of Shri Rajendra Kumar Ajeya, who played a memorable role in the social reform movement of the Meenas, a conference at Neendar-Bainad (Jaipur) was organized. In the same manner, the caste conference of the Rawat-Meenas, was held at Pushkar, Ajmer, in 1946, under the leadership and guidance of Shri Laxmi Narayan Jharwal. Beside these organizations and individuals, there were many other bodies which were trying to bring about awakening amongst the Meenas and aimed at improving their social and political condition. Meena Panchayat, Jaipur, Jaipur Rajya Meena Sudhar Sabha, Meena Kshatriya Mahasabha, Jaipur, Rajasthan Adivasi Meena Sudhar Sabha, Rajasthan Meena Parishad, Harauti, Rajasthan Vimukta Jati Sewak Sangha, Jaipur, Rajasthan Aadim Jati Sewak Sangha, Jaipur, Adivasi Meena Samajik Sudhar Mandal, Bundi, Harauti Adivasi Meena Samajik Sudhar Mandal, Bundi, Meena Aparadh Nivrati Samiti, Sikar, Akhil Bhartiya Meena Adivasi Sabha, Alwar, Madhyabharat Meena Sudhar Sabha, Gwalior, Meena Vikas Samiti, Indore were some of the important organizations, through which an attempt was made by the Meena community, to do away with the various social evils.[87]

Efforts of All-India Khandelwal Vaishya Mahasabha

In order to wipe out the sufferings of the Khandelwal Vaishya community, caused by the various mal-practices prevalent in them, a Mahasabha was formed by the name of Akhil Bharat Varshiya Khandelwal Vaishya Mahasabha and its rules and laws were made obligatory on the various gotras of the Khandelwal-Vaishya community. The Mahasabha held annual conferences to discuss various social issues in order to do away with the prevalent social evils.[88] Following is a record of the work of the Mahasabha.

First All-India Khandelwal Vaishya Conference

The First All-India Khandelwal Vaishya Conference was held at Delhi in December, 1915. It passed many resolutions to encourage community brotherhood, increase female-literacy, encourage parents to send their children (male as well as female) to schools and to prevent child and unequal or mismatched marriages. Resolution number one which was passed by this Sabha, laid emphasis on the establishment of local Sabhas in different places, to carry and propagate the message of the Mahasabha. Resolution number two laid emphasis on education of the female children as well as that of grown-up females and urged the members of the community to open up schools exclusively for the women of the community and further asked the local Sabhas and caste panchayats to make necessary arrangements for the education of the females. Resolution number two, three and four asked the members to refrain from child marriages and oppose it vehemently. The Mahasabha asked the members to contribute at least one rupee on the occasion of the birth of a son and at least two rupees on the occasion of the marriage of son/sons; the collection done thereby, was to be used for the betterment of the community. Request was also made to open one fund for the orphan-children and one for the help of widows, in every home and shop. Resolution number five opposed unnecessary expenditure done on the occasions of birth, death and marriage; and asked the members not to marry their children, especially female children, in lieu of money. It vehemently criticized the marriage of old people with young girls and urged the members to refrain from such inhuman practice.

Second All-India Khandelwal Vaishya Conference

The second conference was convened at Delhi, in December, 1918. In this conference, members were again asked to open or to help in the running of new primary schools, for the betterment of society. The conference expressed its dissatisfaction and discontentment at the fact, that a large number of people were still illiterate in the community. The members were expected to provide money for the establishment of new schools and offer scholarships to intelligent and meritorious students of the community. The conference also proposed to open a fund for the help of poor, destitute, widows and also for the help of poor brethrens of the community for the marriage of their girls. For this aim a committee by the name of Khandelwal Vaishya Sahayta Samiti was established.

Third All-India Khandelwal Vaishya Conference

The third conference was held at Indore in June, 1920. The Mahasabha again expressed its dissatisfaction at the existing state of literacy prevailing in the community. For this purpose it was proposed that a committee of the community brethrens should be formed and the committee asked to submit its report within one year on the following questions. The committee was to identify those places where there was no government or private school (i.e., those schools run by the general public) and also suggest whether schools were required or not by the members of the caste in those areas. The committee was further asked to select an education system for the children. The committee was to deal with questions related to the education of female children. Should there be separate schools or should there be a co-educational system, and further, how to motivate the girls and boys for primary, secondary and higher education – was to be found out by the committee.

Fourth All-India Khandelwal Vaishya Conference

The fourth All India Khandelwal Vaishya Conference was held at Aichelpur (Barar) in October, 1921. The conference expressed its dissatisfaction on the prevalence of child, unequal or mismatched marriages, in the community and asked the members, to discard these social evils. It also criticized the practice of breaking the sagai-contract, in lieu of money. Resolution number one of the conference laid emphasis on the marriage of girls and boys at a mature age and denounced the marriage of male members, after the age of forty. Resolution number two, criticized the practice of marrying the girl to a rich or influential person, in lieu of money, and asked the members to oppose and condemn this contemptuous practice. It read as "unfortunately some mean and irreligious persons are still existent in the Khandelwal-Vaishya community, who by accepting the money, in lieu of their daughters (i.e., selling their daughters to a rich or influential man) are defaming their community. This Mahasabha, looks down upon them and urges its members to put an end to such a practice". Resolution number four and five criticized the unnecessary and superfluous expenditure done on the occasion of marriages and death and framed certain rules for checking this. Resolution number seven, once again, emphasized the need of education for females and asked the members to open Kanya-pathshalas for this purpose. The conference showed its concern about the illiteracy in the Khandelwals of Jaipur region and asked the members to make special efforts, for the abolition of the same.

Fifth All-India Khandelwal Vaishya Conference

It was held in Ajmer in October, 1922. The fifth conference, again, expressed its contempt in strong terms, against child, unequal or ill-matched marriages. It proposed the minimum and the maximum age for the marriage of girls and boys (or men) as 12 and 36 respectively. No marriage was to be performed in the community before and after the prescribed age limits for marriage. It also tried to put a check on the tendency of marrying a girl, in lieu of money, to an old but wealthy or influential groom, and asked the members to severe their connections and boycott the people, whosoever commit this crime or help in the commission of this crime. Similarly, Resolution Number 7 passed by this conference, again brought out the significance of education, for the betterment of the community, and asked the members to open new schools and help the existing schools.

Sixth All-India Khandelwal Vaishya Conference

The sixth All India Khandelwal-Vaishya Conference was held at Kanpur in December 1924. Resolution Number 4 laid down, that the marriage of a girl before 13 years and that of a boy before 18 years should not be performed by the community members. It is significant to note that the sixth conference prescribed the minimum age limits of 13 and 18 for girls and boys respectively, which was somewhat higher than the age limits prescribed by the other castes. While the Pareeks of Merta City fixed it at 10 and 15 years (in 1924), the Pareeks of Kota State, fixed it at 12 and 16 years (in 1927); and those of Jaipur fixed the minimum marriageable age for the girls and boys of the community as 14 and 18 years in 1945. It is also significant to note that the Mers and the Merats of Merwara fixed the minimum age of marriage of girls as 11 years (in 1889); the Rajguru Purohits of Jodhpur and Pushkar and the Brahmins of Bikaner framed rules, providing age for marriage of boys and girls as 15 years and 11 years (in 1890-91); the Vaishya community fixed it as 11 for girls and 15 for the boys in 1894. The Rajputana Provincial Hindu Conference prescribed the minimum marriageable age as 14 for girls and 18 for boys, only as late as November 1928, i.e., after a period of four years after the sixth All-India Conference of Khandelwal

Vaishyas was organized. Similarly, the Rajputana Ladies Conference impressed upon the various governments of the Rajputana to effect legislation prohibiting marriages of boys below 18 years and girls below 14 years of age, in 1928.

Eighth All-India Khandelwal Vaishya Conference

Though the seventh All India Khandelwal Vaishya Conference was held at Mathura, in May 1927; but because of some unexpected problems it could not pass any resolution other than that of opening schools and gymnasium. In the eighth conference, the Mahasabha again criticized and condemned the practice of the selling of child-brides to rich people. It also opposed the prevalent purdah system in the community.

Ninth All-India Khandelwal Vaishya Conference

It was held at Kota in 1930 and resolution number 3 criticized the practice of taking bride-price. The Mahasabha came to know that the caste-panchayat of Manpur (in Jaipur State) had proposed to take one thousand rupees as bride-price. The Mahasabha condemned this measure in harsh words.

Tenth All-India Khandelwal Vaishya Conference

It was held at Agra in May 1933. To see that the resolutions of the previous conferences have been worked out or not, it was proposed that a committee of five to seven members be set up who would see to it and do the needful. Resolution No. 5 emphasized the need for a community census so that the details about the present number of girls and boys, their educational qualifications, their occupation and service could be found out. It was also laid down that the local branches would provide education to those girls and boys who were poor, orphan or destitute. They were also to impart vocational education to the widow for their betterment.

Twelfth All-India Khandelwal Vaishya Conference

It was held at Dausa in April 1936. Resolution No. 1 of this conference once again laid emphasis on the establishment of schools in those areas where there was none. Resolution No. 2 once again condemned the practice of taking bride-price and considered it against religion and community interest. To put an end to this practice the Mahasabha proposed social ostracism of those who commit or help in committing this crime. A resolution was passed which made it compulsory for all the office-bearers of the Mahasabha to abide by the rules framed from time to time.

Thirteenth All-India Khandelwal Vaishya Conference

It was held at Gaya in December 1938. Resolution No. 5 of the conference aimed at the establishment of the industrial building in which arts like soap-making, button-making, weaving, etc., were planned to be taught to widows. Resolution No. 10 tried to put an end to the prevalent practice of *rokani* or *tharava* in which marriage was performed after many years from the day of betrothal ceremony.

Awakening Amongst the Jats

The social changes that were taking place in other castes influenced the peasant community of the Jats. The Jats, in the early decades of the 20th century, felt that they were being oppressed by the higher sections of the society for a long time and the chief cause of this exploitation, according to them, was the prevalence of illiteracy amongst them, besides other socio-political, economic circumstances.[89] Moreover, the influence of Arya Samaj over some of its leaders, motivated them to think about the role of education as an instrument of social change. Moved by a strong desire for the upliftment of the Jat community, on the 9 August 1917, Chaudhry Bahadur Singh Bhaubhia with the help and cooperation of Swami Mansanath and Thakur Gopal Singh Panniwali, established Jat Anglo Sanskrit Middle School at Sarrafon ki Dharmashala in Hanumangarh town. But this was resented by the locally predominant Rajput community, and consequently on the 1 January 1918 this Jat school was transferred to Sangariya and was established at the Dharmashala of Seth Bajrang Das. In those days when this Jat school was established at Sangaria, there was no other school for the Jat community in the whole of Bikaner region as well as other near by regions, including the Hisar region of Punjab. Thus, this was the first and the only Jat school for the Jat boys within the area of 800 miles. Seeing the significance of this institution for the Jat community and sharing concern about their upliftment, Thakur Gopal Singh – one of the enlightened Rajputs, donated 14 *bighas* and 3 *biswas* of his land at Sangaria, for the school building and other socially useful productive works. It was the first instance of its own kind when someone donated his land solely for the purpose of spread of education and that too by a man belonging to the powerful Rajput community for the spread of knowledge amongst the agricultural community of Jats. Chaudhry Bahadur Singh, in order to promote the community consciousness towards education, and for invoking community participation, started touring different places and collected donations not only from the nearby regions but also from distant places like Calcutta and Benaras. In 1919, in order to establish a separate building for school and hostel, he issued an appeal to his Jat brethrens to contribute generously for the purpose of education. For this purpose a meeting was held on 27 March 1921, under the leadership of Chaudhry Sir Chhotu Ram in which, on his fervent appeal, people donated generously and consequently Rs 11,000 was collected. Chaudhry Bahadur Singh also started primary schools at Goluwala, Mattili, and Ghamurwali villages and also started a library, dispensary and *gau-shala* at Sangariya school. After his death at the age of 42 (on 1 June 1924), his work was carried out by Chaudhry Harish Chandra Nain, Chaudhry Jeevan Ram, Chaudhry Harjiram Malot, Chaudhry Sardara Ram Chautala, Chaudhry Maniram Sihag, Chaudhry Gangaram Dhaka, Chaudhry Shivkaran Singh Chautala, etc., To commemorate his untiring efforts in the field of education, it has been rightly said for him that:

> "बहादुरसिंहजी भौभिया, जाट वीर था एक।
> जिसके मन में थी जगी, परोपकार की टेक।।
> लख गांवो की हीनता, ली यह मन मे ठान।
> बिन विद्या जाता नही, अंधकार अज्ञान।।
> सैनानी वह देश का, जागृत पहरेदार।
> लगा जगाने क्षेत्र को, कर विद्या प्रचार।"

The indefatigable efforts of Chaudhry Bahadur Singh, to spread the rays of education amongst the Jats, proved successful and very soon voices in favour of education of children (both male and female children) were heard from different quarters. With this aim in mind, Akhil Bhartiya Jat Mahasabha was organized at Pushkar (Ajmer) in 1925, and it was presided by Krishna Singh, the Maharaja of Bharatpur. The Jat leaders of Marwar like Moolchand Nagaur, Babu Gullaram Ratkudiya, Shri Bhianram Sihag, and Master Dhara Singh and those of Shekhawati like Chaudhry Govindram Hanumanpura, Panne Singh Devrod, Devasingh Bochlya, Ramsingh Kanwarpura, Bhudaram, Chimnaram Sangasi, Chetram Bhaanwarwasi, Laduram

Kisari, Motiram Kotri, Master Ratan Singh, etc., attended this Mahasabha and came to the conclusion that only through spread of education the Jats could rise.

This led the Jat leaders of Shekhawati region to establish Jat Sabha, on the 5 November 1925 and through it they tried to do away with the social evils, and spread education. This initiative of the Jat leaders of Shekhawati, motivated the members of the Jat community of other regions also, and consequently on the 2 March 1927, a meeting was held at Jodhpur under the leadership of Radha Krishna Mirdha. A committee was formed in which Radha Krishna Mirdha was elected as president, Ramchandra Mirdha as secretary and Ramu Ramji (of pargana Mallani) as deputy secretary. It was decided in the meeting, that to educate the sons of the Jat peasants, a boys hostel should be opened at Jodhpur. Chaudhry Gullaram, on this occasion, gave a new mantra *padho aur padhao* (study and teach) to the Jat community. Chaudhry Gullaram gave his own house at Ratanada, Jodhpur, for the above mentioned holy purpose and consequently on the 4 April 1927, Jat Boarding House at Jodhpur came in existence. Similarly, Chaudhry Moolchand, B. R. Mirdha, Bhianram, Master Dhara Singh, Chaudhry Moolchand Nagaur and Chaudhry Gangaram Khileri opened a boys hostel at Nagaur on the 21 August, 1930 and Chaudhry Ramdan Daukia opened a school at Barmer. Boys hostels were also opened at Merta, Deedwana, Maroth, Parbatsar, Khinwasar, Pipaad, Kuchera, Ladnun, Bilara, Ratkudiya, etc. It is significant to note that Chaudhry Moolchand was also a great supporter of women education and he believed that until and unless women are educated, overall development of the society is not possible. With this aim in mind, he opened a girls' hostel at Chenar (Nagaur) and appointed Shrimati Teeja Bai as its first warden. Another girls' hostel was opened at Ratkudiya.

In 1929, Baldev Ram Mirdha started Kisan Shikshan Sansthan and through it the activities of Jat Boarding House, Jodhpur were carried out. In order to highlight the significance of education, B.R. Mirdha made extensive tours in the villages and motivated the Jat boys to study at his hostel. This Jat Boarding House at Jodhpur, proved a lighthouse and soon it was felt that such boarding houses should be opened at other places also. In 1934 a boys hostel was opened at Barmer, by Babu Gullaram, B.R. Mirdha, Chaudhry Moolchand Nagaur, Bhianram Sihag and Chaudhry Ramdan; in 1934-35, at Merta, by Pusaram Kilak, Chaudhry Mahram Kamedia,

Prabhuji Ghatela and Birdharam Maharia; and beside these, such boarding houses were opened at Didwana by Kisnaram and Subedar Pannaram Dhingsari, at Maroth by Ishwarram Chaudhary Maharajpura, at Khinwsar by Chaudhry Hetram, at Bilara by Babu Gullaram, and also at Parbatsar, Ratkudiya, Pipaad, Kuchera, Rol, Ladnun and Jayal. Schools were also opened by Kisan Shikshan Sansthan at the following villages: Baapa, Bhoondana, Madlaya, Kawaspura, Rataau, Amarpura, Bhadwasi, Khadnal, Bodwa, Khudi, Roodu, Shilgaon, Jhadisara, Bhakrod, Bugarda, Dhandesari, Baldu etc.

Baldev Ram Mirdha and Chaudhry Ramdan of Barmer believed that it was because of the prevalent social evils, that the Jats were leading a miserable life. Therefore they vehemently denounced social evils like – child marriage, unequal or ill-assorted marriage, mausar, dowry system, drinking of wine etc. and asked the Jat peasants to shun them. To spread awareness amongst his own people against these malpractices, on the 22 August 1938, i.e., on the day of Teja Dashmi, B.R. Mirdha, along with Chaudhry Mool Chand Nagaur and Babu Gullaram, established Marwar Jat Krishak Sudharak Sabha at the cattle fair of Parbatsar. It is remarkable that the day as well as the place was carefully chosen to establish this Sudharak Sabha. The cattle fairs at Parbatsar, Nagaur, Balotara, Merta etc. – which were attended by thousands of villagers, not only from nearby areas but also from far-flung regions, provided them an audience. It gave them a platform to express their views and share their concern, with their peasant brethrens, for the upliftment of their caste. This again shows the impact of Arya Samaj on the leaders of the Jat community, as it was the Arya Samaj which adopted this strategy, for the first time in the history of the Rajputana, to reach out to the common masses.

Babu Gullaram, became the first President and Moolchand became the Secretary of this Sudharak Marwar Jat Krishak Sudharak. The members of this organization not only conducted meetings at various places (including villages), but also spread the wave of reform through its own bhajan mandalis (groups of devotional song-singers) and upadeshaks (i.e., preachers). The members of these bhajan mandalis, through their bhajans (devotional songs) and sermons, asked the villagers to discard the prevalent social evils of child and unequal marriages, mrityu bhoj or mausar, dowry system, fighting, eating and taking of amal (or opium), tobacco and wine, singing of vulgar and obscene songs at marriage ceremonies, speaking of indecent and improper words (*gaaliyan*) *raati-joga, chura-pratha,* etc., The cattle fairs, which were organized at different places such as Balotara, Nagaur, Merta, Parbatsar etc., where thousands of the villagers appeared and which continued for many days, provided a good opportunity to the members of Sudharak Sabha. In these cattle fairs, Thakur Hukum Singh Parihar, Bhola Singh, Heera Singh Pahadsar, Pt. Dattu Ram Bahadara, Chaudhry Ganpat Ram, Chaudhry Jivan Ram Jetpura, Chaudhry Chandu Lal, Chaudhry Mohar Singh Poonia, Nand Kishore Gajadhar, Balak Ram Thalod, Chain Singh Saharan, Ramdhan Jhakad, Shimbhulal Golya, Pannalal Latiyal, etc., acted as upadeshaks and asked the villagers to denounce the various social evils. Their efforts, gradually, brought good results and the consciousness against these social abuses began to permeate in the Jat society.

But the above mentioned description highlighting the significant role of the enlightened individuals and those of the caste organizations against the prevalent social evils (and especially against female infanticide and child marriage), can never be completed without mentioning the name and work of Onkar Bhatt. In 1832-33, Bhatt wrote *Dissuasive Against Infanticide Addressed to the Rajpoots,*[90] which was written in Braj-bhasha and which was published by Calcutta Baptist Mission Press. It was circulated amongst the various Rajput rulers and the nobles of the Rajputana and also to those of Central India. In this book, Bhatt asked the native rulers to put a stop to the inhuman practice of female infanticide on religious, social and moral grounds. He reminded the Kshatriyas of their chivalry, valour and helpfulness and told them that this obnoxious crime was not even prevalent in the so-called antyaja (lower castes) and malechha castes (foreigners). He dubbed female infanticide as "a crime which is much more heinous and abominable than even the murder of a Brahmin, and of which there is no prashchitta or repentance". Onkar Bhatt requested the Rajput rulers to award severe punishments (even of cutting limbs and other parts) to those who were found guilty of this crime, and wrote that "looking to the seriousness of their crime, the award of rigorous punishment for 12 years to the guilty would not be sufficient". It will be interesting to note his words:

"नाक वास प्रभु देत हैं सुता होत हैं जाहैं
वे पापी धन लोभते उपजत मारता हैं।।
नहि यह धर्म वेदमो गायो रूखि मुनिके मन नहि भायो।
त्रेता द्वापर कलजुग माही यहबिध धर्म कहवी नाही।।

सूरपनो राखे अतिभारीं तजे धीरचतुराई गहरी।
सनमुखलड़े जुद्धमों तयसे रहैं प्रभुमो जोगीमन जयसे।
दानसूनता होय हैं भारी बहुबिध द्विजसंरछनकारी।
एते धर्म कहे छत्रिनके ईनते लागत है सबनीके।।
मृगबधमृगयामों अरू जानो सरनागत संरछन मानों
सनमुख आयो सस्त्रग्रहीता बधताको अति होत पुनीता।।
तिंहा एतेंको छांटिकैं छत्रि करों संधार।
बालवृद्ध गुरू मृगद्रसी रोगी भागनहार।
यह बिध धर्म कह्यो छत्रिन् को नहि कन्याको बध हैं नीको।
असुर यवन जाति हे जेती उनकोवी उपजतहे भीति।।
जयन धर्म्ममों देखो जाकें वेयाकोंनीके नहि भाकें।
अंतिज मलेच्छ जाति बहोतेरी उनमो बी यह नाहि निहारी ।।
अनुचित कर्म बडो यह जानो द्विजबध तैं दूनो करि मानो।
नहि यह देस धर्म्ममों जान्यो जाति धर्म्ममो नहि बखान्यों।।
प्रायश्ति नहि याको लेखो पारासर सुत कतमो देखो।
साधसंतकी खोजो बानी तिनमों याकि नही निसानी ।
अयसे पापिनको उचित राजदंड बहु भांत ।
बंधन द्वादस बरसलों तोनहि दोख मिठात।।"

He considered this crime much more sinful than abortion and asked the rulers to excommunicate the offenders from their respective states. Not only the males but also the females were responsible in one or the other way for this horrible crime, according to him, and as such no leniency should be shown to them on account of their being members of the fair-sex. "Such offenders should be thrown into some deep river or water tank, with a big stone tied on their necks", he wrote.

"गर्भपातमों दोख बखान्यों तासो अधिक दोख यह जान्यो।
प्रायश्चित यांको यह कीजे, नृपने सब सर्वस्व हि लीजे।
देसनिकारो अरू तिहे दूजे अंग भंग कमसों सब कीजे।
नहि यह दंड अकेलो नरको स्त्रिय को वी यह जानोको।
दुष्ट नारि पतिघात जो करें गर्भपात बालकपर हरें।
तिनके सीला बांधिकरि गलमों नृपकरि कोध डारि देवो जलमों ।
यहबिध प्रायश्चित हैं याकें मिताक्षराको देखों जाकें।
गर्भवती नारी जोकरें यहबिध पाप जरा नहि डरें।। 20 ।।
वायप्रसूती होयकें बांधि मंगावें भीक।
नानाविधके त्रासतें पुनि मारे तयकीकं।।
भूपदंडके भय तैं घरमों करि यह पाप डरत नहि मनमों।

आत्मघातकों पातक तिनकों सप्तजन्मलों हैं नहि नीकों।। 21 ।।
नर्कवासवें भुगतैं निहिचैं जे कन्यामारें अरू बेचैं।
पुनि पश्वादिकमों अवतरे तउ पाप उनको नहि जरें।। 22 ।।
यहबिध तातधर्म हैं दुष्टा हिंसाधर्म कहयो अनिष्टा।।
बहुधनषर चहो नसुडरे कन्यावधता सोजे करें ।। 28 ।।
सुता पापते जोंत हैं संचितधन अरू धीर।
उलट होत निश्चयकरी जो बहुषावें धीर।।
जन हिंसाकरि धन उपजावें ताको द्रव्यनिरर्थक जावें ।
जीवदयासो हे नहि दूजो धर्मशास्त्रसगरेमो खोजो।।
पापकर्म्मतैं द्रव्य उपावे द्वाद्स बरस बीच सब जावें।
द्रव्य भये यह फल सब भाषैं परनरको अपनी करि राषैं।।
अपने पुत्रसुताको निहचे परनरनारक बूनहि पोचे।
तासे कूरकर्म्म नहि अयसो बालकनास करत हैं जयसो।।
और सूनो सगरे मन लाई कथा भागवतमो यह गाई।
वारे दुष्टकंसने बेटे बयनदेवकी केछ मोटे।।
स्वसंज्ञा हैं गायकों तासुनू हैं बछ।
ताके मारे नहि बच जैंतन करोको उलछ।।
पुनि ता पापदोखतैं सारे कंसादिक हरिनें सब मारे।
यातें नहि यह उचित बखान्यों कन्यावधनिहचे करि जानों।।
पुत्रमारवेकों मन धारों हरनाकुस प्रभु तबही पछारों।
यह सब मूर्खपनेकी बातैं अधिक दोख दूजोनहि यातैं।।
सबते विद्या पडबोनीको जामे निकसे नाम हरीको।
जाको चोरदुष्टभय नाही यासो धनदूजो अरू नाहीं।।
खरचके अष्टगुण होई पातक पडवेतैं भगजाई।
और द्रव्यसब तुछ बखान्यों।
धीरशूरके यह मन मान्यों।।

Onkar Bhatt was also against the prevalent practice of unequal marriages and believed that poor parents should not marry their girls, in lieu of money or some other expectation, to some unworthy or old grooms. According to him, one way to stop child and unequal marriages was the marriage of poor girls with poor boys and vice-versa. Similarly, the rich persons should try to help their poor son-in-laws, with all their might. Those persons, he believed, should be ostracized from the caste, who refuse to accept the daughters of their poor caste – brethrens in marriage alliance to their sons. In this connection, he expressed his sentiments in the following words:

"होत विनयविद्याते निहचे विनयपात्रताको पुंनि खयचे।
निर्धनके घरकन्याजनम ; तो वह यहैं विचारो मतम।।
केवल कन्यादानहि कीजे कन्याद्रव्य कबू नहीं लीजें।
धनधारी धनव्यय बहु करो जामाताको सब दुःख हरों।।
यथा शक्ति सबकों कह दीनी देखो वेदविधि रंग भीनी।

निर्धनने निर्धनको दीजे निर्धनकी निर्धनने लीजे।।
देवे धनी धनीको बेटी समझ लेत जो अपनिहेटी।
यहबिध कन्यादान बखान्यों रूखि मुनि सबके मन मान्यों।।
यहबिध दान करे कन्याकों स्वर्गवासनिहत्ते होय ताकों।
वाते वृद्वबालसब मिलके कर बिच्चार सारेहिलिमिलिके।।
कन्या निर्धनपुरखकि जो न लेय धनवान्।
किजें वाहेर जातसो योहिं वेदनिरवान्।।
पत्रपठावे सबके नेहरे यथाशक्ति करिके जहिरे।
त्यागे कन्यावधकौ सगरें कीयेंमाफ अबतकजे बिगरे ।।
जेकोईपुनि अयसो अबकर हैं बाकों जातपातपरहरहैं।।
राजपूत यह रीत चलावें वो अब अश्वमेधफल पावें ।।

It is remarkable that this effort of Onkar Bhatt, to motivate and request the Rajput rulers and nobles to shun the age-old practice of female infanticide, is the first of its own kind as it came from a priest and also that it was the first attempt from a common man's side to put an end to this inhuman practice. No common man before him, dared to bring this matter in an unflinching manner before the ruling classes and especially the one, which itself committed this crime, though it is quite possible that some of them might have thought about it. Moreover, at individual level, his was the first common man's voice against certain social evils like – dowry, uneven marriages and the marriage of girls to unworthy and unsuitable grooms (*kanya vikraya*).

Thus, from the above account, it becomes quite clear that the caste organizations played a commendable role in the development of their own community, as they tried to control and eradicate the social malpractices, prevalent in their society. Since the rules framed by these organizations, were made obligatory, on every member, and since the, people were afraid of the punishments given by the caste organizations, therefore, their rules produced desired effects, to some extent, in checking the practice of early and mismatched marriages. But at this juncture, it is also necessary to understand, that sometimes some of these caste panchayats, under the pressure of rich or influential persons, supported the child or uneven or mismatched marriages and forced the parents to marry their sons or daughters at an unsuitable age or to an unworthy fellow. Sometimes they also, on threat of social-ostracism and other punishments, forced the enlightened individuals of their community to stop raising their voices and shut their eyes against such social evils. Except a few examples, it must be written in all fairness to them, that these caste organizations played a praiseworthy role in the development of their communities as they accepted the demands of the changing times and moulded their structure according to the need of the hour.

It is also remarkable to note that the British administered district of Ajmer, had a significant association with the social reform movement in the Rajputana. Many of the reformers started their work, at one or the other time, from this place and made Ajmer as the headquarter of their activities. Perhaps it was the influence of the Arya Samaj, or perhaps the works of Christian missionaries or perhaps the liberal attitude of the government due to which the people made this place conducive for the reform process. Moreover, at that time, Ajmer was the centre of higher education in the branches of modern education in Rajputana which also helped and motivated the enlightened individuals to start their work from that place.

It is also noteworthy, that the Pareek Brahmins of Jaipur were the first to frame rules against certain social vices (like the heavy expenditure done at the time of marriage) as early as Samvat 1600 (1543 A.D.). But it was the Khandelwal Vaishya community, which prescribed the minimum age of marriage for boys and girls as 18 and 13 respectively; which was slightly higher than the age limits, prescribed by other communities. Whereas the Pareeks of Merta city fixed it as 10 for girls and 15 years for boys (in 1924); the Pareeks of Kota State, fixed it as 12 and 16 years (in 1927); the Pareeks of Khinchiwara, Mauthara, Harauti and Umat-wara, fixed it as 10 and 15 years (in 1928); the Mers and Merats of Merwara fixed the minimum marriageable age for girls as 11 years (in 1889); the Rajguru Purohits of Jodhpur and Pushkar and the Brahmins of Bikaner, fixed it as 11 and 15 years respectively (in 1890-91); the Khandelwal Vaishya community prescribed the minimum marriageable age for girls as 13 years and for boys as 18 years in 1924. It is also remarkable that some of the caste organizations of the Rajputana, e.g., that of the Jats and some of the business classes, were influenced by the ideology of Dayanand Saraswati and as such, they adopted the strategies of Arya Samaj (like the use of upadeshaks and bhajan-mandalis, in fairs and specially the cattle fairs) to propagate against the prevalent social evils.

From the above account, it becomes quite clear that there was enough consciousness, against the prevalent social evils, amongst the various castes, though their methods differed from each other owing to the difference in the level of their education, their social position, their commitment and their zeal. Whereas some took initiatives themselves, the others thought it proper, to leave the entire matter on the native rulers and expected them to make rules for the betterment of their subjects. Still, there were some, who believed that these problems will come to an end, as and when the light of education spreads. With this aim in their mind, they established schools, libraries and hospitals for the upliftment of their community. But it must be kept in mind while reviewing the whole scenario, that every caste, because of the structural peculiarity, cared more for its benefits and had no thoughts about the betterment of other castes. Some of the castes were progressive in their outlook (like the Pareek Brahmins) and contrary to the established fact in historiography (which revolves round the works of British officers and gives all credit to them for the social reform process in India and specially in the Rajputana) they played a notable role, much before the arrival of British East India Company in Rajasthan.

Limitations of Non-Governmental Reform Efforts

Though many caste organizations as well as enlightened individuals worked hard to mitigate the sufferings of the women and were even able to get regulations passed, but even then the problem of child marriages, unequal marriages and the sale of bride and that of groom did not end, and are in existence, till date. The first important cause responsible for this, was the orthodox-attitude of the society. The masses, who were mostly illiterate considered the reforms or the above mentioned resolutions as unpractical and believed them to be the works of a few educated youths of their community, who according to them, wished to laugh at the traditions of their society. In the early period the reformers were mostly laughed at and were not taken seriously by the common men. The orthodox attitude of the masses, prevented them to attend the meetings of the so-called reformers of their society. Moreover, these caste organizations and individuals faced a stiff resistance from their own caste-panchayats, which were mostly dominated by the elders as well as the rich men of the community. When questions were raised about the rights of the panchayats and the rights of the panchas – who married twice or thrice on account of their money – these caste organizations came in direct opposition with the caste-panchayats, and the former started opposing the latter.

These caste organizations depended upon the support (moral, material and physical) of their caste members and when they could not get it, there was no other way for them but to face great difficulties. The above mentioned incidents clearly show that many newspapers and caste organizations, later on disappeared from the scene because of lack of support from their own members.

The role played by different native States also caused much damage to the works of these caste-organizations. The Sarda Act, which came into force in British India in 1930, was not applied in the native States for a long time and as such whenever anyone informed any State about the occurrence of some child or unequal marriage, the concerned State tried to pass the matter in total silence by stating that Sarda Act was not in force in their State and therefore they were unable to interfere in that matter. Inspite of all difficulties, these enlightened individuals and the caste organizations ultimately became successful in pressurizing their rulers to pass an Act for the prevention of child and unequal marriages, in their respective States.

Notes

1. Ghurye, G.S., *Caste and Race in India*, Popular Prakashan Pvt. Ltd., Bombay, 1988, pp. 1-2.
2. Mishra, Jai Shankar, op. cit, pp. 148-200.
3. Ghurye, G.S., op. cit., pp. 3-4; and also, Mishra, Jai Shankar, ibid.
4. Ibid.
5. Ibid.
6. Tiwari, Raghunath Prasad, *Pareek Jati Ka Itihaas*, Richa Prakashan, Jaipur, 1992, pp. 54-55.
7. The original document stated that this marriage was performed in Samvat 1600 i.e., 1543 A.D., during the time of Akbar. This document also mentioned Jehangir – the heir apparent. The Mahzar, issued by the Pareek community and approved by the Jaipur Durbar, in Samvat 1940 i.e., 1883 A.D., also mentions Samvat 1600 as the year of that grand marriage. But this is an established fact, that Akbar became the Emperor of India in AD 1556 (and not in AD 1543, as the document mentions) and that Jehangir was born in AD 1569, much after the time given in the document. The original copy of this Mahzar, (beside other original documents regarding the reforms

done in the Pareek community) is still available in Tiwari Madan Lal Pareek Shodh Sansthan, Jaipur, which was founded by Raghunath Prasad Tiwari, the author of *Pareek Jati Ka Itihaas*, in memory of his father. This Mahzar was approved by the Jaipur Durbar, as previously mentioned, and it appears that there was some misunderstanding in reading the original document. But in any case, this incident really happened in the history of the Pareek community, as the *Jooth Ki Bavadi* still exists in Sanganer, Jaipur.

For the reform-efforts done by the Pareek Community, please see Tiwari Raghunath Prasad, *Pareek Jati Ka Itihaas*, pp. 54-73.

RSAB: Mehkama Khas, Jodhpur Records, File no. C/5/1, Vol. II, Social, Marriage Legislation.

8. For more information regarding the reform efforts done by the Pareek community, please see Tiwari, Raghunath Prasad, *Pareek Jati Ka Itihaas*, op. cit., pp. 54-73.
9. R.S.A.B.: Mehkama Khas, Jodhpur Records, File no. C/5/1, Social, Marriage Legislation.
10. 'Jiwan ke vividh kshetron me Kayastha mahaparivar ka yogdan', pp. 33-35, and 'Kayastha Jati aur sam-samayik Samaj', pp. 8-9, in *Volunteer* – a social magazine of Kayastha caste (swarna jayanti visheshank), 1947-97, edited by Chitransha Ajay Prakash, Chitransha Suresh Chandra Shrivastav and Chitransha (Smt.) Anita Saxena, Govind Nagar, Kanpur, U.P., August, 1997. And also, Heimsath, Charles, op. cit., p. 281.
11. 'Jiwan ke vividh kshetron me Kayastha mahaparivar ka yogdan', pp. 33-35, and 'Kayastha Jati aur sam-samayik Samaj', pp. 8-9, in *Volunteer*, op. cit., pp. 33-35.
12. *Chitransha Sandesh* (a social news-bulletin of Kayastha caste), edited by Chitransha Kamal Kant Verma, Lucknow, Jan-March 2006, issue no. 74, p. 3.
13. 'Jiwan ke vividh kshetron me Kayastha mahaparivar ka yogdan', pp. 33-35, and 'Kayastha Jati aur sam-samayik Samaj', pp. 8-9, in *Volunteer*, op. cit.
14. *Chitransha Sandesh*, issue no. 74, op. cit., p. 3.
15. Singh, Sita Ram, *Nationalism and Social Reform in India*, 1885-1920, p. 136.
16. 'Jiwan ke vividh kshetron me Kayastha mahaparivar ka yogdan', pp. 33-35, and 'Kayastha Jati aur sam-samayik Samaj', pp. 8-9, in *Volunteer*, op. cit.
17. Report of the 11th National Social Conference 1897, Poona 1898, p. 58. Cf. Saxena, R.K., op. cit., pp. 202-203.

18. 'Jiwan ke vividh kshetron me Kayastha mahaparivar ka yogdan', pp. 33-35, and 'Kayastha Jati aur sam-samayik Samaj', pp. 8-9, in *Volunteer*, op. cit.
19. 'Chitranshi Patra-patrikayen' in *Volunteer*, op. cit., pp. 33-35.
20. Heimsath, Charles, op. cit., p. 283.
21. Kothari, Rita, *Female Infanticide and Child Marriages in the 19th and 20th Century India*, M.Phil. Dissertation, University of Rajasthan, Jaipur, p. 178.
22. Seventh Report of the Indian National Social Conference, 1893, Part II, p. 41.
23. Singh, S.R., op. cit., p. 163.
24. For the growth and development of journalism in the Jain community, please see Bhanawat, Sanjeev, *Sanskratik Chetna aur Jain Patrakarita*, Siddha-Shri Prakashan, Jaipur, 1990. pp. 60-79.
25. Bhutodiya, Mangilal, op. cit., pp. 454-455.
26. Bhanawat, Sanjeev, op. cit., p. 83.
27. Ibid., pp. 84-86.
28. Ibid., p. 92.
29. Ibid., p. 97.
30. *Jain Samaj*, April, 1917, p. 5.
31. *Jain Samaj*, May 1917, p. 48.
32. *Tarun Oswal*, June 1940, p. 24.
33. *Jain Yuvak*, October 1928, pp. 26-27.
34. Ibid.
35. Bhutodiya, Mangilal, op. cit., pp. 446-451.
36. Sunder Lal, Minister of Kishangarh State and Deewan Nathmal Mehta of Jaisalmer participated in it. Cf. *The Indian Social Reformer*, January 21, 1900, p. 165.
37. *Agrawal Upkarak*, 4th issue, June 1, 1906, Cf. Goyal, Lata, op. cit., p. 172.
38. *Report of Ghaseti Agrawal*, Vedic Yantralaya, Ajmer, 1897, p. 5. Cf. ibid.
39. *Agrawal Upkarak*, 4th issue, June 1, 1906. Cf. ibid.
40. *Second Report of Agrawal Pathshala*, 1905-06, Vedic Yantralaya, p. 1. Cf. ibid.
41. Vidyalankar, Satyaketu, *Agrawal Jati Ka Itihaas*, Vani Prakashan, Bombay, 1972, p. 52.
42. *Report of All-India Marwari Conference*, 1943-47, p. 3.
43. *First Report of Maheshwari Sabha*, 1907-08, Vedic Yantralaya, p. 2.

44. Ibid., p. 3.
45. *Report of Bal Vidhwa Sahayak Samiti*, 1928, Vedic Yantralaya, Ajmer, p. 6.
46. Ibid.
47. *Child Marriage Prohibition Act 'Sarda Act'*, (edited by Pt. Shiv Shankar), Rajputana Press, Ajmer, 1938, pp. 37-38.
48. RSAB: Mehkama Khas, Jodhpur Records, File no. C/5/1, Vol. II, Social, Marriage Legislation (from 1.1. 1936 to 1.1. 1939).
49. Ibid.
50. Ibid.
51. Ibid.
52. *The Times of India*, 22.4. 1938.
53. Ibid.
54. *Bombay Chronicle*, 5.9. 1927.
55. RSAB: M.K.J.R., File No. C-2/10 of 1926-36, Social, Basta No. 6, dated January 31, 1934.
56. Ibid.
57. Ibid.
58. Ibid.
59. *The Hindustan Times*, dated 1-12-1928.
60. *The Hindustan Times*, dated 26-11-1928.
61. *The Times of India*, dated 23-11-1928.
62. RSAJ: Confidential diary of the Sambhar Division, dt. 10 Nov. 1934; General, Social & Religious Basta No. 9 File No. 152, Part-II.
63. RSAJ: Permission to *All India Kshatriya Mahasabha* for preaching its aims and objects in Jaipur State; General, Social & Religious Basta No. 9, File No. 152, Part-II.
64. RSAJ: General, Social & Religious Basta No. 9 1924, File No. 152, Part II.
65. RSAB: Sociology, 43, No. 20227, p. 13.
66. Ibid.
67. *Report of Vidya Unnati*, Oswal Samaj, 1912, pp. 5-6.
68. Bhandari, Sukh Sampat Rai, *Oswal Jati Ka Itihaas*, Vedic Yantralaya, p. 247.
69. Ibid., p. 190.
70. Bhutodiya, Mangi Lal, op. cit., p. 445.
71. Bhandari, Sukh Sampat Rai, op. cit., p. 336.

72. Bhati, Narayan Singh, 'Samaj Ratna Har Bilas Sarda' in *Parampara*, Rajasthani Shodh Sansthan, Chopasani, Jodhpur, 1985, p. 103.
73. RSAJ: General, Social & Legislation Basta No. 1, File No. 156.
74. Ibid.
75. RSAJ: General, Social & Legislation, Basta No. 9, 1943, F. No. 152, Part-II.
76. Ibid.
77. Ibid.
78. RSAB: M.K.J.R., File No. C/5/1, Vol. II, op. cit.
79. Kothari, Rita, op. cit., p. 184.
80. Bhatnagar, V.S., 'Social and political awakening among the Meenas' in Sharma, G.N. (ed.), *Social and Political awakening among the Tribals of Rajasthan*, Centre for Rajasthan Studies, University of Rajasthan, Jaipur, pp. 86-92. And also, Saraswat, Rawat, *Meena Itihaas*, published by – Jhunthalal Nandhla and S.K. Sharma, second edition, Samvat 2057, pp. 126-133.
81. RSAJ: From Dhanna Ram Engineer to the V.P., Council of State, Jaipur dt. 27 January, 1936, General, Social and Religious, Basta No. 9, File no. 152, Pt. II.
82. Ibid.
83. Ibid.
84. RSAJ: General, Social & Legislation, 1924, F. No. 152, Part-II.
85. Ibid., File No. 154.
86. Bhatnagar, V.S. op. cit., And also, Saraswat, Rawat, op. cit.
87. Ibid.
88. Gupta, K.C., and Kedawat, R.P. (Eds.), *Sambhaav* (Book published by the Akhil Bhartiya Khandelwal Vaishya Mahasabha, at its 27th Conference at Alwar, Rajasthan), 1986.
89. For more information on this subject, please see Pemaram and Chaudhry, Vikramaditya, *Jaton ki Gaurav-gatha,* Rajasthani Granthagar, Jodhpur, 2004.
90. The original copy of this book can be seen at Maharaja Sawai Man Singh-II Museum and Library (City Palace Library, Jaipur).

6

Role of the Native Rulers

I
Abolition of Female Infanticide

The practice of female infanticide, as we have seen in Chapter 2, was widely prevalent among the various sections of the society and particularly among the Rajputs, therefore it was difficult for the native rulers and especially for the enlightened ones to overlook it. The magnitude of this crime and the heinous methods which were adopted to do away with the female infants compelled them for introspection and device strategies for its eradication. It is remarkable that the efforts to check the practice of female infanticide, started much before the arrival of the East India Company in the Rajputana and the State of Jaipur was the first to take the lead in its abolition.

As early as Samvat 1787 (1731 A.D.),[1] Maharaja Sawai Jai Singh of Jaipur assembled the fifty-three clans of Kachwahas and the nobles and pundits of his court and explained to them that it was a serious crime on the part of parents to destroy their female offsprings and asked them not to kill their female infants within the 'territory' of Jaipur. Knowing that the root cause of female infanticide among Rajputs was the existence of the practice of giving heavy dowry at the time of marriage of the daughters, Jai Singh tried to regulate the amount of marriage expenses and ordered that it should not exceed 1/8th of the annual income of the chief. In the event of any Kachwaha being destitute and unable to pay the *daheja* (i.e., dowry) he was asked to come to the town of Jaipur and celebrate the marriage ceremony of his daughter there, where arrangements were made by the Raj to provide financial assistance to the needy.

Sawai Jai Singh was also aware of the menace of the Charans and Bhats and to save the Rajputs from their extortionous demands, he laid down that those who suffered from their heavy demands, at the time of the marriage of their daughters, should come to Jaipur to celebrate their marriages. He enjoined upon the Charans that they should not make any demands of tyag from anyone, on a marriage taking place at the capital. To make these rules more effective, he also asked the Vakeels of other States who were in the court of Jaipur, to write to their masters to enforce the same regulations, in their respective States. These rules of Sawai Jai Singh were followed up to the time of Maharaja Sawai Madho Singh,[2] after whose reign many Sardars, in order to have their names emblazoned by the Charans and Bhats, started spending large sums of money on the marriages, in their families.

Thus, for the first time in the recorded annals of the Rajputana, an attempt was made, by a native ruler, to regulate the marriage-expenditure of the Rajputs and to save the people from the exorbitant demands of the Charans and Bhats. It is also significant to note that Sawai Jai Singh of Jaipur was the first ruler who seriously pondered over the issue of female infanticide and tried to curb this practice. The practice of giving heavy amounts of dowry and the demands of Charans and Bhats on the occasions of marriages and the inter relationship of these two factors with the practice of female infanticide was understood and acknowledged by him, much before any other prince or ruler of the Rajputana. It is also remarkable that he took this initiative on his own, without any outside or external influence upon him. It was promulgated much before the advent of the British in the Rajputana and this contradicts the prevalent notion of historical writings which gives all the credit of social reforms to the British officers and depicts the native rulers as insensitive and insouciant towards the social cause. In the absence of any document, it is difficult to determine how far these regulations were able to produce the desired effects and also that whether they were able to induce people to refrain from the evil practice of female infanticide.

Moreover, the number of lives thereby saved is also a matter of conjecture, in the absence of records. But these efforts of Sawai Jai Singh, established beyond doubt, the prevalence of female infanticide among the various clans of the Kachwahas, as well as the willingness of the native rulers to take appropriate action against the prevalent social evils.

In the fourth decade of the 19th century when the English officers came to know about the Act of Sawai Jai Singh, they were very much excited. John Ludlow, the Political Agent at Jaipur, was pleased "to snatch from oblivion" some records of Jai Singh's legislative enactment prohibitory of female infanticide and of the sumptuary regulations which he instituted for reducing the expenditure among the Rajputs.[3] The Jaipur council of regency ascertained from a Bhat, Moolji by name, that Sawai Jai Singh's edict was promulgated in Samvat 1787 (1731 A.D.).[4] It was interesting for Ludlow "to trace to the earliest period, a law the institution of which was honourable to the Rajput period".

On the 12 April, 1844, the Jaipur council of regency submitted a memorandum to John Ludlow,[5] the Pol. Ag. at Jaipur, in which the council lamented the fact that "the practice of infanticide does not appear to have ceased, despite the efforts made in the past by many chiefs in every quarter. The council was of the opinion "that a crime of this magnitude cannot be brought home satisfactorily through any search that can be instituted or by any oral evidence, that can be obtained", yet it believed that "those who are gifted with penetration, could perceive that without striking at the root of the evil, there was little hope of its suppression".

The root of the evil, according to the Jaipur council of regency, lay in the fact that when marriages of the Rajputs and others took place, Charans, Bhats, Dholees, Meerasis and others of the like classes, whether native or foreigners, assembled in crowds from all quarters to demand the tyag, and the expenses incurred by the bride's father in the marriage entertainment and the tyag payments to the Charans, caused the greatest impoverishment to the involved parties, which forced them to opt for female infanticide. "While those entertainers", wrote the council of regency, "who cannot satisfy the claims of these persons, are abused by them from door to door, among the Rajput clans, from which dread and the consequent fear of suffering in character, the Rajputs have no other recourse left, but to destroy their female children at their birth."(sic)

This heavy expenditure, done at the times of marriages created pecuniary difficulties before the Rajputs, which ultimately put pressure upon the peasantry, who were made to suffer every method of extortion. The council therefore suggested Ludlow that for the effectual prevention of the evil and with a view to review the source of distress from families of respectability, the following course be adopted through the aid of the British government and their officers:

"When a marriage shall take place, within any principality, whether in a town or district, the Charans, Bhats, etc., of that village shall alone attend the occasion and the presence of foreigners of the classes in question shall be prohibited." It further suggested that "as regards the allowance claimable by the Charans, etc., of the country, the father of the bridegroom shall pay to them on arrival at the house of the bride, a tithe of the produce of his Jageer, Istimrar, Ijara, Bhoom, Zamindari or other source of wealth that he may posses and the father of the bride shall feed for one day all the Charans, etc., of his own country, who may attend the ceremony."(sic)

The Jaipur council of regency, discussed the course proposed with Colonel Sutherland,[6] A.G.G. and Major Thoresby, Offg. A.G.G., and desired that the project should be brought to bear effectually through the influence of the British government so that no one should henceforward kill his daughter and that the crime may cease to exist. The council asked for the interference of the British government "to confer their boon upon their subjects". It is remarkable that the idea of restricting the movements of Charans and Bhats originated with the authorities at Jaipur Durbar and Rawal Sivii Singh, Thakur Luchman Singh, Thakur Bhopal Singh and Thakur Jutun Singh Foujdar of Jaipur Durbar played a key role in framing the memorandum and originated the suggestion of obtaining concurrence of other States in the Rajputana, as they believed that without the union of three larger States of Udaipur, Marwar and Jaipur, the plan could not well be enforced.[7] It is also significant to note that the submission of this memorandum as well as its contents are of immense importance as it throws new light on the initiation of the reform process in the State of Jaipur. Moreover, it also indicates the difficulties that were being faced by the Jaipur State and its helplessness in controlling the demands and the movements of Charans and Bhats. Its asking for help as well as interference, from the paramount power, is reflective of its dependence on the foreign power. The proposals of the Jaipur council of regency provided the British officers a foundation upon which they could form their policy against female infanticide.

Major Ludlow, believed that the proposals of the council were important for diminishing or annulling the hideous crime of infanticide, and called them "both expedient and practicable".[8] He considered the position of the British at Jaipur as favourable for the adoption of the initiative for placing suitable restraints upon the rapacity of the Charans and Bhats. He called infanticide as an "unholy but a time-honoured custom" and believed that all the chiefs of Rajwara desired the change proposed, if the interposition of British authority would only furnish them with grounds for making it appear that they were acting under the injunctions, emanating from the paramount power. He also suggested the use of Mohammedan intelligentsia at the marriage ceremonies, who would keep a check on the extortions of Charans and Bhats.

Thus, on 30 April 1844, Ludlow sent a letter to the Court of Jodhpur,[9] regarding the course for preventing the destruction of female children among the Rajput clans and restricting the movements of Charans and Bhats. In the document it was set forth that within the territory where the marriage was to take place, whether in a town or in the district, the Charans and Bhats and others of that principality were alone to attend the occasion and those of other territories, were to be excluded from joining the ceremonies. On the receipt of this letter, the Jodhpur Durbar replied on 7 May 1844[10] that the course already decided upon in 1839, for fixing the demands of Charans, Bhats, Dholees and others would continue in force in Marwar, leaving the rates fixed by the Jaipur administration to have effect within their jurisdiction. The Durbar also proposed to pass an enactment, provided the course, which had been proposed, receive the assent of Udaipur and Jaipur to the effect that Charans, Bhats, Dholees, etc., do not quit their own territories, to obtain fees on marriages taking place in foreign principalities and that foreign Charans, Bhats, etc., do not enter Marwar with that motive. It also suggested that should any of these classes proceed to a foreign territory to demand the said payments, the Jagirdar of that country, where the ceremony is to be performed, shall send the offender to the nearest local authority, who will turn him out of the 'territory' and should the person so apprehended, commit any act of outrage in the presence of the Haqim or the master of the entertainment, or inflict wounds upon his person; he will be placed in confinement.

When Ludlow came to know about the willingness of the Jodhpur State to check the activities of Charans and Bhats residing in their own territory and their readiness to limit their movements within their own 'territory', he was very much pleased and he wrote to the Mewar Durbar, asking him to become a part of the team. Major Ludlow asked Lt. Col. Robinson, Political Agent in Mewar, to use his influence over the Maharana of Udaipur to make him accept the rules framed by the Jaipur council of regency.[11] The authorities at Jaipur also told Mewar Durbar that the State of Jodhpur had given their consent. Consequently, on the 24 May, 1844 the Udaipur Durbar issued a proclamation[12] and declared that "henceforward should anyone destroy his daughter, he will be hanged by the neck for the offence".

The proclamation also fixed 10 per cent of the yearly income as alms for the Charans and Bhats. If the Charans collected above the prescribed scale, the money thus taken would go to the State and as a measure of punishment, the estate of the Charans would be confiscated. The Maharana also forbade all the Charans and Bhats of other States from entering Mewar.

In the same year, Major Ludlow wrote similar letters to the Durbars of Harauti, Mahee-Kanta, Bikaner, Jaisalmer, Kishangarh, Alwar, Karauli, Dholpur and Bharatpur.[13] These States expressed their high approbation of the scheme proposed by the Jaipur council of regency, through their *Khureetas*.[14] This shows their willingness to put an end to the heinous practice of female infanticide and also that they themselves were afraid of waging a war against the exorbitant demands of Charans and Bhats, and it also suggests that the influence and the might of British power was accepted and acknowledged by them as decisive in the prevention of female infanticide. Thus Ludlow was right in his belief that "all the Chiefs of Rajwara desire the proposed change, if the interposition of British authority will only furnish them with grounds for making it appear that they are acting under injunctions emanating from the paramount power.[15]

Major Thoresby, the Offg. A.G.G., after receiving the letters of high approbation from the above States, addressed a Khureeta to each of the native princes in which he expressed his satisfaction at finding that they were disposed to place the conduct of the Charans and Bhats in their several jurisdictions, under wholesome restrictions and recommended the exercise of due attention to the means, by which the resolution can be reduced to practice, in lieu of remaining upon record unheeded.[16]

Encouraged by the results and the letters of high approbation, the Jaipur Council of Regency issued a *Mahzarnama* on the 20 February, 1847[17] prohibitory to female infanticide in its principality, in which rates to be received by the Charans, Bhats, Dholees and Meerasis (singers), on the occasion of marriages were fixed. Copies of the proclamation were transmitted through the Agency to all the States of the Rajputana and they were everywhere approved and acted upon and it was made clear that no one should be permitted to receive amounts in excess to the stipulated rates. The Council considered that formerly the expenditure on Charans, Bhats and others was excessive and stated that "suitable rules were enacted to prevent this; but rules have not been enacted to prevent persons possessed of insufficient means and who considered themselves suffering reproach, if they do not expend money proportionate to their ranks(sic)." It was declared therefore that "from the amount which may remain after paying the Charans and Bhats tyag, the eighth of the revenue, of the estate of the person whose nuptials are to be performed, shall be expended in the ceremonial and that nothing shall be paid by anyone in excess to this rate".

By this Mahzarnama, the Jaipur Council of Regency hoped that "female children will no longer be destroyed and that inter-marriages will take place between the children of houses of corresponding rank." It also hoped that from now onwards there will be no occasion for the sending of *dolas* or for alliances with houses of inferior rank, and that having determined the marriage expenses to be one-eighth of the estate, "no one will consider his dignity hurt by paying at a fixed rate and... feel the disbursement burdensome." Besides preparing the Mahzarnama all the Amils were addressed directing that, "no person shall be suffered to pay at rates exceeding the stated limit and that should anyone do so, shall be called upon to answer for so doing, being there-in regarded as an offender against the Raj." It was also arranged in the Mahzarnama that should any person transgress the rules laid down on the same, being proved against him, the party supplying the information shall receive a reward of Rs 300.

Lt. Col. Sutherland was satisfied by the passing of this law. "The sumptuary law, now passed by the Jaipur council of regency", observed Sutherland,[18] "for preventing the expenditure of more than an eighth of the year's land revenue of the father, on the marriage of his daughter, will go a long way to check the lavish expenditure on marriage... If the law should have the effect of producing marriages in families of corresponding rank; a great benefit would be conferred on the social condition of the Rajput people."

The strict measures mentioned above produced the desired effects and went a long way in limiting the demands of the Charans and Bhats. On 20 February 1847 the Jaipur Council of Regency, told the Political Agent that a period of two years, four months and a few days has passed, during which period they have not heard of the Charans, Bhats, Dholees, Meerasis, and others having come in the celebration of marriages among the Rajputs from foreign territories or of these classes having taken amounts exceeding the rates laid down for them or of their having made any violent demands in the hope of obtaining more.[19] However, on one occasion, the council stated, in 1844, when the *barat* of Bijai Singh, the brother of Rawal Shiv Singh, proceeded to the *thikana* of Masooda in the Ajmer district, to marry the daughter of the Thakur, Charans came from foreign territories to demand the amount of tyag, in excess to that which was authorized. On that occasion, a gross amount of rupees 7,700 was given to them. In consequence of this, the Political Agent at Jaipur, addressed the officer of that district and ordered him to adopt requisite steps. With this exception, the Jaipur council heard of no complaints of Charans' excesses or their demanding more than the stipulated amounts. On the contrary, when a chief from Marwar came to Nuraina, to celebrate his marriage, he refused to pay even the regulated dues to Charans. Thus, the Jaipur council received complaints from Charans, "of not obtaining their dues" and it expressed its satisfaction that the Charans have succumbed to the extent of not being able to obtain from some persons, the stipulated rates of payments.

It seems that some of the Charan and Bhat families were not prepared to comply with the royal orders and were bent upon challenging the authority of the Raj. Consequently, in 1863,[20] the Maharaja of Jaipur once again issued orders to restrict their movements from going to other States during the marriage season. Though it had a good effect temporarily, for the orders were issued just before the marriage season commenced and the Charans and Bhats had hardly any time to recover from their surprise before the season was out. The Charans later on adopted vigorous means to enforce their demands by having recourse to mutilation but that was only an exception to prove the rule. Thus by the end of 1870, the expenditure incurred in paying tyag dues, ceased to exist in Jaipur State and with that one of the root causes of female-infanticide was buried deep into the soil.[21]

While this was the state of affairs in Jaipur, similar efforts were being made by the native rulers and the British officers in Jodhpur. It is striking to note that Maharaja Bukht Singh,[22] who died in 1753, after a short reign of three years, also tried to put an end to the heinous practice of female infanticide, much before the English officers. Maharaja Bukht Singh passed an Act, which not only prohibited the crime of infanticide, but also limited the demands of Charans and Bhats on the occasion of marriage and where the father of the bride had not the means of defraying the amount so limited, he fixed a house-tax for the purpose, on the members of the same tribe in the town or village, to which the bride belonged. Where still there would be an insufficient amount, the Maharaja proposed to make good the deficiency from the State treasury.

It appears that the efforts of Maharaja Bukht Singh owing to his short reign, could not produce the desired effects and the terror created by the Charans and the Bhats haunted the minds of the people. Consequently in 1763 (Samvat 1821, *Chey Budi Astume*), Maharaja Bijay Singh[23] of Jodhpur also passed an Act, which prohibited female infanticide in Marwar. The Maharaja of Jodhpur, like Sawai Jai Singh of Jaipur and his predecessor, came to the conclusion that the extortionous demands of the Charans and the Bhats was one of the important causes of the prevalence of crime of infanticide (in Marwar). To curb this heinous practice, he adopted another course of action, for it was impossible to get the marriages solemnized at the capital due to lack of proper provisions in a sandy area.

As he was aware of the fact that the Charans and the Bhats assemble in a large number on the occasion of marriages and also that if their claims remained unsatisfied, they wrote satires against the father of the bride and created great disturbances and ugly scenes to have their tyag dues; Maharaja Bijai Singh tried to regulate the amount of tyag and laid down the fees of the Charans and the Bhats on the occasions of marriages to be paid by the bride's father in proportion to his income or rental in land.

According to the law of 1763, all the Rajput Pattiats were to pay Rs 25 to the Charans and Rs 15 to the Bhats (Rs 8 to Sasan Bhats and Rs 7 to the Bhuldea Jude Bhats) and Rs 5 to the Dhooms, as tyag on every 1000 rupees of rekh or rental of land. Thus, Rs 45 were to be paid as tyag on every 1000 rupees of rekh. The law stated that those whose rekh exceeded or fell short of this amount, were to pay proportionately more or less as the case would be. Similarly, it was laid down, that the Charans would receive Rs 25, the Bhats would receive Rs 9 (Rs 5 to Sasan Bhats, and Rs 4 to Bhuldea Jude Bhats) and Dhooms would receive Rs 5 on every 1000 rupees of rekh on the marriage in the family of the Sardar or Pattiat. Maharaja Bijay Singh also laid down that those Rajputs who paid more than the minimum amount out of vanity and those Bhats and Charans who demanded more than what was their due, were to be punished and those who were found to be guilty of female infanticide were to be banished from the State of Marwar. It was also specified therein that the amount was to be collected by the Akawat i.e., the Chief Charan, who would then distribute it among others. If any person tried to receive money, otherwise than through the Akawat (i.e., the Chief Charan), he was to be held guilty by the administration.

The Maharaja by his proclamation, instructed all the Pargana Hakims to be careful in their duties and warned them that whosoever would be found negligent would be punished by the Raj. In the same way, Maharaja Bijai Singh, instructed the Charans and the Bhats to enter into an agreement with him, which forbade them to demand more than the stipulated amount and also that in case of breach, the law would be free to take its own course. Consequently, Barhat Kerea, Sandoo, Adola, Asiyan, Kavia, Monduree, Melun, Sulux, Ratnoo, Sondaya, Bhutoo, Mheroo, Bogta, Maroo, Goonoo, etc., signed the deed on behalf of the Charan and the Bhat community of Marwar and Godwar. They also agreed that if any Charan violated this agreement, he would be excommunicated and promised that they would motivate the Charans and the Bhats of every village to sign this agreement.

Despite the efforts of these enlightened rulers, the problem of female infanticide could not come to an end in Marwar or Jodhpur and the demands of the Charans and the Bhats remained at the same level, that they were. Seeing this anomaly Lt. Col. Sutherland, A.G.G. in 1839, took upon himself "the correctness of what was then much wrong in the administration of Jodhpur and the mitigation of the evil which prevailed in that country."[24] Sutherland, while viewing the situation from his own angle, came to the conclusion that the Rajputs could be won over to the British side, by a policy of give and take. As he was very much impressed by the prevalent anecdotes about the Rajput character, therefore, he believed that this policy would suit the occasion and would create an atmosphere in favour of the abolition of female infanticide.

With this aim in mind, Sutherland along with Captain Ludlow met Maharaja Man Singh and his nobles in 1839, for the purpose of framing a code of rules for the prevention of this heinous practice in Marwar.[25] Sutherland told them that the English in conformity with the prejudices of the Rajputs, had bound themselves to abstain from the slaughter of kine, and from the killing of pea-fowl and pigeons and other beasts and birds which were sacred to them and that they therefore wanted the Rajputs to stop committing Sati and infanticide, since these practices were looked with horror by the English.[26]

However in the same or at a subsequent meeting, Maharaja Man Singh told Sutherland that a law had already been passed in 1763, by his illustrious predecessor Bukht Singh, which prohibited female infanticide in Marwar.[27] Sutherland, after knowing this, referred to the *Duftar* of that period with much anxiety and found to his great surprise the act, which had come into disuse by then. Thus he was very much pleased to find out this act in the archives of Jodhpur and this discovery motivated him to chalk out a system, which was later on termed as the Marwar System by Sutherland, which in reality was nothing but old wine in a new bottle.

Taking a cue from the Act of the late Maharaja, Sutherland drafted a code of rules in October 1839[28] with the help of Maharaja Man Singh and his nobles. In the conversation, the heads of the Charans and the Bhats were "called into the legislative tent" and there they entered into an agreement with the Maharaja and bound themselves to receive the sums specified in the code of rules.[29] Similarly, all the Chiefs, Bhumias and Rajput householders, through their representatives, bound themselves to pay the sums, as was fixed and mentioned in the code of rules.

Sutherland believed that the effect of being given to the law, infanticide will cease in Marwar. This code of rules was submitted to the Government of India on the 3 January, 1841. Thus, by the 45th Article of the Code of Rules, female infanticide was prohibited in Marwar and "the principal noble of the State down to the Bhumias and those possessing a single dwelling" were instructed to preserve their female children.[30] Similarly, the fees of the Charans and the Bhats on the occasion of marriage, was also fixed.[31] It was fixed that those Jagirdars who had an annual income of 1000 rupees of rekh, would pay Rs 25; those Bhumias (holder of land in lieu of service) who had an annual income of 1000 rupees of rekh, would pay Rs 10 and the ordinary Rajputs, who were not landed proprietors, were to pay Rs 5 to the Charans. Similarly, those Jagirdars who had an annual income of Rs 1000 were to give Rs 9 to Bhats, Pavadiyas and Baladiyas and the Bhumias were to give Rs 5, and the ordinary Rajput would give Rs 4 to these classes. Similarly, Dholee Ranas (singers) were to receive, at marriage ceremonies Rs 5 per 1000 rupees of rekh and it was also specified in it, that they were not entitled to claim a higher payment for their services.

In order to make this rule effective, Maharaja Man Singh ordered that "since these rules have been framed with the consent of all persons, therefore, if a Rajput pays more than the above noted amount or kill his daughter, he will be liable to punishment by the Raj" and also that "if a Charan, Bhat or drummer demands more, he will also be liable to punishment". Maharaja Man Singh also proposed to make up the deficiency, from the State treasury in case a village was too poor to meet the demands of Charans and the Bhats.

Sutherland circulated the copies of this code of rules to other States of the Rajputana and also to the British authorities in the neighbouring provinces of Malwa, Gujarat and Kutch.[32] "Since the legislation on the subject was enacted in Marwar" observed Sutherland, "and from the period of discovery of the act of Maharaja Bukht Singh, I have not doubted that infanticide would be much less prevailing in the Rajputana and that eventually it would cease to be one of those crimes which darkens and degrades the character of the Rajputs". But Sutherland believed that a provision for the limitation of the claims of the Charans and the Bhats was not the only remedy, which was needed to eradicate "a crime and a usage so widely spread and so inveterate as that of infanticide amongst the Rajputs (sic)".

The other causes, which were responsible for infanticide were that of securing a sufficient dowry for the daughters of Rajput families and secondly that of breaking through the usage, which prevented inter-marriages of families belonging to the same communities. For this Sutherland felt that "the first can hardly be legislated for, since it must belong to the head of each family to secure a suitable husband and to make a suitable provision for his daughter. The second is a matter, which must be left to future time and enlightenment."[33] He believed that it would be dangerous for the Britishers to advocate marriages in the same community, "as it was for the emperors of Delhi, in former days to seek the daughters of the houses of Udaipur, Jodhpur or Jaipur in marriage for themselves." But he also came to know that even this great innovation of marrying in the same community was attempted by Maharaja Jai Singh of Jaipur as he himself married into a Kachwahi family.

The Court of Directors, when informed of this measure, declared it to be of the utmost importance, as it opened a new view of the means by which female infanticide could be prevented.[34] Further, they were extremely anxious to know the effects of such a system and directed that Sutherland's arrangements be circulated amongst the Political Officers in India, and also to the Bombay government. The Court of Directors considered the Act very creditable to the ability of the British Officers as well as the good sense and right feeling of the Thakurs of Jodhpur.

In October 1843, some important aspects of these rules specially related to the Rajputs, were inscribed on marble slabs and they were fixed at the district headquarters of the State, and a breach of these rules was declared punishable by the Raj.[35] The promulgation of the proclamation relieved a number of chiefs who had previously suffered from the extortions of the Charans and the Bhats. The members of the Marwar council of regency and other Rajputs of respectability assured Ludlow, the Political Agent at Jodhpur, of the non-existence of female infanticide in Marwar and also that "no difficulty had anywhere been experienced in satisfying the claims of the Charans and the Bhats, since the establishment of the Agency."[36] There were, however, a few instances when the chiefs had voluntarily paid more to the Charans and the Bhats to do honour to the occasion, which was considered "a venial offence" by the Maharaja.[37] In 1840, the son of Thakur of Bhadrajun married a daughter of the house of Rakhee (both places were in Marwar) and in the marriage, Bhadrajun paid five times and Rakhee paid six times than the amount of tyag specified in the code of rules. Similarly, in 1841-42 the Thakur of Ghanerao married two of his five daughters to the chiefs of Shekhawati and Marwar and on that occasion, he gave more than three times the authorized amount to the Charans and the Bhats. These incidents attracted the displeasure of the Maharaja and of his Sardars. Nevertheless the Maharaja, Sardars and the administrators, Ludlow reported, pleaded for indulgence on behalf of the chiefs, who had exceeded the stipulated payments, urging Ludlow that they had been made voluntarily and that the evil would be corrected by degrees. Ludlow was himself convinced of the voluntary nature of the payments, considering the amount paid to them to be much less than what used to be given earlier. It has been stated that the payments formerly made to the Charans by the Rajputs of ranks, on a single marriage varied from 1/3rd to 3/4th of one years income. In 1841-42, the amount paid to the Charans and the Bhats of Marwar by the Thakurs of Ahwa, Bhadrajun, Rakhi and Ghanerao was as follows:[38]

Thakurs of	*Amount of Rekh*	*Produce 3/5th of Rekh*	*Amount paid to Charans, etc.*
Ahwa	40,400.00	24,240.00	1,000.00
Bhadrajun	31,950.00	19,170.00	4,000.00
Rakhee	25,100.00	15,060.00	4,000.00
Ghanerao	60,550.00	36,330.00	5,000.00

On an alliance having been negotiated in the Rajput families, gifts of houses or valuable property were presented by the lady's family. It invariably took place at the paternal estate of the bride elect and a voluntary expenditure was sometimes incurred by the parents of the bridegroom. The charges, which a chief of rank incurred at the marriage of a daughter, is stated at about one year's income of which under fortunate circumstances 2/3rds were allotted as nuptial presents and the entertainment, and 1/3rd on the Charans and the Bhats, as their marriage presents. 2/3rds were fixed on the marriage ceremonies, but the extent of the tyag depended upon the number of marriages, which were taking place in the country, at the same time upon the reputed wealth of the entertainer and of course upon the *Kamdars,* who bargained with the leading persons of the Charans. "It is affirmed", wrote Ludlow, "that upon occasions of an unexpected confluence of this class, their exactions have sometimes amounted to 3/4th of the year's income and thus the estate became involved in debt and difficulty, which for a season threw insurmountable obstacles in the way of future marriages in the same family."[39]

In 1842, Rao Raja Ridmal, the Vakeel of Jodhpur, told Ludlow about the efficacy of the efforts and also that he has not of late heard of any case of female infanticide.[40] "The Thakurs of Pokhran and Khejoorla and the family of Zalim Singh, of which the Kuchamun Thakur is the representative have not for ages destroyed their infant daughters – but the collateral branches of the last named line, have not practiced the same forbearance" – Rao Raja Ridmal told Ludlow.

He also wrote that "two Thakurs Devi Singh and Doorjun Lal, following the example of the Kuchamun family, have abstained from the destruction of their female infants for the past five years. According to Rao Raja, in Samvat 1876 (1819 A.D.), the widow of Sultan Singh of Neemuch, while mounting the pile, pronounced a curse upon her descendants who would destroy their infant daughters and from that day, prohibition has been respected in that family. Ridmal believed that female infanticide was practiced in the house of Asoph and also by some of the Bhatees and Charans of distinction. But the humbler members of these clans "uniformly suffer the existence of their female children in consequence of receiving money payments from the families into which they marry their daughters". Bukhtawar Singh, the Thakur of Bhadrajun never makes away with his offsprings and even abstains from destroying animal life and asks for the same observance from his retainers and others, subject to his authority, observed Ridmal.

He believed that except Rajputs, the Brahmans, Mahajans and all other classes, never destroyed their infant daughters and the Rajputs committed it because of the fear of character-assassination from the Charans. The Brahmans and the Mahajans, according to him, never dreamt of destruction of their daughters, nor considered their existence in the light of misfortune.

"Although it is a point which cannot be declared with certainty", observed Ridmal, "it is believed that a number averaging between 300 and 400 female infants may have been destroyed annually in Marwar, prior to the rule prohibitory to killing them being enacted in Marwar", and also that, "since that period, I have not been able to ascertain that a single child has been made away with", though at the same time he cautioned himself by saying that this crime is of such a nature, that no one would acknowledge its perpetration.

On 7 April, 1846, Capt. Greathead, (Political Agent in Jodhpur during 1845-48) reported certain cases of infringement of rules set by the Durbar of Jodhpur.[41] According to his report, the Thakur of Raipur, on the occasion of marriage of his daughter with a member of the House of Jullya, Jaipur, squandered a large sum on the Charans and the Bhats, who in turn wrote odes in his praise to be chanted around the various places. One of these compositions, fell into the hands of Capt. Greathead, and it particularly commended the Thakur for uprooting the regulations imposed by the British. The main body of the Thakurs complained of this refraction and asserted that if it passed unpunished, they would not be able to resist the importunities of those mendicants and the old practice would once again dominate Marwar. The Maharaja of Jodhpur, consequently attached two villages belonging to the Thakur to be released only on the payment of an adequate fine. Sutherland viewed it with satisfaction and considered it an "act of well timed severity".[42] The law was also twice infringed in the district of Ajmer and Sutherland instructed Major Dixon, on that subject. In the same year, the Maharaja of Bharatpur, represented that although his country was free from the intrusion of Charans and Bhats from the different States of Rajputana, it was not so from those living in the British territories. Understanding the significance of this grievance, Sutherland instructed the Lieutenant Governor of Ajmer, to take necessary action against it.[43]

On Asadh Sudi 1, V.S. 1903 (i.e., July 12, 1847), Maharaja Tukht Singh of Jodhpur,[44] on the advice of the Political Agent, issued a proclamation, forbidding the Charans and the Bhats to practice human sacrifices and self-immolation for extorting tyag dues on peril of suffering imprisonment. He also declared that if any Chief or Rajput paid more than the stipulated amount, he would be held responsible for it. Major Thoresby expressed a belief that the salutary measure of Marwar would be followed by other States too, where such practices were adopted by the Charans.[45] The Maharaja took the proclamation seriously and when the Charans resorted to undo it, he imprisoned some of them for seven years and banished others from Marwar.[46]

In Mewar, Maharana Jawan Singh, in 1831, issued a proclamation prohibiting female infanticide among the Puryar (or Padihar) Meenas of Jahazpur (Bhilwara).[47] It is surprising to note that the Maharana restricted his prohibitory order to the Meenas of

Jahazpur alone and chose to keep quiet over the issue of female infanticide by other sections. The Puryar Meenas were a free and turbulent race and it is said that at times they indulged in robbery and other crimes.[48] The women of Puryar Meenas freely admitted that they did not allow any daughters to live. The Maharana of Udaipur, forbade this practice on peril of punishment but provided a favourable consideration for those, who would preserve their daughters.[49]

The Raj-Rana of Bundi, following the example of Maharana of Udaipur, issued a proclamation as early as Chaitra Sudi 13, 1889 V.S. (1832 A.D.) directing the Meenas to refrain from destroying their daughters and warned them against it.[50] The promulgation assured of some consideration on the part of the Durbar, if they preserved their daughters. It enjoined on the Patels of every village to fix up a stone in their respective villages to that effect. The Raj-Rana, at the suggestion of Wilkinson, the Political Agent at Kota, offered to his Vakeel some presents consisting of silver anklets, bracelets and clothes of the value of Rs 15 to Rs 20 each to be distributed to all who had preserved their daughters.[51] Though the scheme cost the state exchequer to the tune of Rs 300 only, yet it served to focus public attention on the crime.

A more effective step was taken when Maharao Raja Ram Singh[52] on Magh Sudi 3, 1893 V.S. (1836 A.D.), got an agreement executed by the feudal chiefs and Sardars to the effect of preserving their daughters. Thirty-nine Sardars, whose seats were fixed on the left and right side of the Maharao Raja signed this agreement. If the offence was established against anyone, they agreed, that he would be banished from the country or fined to any extent that might be deemed proper. He would also be excommunicated. The Maharao Raja out of the consideration of the rank of the Sardars provided some assistance in negotiating the marriage of their daughters.[53] This agreement was brought into operation strictly and when in the following year the offence of the Thakur of Kuchowala was proved, his entire family was ignominiously expelled from the State of Bundi. Though attempts were made for the remittance of the sentence passed, but Maharao Raja most judiciously remained firm and got his orders executed. This had the desired effect as no instance of practice was reported in the State of Bundi amongst the Solankis after this incident.[54]

Similarly, the ruler of Kota issued strict orders against infanticide among Rajput and Meenas and agreeably with the suggestions made by the Political Agent, the rulers of Bundi and Kota declared the assistance to be provided by the Raj in effecting the marriage of their daughters. But at the same time they were sounded that disregard of the rules would be treated strictly[55] and would receive a fit recompense for the crime. The Maharao of Kota fixed a scale for the distribution of tyag according to the practice prevailing in the other States of the Rajputana. According to it,[56] Jagirdars with a revenue assessment of Rs 1000 were to distribute tyag as follows: Rs 40 each to the Charans and the Raos, Rs 14 to the Dholi; Rs 6 to the Nagarchi, similarly, the Rajputs were to distribute Rs 15 each to the Charans and the Raos and Rs 4 each to the Dholi and the Nagarchi. Other free holder Rajputs were to distribute Rs 5 each to the Charans and the Raos and Rs 2 and Re 1 respectively to the Dholi and the Nagarchi. The Kota Durbar fixed capital punishment for the crime and forbade the Charans of Kota to collect tyag from territories other than their own.

When Lord William Bentinck came to know about the proclamation of Maharana of Udaipur and the co-operative attitude of the rulers of Kota and Bundi, he wrote congratulatory letters to them for showing their willingness to suppress the practice.[57] Bentinck appreciated the conduct and noble feelings of Maharana of Udaipur as also his humanitarian spirit and urged him to extend the proclamation to all classes of people, living within his territory.[58]

In 1836, Wilkinson, informed the Government of the enormity of the crime practiced in Malwa and in some parts of the Rajputana. He was informed by a Rajput Chief, whose name he has not disclosed, that nearly 20,000 infants were annually put to death in these States.[59] He expressed this opinion in a letter written to John Bax, the Resident at Indore but John Bax considered this as un-reliable and un-authentic, as this was based on conjectures and surmises and not on any data.[60] Bax was of the opinion that Rajput chiefs, because of their excessive use of opium and other intoxicants and debauchery had very few children. Moreover, he urged, it was a practice in many families to give away girls to others to be brought up in less noble families. Thus he believed that it was not fair to suspect that every girl whose birth was concealed was put to death.

Wilkinson after his enquiries came to the conclusion that the practice prevailed far more extensively than was previously supposed. He also came to know that the practice had nothing to do with any religion, as the people themselves told that it was a crime against god and nature and said that they were very much afraid of the sin. However, in order to absolve themselves of the sin, they performed penitential rituals like *Seedha-Surriyam* (i.e., giving of a single meal of flour to the family priest).[61]

Lancelot Wilkinson, in order to put a check on the practice of infanticide suggested creating a public opinion against it, with the help of education.[62] It is remarkable that the need of education and its role as a tool of social development and social change was understood and emphasized by Wilkinson as early as the fourth decade of 19th century. He believed that the prevalent prejudices against the girl child, which ultimately forced some of the parents to opt for female-infanticide, could be done away only with the spread of education. "Knowing the inveteracy of habit", he observed, "which had been confirmed by generations of practice, renunciations and prohibitions by the *Rajas* and the chiefs would have little effect." But he admitted that as a preliminary step, they would be useful and even essential for the simple reason that "a sense of consistency and fear of exposure to superior authority" would always operate to a certain degree in securing the observance and enforcement of such public statements. Wilkinson was also in favour of sumptuary regulations, such as reduction of marriage expenses, which aimed at the removal of the causes of infanticide. He also recommended that rewards should be given to those chiefs who aided the government in suppressing the crime.

In 1843, the Maharaja of Jaisalmer, on the insistence of Captain Ludlow, issued a notification dated Shrawan Sudi 5, 1990 V.S.,[63] forbidding the Charans to accept the tyag dues. To make it more effective, it was declared by the beat of drum in the far-off lands and the Charans and Thakurs present at the court were informed accordingly in un-ambiguous terms. Purohit Sardar Mal informed Ludlow that the orders against infanticide had been already promulgated during the time of *Bara-Maharaj*.[64] But it appears that his persuasive measure did not bear fruits and the very next year specific instructions regarding the acceptance of tyag dues were circulated. It was laid down that the Charans would not make a mess at the time of marriage and would accept 10 per cent of the rekh as their largess. Charans would be subjected to heavy punishment in case of break of rules and their villages granted by the Raj would be confiscated as a last resort. They were forbidden to move out of their State to collect tyag dues at the peril of imprisonment.[65] An attempt was again made in V.S. 1910 (1853 A.D.)[66] to regulate the distribution of largess and the Charans were asked to accept whatever the party offered them but in no case more than 10 per cent of the total expenses incurred on the marriage. In the previous promulgation it was taken as 10 per cent of the rekh while according to this it was 10 per cent of the total actual expenses incurred on marriage. It was again announced that the offenders would be liable to punishment.

Similarly in Bikaner, Maharaja Ratna-Singh,[67] during his religious pilgrimage to Gaya in 1837, asked his nobles to take an oath in Gaya, that they would not, in future kill their daughters. Perhaps he thought that the oath taken at a religious and sacred place, would induce his Sardars to refrain from the evil practice of female infanticide and that nobody would break the oath on account of the fear of religion. In 1844, the Maharaja of Bikaner received a Khureeta from the Political Agent, Jaipur,[68] requesting him to take appropriate action against the practice of female infanticide in Bikaner. The Maharaja accordingly framed certain rules.[69] According to them, all of the nobles and other Rajputs would spend only that much amount in the marriage of their daughters, which their circumstances allowed them. Those Sardars who had no land of their own, would spend Rs 100 only, in the marriage of their daughter and out of these 100 rupees, Rs 10 was to be given to the Charans, the Bhats, etc., as tyag.

In November-December 1843,[70] Lt. Col. Robinson, Political Agent in Mewar, communicated with the chiefs of Udaipur, Pratapgarh, Banswara and Dungarpur and apprized them of the "extreme abhorrence with which the British Government regarded the crime of infanticide" and the desire of the British government to put a stop to it and the measures which were in contemplation for that purpose and invited their aid and cooperation for giving effect to the same. Robinson even proposed to organize a panchayat at Samlaji (Abu), to discuss the evils of infanticide. He wanted the panchayat to frame a set of rules for themselves "for fixing among themselves the amount of dowry to be given and taken in their inter-marriages".

In reply to this letter, Maharana Saroop Singh of Udaipur, on 27 December 1843 (*Poosood* 6th)[71] told Robinson that the barbarous practice of female infanticide had been strictly prohibited in Mewar, and as such expressed the futility of deputing a respectable chief from Udaipur to join the proposed panchayat at Samlaji. He also assured the Political Agent that on his insistence, he would once again issue strict injunctions throughout his dominion, for the prevention of the practice of female-infanticide. In April 1844, Major Ludlow, asked Lt. Col. Robinson Political Agent at Mewar, to use his influence over the Maharana to make him accept the rules framed by the Jaipur Council of Regency.

Consequently in 1844, the Mewar Durbar again received a Khureeta from Lt. Col. Robinson,[72] in which it was stated that the Jaipur Council of Regency and the Political Agent at Jaipur had proposed that in whatever country a Rajput marriage shall take place, the Charans, the Bhats and the Dholis of that country shall alone attend the ceremony and that no foreigners (i.e., the Charans, the Bhats of other States) shall be admitted and that the bridegroom who comes to ally himself in marriage shall pay 10 per cent on his income and nothing short of or in excess to that amount and also that should the Charans object to this course, intelligence would be given to the nearest crown pargana, where the recesant would be placed in confinement. It was also told to the Mewar Durbar that the concurrence by the Jodhpur Durbar had already been received. The Mewar Durbar, consequently, gave approval to the same and issued a proclamation on Juet Sudi 7, Samvat 1900, i.e., 24 May, 1844[73] by which 10 per cent of the yearly income was fixed as alms for the Bhats and the Charans to be paid by the bridegroom and laid down that if any Charan collected above the prescribed scale, the money thus taken would go to the State and as a measure of punishment, the estate of the Charan would be confiscated. The Maharana also forbade all the Charans and Bhats of other States from entering Mewar. It also ordered that "henceforward, should anyone destroy his daughter will be hanged by the neck for the offence.[74]

A notification to this effect was again issued in V.S. 1907 (1851 A.D.).[75] The very fact that the order was issued twice, proves that the earlier orders might have remained ineffective. The Maharana again issued a proclamation vide his orders dated Asadh Sudi 3, 1916 V.S.[76] The Officiating Political Agent of Mewar expressed his belief that if carried out earnestly, the proclamation would be fruitful in eradicating infanticide and solicited the cooperation of the neighbouring States to support this desirable measure of the Maharana.[77] It is significant to note that by this order, Maharana got a deed executed by the Bhats and the Charans from outside the State not to collect tyag dues from Mewar. Consequently, Gulab Singh, Ram Lal, Barhat Ram Ratan, Begat Ram, Rao Bukhtawar Singh executed the deed on Shrawan Sudi 2, 1917 V.S.[78] A reminder to this was again effected in 1863 A.D.

It is striking to note that the number of Charans and Bhats in Marwar, Mewar and Jaipur were much more than in other native States of the Rajputana and consequently the problem of infanticide was graver in these States. The issuance of prohibitory orders in quick succession in these States not only reflects upon the persistent existence of the problem but also affirms the desire of the rulers to preserve female infants. These measures of the Mewar Durbar started producing the desired effects soon and the Meenas, in their reply to a letter by Major General Lawrence, handed over a written undertaking from each village promising that every female child would be preserved in future and that in the event of infanticide, it would be reported to the authorities and the guilty would render himself liable to any punishment that may be considered expedient.[79]

The persuasive measures of the authorities, created an effect on the Bhats and the Charans towards their debt to society and consequently they resolved to regulate the scale of payments on occasion of marriage vide letter dated 11 March, 1879.[80] They laid down that on the marriage of an eldest son, 1/10th of the annual income would be paid as tyag dues, while on that of a younger son, it was limited to 1 per cent only. If the younger son happened to receive a separate maintenance, he would be treated at par with the eldest son. It was also laid down that in future, the share of the Charan was to be remitted to Udaipur Durbar which was to be devoted to the education of their sons. In pursuance of this resolution, a school was established at Udaipur in 1880-81, where free boarding, lodging and clothing, apart from other necessities, were provided to the sons of the Charans.[81]

The lead given by Mewar in educating the sons of the Charans out of their share money was adopted by Bundi too. Banswara and Jhalawar States vide their notification dated Oct. 1879 and Feb. 1880 respectively adopted the same rules regulating the dues of the Charans and forbidding them to go outside the State for collecting tyag. Pratapgarh followed suit.

When this was the state of affairs in eastern, western and northern native States of the Rajputana the situation was somewhat different in some of the southern States. The States of Banswara,

Dungarpur and Pratapgarh repudiated the very existence of female infanticide in their respective states and as a proof of their contentions they cited numerous examples of the marriages of their as well as their noble's daughters marriages. As has been discussed above, in 1843, Lt. Col. Robinson, Pol. Ag. in Mewar, addressed a Khureeta to the rulers of Banswara, Pratapgarh, Dungarpur and Udaipur regarding female infanticide and its abolition in their respective States, and invited them for a panchayat to be held at Samlaji (Abu).

In response to this Khureeta, Maharawal Bahadur Singh of Banswara[82] told Robinson about the non-existence of female infanticide in his State and also that "it was considered a great sin" and that the Rajput chiefs of his State have never been known to be guilty of this crime. In support of his contention, he gave the examples of the previous rulers and also of his nobles, who had grown-up daughters. He also told Robinson, about the bridegroom as well as the name of principality or State, in which the daughters of the nobles were married. "Maharawal Ommeyd Singh (Ummed Singh) had two daughters and they were married to the chiefs of Eder. The late Maharawal Bhawani Singh has left a daughter, who is not yet married. My adopted son has an unmarried sister. The Thakur of Moula gave his daughter in marriage to Rawal Bhawani Singh, the two daughters of Rao of Kushalgarh were married in the Deogarh family" (sic) – the Maharawal told Robinson.

Since this practice was not prevalent in Banswara, therefore, Maharawal Bahadur Singh told Robinson, that it was useless to depute any person from the State to attend the proposed panchayat at Samlaji (Abu). It is striking to note that the Maharawal did not consider it necessary to issue a note to re-affirm the prohibition of the practice, as per the wishes of the Political Agent. Had it been so, records would have been there in the archives of Banswara or with the British officers.

Similarly, Maharawal Samut Singh of Pratapgarh[83] also denied the existence of female infanticide in his State. In a letter written to Lt. Col. Robinson, on 29 December 1843, he told that female infanticide was not known amongst the Rajput chiefs, high or low, of his principality and also that it was looked upon with "abhorrence and disgust and whosoever is guilty of this crime, brings disgrace upon his family according to our Shastras". He also told Robinson that infanticide was strictly prohibited by him and as a proof of this contention, he further told that his daughters were married to the chiefs of Eder, Bikaner, Raghavgarh, Lunwara and Jhabua. To refute the existence of this crime in the houses of his nobles, he gave examples of the marriages of their daughters. "The Thakur of Dhumatur of Pratapgarh", he wrote, "married his daughter to the chief of Ahmednagar, the daughter of the Thakur of Roypur (or Raipur) was married to the Sulana chief and that of the chief of Uchlada to the Raja of Seetamhow and the Thakur of Mohangarh gave his daughter in marriage to the chief of Ghurhee in Banswara". These examples were ample proof of the non-prevalence of female infanticide in the State of Pratapgarh – he claimed.

In the same way, Kunwar Dulpat Singh, Regent of Dungarpur[84] told Robinson that infanticide was against the holy Shastras i.e., scriptures of Hindu religion and as such was looked upon as a heinous crime by the Rajput chiefs of his State. He also stated that strict rules existed for the prevention of female infanticide throughout his "territory", but even then, he assured Robinson, that he would give wide publicity to the wishes of the government on the subject in question. He even proposed to depute Solanki Sardar Singh on his part at the proposed panchayat at Samlaji (Abu). On the insistence of British government, Maharawal Udai Singh of Dungarpur issued a proclamation on V.S. 1925, Magh Soodi 4 (i.e., on 17 January, 1869) and forbade the practice of infanticide in his State, and declared it a crime. Thus, the rulers of Udaipur, Banswara and Pratapgarh denied the existence of female infanticide in their respective States and expressed their unwillingness to send their representatives to the proposed panchayat.

The examples above cited clearly establish the fact, that the practice of female infanticide had been abolished in many of the native States of the Rajputana, by the native rulers themselves, even before the British officers started thinking in this regard. Perhaps the initiative of the native rulers in issuance of legislation against infanticide motivated the British officers in the Rajputana, to work against it zealously, as they got a levelled field to play upon.

In Jhalawar, where the practice of infanticide was prevalent among the Rajputs and the Meenas, Raj-Rana Madho Singh in 1834[85] (when Jhalawar was a part of the Kota State), welcomed the proposal of the British government to abolish the cruel practice and issued an order in the same year to that effect. Later, this order was followed by Raj-Rana Madan Singh,[86] the successor of Madho Singh. Even after their sincere efforts to crush this social evil, it could not be eradicated completely. Therefore, when Jhalawar was created in 1838, this cruel practice prevailed there.

To eradicate this practice, Maharaj-Rana Madan Singh issued a proclamation in 1844 declaring it illegal in the territory of Jhalawar. By this declaration, Maharaj-Rana directed the Meenas to refrain from destroying their daughters and warned them against it. This proclamation assured of some consideration on the part of the Durbar if they preserved their daughters. Maharaj-Rana also instructed the Patels of every village to fix up a stone in their respective villages. Lord William Bentinck, the Governor General, appreciated the step of the Durbar in issuing the prohibitory order, which was ample proof of his genuine philanthropy.[87] But as the problem of infanticide was closely linked with the demand of the tyag, by the Charans at the time of marriages, so the evil could not be rooted out as long as this demand stood intact. Hence an action against infanticide involved an operation against the Charans.[88]

In 1880,[89] the Jhalawar Durbar issued a notification to solve the problems of Charans. This laid down that at the marriage of the eldest son, 1/10th of the annual income would be paid as tyag dues, while on that of the younger son, it was limited to 1 per cent only. If however, the younger son happened to receive a separate maintenance, he would be treated at par with the eldest one. Out of 1/10th or 10 per cent charged as tyag dues, 5 per cent were to be given to the Charans, 3 per cent to the Bhats and 2 per cent to others entitled for tyag. The Durbar vide his notification dated February 1880,[90] forbade the Charans to go outside the State for collecting tyag dues.

The aforesaid discussion reveals that the efforts of the native rulers as well as of the British officers produced the desired change and the incidents of female infanticide started declining and a feeling of contempt for it emerged in the human-hearts. Thus, according to the annual Agency reports of Mewar, Jaipur, Marwar, Harauti, Tonk, Eastern States, Alwar, Dholpur, Kota, Jhalawar, Sirohi, Sujangarh[91] and the annual reports of the British administered areas of Ajmer and Merwara[92] for the years 1873-1880 not a single case of female infanticide was reported in the above States. Similarly, in 1891-92, Colonel S.B. Miles, Resident at Mewar, reported the complete absence of infanticide in Mewar in his Administrative Report to the First Asstt. A.G.G.[93] Like wise, Lt. L. Impey, Asstt. Political Agent in Banswara, reported the complete absence of infanticide in Banswara and Pratapgarh in 1892.[94] Col. H.P. Peacock, Offg. Resident at Jaipur, denied the existence of female infanticide in Jaipur and Kishangarh during 1891-92.[95] The same was the case with Eastern Rajputana States, where Lt. Col. N.C. Martelli, Political Agent in the Eastern States, reported the complete absence of infanticide in Karauli.[96] Captain T.C. Pears, Offg. Political Agent in Harauti & Tonk,[97] and C.S. Bayley, Esq., Political Agent in Bikaner,[98] also denied any incidence of infanticide in their respective areas, in their reports to the First Asstt. A.G.G. However, only one case of infanticide was reported in Kota by Major W.H.C. Wyllie, the Political Agent, in the year 1891-92.[99] Similarly, three cases of infanticide were reported in Pratapgarh and one case from Karauli and one from Kishangarh were reported in the year 1883-84.[100]

These examples clearly reveal that a perceptible change had started taking place in the mind set of the people and the practice of female infanticide was looked down upon by them. It is significant to note that when the Desh Hitaishini Sabha was formed by Maharana Sajjan Singh of Mewar on 2 July 1877 and when the Walterkrit Rajputra Hitkarini Sabha was formed by Col. Walter; the problem of female infanticide had come to a virtual end in the Rajputana, as the administrative records of the various native States reveal. Since it was believed that the root cause of female infanticide was the custom of spending large amounts on marriages and the distribution of tyag to the Charans and the Bhats, therefore the DHS and the WKRHS tried to regulate them, and ultimately became successful in reducing them.

Thus from the above account, it becomes quite clear that the practice of female infanticide was prevalent in many sections of the then society of the Rajputana and also that some of the enlightened rulers tried to put an end to this nefarious practice, much before the arrival of British East India Company in the Rajputana. In the absence of any written records, it is difficult to ascertain how far their proclamations were successful in producing the desired effects and in checking this heinous crime. It is also significant to note that while some of the native rulers (e.g., Sawai Jai Singh of Jaipur, Maharaja Bukht Singh and Vijay Singh of Jodhpur, Ratna Singh of Bikaner) instructed the principal Sardars as well as other nobles of their clan and sub-clans, not to kill their female infants; other rulers (e.g., Maharana Jawan Singh of Udaipur and the Raj-Rana of Bundi) issued proclamations directing only one community (Meenas) to refrain from such crimes and deliberately kept quiet over this crime, committed by other sections of the society (e.g., the Rajputs). This can be attributed either to the absence of this crime among other sections (which is difficult to believe) or to the fact that they were hesitant or unwilling to take action against their own kith and kins. It may also be the reason that they were afraid of taking any action against the Charans and the Bhats, for the fear of character assassination always loomed large on their faces. Any action on the part of the ruler, to control and check the practice of female infanticide, would ultimately bring them into a conflict with the Charans and the Bhats and would bring a disgrace to the family. Perhaps this belief forced them to keep mum on this subject. While that was not the case with the British Officers as they were not afraid of any caste or clan and being the paramount power could use force to pressurize the native rulers. Any violation of rules by any caste or clan was dealt by them with complete seriousness and they were not hesitant to punish the offender, be it a ruler or a common man. The fear of punishment created a terror in the hearts of the people and when they saw the nobles being expelled and the Charans and the Bhats imprisoned, they thought it wise to refrain from such practice.

II
Prevention of Child and Ill-Matched Marriages

The movement against child marriage first started in the British Indian province of Bengal as early as 1850. In Bengal, the voice against this evil was raised by the Brahmo Samajis, who took great pains in arousing the conscience of the Bengali educated class. Because of the works of Ishwar Chandra Vidyasagar, Keshab Chandra Sen, B.M. Malabari, Dayaram Gidumal, M.G. Ranade, and many other social workers, a new consciousness was seen in the Indian social structure. Impressed by the humanitarian aspect of social reform movement, the British government helped the reformers in wiping out the evils, by introducing many social legislations in British Indian provinces. But the Indian States were left alone to deal with this problem, with their own resources. Many enlightened individuals, caste-organizations, social reformers endeavoured to prevent the nefarious practice of child and unmatched marriages and through various written and verbal representations, requested the governments of the native States to make some suitable law for the prevention of child marriage in their respective States, and also highlighted upon the issue of providing education to women for their emancipation.

The first step in this direction was taken by the State of Mysore[101] in British India, which passed a Regulation on 5 October, 1894, to prevent infant marriages as well as unmatched or unequal marriages in its territories. Regulation No. X of 1894, or "The Mysore Infant Marriages Prevention Regulation", as it was called, extended to the whole of the territories of Mysore and was made applicable only to marriages among the Hindus. It was to come into operation at the expiry of six months from the date of its publication in the official gazette. According to the Regulation, a girl below eight years of age was an infant and any person who caused the marriage of an infant girl, or who knowingly aided and abetted such a marriage, and any man who had completed eighteen years of age married an infant girl, was to be punished with simple imprisonment for a term which might extend to six months, or with fine or with both. To check the prevalent practice of unequal marriages, it laid down that "any man who having completed fifty years of age marries a girl, who has not completed fourteen years of age, shall be punished with imprisonment of either description for a term which may extend to two years, or with fine or with both." To make this rule more effective, Regulation No. X of 1894 declared that any person who caused the marriage of a girl, who had not completed fourteen years of age, with a man who had completed fifty years of age, and any person who knowingly aided and abetted such a marriage was to be punished with simple imprisonment for a term which might extend to six months or with fine, or with both. No offence, punishable under this Regulation, was to be tried by any Court inferior to that of a Magistrate of the District. Any marriage, which had actually taken place, was not to be deemed to be invalid on the ground of the penalties provided by this Regulation.

Thus, the State of Mysore paved the way for future reforms and created an example before the public in general and native States in particular and motivated them to frame similar rules for their respective States. Though it had some shortcomings, but its importance lies in the fact that for the first time in the history of modern India an attempt was made by a native State to fix the minimum marriageable age for girls and to restrict unequal or ill-matched or ill-assorted marriages. It is significant to note here that emperor Akbar too fixed the minimum marriageable age for girls as 14 years, but it is difficult to ascertain, in the absence of any relevant records, that how far it was successful in producing the desired effects. Its importance also lies in the fact that it was passed, inspite of the huge protests against it, by the orthodox section of the society.

Its impact was soon felt and witnessed by other native States and in 1904 the State of Baroda[102] passed a similar Act which was called Baroda Early Marriage Prevention Act of 1904. It went a step further by laying down twelve (12) as the minimum age of a girl at the time of marriage. In order to respect public sentiment on the subject and to avoid unnecessary inconvenience and embarrassment to the public, this Act provided that if the guardians of a minor girl (i.e., one who had not completed her twelfth year) whose age was above nine, desired to get her married, they might do so with the permission of a tribunal consisting of the local sub-judge and three assessors of the petitioner's case. The parents had to satisfy the tribunal that if the marriage of the minor girl was not allowed, it would possibly not take place at all or not within one year of the bride attaining maturity, or that the parents and guardians of the girl were not likely, owing to old age or infirmity, to survive until she came of age and that she had no other guardian, or that inevitable difficulties of a similar nature were likely to occur. The tribunal if satisfied could grant permission for the celebration of marriage before the girl was twelve. In order that this concession might not be abused it was provided that if the sub-judge disagreed with the assessors the case should be referred to the district judge and his decision was to be final. Similarly, the State of Indore[103] legally regulated the age at marriage in 1918 by prescribing fourteen years and twelve years as minimum marriageable age for a boy and a girl respectively.

The impact of these regulations was witnessed in other parts of the country, as thousands of enlightened people, requested their rulers to pass similar Acts. The works of various social and caste organizations as well as national organizations, had already created a dent in the minds of the people and voices against many nefarious social practices were being raised by them, from different platforms.

Consequently, the States of the Rajputana could not keep themselves aloof from the mainstream and the demand for social reforms, spread like the fire of the forest. As discussed earlier, many caste organizations and social organizations (like the Arya Samaj, DHS, WKRHS), were working in the Rajputana, for social and moral upliftment of the people and especially for the emancipation of women, and because of their sincere efforts, a new consciousness was seen in the social and political milieu of the Rajputana. It is surprising to note that in the Rajputana, the State of Bharatpur took the lead in the prevention of child marriages and also to encourage widow remarriages, despite the fact that it was considered as orthodox, conservative and traditional by the people.

The State of Bharatpur can be considered as the most progressive State of the erstwhile Rajputana, as it was the first native State, which placed upon the statute book a law which dwelt at length on the issue of child marriage as well as on the remarriage of widows and that too the Child Marriage Restraint Act of 1929, popularly known as the Sarda Act, which was applicable to the British Indian provinces.

The Bharatpur Social Reforms Act of 1926,[104] came into effect from 1 January, 1927 and extended to the whole of Bharatpur State. To understand the importance as well as the role played by this Act in motivating others, it would be relevant here to make a detailed study of the Act.

The Bharatpur Social Reforms Act of 1926

Preamble

Whereas it is known, that by the law as administered in civil courts established in the Bharatpur State, widows especially Hindus, with certain exceptions are held to be, by reason of their having once married, incapable of contracting a second valid marriage and the offspring of such widows, by any second marriage, are held to be illegitimate and incapable of inheriting property... and whereas it is expedient in the interest of health and good morals of the people that the child marriages should be stopped:

Title, Extent and Commencement

It is hereby enacted as follows:

1. (1) This Act may be called the Bharatpur Social Reforms Act.

   It extends to the whole of Bharatpur State.

   It shall be promulgated this today the 16th of November, 1926 and shall come into force from the 1st January, 1927.

(Chapter 1 of the Act pertaining to widow remarriage is not being produced here, as it is out of the purview of this study.)

Chapter II
Child Marriages

Age limit for marriages: 10(i) All marriages or remarriages contracted between parties who have not attained the age of 14 in the case of females and of 16 in case of males may be declared void by a court of law.

Exceptions

(a) In case of marriage contracts entered into before this Act came into force, celebration of marriage may be permitted, provided the parents or guardians furnish sufficient security that consummation shall not be allowed till the pair have attained the ages prescribed in clause-I of this section.

In special circumstance, for reasons to be recorded, marriage may be permitted provided the security referred to in exception (a) is furnished.

N.B. Authority to deal with such applications shall be vested in the *Durbar*.

10(ii)(a)

Notwithstanding anything contained in section 190 of the Code of Criminal Procedure, 1898, no court other than that of a *Nazim* shall take cognizance of, or try the offence committed under this Act.

(b)(i) No court shall take cognizance of any offence under this Act save upon complaint made within one year of the solemnization of the marriage in respect of which the offence is alleged to have been committed.

(ii) The court taking cognizance of an offence under this Act shall, unless it dismisses the complaint under section 203 of the Code of Criminal Procedure, 1898, either itself make an inquiry under section 202 of that code, or direct a Magistrate of the 2nd class subordinate to it to make such inquiry.

(iii) At any time after examining the complaint and before issuing process for compelling the attendance of the accused, the court shall, except for reason to be recorded in writing, require the complainant to execute a bond, with or without securities, for a sum not exceeding one hundred rupees, as security for the payment of any compensation which the complainant may be directed to pay under Sec. 250 of the Code of Criminal Procedure, 1898, and if such security is not furnished within such reasonable time as the court may fix the complaint shall be dismissed.

(iv) A bond taken under this section shall be deemed to be a bond taken under the Code of Criminal Procedure, 1898 and Chapter XLII of that Code shall apply accordingly.

(v) A complainant or informer in case of conviction may be granted by the court upto half the amount of the fine imposed, if realized.

Punishment in case of infringement

All persons knowingly abetting a marriage or remarriage contrary to the above age limit contravening the provisions of section 10 shall be liable to imprisonment for any term not exceeding 2 years or a fine not exceeding Rs 3,000 or to both.

Provided

(i) that a male between 16 and 21 contracting a child marriage shall be punishable with fine only which may extend to Rs 1000.

(ii) that notwithstanding anything contained in section 25 of the General Clauses Act, 1897 or Section 64 of the I.P.C. no court shall be competent to direct imprisonment in default of payment of fine under exception (1) of this section.

(iii) that no woman shall be punishable with imprisonment.

A critical analysis of the proclamation reveals certain features, which makes it different from the legislation passed by the other States of the Rajputana. The importance of this Act lies in the fact, that for the first time in the history of the Rajputana, an attempt was made by a native State to abolish the practice of child marriage and to legitimize widow remarriages. Moreover, it dealt upon the procedure of investigation in detail, discussing the intricacies involved in it, along with the punishments to be inflicted. It is worthy to note that the proclamation refrained from enacting against unequal marriages, and passed the matter in complete silence while the other States of the Rajputana, later on, legislated against it along with the practice of child marriage.

The State of Kota, motivated by the Act of Bharatpur State, placed upon the statute book a law with effect from July 1, 1927 against infant marriages, wherein the marriageable age of girls and boys was fixed at 12 and 16 years respectively.[105] This Act was called as Kanoon Shadi (Vivah Sambandhi Niyam). Maharao Ummed Singh, the ruler of Kota, at the time of passing the law, declared it that "though the Durbar is against the interference in the day-to-day affairs of the subjects; but when there is a practice prevalent among the subjects, of marrying their sons and daughters to an unsuitable or elder person, in lieu of money or of breaking the *sagai-contract* in greed of getting more money from some other party, which ultimately causes great harm to the society; the State feels it, that it is its duty to pass an Act to check the evils of child and unmatched marriages." According to Rule No. 2 of this Act, a girl below 18 years of age was not to be married to a man more than double her age.

Rule No. 3 laid down that an engagement should not be broken under normal circumstances but it was allowed only on the following conditions:

(a) physical incapability.
(b) affliction with infectious disease of either the boy or the girl.
(c) bad or immoral conduct of either the boy or the girl.
(d) or, if the boy was deprived of property in lieu of which the engagement had been fixed; or
(e) revelation of a caste distinction, which was not known prior to the engagement.

Rule No. 4 enjoined that the guardians or the parents of a girl, should not take money from the groom's side, on any pretext. The Act also provided a check on unequal marriages by restricting the parents or guardians of a girl above 18 years of age from marrying her to a man above 45 years of age. It also discouraged the prevalent practice of the marriage of old persons with young and virgin girls and laid down that a man, above 45 years of age, should not marry a virgin. To ensure the implementation, it gave special powers to First Class Magistrate, who would hear the cases regarding the violation of these rules. The Magistrate could, in the cases of violation of the rules, impose a fine upto Rs 1,000 or award six months simple or rigorous imprisonment, to the party/parties concerned. The Magistrate was also accorded the authority to prevent a marriage, if necessary. Appeals regarding the stopping of marriages or of interference in such marriages were to be made to the Magistrate. Until the Appellate court decides the matter, it was made clear, such marriages were not to be performed. To make these rules effective, it was laid down that any subject of the State who entered into a marriage in another State contrary to the rules, was liable to punishment on returning to the State. It is significant to note that these rules were not made applicable on those castes, in which the practice of naata was prevalent. Similarly, the Walterkrit Rajputra Hitkarini Sabha was also excluded, as it had its own set of rules. It is significant to note that the Act did not provide either for any security deposits or permission of the State before proceedings could be initiated against an offender. This gave birth to an unpleasant situation because to settle their own personal scores, some provided false information to the State machinery through false or anonymous letters, thereby making the State to act. Such false information created bitterness in the hearts of the subjects towards the State machinery and forced them to protest against this law.

Consequently, on 16 December, 1930, new provisions were incorporated in this Act, to remove some of its defects. It was made clear now that no action would be taken against any party on the basis of false or anonymous letters. But as article no. 9 stated, action would be taken on those petitions which were received by post and which had the details about the name and address of the sender. The court was asked to verify the name and address of the petitioner and if need be, to call him in person before registering his complaint. Article No. 10 provided that if any such letter (or complaint), was found false, then the sender of that letter would be fined upto Rs 200 and this money would be given to the party concerned, against whom the complaint was made, as compensation. But if the complaint was found to be true, then the party concerned would be fined and the money thus collected, would be given to the informer as reward. It was also laid down that in case of any controversy, regarding the age of bride and groom, if the age happened to be near about the prescribed age, then the benefit of doubt could be given to the concerned party/parties. It is strange to note that Article No. 13 repealed the previous provision of 'simple or rigorous imprisonment' and now stated that it would be given, only under certain conditions, and in ordinary circumstances, the court would only fine the offenders. The words 'only under certain conditions' were left unexplained in the amendment made in 1930. In 1928, the Vaishya-Sudharak Mandal[106] made a representation to the Kota

Durbar in which they requested that a sufficient time of almost one year had passed and that by now every caste had understood the real significance of the Act. It therefore prayed that the Walterkrit Hitkarini Sabha and those castes (in which the naata practise was prevalent) should be included within the purview of this Act, and no privilege should be given to them in this respect. As a result of this, the Kota Durbar on 30 August 1928, after much discussions, declared that "henceforward these rules will be applicable on all the castes". But this declaration created great uneasiness in certain sections of the society, which protested against it and consequently the Kota Durbar had to bow before the wishes of certain sections of the society and on 16 January, 1934 it declared that Rule No. 1, 2 and 4 would not be applicable on those castes in which the practice of naata or widow remarriage was accepted.

Though there were some shortcomings in the Act, yet it went a long way in motivating other States. The marriageable age prescribed in the Act for the girl was 12, which was quite low, if we compare it with that of the Bharatpur State (the State of Bharatpur, as discussed above, prescribed the minimum marriageable age for girls as 14 years). Moreover, the rules relating to unequal marriages were quite inadequate as the age-gap prescribed at 18 and 45 years for the girl and the prospective groom was quite high. But even then it can be said that the significance of this Act lies in the fact, that it was the first Act of any native State of the Rajputana, which tried to put restrictions on unequal and ill-matched marriages, through a proclamation.

The examples created by the States of Bharatpur and Kota inspired other States too, and soon the State of Bikaner followed the course. On September 6, 1928, the Maharaja of Bikaner gave his consent to the Hindu Vivah Act. This Act extended to the whole of Bikaner State and was applicable to all the Hindu citizens of the State except the Rajputs and the Charans, who were governed by the rules of the Walterkrit Rajputra Hitkarini Sabha.[107] The Act made clear the meaning of certain terms like marriage, child marriage and minor to avoid the possibility of confusion, at any level. It prescribed 16 and 11 years as the minimum age for boys and girls respectively and forbade the performance of marriage before that age. If any man above the age of 18, contracted a child marriage or anyone who and got the marriage of a minor solemnized, was to be punished by a fine up to Rs 1,000. Further, a girl below 14 years of age was not to be married to a man above 45 years of age. The Act also prevented the marriage of a girl under 18 years of age to a boy younger than herself. The Act provided that the complainant to such a marriage would deposit Rs 500 or furnish security in value thereof, before the proceedings could be instituted.[108] It is remarkable that the minimum age for marriage for girls was quite low, if we compare it with that of the State of Bharatpur and Kota, for they fixed it as 14 and 12 respectively.

In 1927, the Maharaja of Jodhpur contemplated the introduction of legislation to prevent child marriages and marriages between males and females having inordinately great differences in their ages and as such, the copies of Acts passed on the subject were obtained from the States of Baroda, Indore, Bikaner, Alwar, Kota, Kashmir and Mandi.[109]

With a view to ascertain the views of the various communities in Marwar, Sardar Jwala Singh, the Judicial Minister of Jodhpur, convened a meeting of two representatives of each of the communities of Pushkarna Brahmins, Shrimalis, Oswals, Daima Brahmins, Maheshwaris, Agarwals, Charans, Kayasthas, Malis, Rana Rajputs, Khatris, Mohammedans, Sunars, Luhars, Barbers, Ghanchis, Sanchoras, Bhats, Lakharas, Telis, Tambolis, Ganchas, Kasaras and Gandhis. Opinions of all communities, except the Rajputs and the Charans, who were governed by the Rules of WKRHS, were obtained. The consensus of opinion was that most of the communities favoured the introduction of reform "not through legislation" but through social propaganda in their communities gradually. But at the same time, they too accepted the principle that girls below the age of 11 or 12, should not be married. As regards the marriage of males, whether first or subsequent, they were prepared to fix the age limit between 14 and 40 respectively.

In 1929, the Maharaja of Jodhpur again desired to know if the people of Marwar would welcome legislation on the subject of child marriage. And as such, the matter was entrusted to Munshi Himmat Singh, the Revenue Minister, who prepared a draft of the Marwar Marriage Bill and published it in the Marwar Gazette in 1930.[110] The preamble of the Bill emphasized upon the essentiality of an enactment to prevent child and unequal marriages. The main provisions of the Bill were:

(a) That no boy should be married before he completed 16 years and that no girl should be married before she had completed 12 years.

(b) That no girl under 18 years of age, should be married to a male, who was over 45 years of age and that no virgin should be married to a male, who was above 60 years of age.

But the legislation met with great opposition from the orthodox segment of the people and the matter was dropped for the time being. In 1939, Radha Mohan, the Legal Remembrancer again proposed the Act,[111] on the lines of the British Indian Child Marriage Restraint Act, and the same was referred to the District Advisory Boards and the Municipalities for eliciting public opinion. The Municipal Boards at Jodhpur, Jaswantpura, and Siwana expressed their views in favour of the proposal. The Municipal Boards at Phalodi, Didwana, and Barmer were also in favour of the proposal and they made definite suggestions regarding the ages for girls and boys, as 12-16, 11-16 and 14-18 respectively. The proposal was not approved by the Municipal Boards at Pali, Balotra, Nagaur and Ladnu. However, the dissentient members of the Municipal Boards at Pali and Balotra, who were in favour of the proposal had suggested that the marriageable ages for girls and boys, respectively may be fixed at 11-15 and 12-16. The Jalore Municipal Board approved the proposal subject to the amendment that ages for girls and boys for marital relationship in the communities where widow marriage was not allowed and for gauna (consummation) in the communities where widow marriage was permissible, should be fixed at 13 for the girl and 18 for the boy.

The Nagaur District Advisory Board, however, desired that the Government should enlighten the views of the masses by spreading education for a period of at least five years and then introduce the proposed Act so that it might become acceptable. Views of certain public institutions on the proposal in question was also obtained and it was found that 26 public institutions were in favour of the proposal while 6 were against it. The names of those who supported the proposals were:

(i) Hindu Sabha, Nagaur (ii) Jat Boarding House, Jodhpur (iii) Pali All India Jain Shvetambar Conference (iv) Maheshwari Nav-Yuvak Mandal, Pali (v) Arya Samaj, Pali (vi) Arya Samaj, Nagaur (vii) Sojat District Vaidya Conference (viii) Jodhpur Nav-Yuvak Mandal (ix) Joshi Pushkarna Sabha (x) Shri Pushtikar Nav-Yuvak Mandal, Jodhpur (xi) Shri Pushtikar Nav-Yuvak Mandal, Karachi (xii) Shri Pushkarna Yuvak Samaj, Phalodi (xiii) Jain Friend's Club, Phalodi (xiv)

Seva-Sangha, Pali (xv) Arya Samaj, Sur-Sagar, Jodhpur (xvi) Arya Samaj, Barmer (xvii) Marwar Vidyarthi Sangha, Jodhpur (xviii) Mohalla Khagal Public Meeting (xix) Gundi Mohalla Public Meeting (xx) Nai-Brahman Mandal, Nagaur (xxi) Teachers' Association, Nagaur (xxii) Arya Samaj, Sardarpura, Jodhpur (xxiii) Hindu Sabha, Pokaran (xxiv) Shri Nav-Yuvak Mandal, Jaitaran (xxv) Marwar Lok Parishad, Sojat Branch (xxvi) Oswal Hitkarini Sabha, Ladnu.

While the names of those public institutions/caste panchayats who were against the proposed Act were:

(i) Pushkarna Brahman Maha-Mandal, Jodhpur. (ii) Panchas of Pushkarna Community, Jodhpur. (iii) Anjuman Islamia, Jodhpur (iv) Muslim organizations of Pali (v) Shrimali Brahmans (vi) Some organizations at Pali (there names have not been specified in the document).

The amendment moved by Jai Narayan Vyas to stop ill-matched marriages, was also referred to the various Municipalities for eliciting public opinion. All the Municipal Boards favoured the prevention of ill-matched marriages of males above 40 to 45 years with girls of tender age. The District Advisory Board at Phalodi also passed a resolution recommending that marriage of a male above 45 with a girl of tender age should be prohibited.

Thus, opinion of majority of public institutions was in favour of the proposal, though they differed with regard to the age limits (which ranged between 11 and 14 for girls and 16 and 18 for boys).

Consequently, in 1939, the State of Jodhpur, on the insistence of the enlightened people, passed the Marwar Child and ill-matched Marriages Prevention Act, which extended to the whole of Marwar, except the Sambhar Shamlat Area and also applied to all Marwar Durbar's subjects and servants of the Durbar in any part of India and also those who were domiciled in any part of India, wherever they may be. This Act defined the child as one who was under 18 years of age, and if a female, under 14 years of age; and child marriage as "a marriage to which either of the contracting parties is a child". It also defined the term ill-matched marriage and according to it, ill-matched marriage meant the marriage of a man with a woman or girl more than 20 years younger than himself. As regards the punishment, the clause no. 3, 4, 5, 6 & 7 of the Act said:

"Whoever, being a male above 18 years of age and below 21, contracts a child marriage shall be punishable with fine which may extend to 1000 rupees."

"Whoever, being a male above 21 years of age contracts a child marriage shall be punishable with simple imprisonment which may extend to one month, or with fine which may extend to 1,000 rupees or with both."

"Whoever, being a male contracts a marriage with a female more than 20 years younger than himself shall be punishable with simple imprisonment which may extend to one month or with a fine which may extend to 1,000 rupees or both."

"Whoever, performs, conducts or directs any child marriage or ill-matched marriage shall be punishable with simple imprisonment which may extend to one month, or with fine which may extend to 1000 rupees or with both unless he proves that he had reason to believe that the marriage was not a child marriage or an ill-matched marriage."

(a) "Where a minor contracts a child marriage or ill-matched marriage, any person having charge of the minor, whether as parent or guardian or in any other capacity, lawful or unlawful, who does any act to promote the marriage or permits it to be solemnized, shall be punishable with simple imprisonment which may extend to one month, or with fine which may extend to one thousand rupees or with both.

Provided that no woman shall be punished with imprisonment.

(b) For the purpose of this section, it shall be presumed unless and until the contrary is proved, that where a minor has contracted a child marriage, the person having charge of such minor has negligently failed to prevent the marriage from being solemnized."

However, the Act recognized marriage as legal, if the parent or guardian sought permission from the court on the condition that the betrothal was performed before the commencement of the Act, provided that the boy was a child but in no case the girl a child. It also provided the marriage to be legal, if owing to *singhast* year, a girl had no chance of marrying on the date of her ceasing a to be child or within one year from such date provided the boy had crossed the age of 16.

The Act also laid down that no court other than that of a First Class Magistrate shall take cognizance of, or try, any offence under this Act and also that no court shall take cognizance of any offence under this Act after the expiry of one year from the date on which the offence is alleged to have been committed. If need be, the court could ask the complainant to execute a bond with or without sureties, for a sum not exceeding one hundred rupees, as security for the payment of any compensation which the complainant may be directed to pay under section 250 of the Marwar Criminal Procedure Code and if such security was not furnished within such reasonable time as the Court may fix, the complaint was to be dismissed. it is remarkable that the minimum age for marriages for girls and boys was fixed on the lines of the Sarda Act of British India, and it was made applicable on all the subjects, including the Rajputs and the Charans of Marwar.

Qanun Taiyun Umra Shadi of Jhalawar came into force on May 1, 1931 and was applicable on all the subjects of the State.[112] It prohibited marriage before the age of 18 and 14 years of age for the boy and the girl respectively. Simple imprisonment extending to one month or a fine upto Rs 1,000 or both was prescribed for the offenders. In case, where the offender happens to be younger than the age prescribed, punishment in case of conviction would be inflicted on the father, mother or any other legal guardian, but if the offender happens to be above the prescribed age limits then the offender alone would be subjected to punishment. All abettors including the barber, the priest, the *Gaon-guru* and *Shahar Qazi* were subjected to punishment up to a fine of Rs 500 or in default to simple imprisonment extending to one month. Offences under the Act were declared non-cognizable and non-compoundable but bailable. There were certain exceptions in the Act, whereby in the absence of *Sawa* or *Saat Said* within a year after the completion of the prescribed age or on grounds of economy, when a person proposed to solemnize the marriage of one of his children who had not attained the prescribed, age along with the one who had reached such an age or a person who had reached such a condition of infirmity that he had no hope to live long, then the Magistrate on his executing a bond, with or without sureties to the effect, may permit the solemnization of the marriage with certain reservations. The Magistrates were also empowered to issue injunctions against the performance of an illegal marriage if they were convinced. The Magistrates were even allowed to order the police to stop such a marriage. If a marriage was performed after the issue of an injunction order then the accused and the Brahmin or Qazi performing the marriage were to be punished with simple imprisonment upto three months or a fine upto Rs 1,000.

In 1933, an Act controlling Expenditure on Marriage and Funeral ceremonies of the Alwar State was issued.[113] It included the residents of all communities of Alwar State under its jurisdiction. As per the rules of the Act pertaining to child and un-matched marriages, the minimum marriageable age for boy and girl was fixed at 18 and 12 years, respectively. It prohibited the marriage of a girl to a boy five years younger than her; of a girl above the age of 13 years to a boy more than three times her age. Though the age gap in the above three prohibitions was quite high, yet the fact that at least some initiative was taken is noticeable.

The Act No. 1 of 1935, of Dungarpur State entitled Bal Aur Anmail Vivah Act defined child marriage as one in which either the bride or the groom was a minor.[114] It also defined the term minor and according to it a boy below the age of 18 years and a girl below 15 years of age was a minor. If a person, above 18 years of age but less than 21 years contracted a child marriage, the punishment would be a fine ranging upto Rs 1,000 and one above 21 years, committing the offence of child marriage, was punishable with simple imprisonment up to one month or a fine of Rs 500 or both. For a minor (below 18 years) contracting a child marriage, it reads, "any person having charge of the minor whether as a parent or guardian or in any other capacity, lawful or unlawful, who does an act to promote such a marriage or permits it to be solemnized shall be punishable with simple imprisonment up to one month or a fine ranging upto Rs 1,000 or both. It specifically laid down that in no case the woman would be subjected to imprisonment. All cases, under the Act would be dealt by Vivah Committee and the appeals would be with the Administrative council. The Vivah committee was to consist of two members from the public, with Deewan as the chairman.

The Preamble of the Act also emphasized upon the necessity of such a legislation to curb unmatched marriages as it adversely affected the health of the newly borns and the rising number of child widows, and declared unequal marriage to be one in which a girl below 17 years of age was married to a man above 50 years of age.

On infringement to the rule pertaining to unequal marriage, the bridegroom was to be inflicted with one month's imprisonment or a penalty upto Rs 1,000 or both and those participating in such a marriage were to be inflicted with one month's imprisonment or a fine upto Rs 500 or both.

Dholpur Child Marriage Restraint Act of 1937,[115] came into force on 1 October, 1937. It extended to the whole of Dholpur State and was made applicable on all castes and creeds. it defined child marriage as one, to which either of the contracting party was a child i.e., 15 years in case of a boy and 12 years in case of a girl. Any male adult above 18 years of age but below 21 years, contracting a child marriage was punishable with a fine upto Rs 500. Punishment in terms of money (up to Rs 1,000) was also set forth for the parent, guardian etc. as in the case of Dungarpur State.

No court below the 2nd Class Magistrate could take cognizance, try any offence under this Act. A detailed account was made of any offences under the Act. The offence under this Act was non-cognizable. It is striking to note that the Act did not promulgate any rule to abolish the practice of unmatched marriages.

The peculiar feature of the Act was that punishment in terms of imprisonment was deliberately avoided.

Shahpura State Bal Vivah Nishedh Act of 1939 came into force from April, 1, 1940.[116] It provided that a man above 18 years but below 21 years of age contracting a marriage with a child below 14 years of age would be punishable with a fine upto Rs 1,000 but if he had attained the age of 21 and commits the offence, he would be punished with imprisonment upto three months or fine upto Rs 1,000 or both. Anyone who would finalize such a marriage or consent to it, would be imprisoned upto one month or fined up to Rs 1,000 or both. If parent or guardian, lawful or unlawful, performs an Act for the solemnization of such a marriage, he would be subjected to punishment as above. The courts were empowered to issue injunctions against any party if they felt convinced that such a marriage was likely to be solemnized. Only First Class Magistrates were empowered to try such cases.

However, it is important to note that to withhold child and unmatched marriages, certain limits were placed on the grants made to the bride and bridegroom on the occasion of marriage. The limit was on marriage below 18 and 14 years for boys and girls, respectively. And to curb unequal or unmatched marriages, it was also limited, in marriages of men, more than 40 years of age. The Durbar also consented "to penalize the marriages, which may be performed in Shahpura State territory with a view to escape the penalties of Child Marriage Restraint Act in British India". It is significant to note that the minimum age for marriage for girls was fixed as 14 years, which was higher if we compare it with those of Kota, Bikaner, Alwar and Dholpur.

To prohibit child and unmatched marriages in Banswara, an Act called the Dapa Nishedh Rajya Banswara was sanctioned on 13 May, 1940[117] by His Highness, the Maharawal of Banswara.

Samajik Sudhar Act, Karauli of 1940 was enforced from 1 January, 1940 and it was applicable on all the citizens of the State except those castes where widow remarriage was considered as legal. It made a marriage punishable where the boy or the girl was below 16 or 13 years of age respectively.[118] It also prohibited a man above 45 years of age to marry a girl below 20 years of age. This was a prominent feature of the Act as it is the lowest gap prescribed between unequal marriages or the highest gap prescribed for marriage of a girl. It also laid down that anyone who participates in it or actively helps in its solemnization or consents to it in contravention of the Act would also be punished.

The Kishangarh Durbar issued a legislation Kishangarh Child Marriage Prevention Rules 1940 which were sanctioned on 6th Jan. 1941[119] They extended to the whole of Kishangarh State and came into force after two months of publication in the State gazette. It prohibited the marriage of boys and girls below the age of 16 years and 12 years, respectively.

The Undesirable Marriage Prohibition Act 1 of 1941 of Mewar came into force from March 15, 1941 and was applicable on the whole of Mewar and all the subjects of Mewar, wherever they were residing, excepting Merwara.[120] The Act prohibited marriages of males and females below the age of 18 and 13 years of age respectively.

Any male above the prescribed age contracting a prohibited marriage was punishable with simple imprisonment extending to one month or with fine upto Rs 500 or with both. The same punishment was given to the parent or guardian if a person of either sex contracted a prohibited marriage under him. Any person conducting, directing or actively participating in such a marriage was equally punishable. The Magistrates were empowered to issue injunctions against any party, if they were convinced that such a marriage was likely to be solemnized. The Magistrates were also empowered to award costs against the informer or the person informed against, and the appeal against the Magistrates order would lie with the appellate court. Section 9 awarded punishment to those persons who disobeyed the injunction with simple imprisonment extending to three months or with fine upto Rs 1000 or both. Lastly, the offences under the Act were made non-cognizable.

The Jaipur Durbar, in 1938, planned to enact "Child Marriage Restraint Act" and proposed that:

I.(a) This Act shall be called the "Jaipur State Child Marriage Restraint Act (1938)";

It shall extend to the whole of the Jaipur State territory; and

It shall come into force from the date to be specified by the Jaipur Govt. after its publication in the Jaipur Gazette.

II. In this Act, unless there is anything repugnant in the subject or context.

"Child" means a person who if a male, is under eighteen years of age, and if a female, is under fourteen years of age;

"Child Marriage" means a marriage to which either of the contracting parties is a child;

"Contracting party" to a marriage means either of the parties whose marriage is thereby solemnized; and

"Minor" means a person of either sex who is under eighteen years of age.

Whoever, being a male above eighteen years of age and below twenty one contracts a child marriage, shall be punishable with the fine which may extend to one thousand rupees.

Whoever, being a male above twenty-one years of age, contracts a child marriage, shall be punishable with simple imprisonment which may extend to six months, or with fine which may extend to one thousand rupees or both.

Whoever performs, conducts or directs any child marriage, shall be punishable with simple imprisonment which may extend to six months, or with fine which may extend to one thousand rupees or with both, unless he proves that he had reasons to believe that the marriage was not a child marriage.

(a) Where a minor contracts a child marriage, any person having charge of the minor, whether as parent or guardian or in any other capacity, lawful or unlawful, who does any act to promote the marriage or permits it to be solemnized, or negligently fails to prevent it from being solemnized, shall be punishable with simple imprisonment which may extend to six months, or with fine which may extend to one thousand rupees, or with both. Provided that no woman shall be punishable with imprisonment.

(b) For the purpose of this section it shall be presumed, unless and until the contrary is proved, that where a minor has contracted a child marriage, the person having charge of such minor has negligently failed to prevent the marriage from being solemnized.

Notwithstanding anything contained in section 52 of the Jaipur Penal code, a court sentencing an offender under section 3 shall not be competent to direct that in default of payment of the fine imposed, he shall undergo any term of imprisonment.

Notwithstanding anything contained in Section 180 of the code of Criminal procedure, Jaipur State, no court other than that of a Sessions Judge shall take cognizance of, or try, any offence under this Act.

No court shall take cognizance of any offence under this Act save upon complaint made within one year of the solemnization of the marriage in respect of which the offence is alleged to have been committed.

The court taking cognizance of an offence under this Act, shall unless it dismisses the complaint under section 195 of the code of criminal procedure, Jaipur State, either itself make an enquiry under section 194 of that code, or direct a Magistrate of the first class subordinate to it to make such inquiry.

(a) At any time after examining the complaint and before issuing process for compelling the attendance of the accused, the court shall, except for reasons to be recorded in writing, require the complainant to execute a bond, with or without sureties, for a sum not exceeding one hundred rupees, as security for the payment of any compensation which the complainant may be directed to pay under section 236 and if such security is not furnished within such reasonable time as the court may fix, the complaint shall be dismissed.

(b) A bond under this section shall be deemed to be taken under the code of criminal procedure, Jaipur State, and Chapter XXXVIII of that code shall apply accordingly. However, this Act could not be passed in 1938 and it was in 1945, that efforts were again made to issue such an Act.

The Jaipur Child Marriage Restraint Act of 1945 came into force from January 1, 1947 and extended to the whole of Jaipur except the Sambhar-Shamlat area and was made applicable on all the subjects of the State.[121] It prohibited marriages of males and females below the age of 18 and 14 respectively. Under section 3, a male above 18 but below 21 years of age contracting a prohibited marriage was punishable with fine extending upto Rs 1,000. But if a male above 21 years of age contracted a prohibited marriage, he was punishable with simple imprisonment extending to one month or with fine upto Rs 1,000 or both. Any person conducting, directing such a marriage or having charge of a minor was equally punishable as in the later case. It provided that a district Magistrate or a first class magistrate would take cognizance of any offence under this Act.

A statement of objects and reasons was incorporated which went as:

"The Bill is an adaptation of the Child Marriage Restraint Act (XIX of 1929) in force in British India, more commonly known as the Sarda Act. The main object of the Bill, by laying down the minimum marriageable ages of boys and girls, to prevent, so far as may be, their physical and moral deterioration by removing a principal obstacle to their physical and mental development with a view to securing this object, the Bill penalizes marriages of girls below 14 and boys below 18 years of age and seeks also to punish the promoters of such marriages as offence against the aforesaid rule. Sufficient safeguards against malicious prosecutions have also been provided in clauses 9, 10 and 11 of the Bill."

"This piece of legislation has been in force in British India and progressive Indian States for a number of years and has become overdue for the Jaipur State. The necessity for the same has been felt here also in all quarters. Various representations were made to the Government by private persons and public bodies for enacting it and as a matter of fact, the Bill was framed so early as February, 1943, by the Jaipur Laws Committee, constituted by the Government in 1942; but the passing thereof has so far been deferred by the Government as they considered it expedient that social legislation of this nature, should be placed before and passed by the State Legislature."

"In the meanwhile attention of Government has also been drawn by the Political Department of the Government of India for enacting such legislations. In the interests of all concerned, Government consider it desirable that the council should pass the Bill."

This Statement of Objects and Reasons, as it was called, again reflects the hesitation of the Jaipur Durbar to issue a legislation to the effect. Despite the various representations made by the enlightened people, caste and social organizations (like All India Vaish Mahasabha, the Meena community and the Rajasthaniya Gaur Brahmin Sabha) the Jaipur Durbar refrained from taking any action against this malady.

Perhaps it was the pressure of the Government of India, which forced the State of Jaipur to pass the Act. It is striking to note that while the State of Jaipur pioneered the crusade against female infanticide, as early as 1731, (during the period of Sawai Jai Singh) and reflected progressive thoughts and ideas in the fields of astronomy, astrology and other scientific branches; it showed a lukewarm attitude towards the problem of child marriages, unequal marriages and the remarriage of widows. It is difficult to ascertain why it took such a long time to pass an Act, when it was already in force in the States of Mysore, Baroda, Bharatpur, Kota, Bikaner, Jodhpur, Jhalawar, Alwar, Dungarpur, Dholpur, Shahpura, Karauli, Kishangarh, and Mewar; and when it was in force in British India from 1930.

Despite the fact that its rulers were well-learned and highly educated, despite the fact that it became a centre of higher education, despite the fact that it became a stronghold of Arya Samaj; the State of Jaipur presented a sad picture, as far as an act against child or unequal marriages was concerned. The same was the case with the States of Mewar and Marwar, as they too, had prohibited the practice of female infanticide, much before the English officers showed their concerns for it. But as far as child marriages or unequal marriages were concerned they too followed the policy of 'wait and watch', and though they sympathized with the cause, were afraid of initiating the reform-process, in this regard.

To sum up, we can say that the social legislation against child and unmatched marriages, was the result of the efforts of enlightened individuals, and various caste and social organizations of regional and national level, which requested the rulers of native States, time and again, to ponder over the seriousness of the social problems and to wipe out this stigma. These organizations, whose contribution has been described in the previous pages, also highlighted upon the issue of providing education to women for their emancipation and themselves opened many schools, for their betterment.

Although the contribution of the native people is significant in the issuance of proclamations, the contribution of the native rulers also deserves a special mention. Some of them were enlightened rulers, who tried to do away with the various social evil, without any outside pressure. It is significant to note that the initiative to abolish the heinous practices through legal enactments came in the form of indigenous efforts by the native rulers, even prior to the British influence as early as the 18th century. This is in contrast to the prevalent view that the native rulers were apathetic, insouciant or insensitive to the social cause, as was depicted by the records of the English. Maharaja Sawai Jai Singh of Jaipur, issued proclamations in 1731 A.D. (Samvat 1787) against the practice of female infanticide, Sati and reducing the marriage expenditure, much before, the arrival of East India Company in Rajasthan. Similarly, Maharaja Bukht Singh of Jodhpur, who died in Samvat 1809 (1753 A.D.), after a reign of three years, also passed an Act, which not only prohibited the crime of infanticide but also limited the demands of the Bhats and the Charans, on the celebration of marriages. Maharaja Bijai Singh of Jodhpur, too, passed a law in Samvat 1831 (1765 A.D.), which prohibited female infanticide in Marwar. Similarly, the Raja of Pratapgarh and the ruler of Banswara, prohibited the practice of infanticide, within their respective territories even before its advent in the 19th century. Despite the prevalence of social evils, the significance of their initiative lay in the fact that it provided a ground for further reforms. These examples refute the popular belief regarding the conservation and rigidity of the native rulers pertaining to the abolition of various abhorrent practices, then prevalent.

It is significant to note that while the practice of female infanticide came to a virtual end because of the efforts of native rulers and British officers, the practice of infant-child and unequal marriages could be checked by the initiative of the various caste and social organizations, who through their petitions, letters, appeals, demonstrations tried to create pressure on their rulers and ultimately became successful in getting an Act passed in their native State.

Significantly, in the historical records of the 20th century, there is lack of evidence to corroborate a reformist attitude amongst the rulers of the Rajputana, except the Ruler of Bharatpur, who enacted laws to abolish the practice of child marriages and legitimize widow remarriage. Although States like Kota, Bikaner, Marwar, etc., picked up the cue and issued legislations to prevent child and unmatched marriages, but Mewar and Jaipur adopted a rigid stance. Since there was no consensus regarding the age of marriage or about the remarriage of widows, among various communities, therefore, each State recommended a different age and different method to tackle the two problems. Similarly, the punishments to be inflicted on the offenders, too differed from State to State.

The State of Bharatpur was the pioneer, in the erstwhile States of the Rajputana, which passed an Act against child marriages as early as 1926, though it preferred to keep quiet over the issue of unequal marriages. But despite the efforts of such a large number of people, all over Rajputana, as well as in other States, the practice of child and unequal marriages could not be wholly checked, as the cases of child and unequal marriages still come to light even in the 21st century. Every year on the auspicious occasions of Akha-Teej (Akshaya-Tritiya) and Basant Panchami, hundreds of child marriages are performed in Rajasthan. According to a report published in India Today nearly 1,30,000 children are married off in a single day of Akha-Teej. Though this figure can be doubted, yet nobody can doubt its existence and its prevalence in almost all the sections of the society, even today.

Notes

1. NAI: Translation of a note addressed by the Jaipur council of regency to the Pol. Ag., dt. 27th of October, 1847; From Major John Ludlow, Pol. Ag. at Jaipur, to Lt. Col. Sutherland, A.G.G., dt. 30 October 1847; Enclosure No. 227 of 1847; Cons. no. 78; dt. 20 Nov. 1847.
2. Ibid.
3. NAI: From Ludlow to Sutherland, dt. 30 October, 1847; Enclosure no. 227 of 1847; No. 97 of 1847; Cons. no. 78, dt. 20 Nov. 1847.
4. Ibid.

   However in the 20th century, the Mehkama-Khas of Jaipur informed the British authorities that Sawai Jai Singh issued orders against female infanticide in 1728 A.D.

   RSAJ: General, Social & Religious, Mehkama Khas, Jaipur, 11.11.1937; Basta No. 1.
5. NAI: Substance translation of a memo furnished by the Jaipur council of regency to the Pol. Ag.; dt. 12 April 1844; F. & P., Enclosure no. 2 in no. 230 of 1844; Cons. no. 153, dt. 30 Nov. 1844.
6. In a letter to F. Currie, Secy. to G.O.I., dated 10th of March 1847, Lt. Col. Sutherland claimed that he "established the Jaipur Council of Regency in early part of 1839."

NAI: From Sutherland to F. Currie, date 10 March 1847, Encl. no. 297 of 1847, Cons. no. 47, date 17 April 1847.

However, C.U. Aitchison has mentioned that "in 1834... a council of regency, consisting of five of the principal nobles, was formed under the superintendence of the Political Agent, for whose decision all measures of importance were submitted; the army was reduced, every branch of the administration was reformed, and sati, slavery and infanticide were prohibited."

Aitchison, C.U., A Collection of Treaties, Engagements and Sanads relating to States in Rajputana. Vol. III, Calcutta, 1909, p. 91.

7. Ibid.
8. NAI: From Ludlow to Major Thoresby, Offg. A.G.G., dt. 12 April 1844; Enclosure no. 1 in no. 230 of 1844; Cons. no. 152; dt. 30 Nov. 1844.
9. NAI: Trans. of a note from the Vakeel of Jodhpur to Captain Trench, Offg. Pol. Ag. at the court, date 7 May 1844; Encl. no. 7 in no. 230 of 1844; Cons. no. 159; dt. 30 Nov. 1844.
10. Ibid.
11. NAI: Trans. of a proclamation issued by the Durbar of Udaipur, dt. 24 May 1844; Encl. no. 8 in no. 230 of 1844; F. & P. Cons. no. 158; dt. 30 Nov. 1844.
12. Ibid.
13. NAI: From Ludlow to Thoresby, dt. 21 July 1844, Encl. no. 6 in no. 230 of 1844; F. & P. cons. no. 157; dt. 30 Nov. 1844.
14. Ibid.
15. NAI: From Ludlow to Thoresby, dt. 12 April 1844, Encl. no. 1 in no. 230 of 1844; F. & P. Cons. no. 152, dt. 30 Nov. 1844.
16. NAI: From Thoresby to F. Currie, Esquire, Secretary to G.O.I., dt. 7 Nov. 1844, no. 1414 of 1844; F. & P., Cons. no. 151.
17. NAI: Substance trans. of a letter addressed by the Jaipur council of regency to the Pol. Ag. on 20 Feb. 1847; Encl. No. 2 in no. 57 of 1847; F. & P., Cons. no. 48, dt. 17 April, 1847.
18. NAI: From Sutherland to F. Currie, dt. 10 March 1847, F. & P., Cons. no. 47, dt. 17 April 1847.
19. NAI: Substance trans. of a letter addressed by the Jaipur Council of regency to the Pol. Ag., dt. 20 Feb. 1847; F. & P., Cons. no. 48, dt. 17 April, 1847.
20. RSAB: From Commissioner of Ajmer to Secretary, G.O.I., Ajmer Commissioner's office, Basta no. 26, File no. 310 of 1870.

21. Report on the Political Admn. of the Rajput States; Jaipur Agency, Report for 1871-72.
22. NAI: From Sutherland to F. Currie, dt. 10 March 1847; No. 297 of 1847; F. & P., Cons. no. 47, date 17 April, 1847.
23. NAI: Trans. of a letter from Rao-Raja Ridmul, Vakeel of Jodhpur, to Captain Ludlow, dt. 4 Nov. 1841; F. & P., Cons. no. 40, dt. 22 June 1842.
24. NAI: From Sutherland to F. Currie, dated 6 June, 1845; F.& P., Cons. no. 70, dt. 12 September 1845.
25. Ibid.
26. NAI: J. Sutherland to J.H. Maddock, Secretary to G.O.I., dt. 3 June 1841, F. & P., Cons. no. 43, dt. 12 August 1841.
27. NAI: From Sutherland to F. Currie, dated 6 June 1845; F. & P., Cons. no. 70, dt. 12 September 1845.
28. Reu, Bisheshwar Nath, Cf. *Har Bilas Sarda Commemoration Volume*, Vedic Yantralaya, Ajmer, 1937, pp. 522-23.

    However, in another document it has been mentioned that *Maharaja* Man Singh drafted a code of rules in Nov. 1839.

    NAI: Memo. regarding female infanticide in Marwar. Encl. no. 10 in no. 477 of 1842; Cons. no. 40, dt. 22 June 1842.
29. NAI: Memorandum regarding female infanticide in Marwar. Encl. no. 10 in no. 477 of 1842, Cons. no. 40, date 22 June, 1842.
30. Ibid.
31. Reu, B.N., op. cit., pp. 522-23.
32. Ibid.
33. NAI: From Sutherland to F. Currie, dt. 6 June 1845, F. & P. Cons. no. 70, dt. 12 September, 1845.
34. NAI: Court's Political Dispatch to G.O.I., dt. 26 June, 1842; Para 21, F. & P.
35. Reu, B.N., op. cit., pp. 522-23.
36. NAI: From Ludlow to Sutherland, dt. 29 June 1842, no. 250 of 1842, F. & P., Cons. no. 294-295, dt. 28 December 1842.

    Ludlow believed that Dholees or Ranas were not responsible for female infanticide.
37. Ibid.
38. Ibid.
39. Ibid.
40. In the original document the name of Rao-Raja. Rid-mal is also written as Rial Mal.

NAI: Trans. of a note in reply from Rao-Raja Rid Mal, the Jodhpur Vakeel to John Ludlow, dt. 2 June 1842, F. & P., Cons. no. 294-295, dt. 28 December, 1842.

41. NAI: From Sutherland to H.M. Elliot, dt. 14 June 1847, no. 645 of 1847, F. & P. Cons. no. 132, dt. 24 December, 1847.
42. Ibid.
43. Ibid.
44. NAI: Trans. of a proclamation by Maharaja of Jodhpur, dt. *Asadh Sudi* 1, 1903 V.S., (i.e., 12 July, 1847), R.R., List no. 1, File no. 43/1844, General-III.
45. NAI: From Thoresby to F. Currie, dt. 7 Nov. 1847, R.R., List no. 1 (Mewar), File no. 3/1844, Vol. I.
46. NAI: From Sutherland to Currie, Secy. to G.O.I., dt. Jan. 11, 1848, F. & P., Cons. no. 74, dt. 11 February, 1848.
47. NAI: L. Wilkinson, Pol. Ag. at Kota to Lt. Col. Lockett, A.G.G., dt. 26 April 1833, F. & P., Cons. no. 17 date 23 January, 1834.
48. Ibid.
49. Ibid.
50. NAI: F. & P., Cons. no. 17, dt. 23 January, 1834.
51. (a) The mothers of ten to twelve girls, born since were given these presents. Wilkinson himself gave presents to some who had brought their infant daughters but could not receive any presents.

    (b) NAI: F. & P., Cons. no. 67-A, dt. 3 April, 1846.

    (c) NAI: From Captain C.E. Burton, Pol. Ag. at Harauti to Lt. Col. Sutherland, dt. 12 August, 1846, F. & P., Cons. no. 255, dt. 17 Oct. 1846.
52. NAI: Trans. of a copy of the memo., dated 1893 V.S., F. & P., Cons no. 255, dt. 17 Oct. 1846.
53. (a) NAI: R.R. List no. II, File no. 270 of 1844, dated *Shrawan Sudi* 9, 1901 V.S.

    (b) NAI: F. & P., Cons. no. 253.
54. NAI: F. & P., Cons. no. 17, dt. 23 Jan. 1834.
55. NAI: Trans. of a Khureeta from *Mookhtar* of the *Kota-Raj* received on April 22, 1833. F. & P., Cons. no. 255, dt. Oct. 17, 1846.
56. NAI: Copy of promulgation to all Jagirdars, Istimrardars, Free-holders, Charans, etc., R.R., List no. II, File No. 279 of 1844, date not given.
57. NAI: Gov. Gen. to Raj-Rana of Kota, 23 January 1834, F. & P., Cons. no. 22.

And also, NAI: Gov. Gen. to Rao Raja Ram Singh, *Raja* of Bundi, 23 January, 1834, F. & P., Cons. no. 24.

58. NAI: G.G. to Maharana of Udaipur, 23 January 1834, F. & P., Cons. no. 32.
59. NAI: L. Wilkinson to J. Bax, Resident, Indore, 9 July, 1836; F. & P., cons. no. 50, date 1 Aug. 1836.
60. NAI: J. Bax to W.H. Macnaghten, Secy. to G.O.I., 14 July 1836, F. & P. Cons. no. 49, dt. 1 Aug. 1836.
61. NAI: L. Wilkinson to J. Bax, 9 July 1836, F. & P., Cons. no. 50, dt. 1 Aug. 1836.

    And also,

    "After the murder of every infant, the family considers itself an object of displeasure to the deity, and on the 12th day after the birth they send for the *purohit* or family priest and by suitable gratuities obtain absolution. This is necessary whether the family be rich or poor, but when the absolution is given, nothing more is said or thought over the matter."

    Sleeman, W.H. Journey through the Kingdom of Oudh, Cf. Bingley, A.H., *Handbook on Rajputs*, op. cit., pp. 167-168.
62. NAI: L. Wilkinson to J. Bax, 9 July 1836, F. & P., Cons. no. 50, dt. 1 August 1836.
63. NAI: R.R., List no. II, File no. 279 of 1844.
64. The name of the *Bara Maharaj* has not been specified.
65. NAI: R.R., List no. II., File no. 279 of 1844, dated *Shrawan Sudi* 12, 1901 V.S.
66. NAI: R.R. List no. II, File no. 279 of 1844, *Shrawan Sudi* 8, 1910 V.S.
67. He reached Gayaji on *Posh Sudi* 14, 1893 V.S. (Jan. 20, 1837).

    Cf. Dayal Das Ki Khyat, Vol. 2, p. 150, Cf. Ojha, G.H., *History of the Bikaner State*, Part II, Ajmer, 1940, p. 431.
68. NAI: From Ludlow to Thoresby, dt. 21 July 1844, Encl. no. 6 in no. 230 of 1844, F. & P. Cons. no. 157, dt. 30 Nov. 1844.
69. *Dayal Das Ki Khyat*, Vol. 2, p. 150, Cf. Ojha, G.H., op. cit., p. 431.
70. Lt. Col. Robinson in a letter dated 4 January 1844 to Major Thoresby, Offg. A.G.G., informed him that he had worked according to the spirit of instructions conveyed in a letter by Mr. Currie, Secy. G.O.I. bearing no. 1,150, and dated the 18 November 1843. It, therefore, appears, that Robinson addressed *Khureetas* to these native States in the months of November and December 1843. NAI: From Lt. Col. Robinson to Thoresby, dated 4 January 1844, Encl. no. 1 in no. 36 of 1844, F. & P., Cons. no. 40.

71. NAI: Purport in English of a *Khureeta* from Maharana Saroop Singh of Udaipur to the address of Lt. Col. Robinson, dated 27 December, 1843, F. & P., Cons. no. 41, date 2 March, 1844.
72. NAI: Trans. of a proclamation issued by the Durbar of Udaipur, date *Juet Sudi* 7, Samvat 1900, i.e., 24 May, 1844, Encl. no. 8 in no. 230 of 1844, F. & P., Cons. no. 158, dt. 30 Nov. 1844.
    And also, NAI: List no. 1, Mewar Residency file No. 3/1844, Vol., dated Asadh Sudi 3, 1916 V.S., F. & P.
73. Ibid.
74. Ibid.
75. NAI: From Major Taylor, Offg. Pol. Ag. at Mewar to Major Eden, Offo. A.G.G., dated 20 August 1860, F. & P., Cons. no. 542-45, part-A, September 1860.
76. NAI: R.R., List no. 1, file no. 3/1844, Vol. I.
77. Ibid.
78. Ibid.
79. NAI: From Major Lawrence, A.G.G. to Secy. G.O.I., dated 26 August 1862, F.&P. Cons. no. 30-31, Gen. A, dt. September 1862.
80. NAI: *Khureeta* from *Mehkama Khas*, Udaipur. R.R., List no. 1, Mewar Residency, Mewar, File no. 3/1844, Vol. I, dt. March 11, 1879.
81. NAI: From Maharana Sajjan Singh to Even Sumitt, Offg. Resident, Mewar, dt. 29 October, 1882, R.R., List no. 1, Mewar Residency, Mewar, File no. 3/1844, Vol. I.
82. NAI: Purport in English of a *Khureeta* from Maharawal Bahadur Singh of Banswara, Encl. no. 4 in no. 36 of 1844, F. & P., Cons. no. 43 date 2 March 1844.
83. NAI: Purport in English of a *Khureeta* from Maharawal Samut Singh of Pratapgarh to the address of Lt. Col. Robinson, dt. Poos Sud 8th, Samvat 1990 or 29 December, 1843. Encl. no. 3 in no. 36 of 1844; F. & P. Cons. no. 42, date 2 March 1844.
84. NAI: Purport in English of a *Khureeta* from Kunwar Dulpat Singh, Regent of Dungarpur, Encl. no. 5 in no. 36 of 1844, F. & P., Cons. no. 44, dt. 2 March 1844.
85. NAI: F. & P., Cons. no. 151-160, dt. 30 Nov. 1844.
    And also, NAI: Gov. Gen. to *Raj-Rana* Madho Singh, 23 January 1834, F. & P., Cons. no. 22, dt. 23 January, 1834.
86. NAI: Trans. of a *Khureeta* from *Raj Rana* Madan Singh to W. Bentinck, Gov. Gen. dt. 9 April, 1834, F. & P. Cons. no. 21, dt. 1 May, 1834.
87. NAI: F. & P. Cons. no. 151-160, dt. 30 December, 1844.

88. RSAB: Jhalawar Records, Basta no. 2, file No. 145.
89. NAI: From First A.G.G. to the Resident Rajputana States, April 20, 1887. Abu Residency, R.R., List no. 1, 1887-97, File no. E/9/11.
90. NAI: Pol. Ag. Harauti & Kota to Pol. Ag. Mewar. R.R., List no. 1, File no. 3/1844, Vol. I.
91. RSAJ.: *Report on the Political Administration of the Rajputana States (for 1873-1880)*. Selections from the Records of the Government of India, Foreign Deptt., No. CLI.
92. RSAJ: *Report on the Administration of Ajmer and Mhairwara Districts (for 1873-1880)*. Selections from the records of the Govt. of India, Foreign Department, No. CLXIV.
93. "No cases of *Sati* or infanticide have been reported in Meywar during the year 1891-92."
    RSAJ: Mewar Administration Report for 1891-92, p. 37.
94. "There were no cases of infanticide in Pratapgarh and Banswara."
    RSAJ: Report on Pratapgarh, Banswara and Kushalgarh, p. 48.
95. RSAJ: Jaipur Admn. Report for 1891-92, p. 57.
96. RSAJ: Report on the Eastern Rajputana States, 1891-92, p. 69.
97. RSAJ: Harauti and Tonk Admn. Report.
98. RSAJ: Bikaner Admn. Report, p. 108.
99. "A case of infanticide is reported from Kotah..."
    RSAJ: *Report on the Political Admn. of the Rajputana States for 1891-92*, Calcutta, 1892; Selections from the Records of the G.O.I., Foreign Deptt. Serial no. 49, p. 11.
100. NAI: R.A.R., 1883-84, p. 10.
101. RSAJ: General, Social & Legislation, Basta no. 1 F. no. 156.
102. Ibid.
103. Ibid.
104. RSAJ: *Sociology* No. 43, Bharatpur Social Reforms Act of 1926, and also, RSAB., 43, *Sociology*, No. 24.
105. RSAJ.: General, Social & Religious.
106. Sarda, H.B., *Dayanand Commemoration Volume* (ed.), p. 260.
107. RSAB: Law File No. 22 & 31, *Bikaner State Hindu Marriage Act*, Act no. 4 of 1928.
108. (a) *Arya Martand*, Sept. 18, 1928.
     (b) *The Young Rajasthan*, Aug. 1, 1929.
109. RSAB: *Mehkama Khas*, Jodhpur Records, Social Legislation, File No. C/511.

110. Ibid.
111. Ibid.
112. RSAB; Jhalawar Records, Basta No. 28A, File No. 92.
113. NAI: R.R.R., Pol. Br., File No. 553-P/37, 1934, p. 14.
114. RSAB: *Sociology*, No. 43, 918, 1935.
115. RSAB: *Sociology, No. 43, No. 198*, 1937.
116. RSAB: *Shahpura State Bal Vivah Act* of 1939.
    And also, NAI: R.R.R., Jaipur Agency, Legislative, F. No. 246, 1940.
117. NAI: R.R.R., Jaipur Agency, Legislative, F. No. 246, 1940.
118. RSAB., File No. 1006, Law, *Samajik Sudhar Act, Karauli*, 1940.
119. Ibid., p. 7.
120. *Sajjan Kirti Sudhakar* (Mewar Gazette), dt. 30-01-1941, pp. 576-578.
121. *The Jaipur Gazette*, Vol. LXIV, pp. 5-11, dated March 5, 1946.

7

Female Infanticide in Recent Times

Female infanticide, as we have seen in the earlier chapters, was a practice, which was prevalent in different parts of the world at different periods of history. In the recent times, it has taken the shape of female foeticide, i.e., killing the baby inside the womb, more popularly known as abortion. Because of the advancement in the scientific arena, because of sophisticated machines and expertise, it has become easier for the parents, to get rid of their "unwanted child".

Though there have been gender bias and deep rooted prejudice against the girl child and woman down the centuries, what is still more disturbing is that how the discrimination begins in the womb itself. The latest advances in modern medical sciences have only helped in reviving with vengeance the evil practice of killing a girl child and have quickened the pace of the death of a girl child from the born to the unborn stage.

Various techniques of sex determination and sex preselection have been discovered in the last three decades of the 20th century. Techniques such as sonography, foetoscopy, needling, chorion biopsy and the most popular one, amniocentesis, are being used in India and other countries, to detect the sex of the unborn child and, to kill it if is a female.

Amniocentesis, a scientific technique that was supposed to be used mainly to detect genetic deformities, has become very popular in India for detection of the sex of a foetus. For this, 15-20 ml. of amniotic fluid is taken from the womb by pricking the foetus membrane with the help of a special kind of needle. After separating foetus cell from the amniotic fluid, a chromosomal analysis is conducted on it. This test helps in detecting several genetic disorders like mongolism, defects of nevotube in the foetus, retarded muscular growth, Rh incompatibility, haemophilia and other types of abnormalities. This test is to be conducted on women above 40 years because there are higher chances of mongoloid children produced by such women.

In some cases, a sex determination test is required to identify sex-specific deformities such as hemophilia, retarded muscular growth which mainly affect males. This chromosomal analysis also tells the sex of the child. If used as a diagnostic test to prevent giving birth to affected children, amniocentesis is justifiable. However, today it is almost exclusively being used for sex determination and subsequently for female foeticide. This test can give 95-97 per cent accurate results. The test is conducted after completion of 16 weeks of pregnancy and within a week the findings are available. In Bombay (now Mumbai) where this test is conducted on thousands of women, it was noted that the test had affected the foetus adversely in one per cent of the total number of cases. Thus, this test may lead to spontaneous abortions or premature delivery, dislocation of hips, respiratory complications and needle puncture marks on the baby.

In our country, the facility of amniocentesis is available only in the cities and towns, hence patients from villages and small towns get the results by post; that takes one more week. By the time they decide to abort the foetus, it is over 18 weeks of pregnancy. Abortion at such a later stage is quite harmful for the mother.

Chronic Villous Biopsy (CVB) which can be done after the 7th week and before the 11th week is not freely available and also carries the same risks ranging from haemorrhage, maternal and foetal damage and even death as does amniocentesis.

What is Abortion?

Abortion is the termination of pregnancy before birth, resulting in, or accompanied by the death of the foetus. Some abortions occur naturally because a foetus does not develop normally or because the mother has an injury or disorder that prevents her from carrying the pregnancy to term. This type of spontaneous abortion is commonly known as a miscarriage. Other abortions are induced that is, intentionally brought on because a pregnancy is unwanted or presents a risk to a woman's health.

Abortions all, do the same thing, i.e., they kill an innocent unborn child, but there are various methods of doing this. Abortions are of three general types:[1]

(a) Abortion from below.
(b) Abortion from above.
(c) Using drugs to kill the unborn child.

Some of the examples of the above mentioned general types, done according to the term of pregnancy, are discussed below:

First Trimester

Suction Aspiration or Vacuum Aspiration

This method also known as 'vacuum curettage' – is used in 90 per cent of all abortions performed during the first trimester. In this method, the cervix (i.e., the neck of the womb) is stretched open to allow the surgeons to insert a plastic tube, often with a sharp cutting edge, into the womb. This powerful tube is connected to a strong suction apparatus. The powerful vacuum dismembers the tiny baby and placenta, tearing them to pieces and sucking them into a collection bottle. The surgeon uses the suction tube to evacuate the placenta from the womb. Although the baby is extremely small, body parts are often easily identified and the abortionist will typically do so to ensure all contents of the uterus have been removed.

Vacuum aspiration method is called as "safe, early abortion" by the abortion promoters, and is done up to 12 weeks of pregnancy, and it is used for around half of abortions performed between 13 and 19 weeks. When used at 13-19 weeks, it is often necessary to use other instruments to remove or crush parts of the baby that are too large to pass through the tube.

Abortion by Dilation and Curettage (D&S)

These abortions are usually done before 12 weeks. In this method, the cervix, i.e., the neck of the womb is dilated to permit the insertion of a loop shaped knife, called a curette, to cut the baby into pieces and scrape him or her from the uterine wall. The mother's cervix has to be stretched open prior to the abortion and the body parts are pulled out piece by piece through the cervix. The scraping of the uterus typically involves more bleeding than from a suction abortion and increases the risk of uterine perforation and infection. This can cause damage leading to death or premature delivery of a baby in a subsequent pregnancy.

RU 486

This abortion regimen actually involves the use of two synthetic hormones: the French developed "abortion pill" called mifepristone and a labour inducing drug or prostaglandin, usually the generically named misoprostol. Used between the 5th and 9th weeks of pregnancy, this procedure requires at least two visits to the clinic or hospital. On the first visit, women are given a physical exam to rule out contra-indications – smoking, obesity, high blood pressure, diabetes, anaemia, allergies, epilepsy, asthma or age restrictions (under 18 or over 35) – which could make the drugs deadly. The RU 486 drug (mifepristone) is taken to inhibit the production of progesterone, the hormone which prepares the nutrient rich lining of the uterus. As a result the tiny developing baby literally starves to death as the womb's lining sloughs off. At the second visit women are given misoprostol to induce contractions and cause the dead baby to be expelled from the uterus. While most women abort during the waiting period at the clinic, many abort later – up to 5 days later. A third visit includes an exam to determine whether the abortion is complete or a surgical abortion will be necessary to complete the procedure. RU486 can cause severe disabilities in babies who survive the abortion, can injure and possibly kill women and could harm a woman's subsequent offspring. Preliminary findings in clinical trials and other studies reveal serious under-reporting of the abortion techniques adverse side-effects.

Methotrexate and Misoprostol

Researchers have discovered that the prescription drug methotrexate (often prescribed to combat cancer), when used with misoprostol, can induce abortion during the first trimester. Both drugs act on a woman's reproductive system: methotrexate kills the rapidly growing cells of the trophoblast, the tissue which develops into the placenta, and misoprostol causes uterine contractions to expel the baby. This regimen also involves multiple clinic or hospital visits. After receiving an injection of methotrexate the woman returns 3 to 7 days later to receive the misoprostol vaginally. She returns home where cramping and bleeding begin. The baby is usually aborted within 24 hours.

It is worth noting that methotrexate is a highly toxic drug with side-effects and complications such as nausea, pain, diarrhea, bone marrow depression, anaemia, liver damage and lung disease occurring even at low doses.

Dilation and Evacuation (D&E)

Similar to a D&C abortion, this method also necessitates the forced dilation of the cervix. Metal forceps with a sharp cutting edge are used to grasp and pull the baby from the womb. The entire body is removed piece by piece. Because the baby's skull has typically hardened to bone by this time, it must sometimes be compressed or crushed in order to be removed from the uterus. As a result, women undergoing this procedure have a higher risk of cervical laceration. Ironically, even some abortionists find this procedure distasteful, as the process of using forceps to twist and tear the baby's body from the womb is undeniably traumatic.

Saline Injection or Salt Poisoning or (candy apple babies)

A saline or salt poisoning-abortion procedure may be used after sixteen weeks when enough fluid has accumulated in the amniotic sac surrounding the baby. A long needle is inserted through the mother's abdomen to remove and then replace some of the amniotic fluid with a solution of concentrated salt. The baby breathes in and swallows the solution and usually dies in one to two hours – though sometimes death takes many hours – from salt poisoning, dehydration, convulsions, haemorrhages of the brain and literally burned inside and out by the strong salt solution. The corrosive effect of the salt solution often burns and strips away the outer layer of the baby's skin. This exposes the raw, red glazed looking subcutaneous layer of tissue. The baby's head sometimes looks a candy apple and therefore this method is known as candy apple abortion. This technique was originally developed in the concentration camps in Nazi Germany, to traumatize war-victims.

The baby's thrashing, caused by the trauma of the saline, can be physically painful to his or her mother and is often psychologically devastating to her. The mother goes into labour and a dead baby is usually delivered within 24 to 48 hours.

Prostaglandin

This drug causes a woman to go into labour at any stage of pregnancy. It is generally used in middle to late pregnancy to induce abortion. The potent, hormone-like drug is injected into the amniotic sac to produce labour and premature birth. In some cases the unborn baby is born alive and placed aside to die. In order to avoid, what some abortionists call "the dreaded complication of a live birth", it is now customary to kill the child first before "evacuating" him or her from the womb. Using ultrasound, the abortionist directs a needle containing an injection of lethal potassium chloride into the unborn baby's heart. Other abortionists use an injection of dioxin to cause fetal cardiac arrest. Sometimes salt is injected to kill the baby before birth and make the procedure less stressful for the mother. Prostaglandins are accompanied by serious problems of their own, including potentially lethal side-effects.

Dilation and Extraction (D&X or Partial Birth)

Publicly unveiled in 1992, this method is used to kill babies from 20 weeks through full term. Because the baby is considerably larger and better developed at this time, the opening of the woman's cervix must be greatly enlarged in order to perform this abortion. The entire process requires three days. On the first and second visits the woman receives laminaria, cylindrically shaped or tapered devices which are inserted into the cervix and gradually increase in diameter as they absorb water. When the cervix has been sufficiently dilated, the abortion is performed. The abortionist ruptures the amniotic sac and drains the fluid. Using ultra-sound, the abortionist ascertains the baby's position within the uterus. Forceps are used to turn the baby so that he or she is oriented feet first (breech position) and face down. The abortionist then grasps one of the baby's legs and pulls the entire body, with the exception of the head, outside of the uterus. Because the head is usually too large to deliver, the abortionist uses a sharp pair of surgical scissors to stab the base of the living baby's skull, spreading the scissors to enlarge the hole. The scissors are removed and a suction tube is inserted into the skull opening to "evacuate" the brain. This kills the baby and collapses the head, allowing the abortionist to fully deliver the child. It is worth noting that most babies at this stage of development weigh at least a pound, measure approximately 8 inches in length and are fully formed, with feet roughly 1 inch to 1½ inches in length. Babies born at this point in pregnancy (19 or 20 weeks) have survived.

It appears from the report of Pankaj Pachauri, published in *India Today*, October 31, 1988 that the killing of girl babies is still a widespread phenomenon in some parts of Rajasthan. Among the Bhati community, the result of this practice is as dramatic as it is tragic. The sex-ratio in the area which stands as 750 women to every 1000 men, is loaded against women. While the figure for the country was 938, for Rajasthan it was 919 and for Jaisalmer district, which is pre-dominantly populated by the Bhatis, it was a much lower 811. But among Bhatis, it was perhaps the lowest in the world at approximately 550. According to the report, the practice of female infanticide was widespread in the villages of Deora, Baiya, Jhinjhiali, Maudha, Raudha, and Kundu.

Child Sex-Ratio according to the Census of India, 2001

Rajasthan

Child population in the age group 0-6 years constitutes an important segment of the population structure of the society. It not only helps to compute the effective literacy rate but also acts as a trend setter for the future growth of population. One of the significant findings of Census 2001 is the declining child sex-ratio. The child sex-ratio is defined as the number of girls per thousand boys in the age group of 0-6 years. The child sex-ratio in the State of Rajasthan has been recorded as 909 as against 916 in the 1991 census. None of the districts of Rajasthan has recorded child sex-ratio favouring girls. There are 10 districts having child sex-ratio less than 900. The highest child sex-ratio of 972 in Banswara and the lowest, 852 has been recorded in Ganganagar district. Karauli and Sikar are the only districts where child sex-ratio in urban areas is higher as compared to that of rural areas.

At the State level there is a decline of 7 points in child sex-ratio during the decade 1991-2001. The trend is so widespread that out of 32 districts, in 21 districts one can observe the decline. The districts that have shown large declines are Ganganagar (-42), Jhunjhunun (-33), Jaipur (-28), Alwar (-26), Chittaurgarh (-24), Hanumangarh (-24), Sikar (-22), Dausa (-19), Dholpur (-16), Jhalawar (-15), Udaipur (-14), Kota (-12), Baran (-12) and Dungarpur (-11). The tehsil data shows that out of 241 tehsils spread over 32 districts, 74 tehsils have child sex-ratio less than 900. Maximum number of 139 tehsils come within the range of 900-949 and 28 tehsils have child sex-ratio more than 950. There are 4 districts namely Dholpur, Ganganagar, Jaisalmer and Sikar where all tehsils have child sex-ratio less than 900. Kotra tehsil of Udaipur district is the only tehsil having a favourable child sex-ratio, i.e., 1001 girls per 1000 boys. (See Appendix VII)

This imbalance in the child sex-ratio is because of the prevalence of the obnoxious practice of female foeticide in the State of Rajasthan. This paucity of females leads the society to other social situations such as forceful abductions of girl child as well as grown-up females, prostitution, lack of brides in the near future for the marriageable boys, etc.

Child sex-ratio at the national level

The sex-ratio at the national level comes to 933. The national average in terms of the sex-ratio may be one yardstick, but one can realize that the sex-ratio of 933 at the national level in itself is on the lower side by the world standards. Only Kerala and Pondicherry are the two States/Union territories where the sex-ratio is over one thousand. However there are 16 more States/Union territories that have a higher sex-ratio than the national average. Some of the major States with a sex-ratio lower than the national average are Maharashtra (922), Rajasthan (909), Gujarat (920), Bihar (919), Madhya Pradesh (919), Uttar Pradesh (898), Jammu and Kashmir (892), Punjab (876), Haryana (861), and Delhi (821).

Rural sex-ratio

The rural sex-ratio for India stands at 946, which is a better picture as compared to sex-ratio for total or urban population. An observation of the data would reveal that only seven States/Union territories have shown a lower sex-ratio in rural areas as compared to total areas. These are Pondicherry (990), Meghalaya (969), Manipur (967), Tripura (946), Delhi (810), Chandigarh (621), and Daman and Diu (586). It also shows that the male-female imbalances are much less in rural areas as compared to urban areas if these are not on account of sex-selective migration. Kerala is the only State where the total, rural and urban sex-ratios are almost similar.

Urban sex-ratio

India's urban sex-ratio stands at 900, obviously much below the national average. However, there are twelve States/Union territories that show a higher sex-ratio in urban areas as compared to the national average. Three out of these, Kerala (1058), Manipur (1009) and Pondicherry (1007), have an urban sex-ratio of over 1000. Ten States/Union territories, have a sex-ratio between 900-1000. But the gap between Chhatisgarh (932, lowest in the specified range) and Madhya Pradesh (898, highest in the sex-ratio range of 800-900) is too wide. It may be mentioned that there are 19 States/Union territories which fall in this range. There are three States/Union territories, viz., Chandigarh (796), Himachal Pradesh (795) and Dadra and Nagar Haveli (691) with an urban sex-ratio of less than 800. It is generally agreed that there is a sex-selective migration to urban areas and therefore its influence needs to be studied and quantified before jumping to conclusions regarding the imbalance of the two sexes.

Sex-ratio amongst scheduled castes

The sex-ratio of scheduled castes (936) at the national level, is slightly better than the national average (933). Kerala, Pondicherry and Manipur with a sex-ratio of 1048, 1019, 1005 respectively have the highest scheduled castes sex-ratio in the country. There are 15 States/Union territories that have a higher sex-ratio than the national average. The scheduled castes sex-ratio in Arunachal Pradesh and Mizoram is as low as 724 and 283 respectively. However, their population is very small in these two States. Lakshadweep, Nagaland and Andaman and Nicobar islands do not have any scheduled caste population.

Sex-ratio amongst scheduled tribes

The sex-ratio among scheduled tribes (978) is much better as compared to other groups in consideration. It is reasonably high in relation to the national average (933). There are seven states/union territories, i.e., Dadra and Nagar Haveli (1028), Kerala (1021), Chhatisgarh (1013), Lakshadweep (1003), Arunachal Pradesh (1003), Orissa (1003) and Meghalaya (1000) that have the sex-ratio of 1000 or over. Further, there are 20 States/Union territories that have a sex-ratio higher than the national average. Only three States, viz., Bihar (929), Jammu and Kashmir (910) and Goa (893) are below the national average. Five States/Union territories Pondicherry, Punjab, Haryana, Delhi and Chandigarh do not have any scheduled tribe population.

Sex-ratio: religion-wise

(a) *Hindus*: The sex-ratio for Hindus at All-India level stands at 931, which is marginally lower than the national average (933). There are eleven States with a sex-ratio more than the national average. These states in descending order of the sex-ratio are Kerala (1058), Chhatisgarh (990), Pondicherry (987), Tamil Nadu (983), Andhra Pradesh (979), Uttaranchal (978), Manipur (974), Himachal Pradesh (973), Orissa (971), Karnataka (966), and Tripura (949). The major States of Uttar Pradesh, Haryana, Jammu and Kashmir and Delhi have recorded a Hindu sex-ratio below 900 but more than 800. The lowest sex-ratios for Hindus have been recorded in Lakshadweep (251), Mizoram (341), Nagaland (582), Daman and Diu (698), Arunachal Pradesh (749), and Chandigarh (756). Considering all religions, the Hindu sex-ratio is highest (rank one) in two States – Himachal Pradesh and Uttaranchal, whereas it ranks 4th and 5th in nine States each. In no State or Union territory, Hindus occupy the sixth spot (the last rank among the major religion).

(b) *Muslims*: The Muslim sex-ratio at the country level stands at 936, which is marginally higher than the sex-ratio for India (933). There are fourteen States that have a sex-ratio better than the national average and in descending order these are Pondicherry (1097), Kerala (1082), Tamil Nadu (1020), Lakshadweep (1002), Manipur (973), Andhra Pradesh (961), Karnataka (957), Orissa (948), Tripura (945), Bihar (943), Chhatisgarh (943), Jharkhand (939), Assam (938), and Gujarat (937). Incidentally in West Bengal (933) sex-ratio for Muslims is the same as the national average. The major States of Maharashtra, Haryana, Punjab, and Delhi have recorded a Muslim sex-ratio below 900 but more than 800. The lowest sex-ratio is recorded in Sikkim (439) and Mizoram (271) respectively. In Kerala and Lakshadweep, the Muslim sex-ratio is the highest amongst all the six religious groups. In Himachal Pradesh, Punjab, Chandigarh, Delhi and Mizoram it is the lowest among the six religious communities.

(c) *Buddhists*: The sex-ratio for Buddhists in the country as a whole comes out as 953 which is higher than that of the national sex-ratio (933). In Chhatisgarh sex-ratio (1012) amongst Buddhists is over one thousand. Other States with a sex-ratio above national average are West Bengal (981), Arunachal

Pradesh (970), Maharashtra (961), Andhra Pradesh (960), Tripura (956), Madhya Pradesh (949), Sikkim (944), Himachal Pradesh (942), Jammu and Kashmir (941) and Assam (939). There are 13 States where Buddhists sex-ratio falls between 800 to 900. The States/Union territories with less than 800 sex-ratio are Haryana, Nagaland, Pondicherry, Uttaranchal, Dadra and Nagar Haveli, Daman and Diu and Andaman and Nicobar Islands. Lakshadweep has only one female follower of Buddhism. Considering major religions, Buddhists sex-ratio has the highest position (rank one) in Jammu and Kashmir and Tripura. The lowest sex-ratio (sixth rank) among major religious communities recorded by Buddhists is in the States/Union territories of Uttaranchal, Haryana, Rajasthan, Bihar, Sikkim, Daman and Diu and Andaman and Nicobar Islands.

(d) *Jains*: The sex-ratio for the Jains at the country-level stands at 940, which is higher than the sex-ratio for India (933). Their highest sex-ratio (1000) has been recorded in Daman and Diu. Other States with a higher sex-ratio than the national average are Kerala (996), Gujarat (969), Rajasthan (960), Maharashtra (942), Chandigarh (940), Andhra Pradesh (936) and Delhi (935). The Jain sex-ratio in Tamil Nadu and Orissa is the same as the national average. The States with Jain sex-ratio of less than 900 are Dadra and Nagar Haveli, Goa, Himachal Pradesh, Assam, Jammu and Kashmir, Nagaland, Manipur, Mizoram, Sikkim and Arunachal Pradesh. There are no members of Jain community in Lakshadweep. Among major religious communities, there are four States (Punjab, Chandigarh, Daman and Diu and Andaman and Nicobar Islands) where Jains have highest sex-ratio (rank one). They rank lowest (sixth) among major religious communities in Manipur, Tripura, Assam, West Bengal, Chhatisgarh and Andhra Pradesh.

(e) *Christians*: The sex-ratio for the Christians in the country as a whole is 1009, which is quite high as compared to the national average (933) and compares well with the world scenario. There are 27 States in which sex-ratio amongst Christians is higher than the national average. Of these, as many as thirteen States have a sex-ratio of over one thousand – namely Goa, Pondicherry, Delhi, Andhra Pradesh, Kerala, Tamil Nadu, Karnataka, Orissa, Chhatisgarh, Jharkhand, Meghalaya, Arunachal Pradesh and West Bengal. Chandigarh union territory (932) is closest to the national sex-ratio. Sex-ratios lower than 900 among Christians, have been recorded in Punjab (893), Himachal Pradesh (822), Jammu and Kashmir (594) and Lakshadweep (206). There are 25 States where the Christian sex-ratio is ranked first and only one state each where its rank is 5th (Himachal Pradesh) and 6th respectively (Jammu and Kashmir) among all religions.

(f) *Sikhs*: The sex-ratio of Sikhs at India level stands at 893 which is pretty low as compared to the national average (933) and shows a great imbalance between the two sexes, which is a cause of great concern. Delhi has the highest sex-ratio (925) for Sikhs in all the States/Union territories followed by Chandigarh (910). Rest of the States/Union territories have a sex-ratio of less than 800. Among these states/union territories sixteen are between 800-900, five between 700-800, two between 600-700, three between 500-600 and six below 500. Lakshadweep has a negligible population of Sikhs. Amongst the major religious communities, Sikhs do not hold first rank in any of the States. They hold second rank in Punjab only, but here also this sex-ratio is low at 897. There are as many as 21 States where the sex-ratio stands at 6th rank among the major religious communities.

Factors Responsible for Female Foeticide

The first important factor responsible for female foeticide is the increasing dowry demand in daughter's marriage. The parents of a girl child are always reminded (or haunted) of the marriage of the girl child and of the expenditure, which is to be incurred on her marriage. On account of high dowry demands, dowry deaths and harassment to girl, and dominating role of bridegroom's family in marriage negotiations, daughter's marriage is still considered as a big problem for the family, in spite of the high education, beauty or employment of the girl. Further, the daughter's parents do not receive that respect and care in the society, as they get as parents of son or sons. In the eyes of the society, to have a son is a symbol of status. This mentality of the society is reflected in regional sayings like *beta mare kambakht ka; beti mare bhagyawan ki*, and *kun jage beti ro baap*.

The second factor is the prevalent unhealthy social and family environment and the resultant social pressure, which affects women's thinking against women's dignity. It forces them to think that they are inferior beings, as compared to their brothers and thus anathematize their lives. Right from their births, this difference in the mentality and behaviour of the parents and that of the society becomes discriminating and constant as the brothers and sisters receive different treatment for different works. While boys are taken due care of, are considered as apple of the eye or cynosure, or *khandaan ka chirag*, this is not the case with the girls.

The third important factor responsible for female foeticide is the woman's biological structure and a feeling of insecurity for daughters. The responsibilities and the anxieties of parents, especially those of mother, are doubled as they grow up. Due to her biological structure, she can be exploited by undesirable elements of the society even at a very tender age. The fear of a scandal or of the blot on family's name, if something goes wrong with her, is a fear which haunts the Indian families even today.

The fourth important reason is the belief or the faith in Hindu tradition, that a son is essential for the salvation (i.e., *moksha*), for parents care, for continuity of family lineage and for the inheritance of property; while, the daughters are considered as *paraya-dhan* (or the wealth of others). A strong desire for sons is certainly associated with a religious faith to get salvation, if son lights the funeral pyre of his parents. These are some of the important factors, which force the parents to opt for female foeticide. Despite the growth in literacy rates, and despite the efforts of the government and that of the NGOs (non-governmental organizations) and enlightened individuals (including religious saints and preachers), this tendency of eliminating female foetus is increasing, which is really shocking and disturbing. In future, more sincere and serious efforts are needed to put an end to this horrible practice.

Note

1. Data collected from various websites from internet, regarding abortion and methods of abortion.

8

Conclusion

The custom of child marriage and female infanticide has greatly undermined the status of women in India making her position subservient to that of males. While child marriage determines the personal and social space of a girl child and imposes many new negations, restrictions and limitations upon her body and personality, female infanticide aims at systematic eliminating of the female species. While one denies her right to enjoy her childhood and creates obstacles in her education, and income generating skills; the other denies her fundamental right to live.

The heinous practice of female infanticide was prevalent in India and in the erstwhile States of the Rajputana, in certain clans of the Rajputs like the Rathores of Marwar, the Bidawats of Bikaner, the Tanwars of Torawati, the Kachwahas of Jaipur, the Bhatis of Jaisalmer, the Solanki and the Hara Rajputs of Bundi, the "low and the high Rajput classes" of Sirohi, the Rajputs of Jhalawar, and it was also prevalent to a considerable extent in the Shekhawati region. Among the lesser noteworthy families, it prevailed in the house of Asop, Kuchamun and Neemuch. Apart from the Rajputs, this practice prevailed amongst the Charans and the Bhats, the Meenas, the Ahirs and Jats of Bharatpur and the Mers of Ajmer-Merwara. Thus, it was more widely practiced than is usually believed by the scholars and writers of the Rajputana history. It is significant to note that no evidence of this crime has been found in the Brahmans, Mahajans and other classes (except those mentioned above).

It arose out of the social customs, institutions and the prevalent notions of the inferiority or superiority of a particular caste, clan or tribe and to preserve its cohesive character. The endogamous, the exogamous, the hypergamous and isogamous rules related with marriage, the feeling of pride, prejudice, poverty, superstition amongst certain sections, the prevalent system of giving heavy amounts in tika and dowry, the desire to imitate the higher classes as well as the political instability led to the prevalence of the evil practice in the society of the Rajputana.

Although it is difficult to trace the exact period of the emergence of the abominable practice of female infanticide, it became firmly rooted in the medieval period. Infanticide used to be committed in a very secret manner behind the impregnable walls of the palaces and homes and was believed to be affair of the women alone and was not considered a business of men. The female attendants, or *dais,* who were with the expecting lady at the time of delivery, used to convey the news of the new arrival to the male members, and waited for their instructions, if it was a girl. A total silence on the part of the father or father-in-law was considered to imply that the child, if a daughter should be put to death. The mother of the child was accordingly informed to act in conformity with the wishes of her in-laws. While at times, this crime was perpetrated even without letting her know the ill-fate of the newly born. If the husband wished to preserve a daughter, his order was carried out, without any challenges, but if the mother entertained a similar desire, while the husband expressed any opposite view, death was inevitable for the girl child.

Various methods were in use, to do away with the unwanted girl child. Burying alive in sand dunes, or throwing them in dry wells, or trampling them under the leg of the cot, or denying them all sustenance from their birth, or stifling them by filling their mouth with ashes, or giving them a pill of *bhang* or the use of *amal* (opium), or the use of poisonous juice of *ack* or *aakra,* or drowning them in a vessel full of milk were some of the methods used by the people in the past. Seeing the magnitude of this crime and the cruelty done to do away with her, many enlightened rulers, like Akbar, the Great and also those of the Rajputana, took initiative and devised strategies to put an end to this crime. Emperor Akbar, issued orders in

990 A.H. (Hizri), to prevent infanticide as well as to stop child marriages, polygamy and the practice of sati. He was also in favour of widow marriages, though this was against the wishes of most of his subjects. Similarly, Maharaja Sawai Jai Singh of Jaipur issued a proclamation in 1731 A.D., in which he asked the Sardars and nobles of his court, not to kill their infant daughters and requested other rulers also to take appropriate steps in this regard. He also limited the marriage expenditure to 1/8th of the annual income and to save the marriage parties from the extortionous demands of the Charans and the Bhats, asked them to come to Jaipur and celebrate their ceremony in the capital. Likewise, Maharaja Bukht Singh (in 1753) and Maharaja Bijai Singh (in 1763) of Jodhpur issued similar orders against female infanticide, to curb this heinous practice in their State. This is in contrast to the prevalent notion of historical writings, which brand the native rulers as insensitive and insouciant towards the administration, always indulging in war, wine and women. These examples also reveal that they undertook the reform activities on their own without any outside or external pressure. It is difficult to ascertain, in the absence of relevant records, how far their efforts produced desired effects and how many lives were saved thereby.

It appears that the effect of these proclamations and Acts did not prove lasting or it was limited to the capital and nearby areas, and the practice of female infanticide continued unabated. Seeing this contemptuous crime, some of the English officers intervened, and they took upon themselves the correction of what was then wrong, alongwith the native rulers. British paramountcy felt no great difficulty in impressing upon the rulers, the Charans and the Bhats and the people to refrain from this practice. The offenders were punished with imprisonment or confiscation of property and the demands of the Charans and the Bhats were also limited by them and their movements were restricted to the States, to which they belonged. Because of the harsh measures adopted by the English officers and because of the support given to them by the native rulers, gradually, the incidents of female infanticide started declining. But unfortunately, this practice could not be rooted out completely, as some incidents of female infanticide still come to light, even in the 21st century.

In the last quarter of the 20th century, with the change in time and with new scientific inventions and discoveries, the practice of female infanticide again appeared in the garb of the practice of female foeticide, i.e., killing the baby in the womb itself. Those machines, which were invented to determine any deformity in the baby within the womb, were used for sex pre-selective test and this started a process of systematic clearing of the female infants. Consequently, the male-female ratio further declined and new social problems emerged because of this situation. Though the Government of India has banned sex pre-selection tests, yet these are in vogue in certain areas, though they are done clandestinely, with the help of greedy doctors.

Whereas ancient texts did not play any role in the commission of female infanticide, it did play a major role in advocating child marriages in India, as well as in Rajasthan. Child marriages or infant marriages were unknown in the days of the Vedas and the women of the Vedic society had ample opportunities to get education and learn other fine arts and martial arts like their brothers did. The women at that age, used to be well-educated, well-cultivated and as such took active part in socio-political and religious affairs of the society. The presence of *brahma vadinis* and *sadyo-vadhoos* in the Aryan society, speak volumes about the quality of education imparted to women.

There were many reasons for this trend in society. First, the parents of the girls were always keen to avail of the earliest opportunity to get a suitable bridegroom in a caste-ridden society, where the field of selection had become confined to a few sub-castes. Second, by marrying their daughters at a young age, the parents freed themselves from the worry about their daughter's future. In case, the father died and the mother became a sati, the girl had her husband and his family to look after her, if she was married. Third, as a result of the satisfactory economic condition in the society and the prevalence of the joint family system, people did not feel the necessity of postponing the marriage, till the boy became an earning member. Apart from these causes, the prevalence of infant and child marriages can be attributed to some other factors. The old belief of the Hindus to marry off their children within their life time, and the desire to get free from this worldly duty as soon as possible, the desire to protect girl's virginity from the foreign invaders, the financial, social and familial convenience of marrying two or three or more children at the same time or at the same mandap, the dread of famines or the hope of a good harvest, the emotional black mailing or the desire of grandparents to see their grandchildren married within their life time, were some of the important factors which motivated the people to opt for child marriages.

If we take into consideration the Census reports of 1901, regarding the Rajputana and Ajmer-Merwara region, we find that the marriage of children under ten years of age was widely prevalent in Marwar, Sirohi, Jaipur, Kishangarh, Bikaner, Jhalawar, Tonk and also in the British administered territory of Ajmer-Merwara. Similarly, the Census of 1911 also reveals that the marriage of children under 10, among both sexes was more common in the Western Rajputana than in any of the other Divisions, and the Hindus of the Western Division showed much more inclination towards it than in any other Division. It is noteworthy that this practice was not common in both sexes in the Southern Division, which was greatly due to the very large proportion of Animists and Jains in the population, among whom, as religions, the average age of marriage was much higher than among the Hindus or the Muslims.

According to the Census of 1911, the highest proportion of married males under 5 years, was among the Gujars, the Jats and the Balais of Ajmer-Merwara and the Bhambhis and the Rebaris of Rajputana; and of females, among the Rebaris, the Bhambhis, the Kasais and the Jats in Rajputana, and the Jats, the Gujars and the Kumhars in Ajmer-Merwara. Between the 5-11 age group, the Jats, the Gujars, the Kumhars, the Balais, the Charmakars, the Nais and the Malis of Ajmer-Merwara; and the Rebaris, the Kasais and the Bhambhis of Rajputana had the highest proportion of married males; and the Jats, the Gujars, the Malis, the Kumhars and the Charmakars of Ajmer-Merwara, and the Kasais, the Rebaris, the Jats, the Gujars and the Rangrez of Rajputana, had the highest proportion of married females. Excluding the Christians, the Bhils, the Meos, the Mahajans, the Rajputs, the Kayam-Khanis and the Rawats were among those who showed the least tendency to child marriage in the Rajputana among both the sexes; and the Saiyads among females. In Ajmer-Merwara, the Mers, the Rawats, the Merat Kathats and the Mahajans had the lowest proportions of married and widowed children of either sex.

It is significant to note, that according to the Census of 1911, out of every 1000 children in the Rajputana among those under 1 year of age, there were 52 married and 2 widowed males and 135 married and 2 widowed females, and nearly all of them were among the

Hindus. While in Ajmer-Merwara, there were only 10 females and 1 male of this age returned as married, and none as widowed.

It is also noteworthy that the practice of infant marriage or pre-natal marriage was also prevalent in the Rajputana, among the Kunbis (or Kurmis) of Jhalawar, Kota and the Marwar; the Chaubes of Karauli; the Bhambhis, the Jats, the Kumhars, the Malis, the Nais, the Rebaris and very occasionally among the Brahmans and the Maheshwaris and the higher castes in Marwar; and in Ajmer-Merwara, apart from these castes it was also among the Rawats and the Mers.

The Census reports also reflect upon the number of widowed children in different age groups, in different States. According to the Census of 1911, the highest number of widowed children, in the age-group of 0-4, was in the State of Marwar, where 91 children (45 were males and 46 were females) were reported as widowed. While in the State of Mewar, 30 children (7 males and 23 females), in the same age group, were reported as widowed. Similarly, in the age-group of 5-9 years, the highest number of widowed children was in the State of Marwar where 556 children (221 were males and 335 were females) were registered as widowed. While in Jaipur 285 children (75 males and 210 females) were registered as widowed in the same age group. The same picture emerges from the Census of 1921, where Alwar, Mewar and Jaipur, had the highest number of widowed children in the age-group of 1-5 years. While Alwar had 162 children (64 were males and 98 were females), Mewar had 133 children (40 were males and 93 were females) and Jaipur had 98 widowed children (26 were males and 72 were females). It is remarkable that the number of child-widows was greater than those of child-widowers in every State. This forces us to think about the pitiable condition of child widows, as they were not allowed to remarry and were expected to lead a life of austerity and penance. Though the pain of losing a partner is often felt by both males and females, yet while the child widowers were married off again, this was not the case with the child widows. It is unfortunate that the stigma was attached to the widows as they were considered as inauspicious and were not allowed to participate in social and family functions, or to eat green vegetables or sleep on soft beds or wear colourful clothes. Thus their life became a sad tale of insults, humiliations and utter neglect, without any fault of their own.

Some social scientists believe that the State of Rajasthan has been needlessly denigrated for child marriages and the media (especially the foreign media) has flaunted this visual to project the backwardness of Rajasthan amongst the States of India. According to them, unlike in Bengal, where the child bride after marriage goes to the husband's place and the marriage is consummated; in Rajasthan child bride never goes to the husband's place after the marriage ritual. The husband has to wait for the ceremony of gauna or muklawa, only after which she is allowed to go to the husband's place. According to them, the age entered in the Census records is the age at marriage ceremony and not the age at gauna. If the age at gauna were taken into consideration, the mean age at marriage of females, will be no different than in other States and perhaps better than several States, according to them.

This seems quite convincing, as the Census reports bear testimony to the same fact. According to the *Census report of 1911,* regarding the Rajputana and Ajmer-Merwara, (p. 164), among Ahirs, the average age at which consummation took place was 15-20 for boys and from puberty to 16 among girls. Among the Bhils, the average age for consummation was 14 to 15 for girls and 18 or 20 for boys. Similarly, among the Gujars, the age of consummation was from 13 to 15 for the girls and 16-18 for boys; while among the Jats, it was 13 to 16 for girls and 16 to 20 for boys. Among the Minas, it was 12 to 14 for girls and 15 to 18 for boys. While among the Rajputs it varied from 13 to 18 for girls and 16 to 20 for boys and among the Rawats (of Ajmer-Merwara) it varied from 13 to 15 for girls and 17 to 21 for boys. But despite these figures, it cannot be denied that there would have existed certain cases, where consummation took place immediately after marriage (e.g., in the case of an unequal or ill-assorted marriage, where the bride or the girl used to be much younger than her husband).

Seeing this gross injustice and discrepancy, many enlightened persons, social organizations and caste-organizations tried to ameliorate the condition of women by waging crusade against child and un-equal marriages, polygamy, and certain other malpractices, such as chandni, dance of the bhagtans (i.e., prostitutes), dowry, tika etc., which were deteriorating the position of women of Rajputana. While the social organizations like Desh Hitaishini Sabha, Walterkrit Rajputra Hitkarini Sabha played a commendable role in the abolition of polygamy, child and unequal marriages and in limiting the dowry, tika and tyag expenses; the Arya Samaj played a major role in eradicating these social evils, through the spread of education. It was because of the special efforts of Arya Samaj, that many schools, libraries and other educational institutes were opened in the Rajputana, which provided education (and other arts and crafts) to boys and girls, apart from the general public.

The same can be said about various caste organizations or caste panchayats, as they too, worked hard for the upliftment of women and for the eradication of various social evils. Infact, they were the pioneers in the social reform process or movement in the Rajputana, as the Pareek Brahmins of Jaipur were the first, in the recorded annals of the Rajputana, who made certain rules as early as Samvat 1600 to limit the heavy expenditure, incurred at the time of marriages. This again contradicts the prevalent notion which considers caste organizations as oppressive of free and liberal thoughts. These caste organizations also opened schools and libraries for their caste-brethren and also requested the ruler of their States to ponder over various social issues and to frame rules for the abolition of social malpractices.

It is remarkable to note that while the practice of female infanticide came to a virtual end because of the efforts of native rulers and British officers, the practice of child and unequal marriage could be checked due to the efforts of these social and caste organizations, as it were they, who time and again, brought these issues to the notice of their rulers, through open letters, pamphlets, hunger strikes, *dharnas* and demonstrations.

It was because of their pressure, that the rulers of various States, had to pass Acts prohibiting child and unequal marriages, in their respective States. It is also significant, that while the States of Jaipur and Jodhpur, pioneered the crusade against female infanticide, it was not so in the case of Acts pertaining to child and unequal marriages. In fact, they were among the back-seaters, as many States of the Rajputana had already issued an Act, much before them. Similarly, the State of Bharatpur took the lead in the issuance of an Act prohibiting child marriages and legitimizing widow-remarriages, in the Rajputana.

Despite the commendable efforts of all these enlightened individuals, social organizations and caste organizations, the problem of child marriage (and also that of female infanticide and foeticide) is still prevalent in the society, even in the 21st century, and several cases of child marriages come to light on the occasions of Akha-Teej and Basant-Panchami.

Appendices

Appendix I

Number of Rajputs, Charans and Bhats in Rajputana in 1911

State	No. of Rajputs		No. of Charans		No. of Bhats	
	Male	Female	Male	Female	Male	Female
Alwar	16272	13855	136	118	88	95
Banswara	1874	1734	82	88	214	213
Bharatpur	6493	4910	-	-	434	408
Bikaner	49423	37243	2117	1762	1544	1227
Bundi	2900	2439	873	898	179	175
Dholpur	15202	11262	-	-	345	278
Dungarpur	5068	5021	93	116	321	313
Jaipur	68660	49297	2802	2645	1080	1193
Jaisalmer	19503	14605	482	408	31	11
Jhalawar	1775	1551	92	101	69	62
Karauli	3482	2610	-	-	5	9
Kishangarh	2545	2229	228	214	236	207
Kota	7921	6826	2136	2197	526	530
Kushalgarh (Chiefship)	299	345	4	4	15	12
Lawa (Estate)	46	46	-	-	-	-
Marwar	109734	85995	8311	7379	9068	8484
Mewar	58088	48795	1259	1260	2003	1905
Pratapgarh	1662	1509	42	41	268	266
Shahpura (Chiefship)	869	768	11	12	81	75
Sirohi	8009	6701	495	489	1194	1119
Tonk	5299	4427	347	332	141	109
Total	385124	302168	19510	18064	17842	16691
Ajmer	7548	5644	151	136	393	340
Merwara	677	433	17	11	150	121
Ajmer-Merwara	8225	6077	168	147	543	461

Appendix II

Total Population of Main Rajput Clans in 1911

Clans	*Persons*	*Males*	*Females*
Total Rajputs in 1911	701,594	393,349	308,245
Rathore	176,462	101,248	75,214
Chauhan	106,510	56,410	50,100
Kachwaha	96,242	61,076	35,166
Jadon	71,957	38,771	33,186
Sisodiya or Gehlot	63,964	35,424	28,540
Solanki	22,412	12,352	10,060
Tanwar	21,527	12,047	9,480
Parihar	16,367	8,702	7,665
Gaur	5,662	3,339	2,323
Jhala	4,105	2,494	1,611
Bais	546	269	277
Doubtful	27,284	13,548	13,736
Miscellaneous	33,577	18,045	15,532
Unspecified	12,668	6,552	6,116

Among the five largest clans, the greatest scarcity of females was among the Kachwahas, where there were only 576 females to 1000 males; then among the Rathores (743 females per 1000 males); then the Sisodiyas (806); the Jadons (856) and the Chauhans (888).

Appendix III

Proportion of Males and Females in Rajputs

Provinces and State or District	*Proportion of females per 1000 males in Rajputs (.)*		
	1891	*1901*	*1911*
Rajputana	762	802	785
Alwar	778	830	851
Banswara	+	1120	925
Bharatpur	721	792	756
Bikaner	737	768	753
Bundi	813	882	841
Dholpur	743	745	752
Dungarpur	887	984	990
Jaipur	667	734	718
Jaisalmer	782	815	748
Jhalawar	++	852	873
Karauli	803	741	749
Kishangarh	792	818	875
Kota	820*	844	861
Kushalgarh	+	839	1153
Lawa	1098	1102	1000
Marwar	793	835	783
Mewar	776	817	840
Pratapgarh	+	921	907
Shahpura	753	821	907
Sirohi	869	840	836
Tonk	755	814	873
Ajmer-Merwara	755	731	748
Ajmer	+	712	748
Merwara	+	981	640

(.)Excluding Parganas of Chhabra, Pirawa, and Sironj, and Rajakhera Rajputs of Dholpur, and including Raths.

+Data not available.

*Includes Jhalawar.

++Included in Kota

Contd...

Contd...

According to the Census of 1911, the lowest proportions of female Rajputs were in Jaipur (718), Jaisalmer (753), Bharatpur (756), Marwar (783), and these figures were all below the average one for the caste in the whole province. The same was the case in these States in 1901, except in Jaisalmer and Marwar. Out of these seven States, five (Karauli, Dholpur, Bharatpur, Jaisalmer & Bikaner) were the States with the lowest proportion generally of females in their actual population (excluding Rajputs). The remaining two, Jaipur and Marwar, held a much lower position relatively in the ratio of females among Rajputs than they did in that among all females.

Out of the remaining States, the proportion ranged between 800 and 900 in nine, between 900 and 1000 in three, and was over 1000 in Kushalgarh. There were however, only 644 Rajputs in this Chiefship. In Lawa Estate, where the sexes were equal, there were only 92 all told. Excluding Kushalgarh and Lawa, the proportion of females reached its highest in Dungarpur (990), where the caste numbered 10,089. Next came Banswara, where they numbered 3,608 and females were in the ratio of 925 to 1000 males; then Pratapgarh, where there were 3171 Rajputs and the proportion of females was 907. It is remarkable that all these States were in Southern Division.

Appendix IV

Number of Males and Females in Different Rajput Clans and Sub-clans (according to Census of 1911)

Clan	Sub-Clan	Population		
		Persons	Males	Females
Chauhan	Total	106510	56410	50100
	Bhadoria	865	275	590
	Chatarbhuji	147	119	28
	Chauhan	81186	42989	38197
	Devra	4866	2591	2275
	Hara	4530	2253	2277
	Khinchi	1834	874	960
	Tank	1021	939	82
	Songara	557	252	305
	Somra	79	9	70
Gaur	Total	5662	3339	2323
	Gaur	5652	3329	2323
	Kangordh	10	10	-
Jadon	Total	71957	38771	33186
(Jadu or Yadu)	Barela	91	25	66
	Bhati	58825	31643	27182
	Jadon, Jadu & Yadu	12285	6816	5469
	Tomar	413	147	266
Jhala	Total	4105	2494	1611
	Jhala	4094	2490	1604
	Makwana	11	4	7
Kachwaha	Total	96242	61076	35166
	Bakawat	715	467	248
	Bikawat	234	33	201
	Dhirawat	280	124	156
	Hamirda	998	616	382
	Jogi	83	59	24
	Kachhar	103	94	9

Contd...

Contd...

Clan	Sub-Clan	Population		
		Persons	Males	Females
	Kachwaha	62002	38331	23671
	Khangarot	1489	971	518
	Kilanot	1586	884	702
	Kumawat	252	166	86
	Ladkhani	34	32	2
	Naruka	7942	4561	3381
	Pichanot	989	588	401
	Rajawat	4346	2549	1797
	Shekhawat	13725	10756	2969
	Sheobrampota	189	124	65
	Sultanot	527	362	165
Padihar (or Parihar)	Total	16367	8702	7665
	Padihar	14997	8073	6924
	Patyar	42	3	39
Panwar (or Parmar)	Total	42311	23072	19239
	Panwar	33052	18651	14401
	Parmar	6325	3036	3289
	Sodha	1639	709	930
Rathore	Total	176462	101248	75214
	Bidawat	329	38	291
	Bijawat	123	44	79
	Bika	87	1	86
	Champawat	274	101	173
	Jasawat	227	139	88
	Jodha	629	118	511
	Mertia	976	242	734
	Rathore	172878	100090	72788
	Sindhal	85	53	32
Sisodiya (or Gahlot)	Total	63964	35424	28540
	Ara (Ada)	163	106	57
	Balbhadrot	32	22	10

Contd...

Contd...

Clan	Sub-Clan	Population		
		Persons	Males	Females
	Bargujar	3446	1829	1617
	Bhakrot	92	72	20
	Chundawat	374	251	123
	Gahlot	4386	2318	2068
	Mangalia	215	44	171
	Purawat	91	65	26
	Ranawat	1318	685	633
	Sagawat	91	34	57
	Sisodiya	49550	28314	21236
	Unther	1658	367	1291
Solanki	Total	21527	12047	9480
	Jatu	352	111	241
	Tanwar	21104	11893	9211
Doubtful	Total	27284	13548	13736
	Bachhal	70	8	62
	Bagela	310	72	238
	Bishnu	65	51	14
	Bundela	100	38	62
	Chandawat	608	82	526
	Daima	663	276	387
	Dodiya	500	230	270
	Raghu-bansi	329	191	138
	Rangar	753	546	207
	Rawat	176	100	76
	Sengar	425	257	168
	Sikarwal	4567	2002	2565
	Thakur	1661	992	669
	Udawat	163	32	131

Appendix V

No. of Married and Widowed Children in Rajputana in 1911

S. No.	State and Age	Total Population in 1911 (M+F)	Married			Widowed		
			Children	Male	Female	Children	Male	Female
1.	Alwar	791688						
	0-4		60	18	42	2	-	2
	5-9		2078	536	1542	79	26	53
	10-14		19205	4660	14546	469	183	286
2.	Banswara	165463						
	0-4		7	-	7	-	-	-
	5-9		255	53	202	3	-	3
	10-14		1821	408	1413	30	7	23
3.	Bharatpur	558785						
	0-4		14	5	9	-	-	-
	5-9		3316	807	2509	117	45	72
	10-14		19797	6251	13546	813	376	437
4.	Bikaner	700983						
	0-4		198	54	144	4	2	2
	5-9		2250	427	1823	71	10	61
	10-14		13854	2724	11130	349	72	277
5.	Bundi	218730						
	0-4		-	-	-	-	-	-
	5-9		988	200	788	50	18	32
	10-14		3268	548	2720	80	33	47
6.	Dholpur	263188						
	0-4		-	-	-	-	-	-
	5-9		1983	442	1541	40	23	17
	10-14		10869	3318	7551	259	96	163
7.	Dungarpur	159192						
	0-4		45	12	33	2	-	2
	5-9		393	79	314	4	2	2
	10-14		2220	489	1731	39	8	31
8.	Jaipur	2636647						
	0-4		566	159	407	20	3	17
	5-9		10858	2135	8723	285	75	210

Contd...

Contd...

S. No.	State and Age	Total Population in 1911 (M+F)	Married Children	Married Male	Married Female	Widowed Children	Widowed Male	Widowed Female
	10-14		68114	15722	52392	1409	463	946
9.	Jaisalmer	88311						
	0-4		43	7	36	1	1	-
	5-9		163	31	132	6	2	4
	10-14		1248	234	1014	63	14	49
10.	Jhalawar	96271						
	0-4		90	15	75	-	-	-
	5-9		1133	197	936	23	14	9
	10-14		2253	507	1746	62	9	53
11.	Karauli	146587						
	0-4		-	-	-	-	-	-
	5-9		737	154	633	7	3	4
	10-14		4762	1271	3491	104	38	66
12.	Kishangarh	87191						
	0-4		187	44	143	10	7	3
	5-9		869	247	622	40	20	20
	10-14		2175	640	1535	103	47	56
13.	Kota	639089						
	0-4		34	25	9	-	-	-
	5-9		2557	597	1960	65	25	40
	10-14		11858	2604	9254	185	66	119
14.	Kushalgarh	22003						
	0-4		-	-	-	-	-	-
	5-9		15	4	11	-	-	-
	10-14		132	30	102	3	-	3
15.	Lawa	2564						
	0-4		1	-	1	-	-	-
	5-9		23	5	18	-	-	-
	10-14		60	9	51	2	1	1
16.	Marwar	2057553						
	0-4		3299	780	2519	91	45	46
	5-9		14967	4721	10246	556	221	335
	10-14		40381	11299	29082	1251	498	758

Contd...

Contd...

S. No.	State and Age	Total Population in 1911 (M+F)	Married			Widowed		
			Children	Male	Female	Children	Male	Female
17.	Mewar	1293776						
	0-4		666	212	454	30	7	23
	5-9		4874	1306	3568	188	79	109
	10-14		18286	4349	13937	529	209	320
18.	Pratapgarh	62704						
	0-4		97	26	71	1	-	1
	5-9		360	88	272	5	-	5
	10-14		1031	240	791	29	8	21
19.	Shahpura	47397						
	0-4		62	14	48	-	-	-
	5-9		329	91	238	7	5	2
	10-14		770	201	569	19	9	10
20.	Sirohi	189127						
	0-4		343	70	273	7	1	6
	5-9		937	243	694	22	8	14
	10-14		2396	677	1719	79	36	43
21.	Tonk	303181						
	0-4		413	130	283	26	11	15
	5-9		2130	486	1644	67	18	49
	10-14		6508	1635	4873	169	57	112
22.	Ajmer	380384						
	0-4		489	98	391	15	4	11
	5-9		2652	815	1837	123	58	65
	10-14		7992	2246	5746	321	166	155
23.	Merwara	121011						
	0-4		79	32	47	-	-	-
	5-9		441	140	301	13	7	6
	10-14		1377	283	1094	38	12	26

Appendix VI

No. of Married and Widowed Children in Rajputana in 1921

S. No.	State and Age	Total Population in 1921 (Male+ Female)	No. of married Children	Male	Female	No. of widowed Children	Male	Female
1.	Abu	3606						
	0-1		-	-	-	-	-	-
	1-5		2	-	2	1	-	1
	5-10		14	4	10	2	1	1
2.	Alwar	701154						
	0-1		36	6	30	1	-	1
	1-5		641	274	367	162	64	98
	5-10		2800	661	2139	460	166	294
3.	Banswara	190362						
	0-1		-	-	-	-	-	-
	1-5		40	19	21	3	-	3
	5-10		572	103	469	22	1	21
4.	Bharatpur	496437						
	0-1		-	-	-	-	-	-
	1-5		5	2	3	3	3	-
	5-10		2974	734	2240	77	41	36
5.	Bikaner	659685						
	0-1		5	-	5	-	-	-
	1-5		459	122	337	22	13	9
	5-10		3918	757	3161	257	257	180
6.	Bundi	187068						
	0-1		-	-	-	-	-	-
	1-5		8	1	7	-	-	-
	5-10		811	72	739	33	3	30
7.	Dholpur	229734						
	0-1		-	-	-	-	-	-
	1-5		8	2	6	-	-	-
	5-10		1575	370	1205	88	39	49
8.	Dungarpur	189272						
	0-1		-	-	-	-	-	-
	1-5		13	6	7	1	-	1
	5-10		774	146	628	20	3	17

Contd...

Contd...

S. No.	State and Age	Total Population in 1921 (Male+ Female)	No. of married Children	Male	Female	No. of widowed Children	Male	Female
9.	Jaipur	2338802						
	0-1		100	78	22	4	1	3
	1-5		1352	634	718	98	26	72
	5-10		14400	3004	11396	787	225	562
10.	Jaisalmer	67652						
	0-1		-	-	-	-	-	-
	1-5		16	8	8	5	2	3
	5-10		294	50	244	28	2	26
11.	Jhalawar	96182						
	0-1		-	-	-	-	-	-
	1-5		62	5	57	3	-	3
	5-10		1511	212	1269	70	15	55
12.	Karauli	133730						
	0-1		-	-	-	-	-	-
	1-5		-	-	-	-	-	-
	5-10		813	171	642	5	3	2
13.	Kishangarh	77734						
	0-1		1	-	1	-	-	-
	1-5		195	47	148	19	5	14
	5-10		1393	384	1009	111	48	63
14.	Kota	630060						
	0-1		39	22	17	6	5	1
	1-5		328	158	170	57	28	29
	5-10		2764	564	2200	258	84	174
15.	Kushalgarh	29162						
	0-1		-	-	-	-	-	-
	1-5		5	1	4	-	-	-
	5-10		36	17	19	5	4	1
16.	Lawa Estate	2262						
	0-1		-	-	-	-	-	-
	1-5		6	1	5	-	-	-
	5-10		21	5	16	-	-	-

Contd...

Contd...

S. No.	State and Age	Total Population in 1921 (Male+ Female)	No. of married			No. of widowed		
			Children	Male	Female	Children	Male	Female
17.	Marwar	1841642						
	0-1		20	13	7	-	-	-
	1-5		700	130	570	51	23	28
	5-10		16982	4432	12550	917	360	557
18.	Mewar	1380063						
	0-1		51	17	34	3	-	3
	1-5		2280	532	1748	133	40	93
	5-10		13918	3978	9940	677	240	437
19.	Pratapgarh	67110						
	0-1		1	-	1	-	-	-
	1-5		53	14	39	-	-	2
	5-10		583	111	472	25	8	17
20.	Shahpura	48130						
	0-1		-	-	1	-	-	-
	1-5		118	14	104	2	1	1
	5-10		791	224	567	27	14	13
21.	Sirohi	186639						
	0-1		65	5	60	24	-	24
	1-5		321	36	285	17	8	9
	5-10		1581	254	1327	71	18	53
22.	Tonk	237898						
	0-1		17	7	10	-	-	-
	1-5		380	133	247	30	14	16
	5-10		2690	570	2120	129	36	93
23.	Ajmer-Merwara	495271						
	0-1		1	-	1	-	-	-
	1-5		683	163	520	47	20	27
	5-10		4922	1465	3457	321	156	165

Appendix VII

Child Sex-Ratio in the Age Group 0-6 Years, State/Districts, Rajasthan (1991-2001)

S. No.	State/Districts	Child Sex-Ratio in the Age Group 0-6 Years		
		1991	2001	Absolute Change
	Rajasthan	916	909	-7
1.	Ajmer	913	923	10
2.	Alwar	914	888	-26
3.	Banswara	976	972	-4
4.	Baran	930	918	-12
5.	Barmer	901	922	21
6.	Bharatpur	879	875	-4
7.	Bhilwara	953	951	-2
8.	Bikaner	914	915	1
9.	Bundi	915	908	-7
10.	Chittorgarh	951	927	-24
11.	Churu	904	912	8
12.	Dausa	919	900	-19
13.	Dholpur	875	859	-16
14.	Dungarpur	974	963	-11
15.	Ganganagar	894	852	-42
16.	Hanumangarh	897	873	-24
17.	Jaipur	925	897	-28
18.	Jaisalmer	851	867	16
19.	Jalor	909	924	15
20.	Jhalawar	944	929	-15
21.	Jhunjhunun	900	867	-33
22.	Jodhpur	913	920	7
23.	Karauli	873	876	3
24.	Kota	914	902	-12
25.	Nagaur	918	920	2
26.	Pali	896	927	31
27.	Rajsamand	943	935	-8
28.	Sawai Madhopur	894	900	6
29.	Sikar	904	882	-22
30.	Sirohi	918	918	0
31.	Tonk	931	922	-9
32.	Udaipur	958	944	-14

Appendix VIII

Basic Population Data

Census of India 2001	*(India, States & Union Territories)*

Population in the age group 0 – 6 years by sex and sex-ratio (0-6)

State Code	*India/State/UTs*	*Persons (0-6)*	*Males (0-6)*	*Females (0-6)*	*Sex-ratio (0-6)*
	India@	163,819,614	84,999,203	78,820,411	927
01	Jammu & Kashmir	1,485,803	765,394	720,409	941
02	Himachal Pradesh	793,137	418,426	374,711	896
03	Punjab	3,171,829	1,763,801	1,408,028	798
04	Chandigarh	115,613	62,664	52,949	845
05	Uttaranchal	1,360,032	712,949	647,083	908
06	Haryana	3,335,537	1,833,655	1,501,882	819
07	Delhi	2,016,849	1,079,618	937,231	868
08	Rajasthan	10,651,002	5,579,616	5,071,386	909
09	Uttar Pradesh	31,624,628	16,509,033	15,115,595	916
10	Bihar	16,806,063	8,652,705	8,153,358	942
11	Sikkim	78,195	39,842	38,353	963
12	Arunachal Pradesh	205,871	104,833	101,038	964
13	Nagaland	289,678	147,524	142,154	964
14	Manipur@	308,585	157,682	150,903	957
15	Mizoram	143,734	73,176	70,558	964
16	Tripura	436,446	222,002	214,444	966
17	Meghalaya	467,979	237,215	230,764	973
18	Assam	4,498,075	2,289,116	2,208,959	965
19	West Bengal	11,414,222	5,824,180	5,590,042	960
20	Jharkhand	4,956,827	2,522,036	2,434,791	965
21	Orissa	5,358,810	2,744,552	2,614,258	953
22	Chhattisgarh	3,554,916	1,800,413	1,754,503	975
23	Madhya Pradesh	10,782,214	5,579,847	5,202,367	932
24	Gujarat	7,532,404	4,000,148	3,532,256	883
25	Daman & Diu	20,578	10,685	9,893	926
26	Dadra & Nagar Haveli	40,199	20,308	19,891	979

Contd...

Contd...

27	Maharashtra	13,671,126	7,146,432	6,524,694	913
28	Andhra Pradesh	10,171,857	5,187,321	4,984,536	961
29	Karnataka	7,182,100	3,690,958	3,491,142	946
30	Goa	145,968	75,338	70,630	938
31	Lakshadweep	9,091	4,641	4,450	959
32	Kerala	3,793,146	1,935,027	1,858,119	960
33	Tamil Nadu	7,235,160	3,725,616	3,509,544	942
34	Pondicherry	117,159	59,565	57,594	967
35	Andaman & Nicobar Islands	44,781	22,885	21,896	957

Source: Primary Census Abstract: Census of India 2001

Note: @ Excludes Mao-Maram, Paomata and Purul sub-divisions of Senapati district of Manipur

Plate I (a-b)

Copy of the Memorandum, issued by the Jodhpur Durbar, regarding the abolition of female infanticide in Marwar. (p.359)

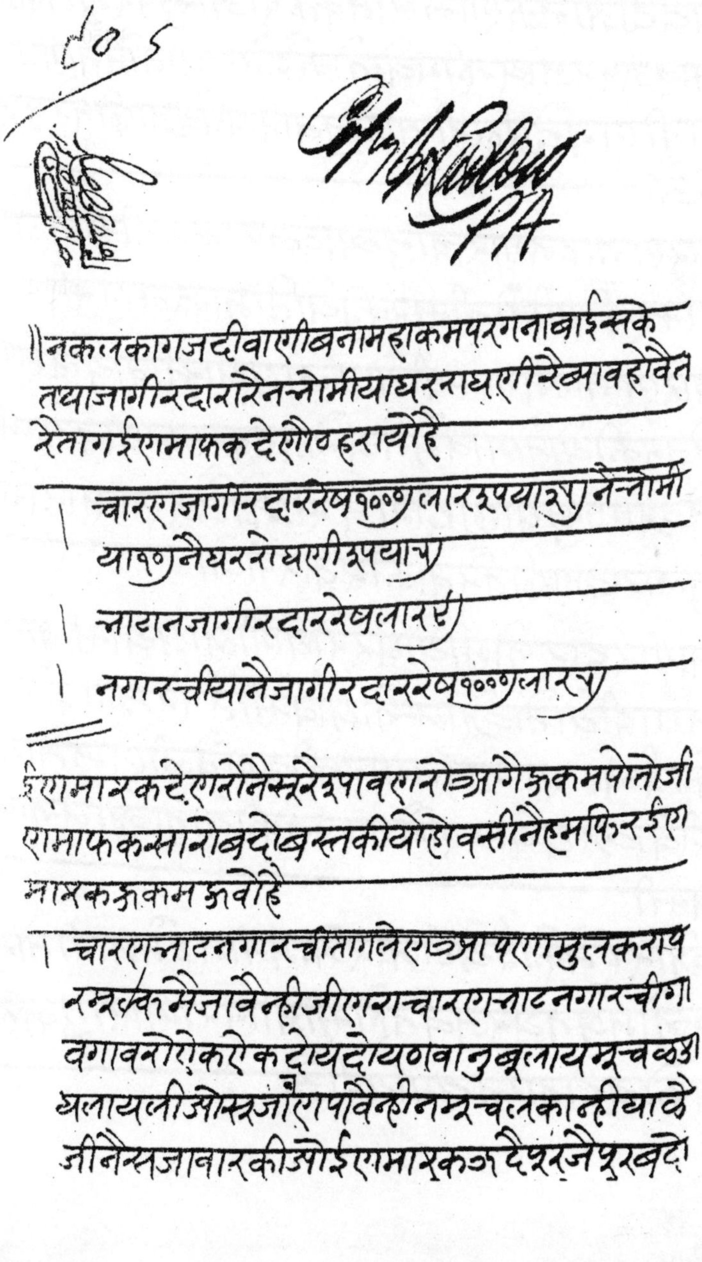

॥नकलकागजदीवाणीबनामहाकमपरगनाबाईस्तके
तथाजागीरदारारैनन्नोमीयाघररायणीरैब्भावहोवेत
रैतागईणमाफकदेणोठहरायोहै

चारणजागीरदाररेष१०००लाररुपया२) नैन्नोमी
या१०) नैघररायणीरुपया२)
भाटानजागीरदाररेषलार४)
नगारचीयानैजागीरदाररेष१०००लार१)

ईणमारकदेणरोनैसरैरुपावणरोआगेहुकमपोनोजी
णमाफकसारोबंदोबस्तकीयोहोवसीनैहमपिरईण
मारकहुकमहुवोहै

चारणभाटनगारचीतागलेणआपणामुलकराय
रस्तमैजावैन्हीजीणराचारणभाटनगारचीगा
वगावरोएकएकदोयदोयणवानुबुलायमुचलका
थलायलीजोसरजोणपावैन्हीनमुचलकान्हीयावै
जीनैसजाबारकीजोईणमारकऊदैपुरजेपुरबंदी

बस्तबंदगयोहैस्रहमञणीहैआछीतरैबदोबस्त
बादद्दीओनैऊएगसारानैकहदीओसुपरमुलकमै
ब्यावऊपरजायन्हीगयोतोऊठैजलषानामैनषीजै
लाजीएगमुदैपहलीसारानुवाकफीआछीतरैऊर
दीज्यो

चारएनाटनगारचीनुब्यावऊपरकमदीरीजैजी
एगस्रकीएगीरोबीस्तरकीयोतोमाकूलहोसी
चारएनाटनगारचीलागलीषयासीवायलेएरो
मैजरकीयोतोगावषेतऊरोऊदकसाराजबतहोसी
नैआगासुपाछादीरीजसीन्हीनैऊएगसारानै
बुलायआछीतरैवाकीरकरदीजो

जागीरदारनोमीयोघररोघणीलीषयासीवाय
लगगदीयोतोओलनोषावसीनैपरम्लकनै
कोईचारएनाटनगारचीआवेजीएगनुलाग
दीयोअथवाऊएनैजाहरनकीयोतोओलनोषा
वसी

औरहमैकोईबेटीमारज्योमतीनहमैमारीनोग।
वनोमषेतयरजबनहोसीजीएगरोसारौनुकहै
पकोबदोबस्तबयायदीजो

Plate II

Copy of the Khureeta from Maharana Saroop Singh of Udaipur to Lt. Col. Robinson, dated 27 December, 1843, (pp. 368-69).

Enclosure . No. 2 in . No. 31 of 1844

Enclosure . No. 1 in No. 5 of 1844

Purport in English of a Khureeta from Maha Rana Saroop Sing of Oodypore to the address of Lieutenant Colonel Robinson Political Agent in Meywar dated Poassood 6th or 27th December 1843.—

After Compliments

I have received your Khureeta dated Poosbud 6th and have understood its contents— You state that it has been brought to the notice of the British Government that the Rajpoots are in the habit of destroying the lives of their female infants which is a most inhuman custom, and it is the wish of the Sirkar to see it entirely abolished.

This barbarous practise has always been strictly prohibited in Meywar and as you have now so strongly recommended its extinction—strict injunctions will be issued throughout my dominion for the prevention of the practice in question— as I have already stated that infanticide is not known in Meywar it seems unnecessary to depute a respectable person from hence to join the proposed Punchayut at Samlajee.

(Translated)

(Sd.) J. Robinson

Political Agent

True Copy

[signature]

Offg. Agent Govr. Genl.

Plate III

Copy of the Khureeta from Maharawal Bahadur Singh of Banswara to Lt. Col. Robinson, Political Agent in Mewar (pp. 368-371)

Enclosure No. 2 in No. 31 of 1841
Enclosure No. 3 in No. 25 of 1841.

Purport in English of a Khureeta from Maha Rawul Buhadoor Sing of Banswara.

After Compliments

Your Khureeta dated Pos 5th with its enclosures has been received. You wish to know if the practice of female Infanticide prevails in Banswara, and if so, to use my best endeavors to put a stop to it, at the same time requesting me to send an influential Chief to Samlajee to join the Punchayut about to be assembled there for the purpose of discussing the said question.—

I am glad to say infanticide is not prevalent in this country—it is considered a great sin, and the Rajpoot Chiefs of this state have never been known to be guilty of this crime. Maha Rawul Oomed Singh had two daughters and they were married to the Chief of Edur. The late Maha Rawul Bhowany Sing has left a daughter who is not yet married. The adopted son has a sister unmarried. The Thakoor of Moula gave his daughter in marriage to Rawul Bhowany Sing. The two daughters of the Sire of Soorajgurh were married in the Doongurh family.—

You will observe from the foregoing that female Infanticide is not practised amongst the Rajpoots of Banswara and under these circumstances it is useless to depute any person from hence to meet the proposed Punchayut at Samlajee.

Translated
(Sd) J. Robinson
Political Agent

True Copy
[illegible]
Offg. Agent Govr. Genl.

Plate IV

Copy of the Khureeta from Kunwar Dulpat Singh, Regent of Dungarpur to Lt. Col. Robinson (pp.368-373)

Enclosure No. 3 in No. 36 of 18[illegible]
Enclosure No. 4 in No. 5 of 18[illegible]

Purport in English of a Khureeta from Koonwur Dulput Sing Regent of Doongurpore

After Compliments

I have been favored with your communication together with the purport of a letter from Captain Lang on the subject of the female infanticide said to prevail among certain Rajpoots and pointing out measures to suppress this barbarous practice.

I beg to assure you that infanticide is against our Shasters and is looked upon as a heinous crime among the Rajpoot Chiefs of this State. Although strict rules exist for the prevention of female infanticide throughout this Ilaqua yet I will agreeably to your [illegible] of Government on the subject in question, and will depute Sownkhan Sirdar Sing on my part to Captain Lang to be present at the Punchayet proposed to be assembled at Samlayee.

(Translated)
(Sd) J. Robinson
Political Agent

(True Copy)
[illegible]
Offg. Agent Govr. Genl.

Plate V (a-d)

Copy of the mahzarnama, issued by the Jaipur Durbar to all Sardars i.e., principal nobles (pp. 354-355).

गपेन्चातेहेक्रिचाररगोक्रीमरजीमाफीकतौतागत्मेरगोक्रात्ता
ओ रलड्न्क्रीजी तीरहडीतोसादीवीक्ररगापड्इेसवास्तैन्करतपदालोतीइ के
मारड्नलरगाचाबेक्रिजसमनेसादीश्ररनापड्ग्भोरनेत्यागदेरगाप्कड्ज
वपेन्चसीरदारानेइीसराजनेपेहतवबीजटहराइेक्रिइीसवातकुमोकु
फक्ररगाग्भोरइीसक्रामक्रीजड्ब्बोदरगान्चाहीयेक्रिजीसमेफीरवातछा
नभाचोड्ग्भ्रीक्रहीहोनेहीपावेग्भोरपेह लोगचाररगोक्रेदूप्रसपेहवात
क्ररतेहैतोत्यागकाग्प्रसावदोवस्तेग्भोरइसतुरमूकररहोजावक्रीइसइ
पेक्रमउड्पैदावारपेकसालसेज्यादेत्यागमैन्चाररगोकुन्हीदीपाजावग्भ
रगाइेलाकेसन्चाररगन्हीग्भापाक्ररग्भोरपेतजवीजक्रलमवघ्रहोक्ररसा
पेषग्भजटवाहाइकेपासवेजीग्भोरसाहैवग्भजटवाहइनेइीसतज्वी
जकुसवराजसघ्यानूमेमाफीकररखुवासतैपन्चसीरदारोइीसराजकेमेगी
ग्भोरसवरीपासदुक्रेरइसुनेइीसतजवीजकुवराहमूनकीग्भोररहैमोइी
ग्भोरम्हरवानगीवमहालल्नड्क्रीपोक्रेक्रीपराहोबीहीमारीजातीथीइीस
तजवीजकुमज्रुरकरैमाक्रस्चाररगोक्रेत्यागश्रावदोवस्तेफरमादीपाग्भोरइ
सवातमेसवक्री नेकनामिक्रइीग्भोरग्भागजीतीलड्क्रीपोमारिजातीथीजी
सवीन्यवलोतवदोवस्तेहोगपाग्प्रतग्भवतकजीछानेचोरीक्रहीक्रीहीपेना
तजाहरसुरगीजातीहग्भोरइीसक्रीपूरीमनाइीग्भोरग्भसीताक्रीइक्रीजो
क्रीइीसक्रेसाक्रामक्ररगाग्भोरउसप्रसावताहोजावगावोसजासगीनपा
वगाग्भोरन्चाररगोक्रात्यागक्रावदोवस्तेहोगपाजीसप्रनीपेहवातक्रहीक्रली
जाहरीहैतोग्भवइीसक्रेवदोवस्तेमैपेक्रवातवाक्रीमालुमहोतीहैक्रीग्भ
पसमैसीरदारप्रेसनमदहोताहैसोवरावरक्रेडीक्राएउमहोताहैग्भोरवारसर

हीसादीवेहुठीआगेबराबरकेमेहोनेसइीसनाखरचहोताहैइीकसइीअज
दारीइीतकलीफतमामउमरतकहैतीहैऔरलड़केलड़कीयोइीसादीवासते
बरकेठीकागेमेकरणेकीताकतन्हीरखेहोऔरइीसमयेलदाखतीहैइीमे
सलनेबड़ेठीकागेमेदोबराबरकेसीरदारहैयेकसीरदारकतोपाचलड़·
केहैऔरयेइसीरदारकेपाचलड़कातोबोसीरदारइीजीसकेपान्चवेटेरखे
पेइथातोबड़ेठीकागेबराबरकेमजीसतरसजीसत्रइरऔरआजकरनीदकऔ
रवाइीन्चारवेटोकाव्याहछोटीठीकागोमेकीजेहाथोड़ाइपपाखरन्नहोवा
इरपरतजैसबड़ेसीरदारकामिलनीजावऔरवाकीमारकुबराबरकेठीका
गेज्यादेसबबसन्हीमिलऔरछोटेठीकागेमवोसंनमदकरन्हीसकतो
वोलड़कीयोइवारीहीरहइीइीसखपालसमोतऔरजुवन्हीकीजवकेइी
सवातकावदेवस्तैपकानहोवजवतकजानसमारजागेलड़कीयोजा
तीइीइीकाजारीरहैइीसवास्तयेहैयेतजवीजमरूनासबमालुमहोताहै
कीन्चारगुइत्यागइावदवस्ततोहोगयाऔरवासादीमेखरचकावदोव
स्तऔरसाहोजावकीलड़काऔरलड़कीकावापसीवायेखरचत्यागाचा
रगोकेकीबोवेटीकेवापकेजीमहोताहैऔरसवखरचसादीकेमै
औरआपनीजागीरन्नोमवागरज्याहोवजीसकेसालतमामकीयदावारी
सऔरआठवाहीसाकेइपयेतोखरचकीपाकरऔरइीसज्यादेसादीमेखरच
कुछन्हीकरैकनोकेइीसइसलुरकेमूकररहोनेमेदेखादेखजोरसमेऔ
रदीनदीनज्यादाहोताजाताहैऔरयेवातसीरफयेकदीनकेनाम
औरतमानाकीअसीहैकीजीसतकलीफदेखादेखीसबठमरतक
न्भतरगीपड़ंतीहीजीसमखराबीऔरवदनामिहोतीहैऔरअ

षरकोईसदूषकेसववसलोगलङ्कीपोकुजानसमारडाले
औरईसमवेडापापऔरअजावेहोताहेऔरजवपेवातलीषी
जावगीवन्नीईसवातकुनेकऔरसवावकीसमजकरपहली
तजवीजमजकुरफुरमाईजीमैतीनपेहवातवाकीजीसकुमजुर
फुरमानेमपूरवदोवस्तौहोनासमककरकेवुल्लफुरमावगेफीरई
सवालछेवदोवस्तकेवदोवस्तकोईवातवाक्कीनेरहेगीऔरईसमै
ईत्तनीवातकेकामेदेहोवगेअवलतोलङ्कीपोकामारनावीलकु
लमोकुफहोजावगादूसरेलङ्कीपोठीकाणेमैसनमदरुवाअरगाऔर
वरन्धबेवाजववाजवलगानेमजोदीकतऔरकरजदारहोतेहसो
न्हीऊवाअरगीऔरजवतकईसकावदोवस्तौन्हीहोवगाजवतकल
ङ्कीपोकेजानसमारकीजाएगेकावदोवस्तकीज्योमाफीकतजवी
जईहांकेसवराजमुध्यानुमैमजुरऔरपसंदरुवान्हीहोगाहीईस
स्तपेहैमजरनामाअपणेराजीकुसीसवास्तैवदोवस्तजानसन्ली
मारेजानेलङ्कीपोकेलीषणेमआपासोहमसबऔरहमारी
आलऔलादईसमैहजरीनामाकुमजमुनमुजवअमलरामद
वेगोजोईससोफेरसोघरमसवेमूषहोवला

Plate VI

Copy of the cover page of the book written by Onkar Bhutt, in 1833 (pp. 332-336).

A

DISSUASIVE

AGAINST

INFANTICIDE,

ADDRESSED TO

THE RAJPOOTS.

BY

SHREE ONKAR BHUTT.

ब्रजभाषामों

राजपुतलोगोंकौ वालककौ वध निषेधग्रन्थ ।

श्रीओङ्कार भट्टकर्द्दकरचितभयौ ।

कलिकत्ता बापटिष्ट मिश्यन छापाखानामें छापा गयौ

ईं सन १८३३

Plate VII (a-b)

Copy of the Memorandum, issued by the Jodhpur Durbar, regarding female infanticide in Marwar (pp. 359-361).

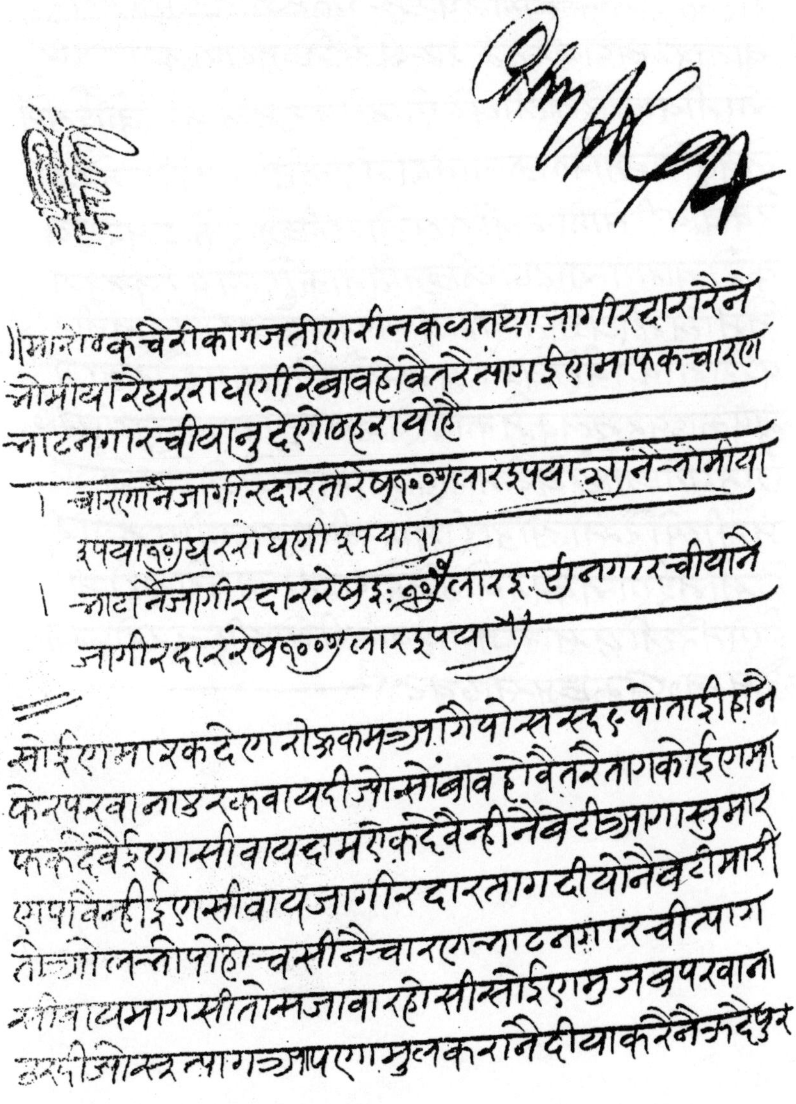

परामुलकसीवायपरमुलकमत्यागलवणनजावसा
हीसुहमैजठेईईणतरैराषणरोहुकमहुवोहैसोअठै
राहीकोरीत्यामत्वेचणनैपरमुलकमैजावैनहीजीणरापर
वानाउरबंदोबस्तकरायदीज्यौनैअमराजागीरदार
भोमीयावगैरैनैलीषदेणोसोपरमुलककरोकोईत्याग
लेवणनैआवैतोहुणनैदामएकदेणोनहीईणतरैसा
रैकवायसीज्योगाफलीराषज्योमतीओरकोईपरमुल
करोन्चारणन्याटठोलीआवैतोकहदेणोपरमुलउरा
नैमीत्लेनहीयेजातारोहोजीणपरवैहुजतउरैतानजीउ
परगनावगैरैहोवैजठैषबरदैसोहाकमवगैरैहुणा
नुपकडपरमुलकमैकाढदेवैआपणाकाकडसुबारैउठ
छोडदेणोओयेवेटीमारणीसासतरमैबोहोनच्यो छै
मलीयोहैसोज्योओईमारसीनोराजरोगुनहगार
होसीनैईणनबपरलोउमैदोनाजगाओलोमुहोसी
ईणतरैलीषसारीजगाउवायदीज्योश्रीहजूररोहुकम
छैसम्वत१८००काअसाढवद११ ——

Plate VIII (a-b)

Copy of the proclamation, issued by the Mewar Durbar, regarding the abolition of female infanticide in Mewar. (pp. 369-370).

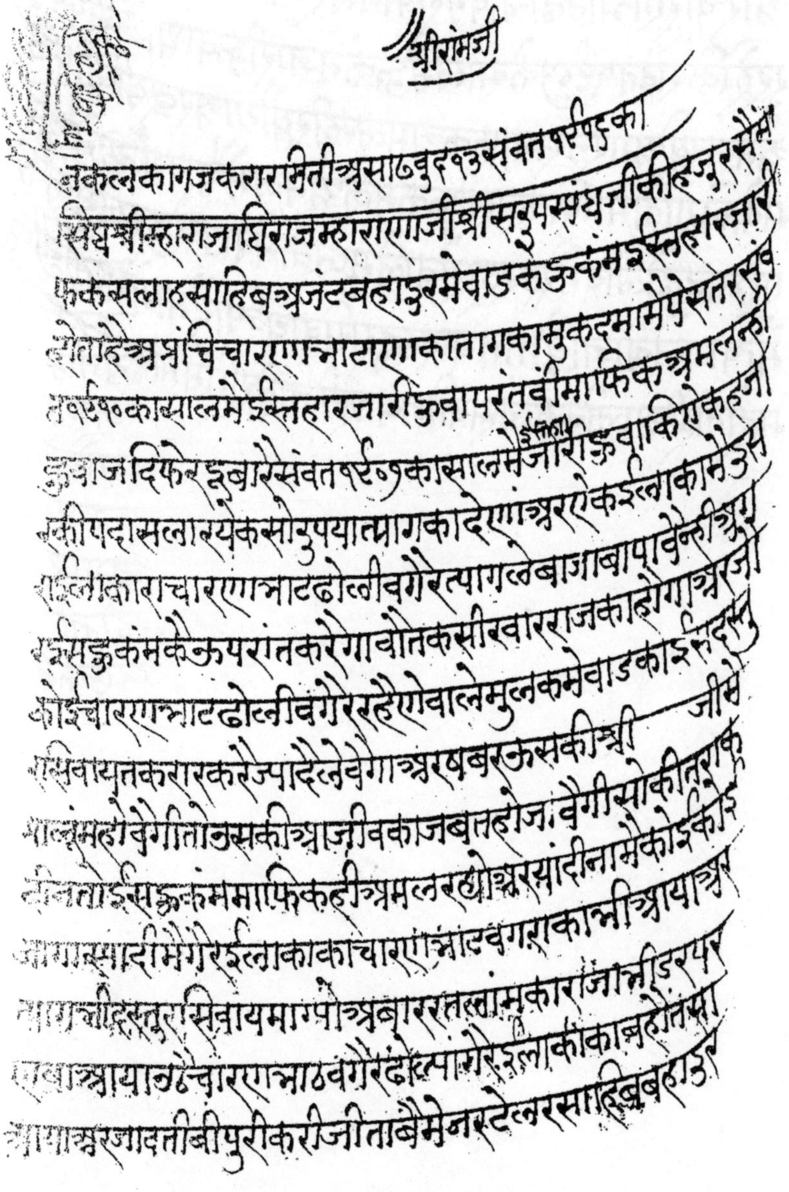

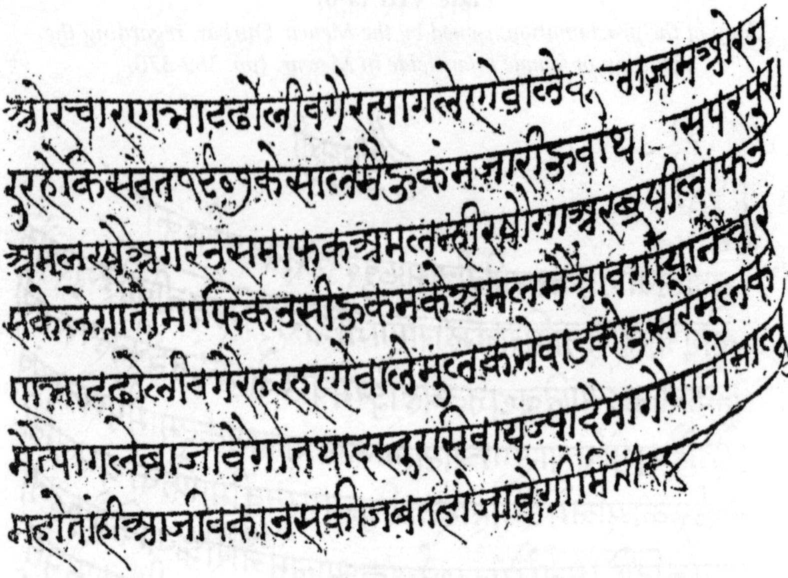

श्रोरचारणभाटढोलीवगेरेत्यागलेएगेवालेव, गगतमश्रोरज
पुरहोकेसंवत१८०७केसालमेंहुकमजारीहुवाथ। सपरपुर
अमलरखेअगरनुसमाफकअमलनहीरखेगाअरखुसीलाफऊ
सकेलेगातोमाफिकउसीहुकमकेअमलमेंआवेगोयानेचार
णभाटढोलीवगेरेहररलएगेवालेमुल्कमेवाडकेउसरेमुलक
मेंत्यागलेबाजावेगातथादस्तुरसिवायज्यादेमांगेगातोमालु
महोतांहीआजीवकाउसकीजबतहोजावेगीमितीसर

Plate IX (a-d)

Copy of the Ishtihar (advertisement), issued by the Jaipur Durbar, regarding the abolition of female infanticide in Jaipur. (pp. 349-350).

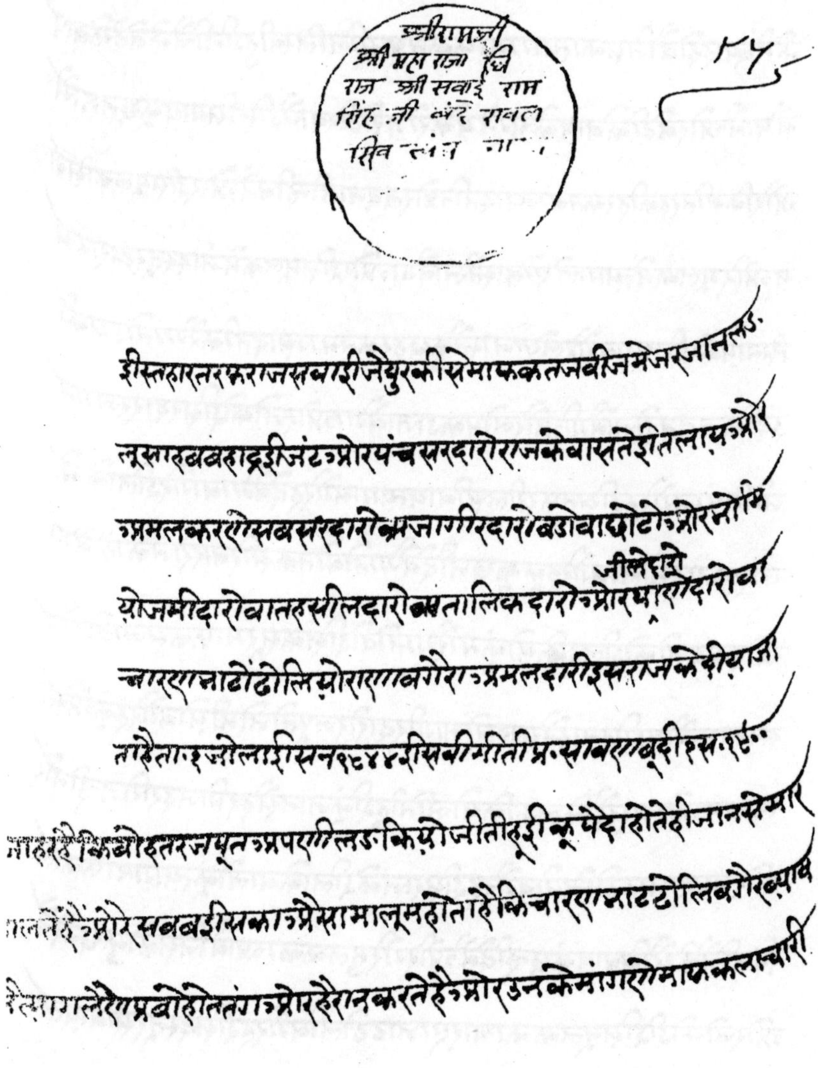
ईस्तहारतरफराजसवाईजैपुरकीसेमाफकतजनाबजिमेजरज्जानलडे
लूसाहबबहादुरईजंटऔरपंचसरदारोराजकेवास्तेईतलायऔर
अमलकरणेसबसरदारोंकाजागीरदारोबडोवाछोटोऔरभोमि
येजमीदारोवातहसीलदारोवातालिकदारोऔरथालीदारोवा
चारणभाटढोलिमोराणावगैराअमलदारीइसराजकेदीयाजा
ताहैतारीखजोलाईसन१८४४ईसवीमीतीअसाढसुदी
...किबोहतरजपूतअपणीलडकियोंजीतीलडकीकूपैदाहोतेहीजानसेमार
...डालतेहैंऔरसबबईसकाऐसामालूमहोताहैकिचारणभाटढोलिवगैरहबाव
...ईलागलेतेंगअवोहोतंगऔरहैरानकरतेहैंऔरउनकेमांगणेमाफकलाचारी

दस्तूरईसईसतहारकेनीचेलिखाहैसोचारणभाटढोलीमीरासीवगैरहईसीसें
जकेईलाकेकेजोब्याहमेंजायाऔरत्यागपायाकरतेहैंसोईसराजकेईली
केमेंब्याहहोवेजिसकात्यागमाफकतफसीललिखीहुईनीचेकेबेटेकेबाप
सेपावेऔरबेटीकेबापकेघरमेंयेकरोजरोटीखावेंईससिवायकुछनमांगें
औरकिसीतरहकीहरकतबाज्यादतीऔरबदनामीनहीकरेंऔरईसमूलककेसिवा
यऔरमूलकमेंत्यागलेणेवास्तेजावेगाऔरईसमूलकमेंजोदस्तूरठहराउस
सिवायकोईत्यागवगैरहलेणवास्तेकुछहरकतबाज्यादतीकरेगातोउसकी
उदूलिजबतहोजावेगीऔरवोपकडाजावेगाऔरजोकोईसरदाररजपूत
ओसोमिणांवगैरहईसतफसीलसीवायत्यागवगैरहदेवेगावागैरईलाकेके
चारणभाटढोलीवगैरहकूकुछनीदेवेगातोवोतकसीरवारराजकाहोवेगा
औरअबजोकोईलडकियोंकूमारेगातोवोईसकसूरमाफकसजाबोहोत
सखतपावेगाईसवास्तेसरदारोंजागीरदारोंरजपूतोंओसोमीयोंवगैरहकूंअैसा
लाजमऔरजरूरहैकिलडकियोंजीतीहुईकूंजानसेहरगिजहरगिजनहीमारें
औरचारणभाटढोलियोंवगैरहईसराजकेईलाकेवालोंकूंत्यागमाफकलि
खेनीचेकेरेसिवायकुछनहीदेवेऔरगैरमुलककाआवेजिसकोकुछनदेवें
औरजोकोईईसमूलककाचारणभाटढोलीवगैरहईसदस्तूरसीवायलें

तलाकरैंगेसोउनकूंजोमुनासिबहोगीसोसजामिलजावेगीऔरईसईलाके
वालोंकीउदिकजबतऔरआयंदासैमिलनात्यागकाउनकोंबंधहोजावेगा
औरचारणभाटढोलीवगैरेकूंऐसालाजिमहैकिइसदस्तूरसिवायकूंधनमांगेऔर
अमूलककेचारणभाटढोलीवगैरहआवैतोउनकूंराजकेतहसीलदारोंवाजिलेदारों
वगैरहसेइतलाकरयकडायदेवैछिपावैन्हीन्हींतोमाफकलिखेउपरकेउनकूंसजा
जरूरहोगीऔरतहसीलदारोंजिल्लेदारोंथाणेदारोंतालिकदमरइसईस्तहारके
मतलबकूंसमझकरपूरीखबरदारीऔरबंदोबस्तऐसारखैंकिइसईस्तहार
केमजमूनसीवायकोईबातन्हींहोणेपावैऔरजोकहींहोवेतोवो[छीपी]न्हीरहैऔर
इसकाबदलाऔरसजाजिस्तरहकिउपरलिखाजरूरहोजावेन्हींतोजबाबदेही
उसकीतहसीलदारोंतालिकदारोंवाजिलेदारोंथाणेदारोंकेजीजिम्मेंहोवेगीऔर
तहसीलदारोंतालिकदारोंवाजिलदारोंवाथाणेदारों......हूकमहैकिसब
चारणभाटढोलियोंमीरासीयोंवगैरहकूं.......करैंकिजैपूरजोधपूरउदेपूर
वगैरहराजस्थानोंमेंएकसलाहहोकरठहरगईहैकिजिसईलाकेमेंसादीहोवे
उसईलाकेकेचारणभाटढोलीवगैरहजोत्याग[लेने]जातेआपसेजावेऔर
येकईलाकेवालेदूसरेईलाकेमेंन्हींजावेसोइसबातमेंतुम्हाराकुछनूकसान
न्हीहै......बीचकायदासिवायहैकिसबास्तेकिजबतूमलोगोंकीतरफ

लड़के रैन आवेगा नोवो नीरजर पावेग्य और जो मामूल ठहरा है सो तुम लोगों
कूं पूरा मिल जावेगा और लड़ाकि ये राजपूतों में मारी जाती है सो तुम्हारे सब बस्ती
री जाती हैं जिनकी हत्या से तुम और तुम्हारे जुजमान सब दूर जावेंगे और राज
पूतों में लड़कियों की नसल बरगिर हैंगे और उदेपूर जोधपूर सें इसरदार इस
मुकदमें जारी हुवे जिन दोनूं की न कलमी इस इसरदार के साथ है इस
के मजमून से नी खबर हो जावे और ये नीसब किरदार जागीरदार जमींदार मो
मिया और तहसीलदार जिलादार थाणादार खबरदारी रखें कि चारण भाट
ढोली मीरासी वगैरह अपणी कोमसी वाय दूसरी जात के कूं अपणी जात के
बताय उनके और घोड़े पोषाक वगैरह के त्याग न ही लेणे पावें—

५०) जागीरदार पांचसै की पैदावार वाले सै दस बेटी से के रूपये पचास के हिसाब—

चारणने	रावाने	ढोलीराण	नगारचीमिरासी
२०)	२०)	७)	३)

५०) इस्तमरारदार सीकरखेतड़ी ऊपरमाई सरदार सीवाड वगैरे ईसमुजब
देवे पांचसै की पैदावारी के हीसाब—

चारणने	रावाने	ढोलीराण	नगारचीमिरासी
२०)	२०)	७)	३)

२०) जो मा जमीदार पाचसै की पैदावारी पर

चारणने	रावाने	ढोलीराण	नगारचीमिरासी

Plate X (a-b)

Copy of the letter from Jaipur council of regency to Major Thoresby, dt. October 8, 1840 in which it was told that they received a complaint from Torawati that one Samandar Singh son of Ranjit Singh, killed his infant daughter ten days ago (p.60).

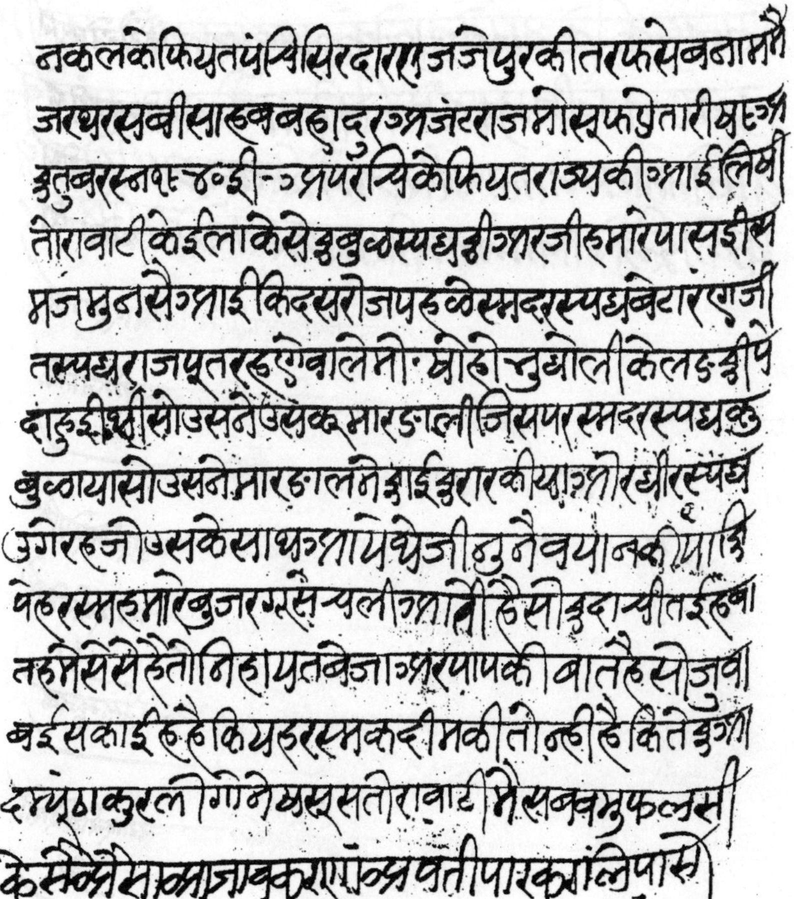
नकलकेफियतपंचिसिरदारांजेपुरकीतरफसेबनामे
जरथरसवीसाहबबहादुरअंजेरराजमोसूफप्रेतारीख८ अ
कुतुबरसन१८४०ई-७अपरंचिकेफियतराज्यकीआईलिषी
तोरावाटीकेइलाकेसेठकुरांसंघधीआरजीहमारेपासईसे
मजमुनसेआईकिदसरोजपहलेसमंदरस्यंघबेटारणजी
तस्यंघराजपुतरहणेवालेमोजेबोहोजुबोलीकेलडकीपै
दाहुईथीसोउसनेउसेकूमारडालीजिसपरसमंदरस्यंघकू
बुलायासोउसनेमारडालनेकाइकरारकीयाओरयोरस्यंघ
उगेरहजोउसकेसाथआयेथेजीनुनेबयानकीयाकि
पेहलरसमहमारेबुजरगोंसेचलीआवीहैसोकुदाचीतईहवा
तहमेसेसेहैतोनिहायतबेजाओरपापकीबातहैसोजुवा
बईसकाईहहैकियहररसमकदीमकीतोनहीहैकितेइआ
दस्यंघठाकुरलोगोंनेइसरसतोरावाटीमेंसब्बमुफलसी
केसबबसेसाआजावककरणीअपतीपारकरलीपासो

ये बात सरासर अयरम की छे ईस वास्ते फोजदारी मे
हमने पेलि लिख्या जा हे कि मारफत कबुल स्पेशक की
सलुक की के मारने वाले के अदालत फोजदारी मे
बुलाया तजवीज मुकदमे की कीजा बे अर आयंदे के
वास्ते तमाम अमलदारी राज मे ईस्तहार जारी हो जावे
कि कोई ओसा काम न कीसन कर सके तारीख ५

Bibliography

Original Sources

Archival Records (Unpublished)

I. Records in the National Archives of India, New Delhi

(a) Proceedings of the Foreign and Political Department of the Government of India from 1818 to 1900.

(b) Political despatches to and from the Court of Directors from 1818 to 1900.

(c) Despatches from the Governor General in Council to the Secretary of State from 1818 to 1900.

(d) Despatches from the Secretary of State to the Governor General in Council.

(e) Rajputana Residency Records.

II. Records in the Rajasthan State Archives, Bikaner

(a) Records of the Ajmer Commissioner's Office.
(b) Records of Mehkama-Khas, Jodhpur.
(c) Dastur Kaumwar, Byah-Bahis of Various States.
(d) Jhalawar Records.
(e) Prevention of marriages of children and persons of incompatible ages, etc.

III. Records in the Rajasthan State Archives, Jaipur (Secretariat Library)

Files regarding

(a) Births and marriages in the family of Imperial Sovereign.
(b) Births, marriages and deaths in the family of the ruling prince.
(c) Births, marriages and deaths among Zenani Sarkars.
(d) Provincial, communal, social and religious conferences.
(e) Purohit social rules.
(f) Request of certain communities for introduction of legislation penalising child marriage in Jaipur State.
(g) Prohibition of *nukta* feasts in Jaipur.
(h) Female infanticide Act in Jaipur.
(i) Records of Mehkama Khas, Jaipur.
(j) Prohibition regarding 'Chandi-Chigda', etc., in Jaipur State.
(k) Proposed abolition and reconstitution of WKRHS.
(l) Complaints in the matter of marriages and betrothals.
(m) Rajput and Charan tika rules.
(n) Rules to deal with cases of breach of promise of marriages among Charans.
(o) Nata-Dharicha.
(p) Annual General Report of *WKRHS for 1905, 1909 and 1912-13.*
(q) Report on Political Administration in Rajputana (1894).

IV. Records of Abu Collection, University of Rajasthan, Jaipur

Report on the Political Administration of the Rajputana States; Selections from the Records of the Govt. of India, Foreign Department:

(a) Rajputana Administrative Report: Ajmer-Merwara, 1895-1935.
(b) Rajputana Administrative Report: Marwar State, 1894-95 to 1944-45.
(c) Rajputana Administrative Report: Bharatpur State, 1897-98 to 1941-42.
(d) Rajputana Administrative Report: Alwar State, 1904 to 1940.
(e) Rajputana Administrative Report: Mewar State, 1895 to 1940.
(f) Rajputana Administrative Report: Jhalawar State, 1905-1939.
(g) Rajputana Administrative Report: Kota State, 1900-01 to 1944-45.
(h) Rajputana Administrative Report: Karauli State, 1895-96 to 1938-39.
(i) Rajputana Administrative Report: Shahpura State, 1990-01 to 1944-45.

(j) Rajputana Administrative Report: Dholpur State, 1894-95 to 1938-39.
(k) Rajputana Administrative Report: Sirohi State, 1895 to 1939.
(l) Rajputana Administrative Report: Tonk State, 1890 to 1942-43.
(m) Rajputana Administrative Report: Bundi State, 1900 to 1944-45.
(n) Rajputana Administrative Report: Dungarpur State, 1867-68 to 1938-39
(o) Rajputana Administrative Report: Banswara State, 1896 to 1942.
(p) Rajputana Administrative Report: Jaipur State, 1905-06 to 1939-40.
(q) Rajputana Administrative Report: Kishangarh State, 1900 to 1942-43.
(r) Rajputana Administrative Report: Jaisalmer State, 1895 to 1940.
(s) Rajputana Administrative Report: Bikaner State, 1895 to 1944.

V. Gazetteers and Gazettes

(a) Rajputana Gazetteers, 1879
(b) Imperial Gazetteers, 1906, 1908, 1909, 1910.
(c) Gazette of India, 1929, 1938.
(d) Marwar State Gazette: 1884, 1894, 1914, 1926, 1929-30, 1939-40, 1943.
(e) Mewar State Gazette: 1882-83, 1930, 1939, 1940
(f) Jaipur State Gazette: 1926, 1927, 1930-31, 1934, 1936, 1939, 1945.
(g) Bharatpur State Gazette: 1912, 1916, 1920, 1924, 1928, 1929, 1930, 1932.
(h) Alwar State Gazette: 1912, 1916, 1920, 1924, 1928, 1929, 1930, 1932.
(i) Dholpur State Gazette: 1913, 1915, 1916, 1917, 1918, 1930, 1937.
(k) Kota State Gazette: 1926.

VI. Interviews

(a) Shri Nath Ji Maharaj (Head-priest of the Charan community).
(b) Shri Shiv Charan Das (a member of the Charan community and a great grandson of Mahakavi Shyamal Das).
(c) Rani Laxmi Kumari Chundawat (eminent writer of Rajasthani folk-tales).
(d) Devarshi Kalanath Shastri, eminent scholar of Sanskrit language and former Director of Rajasthan Sanskrit Academy.
(e) Prof. N.K. Singhi, eminent Sociologist and former Head of the Deptt. of Sociology, University of Rajasthan, Jaipur.
(f) Shri Raghunath Prasad Tiwari 'Umang' (author of Pareek Jati Ka Itihas).
(g) Shri Brij Mohan Javalia (Arya Samaj, Jaipur).

(h) Prof. Vasudhaksr Goswami, Sociologist and Former Vice Principal, Government P.G. College, Dausa (Rajasthan)

(i) Dr. Sanjeev Bhanawat, Director, Centre for Mass Communications, University of Rajasthan, Jaipur.

VII. Census Reports

(a) *Census of India, 1891*, Report on the Census of the Districts of Ajmer-Merwara, Calcutta, 1893.

(b) *Census of India, 1901*, Volume I-A, India, Part-II, Tables, by H.H. Risley and E.A. Gait, Calcutta 1903.

(c) *Census of India, 1901*, Volume XXV-B, Rajputana, Part III, Provincial Tables by Captain A.D. Bannerman, (Superintendent of Census Operations), Nawal Kishore Press, Lucknow, 1902.

(d) *Census of India, 1911*, Vol. XXII, Rajputana and Ajmer-Merwara, Part-II, Tables, Calcutta, 1912.

(e) *Census of India, 1911*, Jaipur State Part-I, by Munshi Govind Sarana. Pioneer Press, Allahabad, 1914.

(f) *Census Report of Marwar State, 1911*, Part-III, Administrative Report, Jodhpur, 1917.

(g) *Census of India, 1921*, Vol. XXIV, Rajputana & Ajmer Merwara, Part-II, Tables.

(h) *Census of India, 1921*, Vol. XXIV, Rajputana and Ajmer Merwara, Part-III, Administrative Volume, Calcutta, 1923.

(i) *Census Report of Karauli State*, 1921, Lucknow, 1923.

VII. Data from Internet

Saw more than 1000 websites on internet about child and unequal marriage, social reform movement in various parts of India, female infanticide, female foeticide and abortions.

VIII. Ph.D Theses

(a) Sharma, Sangeeta, *Arya Samaj and Women Emancipation*, U.O.R., Jaipur.

(b) Puniya, Pramilla, *Jaipur Rajya ke shasan mein raniyon ki bhumika (1768-1835)*, U.O.R., Jaipur.

(c) Singh, Raghvendra, *Atharvein sadi mein Rajasthan ke Rajput-gharanon Ki sanskritik paramparaon evam samajik riti-rivajon ka adhyayan*, U.O.R., Jaipur.

(d) Goyal, Lata, *Rajasthan mein Arya-Samaj aur uske karya (1883-1949)*, U.O.R., Jaipur.

(e) Bhargava, Hembala, *Socio-economic conditions of Rajasthan during 19th century as depicted by foreign travellers*, U.O.R., Jaipur.

(f) Bhasin Narang, Rajni, *Bikaner Rajya mein samantigathan va jiwan (1700-1818)*, U.O.R., Jaipur.

(g) Joshi, Rajendra, *Century of British rule in Ajmer-Merwara*, U.O.R., Jaipur.

(h) Kapoor, Pawan, *Arya Samaj ka Rajasthan ke samajik evam dharmik jivan par prabhav (1875-1947)*, U.O.R., Jaipur.

(i) Ram, Pema, *Madhyakalin Rajasthan mein dharmik andolan*, U.O.R., Jaipur.

(j) Bhargava, Vijay Lakshmi, *British policy towards the State of Rajasthan (1818-1947)*, U.O.R., Jaipur.

Published Books in English and Hindi

'Acharya', Pt. Shri Ram Sharma – *Rig Veda*, Vol. I, II, III, IV. And also, (a) *Sam Veda* (b) *Yajur Veda* (c) *Atharva Veda* Sanskriti Sansthan, Khwaja Kutub, Bareilly, U.P. 1973.

Agrawal, C.M. (ed.), *Dimensions of Indian Womanhood*, Vol. III, Shri Almora Book Depot, Almora, 1993.

Altekar, A.S., *Position of Women in Hindu Civilization*, Moti lal Banarsidas, Delhi, Varanasi, Patna, 1973.

Allen, Charles and Dwivedi, Sharada, *Lives of the Indian Princes*, Business Publications Inc, Mumbai 1998.

Arora, Shashi, *Rajasthan Mein Nari Ki Sthithi*, Bikaner, 1981.

Bahadur, K.P., *History, Caste and Culture of Rajputs*, Delhi, 1978.

Banerjee, Anil Chandra, *Aspects of Rajput State and Society*, Rajesh Publications, New Delhi, 1983.

Barhat, Krishna Singh, *Rajputana Ka Itihas*.

Ballahatchet, K.A., *Social Policy and Social Change in Western India (1817-1830)*, Oxford, 1917.

Basu Krishna et al., *Role and Status of Women in India*, Firma, K.L. Mukhopadhyaya (P) Ltd., Calcutta, 1978.

Basu, Jogiraj, *India in the Age of Brahmanas*, Calcutta, 1963.

Bhanawat, Sanjiv, *Sanskratik Chetna Aur Jain Patrakarita*, Siddhashri Prakashan, Jaipur, 1990.

Bhandari, Sukh Sampat Rai, *Oswal Jati ka Itihaas*, Vedic Yantralaya, Ajmer.

Bhutodiya, Mangilal, *Itihaas Ki Amar Bel: Oswal*, Priyadarshi Prakashan, Ladnun (Raj.) and Calcutta, 1988.

Bingley, A.H., *Handbook on Rajputs*, Asian Educational Services, 1986.

– *History, Caste and Culture of Jats and Gurjars,* Ess Ess Publications, New Delhi, 1978.

Bose, P.N., *A History of Hindu Civilization during British Rule,* Vol. I, II & III, Asian Publication Services, New Delhi, 1978 (Reprint).

Brown, J.C., *Indian Infanticide: Its Origin, Progress and Suppression,* W.N. Allen & Company, London, 1857.

Castes and Tribes of Marwar: Marwar State Publications, 1894.

Chattopadhyaya, Kamla Devi, *Indian Women's Battle for Freedom,* Abhinav Publications, Delhi, 1983.

'Chetan', Chandra Singh, *Maharao Shekha: Vansha Parampara, Khampen, aur unke Gaon,* Sahitya Kala Evam Sanskriti Parishad, Sikar (Rajasthan), 2003.

Chintamani, C.V., *Indian Social Reform,* Thompson & Co. Popham's Broadway, Madras, 1901.

Choudhary, Ram Narayan, *Beesvien Sadi Ka Itihaas,* Rajasthani Granthagar, Jodhpur, 1998.

Chiefs and Leading Families of Rajputana, III rd edition, Calcutta, 1912.

Chundawat, Rani Lakshmi Kumari, *Sanskritik Rajasthan,* Rajasthan People's Publishing House, Jaipur, 1994.

Crooke, W., *The Tribes and Castes of the North Western Provinces and Oudh,* Cosmo Publication, Delhi, 1974.

Dandiya, C.Y., *Position of Women in Rajasthan,* 1975.

Das, S., Purdah: *The Status of Indian Women,* Ess Ess Publications, New Delhi, 1979.

Das, Shyamal, *Vir Vinod,* Vol. I & II, Motilal Banarsidas.

Das, Abinas Chandra, *Rig Vedic Culture,* Calcutta, 1925.

Datta, Kali Kinkar, *A Social History of Modern India,* Macmillan, New Delhi, 1975.

Devendra Kiran, *Status and Position of Women in India, with Special Reference to Women in Contemporary India,* Shakti Books, Vikas Publishing House, New Delhi, 1985.

Devra, G.L., *Some Aspects of Socio-Economic History of Rajasthan,* Jodhpur, 1979.

Dua, Shiva S., *Society and Culture in Northern India, 1850 – 1900,* Indian Publishers Bureau and Balaji Enterprises, Delhi, 1985.

Dubois, Abbe J.A., *Hindu Manners, Customs and Ceremonies* (Translated into English by Henry Beauchamp), Oxford Clarendon Press, Oxford, 1906 (Third edition).

Dundlod, Harnath Singh, *The Sheikhawats and Their Lands,* Rajasthan Educational Printers, Jaipur, 1970.

Encyclopaedia of Religion and Ethics.

Erskine, K.D., *Rajputana Gazetteers,* Vol. II-A and II-B (Mewar), Scotish Mission Industries Co. Ltd., Ajmer, 1908.

Erskine, K.D., *Rajputana Gazetteers,* The Western Rajputana States Residency and Bikaner, Vintage Books, 1992.

Farquhar, J.N., *The Crown of Hinduism,* Oriental Books Corporation, New Delhi, (Reprint 1971).

Fuller, Marcus B., *The Wrongs of Indian Womanhood,* Inter-India Publications, New Delhi, 1984.

Gahlot, Jagdish Singh, *Rajasthan Before Second World War (A Socio-economic Study),* Rajasthani Granthagar, Jodhpur, 1986.

Gahlot, Sukhbir Singh and Dhar, Banshi, *Castes and Tribes of Rajasthan,* Research Publishers, Jodhpur, 1989.

Gahlot, Sukhvir Singh, *Rural Life in Rajasthan,* Books Treasure, Jodhpur, 1995.

Gaur, Albertine, *Women in India,* The British Library, London, 1980.

Meena, *Sati and Social Reforms in India,* Publication Scheme, Jaipur, 1989.

Ghurye, G.S., *Caste and Race in India,* Popular Prakashan Pvt. Ltd., Bombay, 1988.

Ghosh, S.K., *Indian Women Through the Ages,* Ashish Publishing House, New Delhi, 1989.

Ghosh, Vinay, *Ishwarchandra Vidyasagar* (Hindi Translation by Devi Shankar Avasthi), Publication Division, Government of India, New Delhi, 1959.

Gidumal, Dayaram, *Behramji M. Malabari: A Sketch,* T. Fisher Unwin, London, 1892.

Status of Women in India, Ford Printing Press, Bombay, 1959.

Goyal, R.P., *Marriage Age in India,* B.R. Publishing Corporation, Delhi, 1988.

Griffith, M.A., *Rajput's Observation on Social Reforms in Rajputana: Initiated by 'The Walterkrit Rajputra Hitkarini Sabha',* Delhi, 1893.

Grover, B.L. and Grover, S., *A New Look at Modern Indian History,* S. Chand and Company Ltd., New Delhi, 1992.

Gupta K.C. and Kedawat, R.P. (ed.), *Sambhaav* (Book published by the Akhil Bhartiya Khandelwal Vaishya Mahasabha, at its 27th Conference at Alwar, Rajasthan), 1986.

Har Bilas Sarda Commemoration Volume (edited by P. Sheshadri), Vedic Yantralaya, Ajmer, 1937.

Hiemsath, C.H., *Indian Nationalism and Hindu Social Reform*, Oxford University Press, Bombay, 1964.

Indra Prof., *The Status of Women in Ancient India*, 1940 (Place not mentioned).

Jawalia, Brij Mohan, *Socio Economic Conditions in Rajasthan*, Books Treasure, Jodhpur, 2002.

Jagirdar, P.J., *Mahadev Govind Ranade*, (Hindi translation by Shakuntala Mathur), Builders of Modern India Series, Publication Division, New Delhi, 1981.

Jain, M.S., *Adhunik Rajasthan Ka Itihaas*, Panchsheel Prakashan, Jaipur, 1988.

Jain, Pratibha, *Gandhi Chintan, Aitihasik Pariprekshya*, Rajasthan Hindi Grantha Academy, Jaipur, 1984.

Jain, Pratibha, and Sharma, Sangeeta, *Bhartiya Stri: Sanskratik Sandarbha*, Rawat Publications, Jaipur, 1998.

Kane, P.V., *History of Dharma Shastra*, Poona, 1941.

Kanota, Thakur Mohan Singh, *Champawaton Ka Itihas*, Ran Bankura Prakashan, Jaipur, 1991.

Kapur, Promilla (ed.), *Girl Child and Family Violence*, Har Anand Publications, N. Delhi, 1993.

Kapil, F.K., *Rajputana States (1817-1950)*, Book Treasure, Jodhpur, 1999.

Kapadia, K.M., *Marriage and Family in India*, Oxford University Press, Bombay, 1958.

Kapoor, Devendra Kumar, *Success Motivating Vedic Lores*, Deva Vedic Prakashan, Bombay, 1978.

Kumar, Vijay, *British Paramountcy in Rajputana*, Books Treasure, Jodhpur, 1991.

Kurmi, Shiv Kumar Patidar, *'Arya Samaj Jaipur Ke Samaj Sewi'*, published by Kurmi, Shiv Kumar Patidar (former Head, Arya Samaj Krishnapole Bazar Jaipur), 1990

Lawrence, W.R., *The India We Served*, Cassell & Company Ltd., 1929.

Liddle Joanne and Joshi, Rama, *Daughters of Independence: Gender, Class and Caste in India*, Kali for Women, Delhi, 1986.

Malley, O.L. S.S., *Modern India and the West*, Oxford University Press, London, New York, 1941.

Maheshwari, Hari Vallabh, *Jaisalmer Rajya Ka Madhyakalin Itihaas*, Rajasthani Granthagar, Jodhpur, 1997.

Manglani, H.J., *History, Culture and Administration of Jhalawar State*, Jaipur Publishing House, Jaipur, 1993.

Marten, J.T., *Census of India, 1921*, Vol. I, Government Printing Press, Calcutta, 1933.

Mardum Shumari, Raj Marwar, 1890.

Majumdar, R.C., Pusalkar, A.D., Majumdar A.K., (ed.) *The Vedic Age (The History And Culture of the Indian People)*, Bhartiya Vidya Bhawan, Bombay, 1971.

Pt. Baldev Prasad, *Rajasthan Ka Itihaas* (commentary on the Annals and Antiquities of Rajasthan, by Col. James Tod), Shri Venkateshwar Steam Printing Press, Bombay, Samvat 1982.

Mishra, G.S.P., *Pracheen Bhartiya Samaj evam Arthavyavastha*, Rajasthan Hindi Grantha Academy, Jaipur, 1983.

Mishra, Jaishankar, *Pracheen Bharat Ka Samajik Itihaas*, Hindi Madhyam Karyanvaya Nideshalaya, Delhi, 1974.

Mishra, Ratan Lal, *Shekhawati Ka Navin Itihaas*, Kutir Prakashan, Mandawa (Jhunjhunu, Raj.), 1998.

Mishra, Ratan Lal, and Sharma, Mahaveer Prasad, *Shekhawati: Arya Samaj Ke Char Stambha*, Dr. Ghasi Ram Verma (pub.), America.

Muni, Jin Vijay (ed.), *Rajasthani Sahitya Sangraha*, Vol. I, II, III, Rajasthan Oriental Research Institute, Jodhpur, 1966.

Mukherjee, Prabhati, *Hindu Women: Normative Models*, Orient Longman Limited, New Delhi, 1978.

Nag, Ravi Prakash, *Rajasthani Geetan Ro Gajro (Paramparik Rajasthani Lokgeeton Ka Sankalan)*, Sahityagar, Jaipur, 1987.

Nagar, Mahendra Singh, *Marwar Ke Rajvansha Ki Sanskritik Paramparaen*, Rajasthani Granthagar, Jodhpur, Vol. I & II, 2001.

Nanda, B.R. (ed.), *Indian Women: From Purdah to Modernity*, Vikas Publishing House, Delhi, Bombay, Bangalore, Calcutta, Kanpur, 1976.

Natrajan, S., *A Century of Social Reform in India*, Asia Publishing House, Bombay, Calcutta, Madras, N. Delhi, 1959.

Newatia, Radha Krishna, *Bara Bazar Ke Karyakarta: Smaran evam abhinandan*, Shri Bara Bazar Kumar Sabha Pustakalaya, Calcutta, 1982.

Ojha, Gaurishankar Hirachand:

– *Udaipur Rajya Ka Itihaas*, Vol. I & II.

– *Jodhpur Rajya Ka Itihaas*, Vol. I & II.

– *History of Rajputana*.

– *Dungarpur Rajya Ka Itihaas.*

– *Bikaner Rajya Ka Itihaas.*

– *Banswara Rajya Ka Itihaas.*

– *Pratapgarh Rajya Ka Itihaas.*

– *Rajput Kalin Sanskriti*, Rajasthani Granthagar, Jodhpur, 2002.

Paliwal, D.L., *Mewar and the British (1857-1921 A.D.)*, Bafna Prakashan, Jaipur, 1971.

Panigrahi, Lalita, *British Social Policy and Female Infanticide in India*, Delhi, 1972.

Parvate, T.N., *Mahadev Govind Ranade, A Biography*, Asia Publishing House, Bombay, Calcutta, New Delhi, Madras, Lucknow, London, New York, 1963.

Peggs. J., *India Cries to British Humanity* (Reprinted as *Cries of Agony)*, An Historical account of Suttee, Infanticide, Ghat murders & Slavery in India, Discovery Publishing House, Delhi, 1984.

Pemaram and Vikramaditya, *Jaton Ki Gaurav gatha*, Rajasthani Granthagar, Jodhpur, 2004.

Phadke, Y.D., *Social Reformers of Maharashtra*, Maharashtra Information Centre; Bombay, 1985.

Pinkham, M.W., *Women in the Sacred Scriptures of Hinduism*, Columbia University Press, New York, 1941.

Pradhan, M.C., *The Political System of the Jats of Northern India*, Oxford University Press, Bombay, 1966.

Prasad, Bisheshwar (ed.), *Ideas in History: Proceedings of a seminar on ideas motivating social and religious movements and political and economic policies during the eighteenth and nineteenth centuries in India*, Asia Publishing House, Bombay, 1968.

Prasad, Durga, *An English Translation of the Satyarth Prakash of Maharshi Dayanand*, Jan Gyan Prakashan, Delhi, 1983.

Purohit, Purushottam Das, *Pushkarno Ke Samajik Geet*, Rajasthan Law Weekly Press, Jodhpur, Samvat 2017.

Purohit, D., *Mewar Ka Sankshipta Itihaas*, Udaipur, 1934.

Qanungo, Kalika Ranjan, *Studies in Rajput History*, S. Chand and Company, Delhi, 1960.

Raghuvanshi, V.P.S., *Indian Society in the Eighteenth Century*, Associated Publishing House, New Delhi, 1969.

Rai, Lala, Lajpat, *The Arya Samaj*, Longmans Green and Company, London, 1915.

Rajguru, Ira Das, *Women's Education in Rajasthan*, Shodhak, Jaipur.

Rathore, V.S., *Rajpoot Nariyan*, Rajasthani Saahitya Sansthan, Jodhpur, 1985.

– *Rajasthan Ki Sanskriti mein Nari*, Rajasthani Granthagar, Jodhpur, 1995.

Ratnawat, S.S. and Sharma, K.G., *Charan Sahitya Parampara (Essays on Bardic Literature)*, Centre for Rajasthan Studies, Jaipur, 2001.

– *History and Culture of Rajasthan (from earliest times upto 1956 A.D.)*, Centre for Rajasthan Studies, Jaipur, 1999.

Rawat, Saraswat, *Meena Itihaas*, Jhunthalal Nadhla, and S.K. Sharma (publishers), Samvat 2057.

Reu, Pandit Bishveshar Nath, *Marwar Rajya Ka Itihaas*, Rajasthani Granthagar, Jodhpur.

– *Rathoron ka Itihaas*, Rajasthani Granthagar, Jodhpur, 1993.

Risley, H.H., *The People of India*, II edition, (edited by William Crooke) Oriental Books Reprint Corporation, Delhi, 1969.

Russel, R.V. and Hira Lal, *Tribes and Castes of Central Provinces of India*, Reprint, Delhi, 1975.

Saraswati, Dayanand, *Rig Vedadi-Bhashya Bhoomika*, Sarv-deshikarya Pratinidhi Sabha, Delhi, 1991.

Satyartha Prakash, Arya Sahitya Prachar Trust, Delhi, 1980.

Sarda, Har Bilas, *Life of Dayanand Saraswati*, Vedic Yantrayalaya, Ajmer, 1943.

–, *Commemoration Volume of Dyanand Saraswati*, Vedic Yantrayalaya, Ajmer, 1943.

–, *Ajmer Arya Samaj and Swami Dayanand*, Vedic Yantrayalaya, Ajmer, 1943.

Saxena, R.K., *Social Reforms: Infanticide and Sati*, Trimurti Publications Pvt. Ltd., N. Delhi, 1975.

– *Education and Social Amelioration of Women (A Study of Rajasthan)*, Sanghi Prakashan, Jaipur, Udaipur, 1978.

Sen, Amiya P., *Hindu Revivalism in Bengal, (1872-1905, Some Essays in Interpretation)*, Oxford University Press, 1993.

– *Social and Religious Reforms (The Hindus of British India)* ed., Oxford University Press, 2003.

Shankar, Pt. Shiv, *Child Marriage Prohibition Act 'Sarda Act'*, Rajputana Press, Ajmer, 1938.

Sharma, B.N., *Social Life in Northern India (AD 600 to 1000)*, Munshiram Manoharlal, Delhi, 1966.

Sharma, Gopi Nath, *Social and Political Awakening Among the Tribals of Rajasthan*, Centre for Rajasthan Studies, Jaipur.

Sharma, Padmaja, *Maharaja Man Singh of Jodhpur and his times*, Shiv Lal Agrawal & Company, Agra, 1972.

Sharma, Pandit Hanuman, *Jaipur Rajya Ka Itihaas*, Shabda Mahima Prakashan, Jaipur, 1996.

Sharma, Tripat, *Women in Ancient India*, Ess Ess Publications, New Delhi, 1988.

Sharma, S.R., *Mughal Empire in India*, Lakshmi Narain Agarwal, Agra, 11th edition, (year not mentioned).

Sharma, C.L., *Bhil Society: Art and Culture*, Malti Prakashan, Virat Nagar, Jaipur, 1998.

Sharma, Pt. Jhabar Mal, *Khetri Ka Itihaas*, Rajasthan Agency, Calcutta, 1984 V.S. (A.D. 1927).

Shastri, Shakuntala Rao, *Women in the Vedic Age*, Bhartiya Vidya Bhawan, Bombay, 1952.

Sherring, M.A., *Hindu Tribes and Castes*, Vol. III, Cosmo Publications, Delhi, 1974.

Shrivastava, Bindeshwari Prasad, "All India Kayastha Conference" (unpublished), Vol. I, 1887-1939. Excerpts published in *Chitransh Sandesh Prakashan*, Lucknow.

Singh, Bawa Chhajju Singh, *Life and Teachings of Swami Dayananda*, Dayanand Sansthan, New Delhi, 1997.

Singh, K.B.K., *Marriage and Family System of Rajputs (A Study of Tradition and Change)*, Wisdom Publications, N. Delhi, 1988.

Singh, S.R., *Nationalism and Social Reform in India*, Ranjit Printers and Publishers, Delhi, 1968.

Singh, Thakur Bhagwat, *Champawat Rathore*, (pub. by) Thakur Bhagwat Singh, Jodhpur, 1972.

Singh, Raghubir and Ranawat, Manohar Singh, *Jodhpur Rajya Ki Khyat*, I.C.H.R., Delhi and Panchasheel Prakashan, Jaipur, 1988.

Srinivas, M.N., *Social Change in Modern India*, Allied Publishers, New Delhi, Calcutta, Madras, 1972.

The Publications Division, Government of India, *Social Legislation, its Role in Social Welfare*, N. Delhi, 1956.

Tiwari, Raghunath Prasad, *Pareek Jati Ka Itihaas*, Richa Prakashan, Jaipur, 1992.

The New Encyclopaedia Britannica 15th edition, Vol. 6, 22, 25.

Thomas, P., *Indian Women Through the Ages,* Asia Publishing House, Bombay, Calcutta, New Delhi, Lucknow, London, New York, 1964.

– *Hindu Religion and Manners,* D.B. Taraporevala Sons & Co. Pvt. Ltd., Bombay, 1960.

Tod, Col. J., *Annals and Antiquities of Rajasthan,* Vol. I & II, Delhi, 1968.

Trevor, Col. G.H., *Rhymes of Rajputana,* Macmillan & Company, London, 1894.

Upadhyaya, B.S., *Women in the Rig Veda,* Benaras, 1941.

Vasishta, V.K., *Rajputana Agency (1832-58),* Aalekh Publishers, Jaipur, 1978.

Vedalankar, Ramnath, *Vedic Nari,* Samarpan Shodh Sansthan, New Delhi, 1984.

Verma, V.P., *Lokmanya Tilak: Jiwan aur Darshan,* Laxmi Narayan Agrawal, Agra, 1982.

Vidyavacahspati, Indra, *Arya Samaj Ka Itihaas,* two Volumes, Sarvdeshik Arya Pratinidhi Sabha, New Delhi, 1957.

Vidyalankar, Dharma Chandra, *Jaton Ka Naya Itihaas,* Akhil Bharat Varshiya Jat Mahasabha, New Delhi.

Vidyalankar, Satyaketu, *Agrawal Jati Ka Itihaas,* Vani Prakashan, Bombay, 1972.

--, *Arya Samaj Ka Itihaas,* two volumes, Delhi, 1984.

Vijay, Dr. Om Sharan, *Arya Samaj Krishna Pole Bazar, Jaipur: Arya Samaj Ka Itihaas,* Arya Samaj Krishna Pole Bazar, Jaipur.

Vyas, Kailash Nath and Gahlot, Devendra Singh, *Rajasthan Ki Jation Ka Samajik evam Arthik Jivan,* J.S. Gahlot Research Institute, Jodhpur, 1992.

Vyas, K.C., *The Social Renaissance in India,* Vora & Company, Bombay, 1957.

Vyas, Prakash, *Adhunik Mewar Ka Itihaas,* Panchasheel Prakashan, Jaipur, 1990.

Weber, A., *History of Indian Literature,* (Eng. translation by J. Mann and Th. Zachariae), II edition, London, 1882.

Wilson, J., *History of Suppression of Infanticide in Western India (Under the Government of Bombay),* Bombay, 1855.

Yadav, Santosh, *Unnisvien Aur Bisvin Shatabdi Mein Strion Ki Stithi,* Printwell Publishers, Jaipur, 1987.

Index